Bad Days
in History

Also by Michael Farquhar:

*Secret Lives of the Tsars: Three Centuries of Autocracy, Debauchery,
Betrayal, Murder, and Madness From Romanov Russia*

*Behind the Palace Doors: Five Centuries of Sex, Adventure,
Vice, Treachery, and Folly From Royal Britain*

*A Treasury of Foolishly Forgotten Americans: Pirates,
Skinflints, Patriots, and Other Colorful Characters Stuck
in the Footnotes of History*

*A Treasury of Deception: Liars, Misleaders, Hoodwinkers,
and the Extraordinary True Stories of History's Greatest Hoaxes,
Fakes, and Frauds*

*A Treasury of Great American Scandals: Tantalizing True Tales
of Historic Misbehavior by the Founding Fathers
and Others Who Let Freedom Swing*

*A Treasury of Royal Scandals: The Shocking True Stories
of History's Wickedest, Weirdest, Most Wanton Kings,
Queens, Tsars, Popes, and Emperors*

Bad Days *in* History

A GLEEFULLY GRIM CHRONICLE *of* MISFORTUNE, MAYHEM, *and* MISERY *for* EVERY DAY *of the* YEAR

MICHAEL FARQUHAR

ILLUSTRATIONS BY GIULIA GHIGINI

NATIONAL GEOGRAPHIC

Washington, D.C.

Published by National Geographic Partners, LLC
1145 17th Street NW, Washington, DC 20036

ISBN 978-1-4262-1807-1 (paperback)
First paperback printing 2017

The Library of Congress has cataloged the hardcover edition as follows:

Farquhar, Michael.
  Bad days in history : a gleefully grim chronicle of misfortune, mayhem, and misery for every day of the year / Michael Farquhar.
     pages cm
  Includes bibliographical references and index.
  ISBN 978-1-4262-1268-0 (hardback)
  1. History--Anecdotes. 2. World history--Anecdotes. 3. Biography--Anecdotes. 4. Errors--History--Anecdotes. 5. Disasters--History--Anecdotes. 6. Curiosities and wonders--History--Anecdotes. I. Title.
  D10.F33 2015
  909--dc23
                              2014040554

Since 1888, the National Geographic Society has funded more than 12,000 research, exploration, and preservation projects around the world. National Geographic Partners distributes a portion of the funds it receives from your purchase to National Geographic Society to support programs including the conservation of animals and their habitats.

National Geographic Partners
1145 17th Street NW
Washington, DC 20036-4688 U.S.A.

For information about special discounts for bulk purchases, please contact National Geographic Books Special Sales: specialsales@natgeo.com

For rights or permissions inquiries, please contact National Geographic Books Subsidiary Rights: bookrights@natgeo.com

Interior design: Melissa Farris / Katie Olsen

Printed in the United States of America

17/QGF-LSCML/2

To my friend Andy Sullivan—a good man who has proved that through courage, faith, and magnificent humor, even the worst days can be transcended.

*"Life is full of misery, loneliness, and suffering—
and it's all over much too soon."*

—Woody Allen

Contents

Introduction

———✦———

At first glance, the title of this collection seems so simple and direct: It's all about bad days in history. Yet, on deeper examination, it's bewilderingly broad. There are literally billions of miserable episodes throughout human history from which to choose; a single year of the 20th century alone could fill hundreds of volumes. Thus, the subtitle. But that, too, is a bit murky. "Gleefully Grim"? What exactly does that mean? Well, take genocide—a decidedly dark topic not often associated with mirth. *Unless* . . . unless a perpetrator of such a gross atrocity is having a bad day, just as Nazi propagandist Joseph Goebbels was on October 26, 1928, when he whined in his diary: "I have no friends." Or when a State Department spokesperson blathered her way through a press conference on June 10, 1994, desperately trying to avoid using the word "genocide" to describe the mass slaughter in Rwanda.

Still, while the ugliest moments in history are largely avoided here, at least in their rawest form, some days recounted were certainly grimmer than others. A child killer is a child killer, for example, despite the irresistible irony that Gilles de Rais was Joan of Arc's close ally and, on August 15, 1434, personally dedicated a lavish place of worship that he had funded: the Chapel of the Holy Innocents. To the reader, the juxtaposition of this unholy day with the firing of Beatles drummer Pete Best on the next calendar day, in 1963, might be a bit jarring. And so it goes throughout this

"Chronicle of Misfortune, Mayhem, and Misery for Every Day of the Year," as the rest of the subtitle reads: the sublime, grotesque, unsettling, and absurd, all jumbled together in an awkward waltz through time.

Plucked from all eras of history, and from around the globe, the bad days in this book are intended to amuse, tantalize, and enlighten—without being predictable. Thus, to cite one famously rotten day, Lincoln's assassination gets short shrift. Look instead for the deleterious effect it had on two ex-presidents several days later. Or discover how surviving the *Titanic* actually sank the reputation of one of its passengers later that week. Finally, as you peruse this collection, just remember: No matter how lousy your day has been, you can be sure that somewhere in time someone else's was so much worse.

—Washington, D.C.
November 2014

January

"January, month of empty pockets!
Let us endure this evil month,
anxious as a theatrical producer's forehead."

—COLETTE

Crappy New Year!

Ah, New Year's: a day filled with new hope and fresh starts—except when it wasn't. For some unfortunates in history, January 1 was a dead end. And a rather ghastly one. Take the fifth-century monk and martyr Telemachus, who stepped into the middle of a gladiatorial fight in Rome and tried to stop the human slaughter, only to be stoned to death by the bloodthirsty audience unappreciative of the effort. Or Charles II of Navarre, known as "the Bad," who in 1387 burned to

death in his own bed after an attendant accidentally ignited the brandy-soaked bandages with which the king had been bound head to foot as a remedy for his ailments.

Then there was Louis XII of France, who, though aging and decrepit, was lucky enough to wed a young and beautiful English princess, Henry VIII's younger sister, Mary, in 1514. Alas, the vigorous attempts to sire an heir proved too much for the gouty old king, and he dropped dead from exhaustion just three months after the wedding. Yet unlike those others whose grim demise fell on the New Year, at least Louis had fun on the way out.

JANUARY 2, 1811

Swatting the Gadfly
Who Stung With the Truth

Timothy Pickering was an early American pest; a persistent, self-righteous mosquito who, among other offenses, urged the secession of New England and assiduously undermined the first four U.S. presidents. He called George Washington "a much overrated, semi-literate mediocrity." John Adams was forced to fire him as secretary of state because of his disloyalty to the administration—and after that he stubbornly refused to resign. Indeed, Pickering was so obnoxious even his own biographer couldn't stand him. But it wasn't just his odious personality that earned the obscure Founding Father his most enduring distinction: being the first of only nine U.S. senators ever officially censured. That happened because Timothy Pickering dared to tell the truth.

On October 27, 1810, President James Madison issued a proclamation declaring the annexation of West Florida, a Spanish possession, claiming the region had been part of the Louisiana Purchase. Pickering objected to such a unilateral exercise of executive power.

In typical gadfly fashion, he produced before the Senate an old document from France's then foreign minister, Charles Maurice de Talleyrand, stating emphatically that West Florida was not part of the Louisiana Purchase. Only problem was, the document had yet to be declassified—despite the fact that it dated back to the Jefferson Administration. Revealing the classified document was a petty violation, but Pickering's enemies pounced on it.

Henry Clay, the aggressively expansionist senator from Kentucky, introduced a resolution of censure. Pickering called it a "put-up affair," which indeed it was. Had the motion been made against someone less unpleasant to his peers, it probably wouldn't have passed. But Pickering was Pickering, and on January 2, 1811, he became the first entry in the Senate's official annals of infamy.

Apple Dumpling: A Co-Founder's Small Sliver of the Pie

Ronald Wayne considered himself a lucky man when Apple Computers was incorporated on January 3, 1977. Not because of the potential windfall, but because he had extricated himself months earlier from what he considered a potentially risky partnership with Steve Jobs and Steve Wozniak. As the company's co-founder, as well as the most mature and experienced of the three, Wayne had been given a 10 percent stake to essentially serve as Apple's parent, charged with keeping the two other eccentric geniuses under control. But that, as Wayne later recounted, "was like having a tiger by the tail." Two of them, actually, and as the only partner with any assets that could be seized, Wayne decided that the risk was too hazardous. So he was grateful to be set free, and with a check for

$800 to boot! That amount more than doubled when, to avoid any potential legal issues, the new company formally bought out the old. The co-founder thought he was flush with cash, and though his relinquished slice of the Apple pie eventually became worth in excess of $30 *billion,* Wayne always insisted he wasn't bitter. As he told the U.K.'s *Daily Mail* in 2013, "If I had stayed with Apple and accepted the limitations on my philosophy of life I could have well ended up the richest man in the cemetery." Instead, Wayne remained alive and well, selling stamps and coins out of his mobile home in Nevada. And collecting Social Security.

JANUARY 4, 1903

Topsy's Last Stand: The Shocking Execution of an Elephant

Amid the frenzy of invention and astonishing technological advances that characterized the later 19th century, Thomas Edison launched what became known as the War of Currents. It was a ferocious campaign against the use of alternating current (AC)—a system of electricity distribution, perfected by the inventor's onetime employee Nikola Tesla and backed by George Westinghouse—that threatened to make obsolete Edison's own direct current (DC) system in powering American homes and industry. Money and prestige were both at stake, and the Wizard of Menlo Park wasn't about to lose either.

Contrary to his folksy image, the famed inventor was absolutely ruthless in his efforts to discredit the rival system of alternating current, which he sought to portray as being just as lethal as lightning. To that end, Edison's associates staged a number of unsavory public spectacles in which dogs and other animals were electrocuted using the dreaded rival current.

The war reached its grotesque climax in 1890 when Edison used his considerable influence to ensure that convicted ax murderer William Kemmler would be executed by the newfangled electric chair. Of course, alternating current would be used to demonstrate just how dreadful it could be. Edison, in fact, coined the term for death by electric chair as being "Westinghoused," hoping it would enter the national vernacular. It didn't.

By the beginning of 1903, the War of Currents was all but lost as Edison's DC system was rapidly eclipsed. Still, the ever inventive Wizard conjured one last stunt to prove to the world that alternating current would be the bane of mankind. A misbehaving circus elephant named Topsy had killed three of her handlers—one of them after he put a lit cigarette in her mouth. Such aggression could no longer be tolerated, and it was decided that Topsy would have to die for her crimes. The plan was to publicly hang her at Coney Island. But when the American Society for the Prevention of Cruelty to Animals objected, Edison suggested Topsy be "Westinghoused" instead. And so on the appointed day, January 4, 1903—in what *The New York Times* described as "a rather inglorious affair"—the homicidal pachyderm was felled in front of a huge crowd by a 6,600-volt AC charge. And Edison, who had staged the whole sordid episode, captured it all with one of his greatest inventions: the motion picture camera.

JANUARY 5, 1895

Stripped of All Dignity: The Dreyfus Affair

It was just one episode in the prolonged saga of miscarried justice and virulent anti-Semitism that was known as the Dreyfus Affair. But for a man of honor, it was perhaps the most agonizing.

On the morning of January 5, 1895, Alfred Dreyfus, an artillery captain of Jewish descent attached to the French General Staff, having been secretly court-martialed and convicted of treason based on manufactured evidence, was forced to undergo an excruciating ritual of degradation before being shipped off to serve a life sentence on the fearsome penal colony Devil's Island.

At 9 a.m., Dreyfus was marched into the center of the École Militaire courtyard, where, before representatives of all France's armed forces and stands full of distinguished guests, his self-described "horrible torture" began. "I suffered agonizingly, but held myself erect with all my strength," he recalled. "To sustain me I called up the memory of my wife and children."

The sentence of degradation was read aloud, after which Dreyfus suddenly cried out to his comrades, "Soldiers! . . . I am innocent, I swear that I am innocent. I remain worthy of serving in the army. Long live France! Long live the army!"

Despite his protests, guards stripped Dreyfus of his buttons, braids, and epaulets until his uniform was bare of decoration. Then, as the final humiliation in what one witness described as "a more exciting spectacle than the guillotine," they broke his saber in two. The ceremony ended with a parade—a walk of shame. "I was compelled to make the whole round of the square," Dreyfus recounted. "I heard the howls of the deluded mob, I felt the thrill which I knew must be running through those people, since they believed that before them was a convicted traitor to France; and I struggled to transmit to their hearts another thrill—belief in my innocence."

After five years spent rotting on Devil's Island, and many more years struggling to rehabilitate his good name, Dreyfus was eventually officially exonerated in the affair that came to sharply divide France. But the French military that had framed him was never quite reconciled to its own dishonor, and in 1985 it rejected a statue of Dreyfus—holding his broken sword—that was to be placed in the École Militaire courtyard where the much maligned soldier had been so cruelly dishonored. Defaced with the slogan "Dirty Jew" in 2002, the memorial now stands forlorn on an obscure Parisian traffic island.

JANUARY 6, 1540

Sooo Not Hot: Henry VIII Meets His Match, Kills His Matchmaker

Thomas Cromwell was Henry VIII's most adept henchman. He was the ruthless engineer of the English king's divorce from his first wife, Katherine of Aragon, his split from Rome, and the destruction of his second wife, Anne Boleyn. But as a matchmaker, Henry's otherwise able minister was a dismal failure—a shortcoming that would cost him his head.

Henry had married three times for love, but after the death of his third queen, Jane Seymour, the king's influential minister determined a political match was in order to help shore up England's Protestant alliances in Germany. Cromwell settled on Anne, a princess from the duchy of Cleves. And though he had never set eyes on her, Henry agreed to the match based on the glowing reports of her beauty and grace he had received from his closest adviser and others—as well as a somewhat flattering portrait of the princess by the court painter Hans Holbein.

Having successfully finessed the political alliance with Cleves, Cromwell anxiously awaited his master's romantic response to his handiwork. It was not a good one. Henry had eagerly set off to the coast to meet his intended and, as he put it, "to nourish love." But upon first seeing Anne, the king blanched. "I like her not!" he stormed ominously, no doubt leaving Cromwell quaking.

What exactly it was about poor Anne of Cleves that so repelled the king remains a mystery. Perhaps it was simply chemistry—an intangible quality that would have been impossible for Cromwell to detect or convey. All that is certain is that Henry was very unhappy. "I see nothing in this woman as men report of her," he fumed, "and I marvel that wise men would make such report as they have done!" To Cromwell he railed, "If I had known so much before, she had no coming hither [to England]. But what remedy now?"

Unfortunately, there was no remedy without imperiling the vital Cleves alliance. King Henry VIII, a monarch whose will was rarely thwarted, now found himself stuck: "If it were not that she had come so far into my realm, and the great preparations and state that my people have made for her, and for fear of making a ruffle in the world and of driving her brother into the arms of the Emperor and the French King, I would not now marry her. But now it is too far gone, wherefore I am sorry."

Having placed his master's "neck into the yoke," as Henry put it, Cromwell could only meekly offer his regrets that the king was "no better content."

By his wedding day on January 6, 1540, Henry had hardly mellowed to the idea of Anne. "My lords," he said, pausing in front of the chapel at Greenwich Palace, "if it were not to satisfy the world and my realm, I would not do this day what I must do this day for any earthly thing." And if Cromwell hoped the king's mood might improve after he actually bedded Anne, he was sorely disappointed the next morning.

"I liked her before not well," Henry told him, "but now I like her much worse." Indeed, the king made it clear that the wedding night had been exceedingly unsexy. "I have felt her belly and her breast and thereby, as I can judge, she should be no maid, which so struck me to the heart when I felt them, that I had neither will nor courage to proceed further in other matters. I left her as good a maid as I found her."

Mercifully, Anne never felt the sting of her new husband's rejection because, having been overly sheltered as a young woman, she was entirely ignorant about what was *supposed* to have happened.

Henry made no effort to educate her further, which, given how fat and ornery he had become, was probably a blessing. Still, it did make Anne look a little silly, believing as she did that her marriage was fully realized.

"Why, when he comes to bed he kisseth me," she told her senior ladies-in-waiting, "and taketh me by the hand, and biddeth me 'Goodnight, sweetheart'; and in the morning kisseth me and biddeth 'Farewell, darling'. . . Is this not enough?"

It was left to one of the women to explain to the queen that, no, it wasn't enough at all. "Madam," she said, "there must be more than this, or it will be long ere we have a Duke of York [a second son for the king], which all this realm most desireth."

Six months after this farce of a marriage began, Henry had it annulled on the grounds on non-consumation, as well as an

Anne of Cleves: What's wrong with this picture?

alleged premarital contract Anne's family had arranged with someone else. Wisely, the king's fourth wife willingly agreed to the dissolution of her marriage, in return for which the grateful king handsomely rewarded her with a hefty settlement and superior status at court as his "good sister."

Cromwell, however, wasn't so lucky. While the king did elevate his lowly born chief minister, the son of an alehouse keeper, to the status of an earl in the aftermath of the Cleves debacle, it was merely a prelude (and perhaps a setup) for his ultimate undoing. The nobles of the realm, always resentful of the power and influence of the upstart Cromwell, now violently turned against him.

The once mighty minister was arrested on a false charge of heresy, and from his prison cell in the Tower of London he provided valuable testimony in the king's effort to shed his fourth wife. It was his last service to the sovereign he had helped make all-powerful. Less than three weeks after Henry's marriage to Anne of Cleves was annulled, Cromwell was beheaded on July 28, 1540—his pleas for "mercy, mercy, mercy" ignored.

With his head impaled on a spike atop London Bridge, the fallen minister could take no comfort in Henry's eventual change of heart, nor in the king's lament, reported by the French ambassador, that "he had put to death the most faithful servant he ever had."

JANUARY 7, 1945

Blather of the Bulge: The Fool Monty

It was the last gasp of Hitler's dying Third Reich, an unexpected, exceptionally violent thrust through the thinly defended Allied lines in southern Belgium that became known as the Battle of the Bulge. And though U.S. forces bore the brunt of the ferocious attack—bravely striking back under horrific conditions in the biggest and bloodiest single battle ever fought by American soldiers—it was the pompous British field marshal Bernard Law Montgomery who stepped forward in a press conference on January 7, 1945, to take undeserved credit.

Montgomery had been given temporary command of the northern flank of Allied forces, but was hesitant to attack aggressively. "Monty is a tired little fart," Gen. George S. Patton seethed in his diary. "War requires the taking of risks and he won't take them." Yet despite his marginal participation in the battle, and the overwhelming American sacrifices that actually had been made, the field marshal still made his grandstanding press conference appearance.

Wearing a double-badged maroon beret and a parachute harness—"dressed like a clown," as one journalist described him at the time—Montgomery grandly declared before the gathered reporters, "As soon as I saw what was happening [on the first day of the battle], I took certain steps myself to ensure that if the Germans got to the Meuse they would certainly not get over the river . . . I was thinking ahead . . . [The Bulge was] possibly one of the most interesting and tricky battles I have ever handled . . . You must have a well-balanced, tidy show when you are mixed up in a dog fight . . . you can't win the big victory without a tidy show."

The field marshal also implied that it was the British who saved the Americans from an impossible situation, though, as a sop, Montgomery gave a patronizing pat on the head to the Americans soldiers who had, in reality, done most of the fighting. Then came the message that "nearly destroyed Allied unity," as historian Stephen Ambrose wrote: "Montgomery said the GIs made great fighting men, when given the proper leadership."

"Even after sixty years, it remains astonishing that a highly intelligent man who had reached the summit of command could be capable of such vainglorious folly," wrote historian Max Hastings. "From Eisenhower downwards, every American who read Montgomery's words reacted with disgust."

Indeed, long simmering tensions among the Allied High Command—largely caused by Montgomery's incessant hectoring about his own position in the hierarchy—now seemed ready to explode. "This incident caused me more distress and worry than did any similar one of the war," wrote Supreme Allied Commander Dwight D. Eisenhower.

Winston Churchill was left with the task of restoring some semblance of Allied harmony. Using all his oratorical skills in a speech before the House of Commons 11 days after Montgomery's grandiose debacle, the British prime minister made it clear who the real heroes of the Bulge really were:

"I have seen it suggested that the terrific battle which has been proceeding . . . is an Anglo-American battle. In fact, however, the United States troops have done almost all the fighting and have suffered almost all the losses . . . The Americans have engaged thirty or forty for every one we have engaged, and they have lost sixty to eighty men for every one of ours."

Churchill then continued, with what seemed to be a message aimed directly at the credit-hogging Montgomery: "Care must be taken in telling our proud tale not to claim for the British Army an undue share of what is undoubtedly the greatest American battle of the war, and will, I believe, be regarded as an ever famous American victory."

JANUARY 8, 1992

And Now, the Ceremonial Tossing of the Cookies: Bush's Public Pukefest

The State Dinner held at the Japanese prime minister's home was a delectable array of cold salmon with caviar, a clear soup with mushrooms, medallions of beef with pepper sauce, and passion fruit ice cream. Unfortunately, most of the meal landed down President George H. W. Bush's front as he vomited at the table after becoming suddenly and violently ill from the flu. The rest ended up on the lap of his host, who cradled the stricken president's head as he proceeded to pass out. What was worse, while most people have the luxury of hurling in the privacy of their own homes, President Bush's projectile vomiting was captured on camera and endlessly replayed on television. Late-night talk show hosts feasted on the mortifying moment, while a new word for throwing up entered the Japanese lexicon: *Bushu-suru,* which literally means "to do the Bush thing." But it was the president himself who defused the awkward diplomatic incident with grace and humor. "Why don't you roll me under the table," he reportedly said to the prime minister as he lay on the floor, "and I'll sleep it off while you finish the dinner."

JANUARY 9, 1980

Off/On With Their Heads:
Saudi Slice and Splice

It was a busy day for beheadings in Saudi Arabia when, on the morning of January 9, 1980, 63 fanatical terrorists were publicly decapitated for having seized the Grand Mosque of Mecca the previous November. And just to ensure the entire kingdom got the government's message of retaliation for such sacrilege, the executions were carried out simultaneously in eight Saudi cities. Alas, the hectic day wasn't over once all the ornamented swords had sliced through their targets: 63 severed heads now had to be sewn back on for burial, as was the customary and decent thing to do. The year, again: 1980.

You've Got Fail:
The Doomed Merger of AOL
and Time Warner

It was the largest corporate merger in history, reported in the business press as breathlessly as a dazzling royal wedding. On January 10, 2000, came the announcement that AOL, the nation's dominant Internet provider, was to unite with communications giant Time Warner to form a seemingly perfect consolidation of old and emerging media. The future, it appeared, had arrived in an instant.

"Shortly before 9:00 last night, I had the honor and privilege of signing a piece of paper that irrevocably cast a vote taken, a vote of my 100 million shares, for this merger," gushed Ted Turner, a Time Warner director. "I did it with as much or more excitement and enthusiasm as I did on that night when I first made love some 42 years ago."

What followed, however, can only be likened to the regret of a hungover couple waking up to face one another in the harshest light of morning. "Dumbest idea I had ever heard in my life," Don Logan, then head of Time Inc., later said to *The New York Times*. Logan hadn't been told of the merger until the last minute. Neither had Timothy A. Boggs, then head of government relations at Time Warner, who received the news with "real regret and dread," as he later told the *Times*. "I was very leery about this deal."

As became increasingly clear, AOL wasn't half the Romeo it appeared to be. Certainly its stock price was soaring, but there were some real hidden warts—not the least of which was *The Washington Post*'s discovery that the company had been inflating its advertising revenue. Subsequent investigations by the Securities and Exchange Commission and the Justice Department resulted in hefty fines. Plus, the merger (which was in reality a takeover by AOL) coincided with the bursting of the tech bubble and the increasing obsolescence of AOL's dial-up Internet service. And, as *Times* reporter Tim Arango wrote in 2010, "The companies had another problem: Both sides seemed to hate one another."

During what Arango described as "the trail of despair in subsequent years," corporate values plummeted, many employees lost their jobs or the bulk of their retirement funds, and feuding executives were shuffled in and out. Divorce was inevitable. And, like most bad marriages, the end came amid bitterest recriminations.

"I'd like to forget it," Ted Turner told the *Times*. As the combined company's largest stockholder, Turner lost the most from the relationship he had once likened to his first time making love— 80 percent of his net worth, or about eight billion dollars. "The Time Warner–AOL merger should pass into history like the Vietnam War and the Iraq and Afghanistan wars," he said. "It is one of the biggest disasters that have occurred to our country."

JANUARY 11, 1877

Wire Fraud: Boy, Did This Guy Ever Have a Bridge to Sell

The Brooklyn Bridge, or the "Eighth Wonder of the World," as the engineering marvel of its day was once called, still stands today as an enduring monument to 19th-century aspiration and ingenuity—no thanks to one grossly corrupt character with a pivotal role in its construction.

On January 11, 1877, the bridge's board of trustees awarded one J. Lloyd Haigh the contract to provide the critical steel wiring that would actually support the mile-plus span. Chief engineer

Washington Roebling had repeatedly warned the board that Haigh couldn't be trusted, but his bid had been championed by board member and future New York City mayor Abram S. Hewitt, of whom Roebling wrote, "His success will prove a source of endless trouble and vexation." As it turned out, Hewitt just happened to hold the mortgage on Haigh's steel mill, and as a result of the lucrative cable wire contract, he would be assured of steady monthly payments.

Haigh was now in a position to perpetuate a massive fraud, one that could have fatally undermined the impressive span—the longest ever attempted, by far—in an era when far less ambitious suspension bridges routinely failed. And Roebling, previously debilitated by decompression sickness (or "the bends") while working under the East River on the bridge's foundations, wasn't there to stop him.

"The deception, once discovered, was painfully simple," historian David McCullough wrote. Haigh had a certain amount of high-quality steel wiring on hand, which he presented for inspection at his mill. But before the approved wiring made it to the nearby construction site, it was diverted on the way to a building and there replaced with inferior wire that was then applied to the bridge. Meanwhile the previously approved roll was secretly returned to the mill and the whole nefarious process began anew.

Fortunately, the design specifications for the bridge called for far more cable support than was necessary to support the span, so Haigh's inferior steel didn't have to be replaced—a nearly impossible undertaking anyway. "Yet the thought that such corruption was literally woven into the bridge could never be forgotten," wrote McCullough, "and least of all by Roebling himself."

JANUARY 12, 1915

Male Fraud: "Protecting" Women From Voting Rights

On January 12, 1915, Representative James Thomas "Cotton Tom" Heflin, the proudly bigoted Klansman from Alabama,* rose to add his voice to the sexist spectacle unfolding in the United States House of Representatives. At issue was a constitutional amendment that would give women the right to vote—an appalling prospect for the majority of the all-male lawmakers. "Most women now control one vote," the famously flamboyant Heflin addressed his colleagues, playing to the packed visitor galleries as well. "As I told a blushing suffragette the other day, if you are given the franchise you'll control two votes in every household—and that's too many."

Many of the congressmen were perfect gentlemen during the course of the debate, declaring themselves to be interested only in protecting women from the evils of enfranchisement and in sustaining their divinely ordained place—at home. Very chivalrous, at least for the 13th century, but as the *New Republic* noted later that month, the speakers "never for a moment descended to sordid facts as to the actual place of millions of American women in industry. Such facts would disturb their oratory." Furthermore, the editorial continued, "with all this regard for sainted mothers, loyal wives, and womanhood honored at large, such men as Mr. Bowdle seem incapable of sustaining ten minutes' talk without revealing the satyr's hoof."

The congressman referred to by the magazine was Stanley E. Bowdle, the outgoing representative from Ohio, who, among

---

* *See March 27 for an example of Heflin's enlightened approach to race relations.*

much cheering from his fellows (and nary an objection from the southern "gentlemen" present), offered his rather salacious take on the whole voting issue: "The women of this smart capital are beautiful. Their beauty is disturbing to business; their feet are beautiful; their ankles are beautiful, but here I must pause—for they are not interested in the State."

And Bowdle had much more to say, so much so that his allotted time was graciously extended. "Men and women are different," he noted. "They are different in every atom. Right here is where women set up a grouch. Many women resent the limitations of sex. But why quarrel with God when He has the final word? I might as well weep because I cannot gestate a child."

The voting measure failed passage that day, 204-174.

JANUARY 13, 1920

Yes, It *Was* Rocket Science

"We know that the nature of genius is to provide idiots with ideas twenty years later," the French poet and novelist Louis Aragon once wrote. He had a point. It has often been that some of the most brilliant minds have gone unheralded in their own lifetimes. Van Gogh was a failed, starving artist who sold only a couple of paintings before committing suicide in 1890. People liked Bach's organ playing but largely ignored his compositions. Edgar Allan Poe barely made a living writing his classic tales of the macabre.

And sometimes genius has actually been scorned. This was perhaps most egregiously evident in the ridicule Robert H. Goddard endured when his pioneering ideas and practical applications for space travel became public in 1920. *The New York Times* was particularly harsh. In an editorial titled "A Severe Strain on Credulity," published on January 13, 1920, the newspaper declared that Goddard "only seems to lack the [basic scientific] knowledge ladled out daily in high schools." Stung by the unwarranted criticism, Goddard responded several days later. "Every vision is a joke until the first man accomplishes it," he said to a reporter; "once realized, it becomes commonplace."

Just 24 years after Goddard's death in 1945, man first walked on the moon—propelled there by the rocket technology originated by the much derided physicist. The day after that historic event, the *Times* saw fit to publish a correction of its scathing editorial written nearly a half century earlier: "Further investigation and experimentation have confirmed the findings of Isaac Newton in the 17th century and it is now definitely established that a rocket can function in a vacuum as well as in an atmosphere. The *Times* regrets the error."

Off to the Racists: George Wallace's Terrible Turnaround

"It is very appropriate that from this cradle of the Confederacy, this very heart of the great Anglo-Saxon Southland, that today we sound the drum for freedom as have our generations of forebears before us time and again down through history. Let us rise to the call for freedom-loving blood that is in us and send our answer to the tyranny that clanks its chains upon the South. In the name of the greatest people that have ever trod this earth, I draw the line in the dust and toss the gauntlet before the feet of tyranny, and I say segregation now, segregation tomorrow, segregation forever."
—*Inaugural speech delivered by Alabama governor George Wallace, January 14, 1963*

Well before he became the very embodiment of the fierce racial segregationist, George Wallace was a much more moderate man. "If I didn't have what it took to treat a man fair, regardless of his color, then I don't have what it takes to be the governor of your great state," he declared during the Alabama gubernatorial campaign of 1958. But then Wallace decisively lost that race to his bile-spewing, Klan-backed opponent John Patterson. It was a bitter experience for the ambitious politician who had vowed at age 14 that he would one day head the state.

Out of the wreckage of his 1958 campaign—during which he had actually been backed by the NAACP—Wallace reinvented himself as a fire-breathing segregationist. "You know," he said at the time, "I tried to talk about good roads and good schools and all these things that have been part of my career, and nobody listened. And then I began talking about niggers, and they stomped the floor."

Having "made a Faustian bargain," as his biographer, Emory University professor Dan Carter, described the tawdry transformation in the *Huntsville Times,* and "sold his soul to the devil on race," Wallace won his long-coveted place in the governor's mansion. And on January 14, 1963, he delivered the inauguration speech that would forever define him.

JANUARY 15, 1919

The Sweet Smell of Distress: A Tidal Wave of Molasses

Death came suddenly on January 15, 1919, in a terrible surge of sweet, sticky goo. Residents and workers in Boston's North End bustled about their regular routines on this unseasonably warm day when, at about 12:30 p.m., a loud rumbling, like an overhead train, could be heard, accompanied by what sounded like the *rat-a-tat* of machine-gun fire—the popping of rivets, as it turned out. The noise came from a massive storage tank that had loomed over the neighborhood for three years and contained more than two million gallons of raw molasses. It was breaking apart.

The tank's collapse sent a massive wave of molasses—about 8 to 15 feet high, and significantly heavier than seawater—hurtling through the surrounding streets at 35 miles an hour, destroying everything in its path. Railroad cars were lifted from their tracks; buildings were knocked off their foundations and crushed. People in the path of the relentless brown swell never stood a chance. All told, 21 people perished—some not uncovered from the viscous mass for days—and another 150 were injured.

"The sight that greeted the first of the rescuers on the scene is almost indescribable in words," a *Boston Post* reporter wrote.

The aftermath of the two-million-gallon molasses swell over Boston's North End

"Molasses, waist deep, covered the street and swirled and bubbled about the wreckage. Here and there struggled a form—whether it was animal or human being was impossible to tell. Only an upheaval, a thrashing about in the sticky mass, showed where any life was . . . Horses died like so many flies on sticky fly paper. The more they struggled, the deeper in the mess they were ensnared. Human beings—men and women—suffered likewise."

The owner of the tank, United States Industrial Alcohol, tried to disclaim responsibility for the disaster, blaming it instead on an anarchist's bomb. But after years of investigation, the company was found to have been negligent in both the construction and maintenance of the tank and forced to pay a hefty settlement to the survivors. And though the site of the disaster has long since been transformed into a park, some people swear that on a warm day the sweet smell of molasses still wafts through the air.

JANUARY 16, 1547

Tsar Struck: They Didn't Call Ivan "the Terrible" for Nothing

Before Ivan IV became "the Terrible"—when he was ruling as the relatively powerless Grand Prince of Moscow while still a child—only the animals suffered: dogs and cats hurled from high towers by the gleeful little monster-in-the-making. But things started to get nasty when, on January 16, 1547, Ivan was crowned at age 16 as the first "Tsar of All the Russias." Soon enough, the new sovereign transformed his realm into one vast chamber of horrors.

Entire cities suffered from the tsar's increasingly unbalanced fury—most notably Novgorod in 1570. The dangerously paranoid Ivan, convinced that the people of Novgorod planned to betray him to the king of Poland, ordered the city to be sacked with horrifying thoroughness. Thousands of men, women, and children from all levels of society—from the elite down to the lowliest peasants—were systematically massacred, while the food supplies of those who managed to escape the butchery were destroyed. Little was left of Novgorod after Ivan's six-week assault, which just happened to coincide with the 23rd anniversary of his coronation. The festivities continued in Moscow that summer when hundreds of the tsar's enemies were skinned, boiled, burned, or broken in an orgy of retribution on Red Square.*

JANUARY 17, 1912

Sitting on the Bottom of the World: Scott's South Pole Debacle

It was one of the greatest feats in the history of exploration: an arduous trek to the very bottom of the world. Unfortunately, as Robert Falcon Scott discovered to his horror upon reaching the South Pole on January 17, 1912, he and his British team weren't the first to make it there.

---

* *In one more lowlight of his barbaric reign, Ivan killed his oldest son in a fit of fury. Apparently the ill-fated heir objected to his father kicking his pregnant wife and was beaned on the head with an iron staff for his effrontery. Three years later, in 1584, Ivan the Terrible was himself dead, but certainly not forgotten. In fact, the equally ferocious Stalin honored him over three centuries later as his favorite tsar.*

"The worst has happened, or nearly the worst," Scott recorded in his journal after spotting some of the first, uncertain signs that another team had already arrived. Soon enough, the evidence became unmistakable. "We marched on," Scott continued, and "found that it was a black flag tied to a sledge bearer; near by the remains of a camp; sledge tracks and ski tracks going and coming and the clear trace of dogs' paws—many dogs. This told us the whole story. The Norwegians [led by Roald Amundsen] have forestalled us and are first at the Pole."

Nature seemed to mock the British adventurers' failure that bitter January day, as a fierce gale set in and already freezing temperatures plummeted. "Great God! This is an awful place and terrible enough for us to have laboured to it without the reward of priority," Scott lamented in his journal.

With their dreams of glory in ruins, and no flag to plant at the Pole, the frostbitten explorers had nothing to do now but turn around. "It will be a wearisome return," Scott wrote. In fact, it proved deadly. One by one, each member of the five-man expedition succumbed to cold, disease, and exhaustion. Before he died, though, Scott managed to jot a final "Message to the Public":

"I do not regret this journey, which has shown that Englishmen can endure hardships, help one another, and meet death with as great a fortitude as ever in the past. We took risks, we knew we took them; things have come out against us, and therefore we have no cause for complaint, but bow to the will of providence, determined still to do our best to the last . . . Had we lived, I should have had a tale to tell of the hardihood, endurance, and courage of my companions which would have stirred the heart of every Englishman. These rough notes and our dead bodies must tell the tale."

Copy and Pissed: Karma for the Light-Fingered Historian

Historian Doris Kearns Goodwin was in quite a snit when, in 1993, she publicly accused author Joe McGinniss of lifting passages directly from her best-selling 1987 book, *The Fitzgeralds and the Kennedys: An American Saga,* for his own biography of Senator Edward Kennedy. "He just uses it flat out, without saying that it came from my work," Goodwin complained to *The Boston Globe.* "You expect that another writer would acknowledge that," she continued. "It's inexplicable why it wasn't done."

But, as it turned out, *The Fitzgeralds and the Kennedys* wasn't entirely Goodwin's work to begin with. In fact, she liberally used the words of other authors in numerous instances. One glaring example was Goodwin's appropriation of Rose Kennedy's own prose, reproduced nearly word for word.

On January 18, 2002, 15 years after *The Fitzgeralds and the Kennedys* was first published, *The Weekly Standard* exposed Goodwin's overt plagiarism—not only of Rose Kennedy and several others, but perhaps most egregiously of author Lynne McTaggart's 1983 biography of Kathleen Kennedy. The magazine included a damning list of comparative passages, and an explanation, of sorts, from Goodwin:

"I wrote everything in longhand in those days, including the notes I took on secondary sources. When I wrote the passages in question, I did not have the McTaggart book in front of me. Drawing on my notes, I did not realize that in some cases they constituted a close paraphrase of the original work."

Goodwin also acknowledged that she later made an agreement with McTaggart to include more footnotes and a paragraph crediting her book for the subsequent paperback addition, though without quotes added to the purloined passages. What she neglected to mention, however, was that a financial settlement had also been reached with McTaggart. That was revealed several days later in a *Boston Globe* article in which Goodwin insisted she was "absolutely not" a plagiarist and lamely defended her mistakes by explaining that *The Fitzgeralds and the Kennedys* was the "first big work of history I have ever done." But, as the newspaper helpfully pointed out, she had actually published *Lyndon Johnson and the American Dream* in 1976—11 years before.

Goodwin seemed to make more of a mess of her reputation as she struggled to redeem it. Her euphemistic description of her acts of plagiarism as "borrowing," as well as her continued excuse of faulty note-taking, only inflamed her critics further. When she tried to salvage the credibility of her Pulitzer Prize–winning *No Ordinary Time: Franklin and Eleanor Roosevelt* by repeatedly asserting that it was uncontaminated by plagiarism, the *Los Angeles Times,* among other publications, revealed several instances of "borrowing" in that book. Then there was her promise to have the remaining offending copies of . *The Fitzgeralds and the Kennedys* pulped, which remained unfulfilled.

Bo Crader, who originally broke the story for *The Weekly Standard,* summarized the situation to devastating effect when he used Goodwin's own indictment of Joe McGinniss to conclude his piece: "There's nothing wrong with an author building on material from a previous book," Goodwin had said. "That's the way history is built, as long as you credit the source . . . I just don't understand why that wasn't done."

JANUARY 19, 1990

The Mayor Crack'd: D.C.'s Smoking Top Gun

Marion S. Barry, the mayor of Washington, D.C., was soaring high, buzzing on his own sense of invincibility, even as his city was consumed by a murderous crack cocaine epidemic and rumors of his own chemical indulgences ran rampant. "Co-caaaane?" the self-proclaimed "Night Owl," frequenter of sleazy strip joints and hotel rooms turned drug dens, exclaimed in a *Los Angeles Times* profile. "How folks use that stuff, anyhow? You put it up your noooose? No! Ooooooeeeeeee!" Mayor Barry's expressed distaste for the drug was delivered, as the *Times* reporter noted, "mockingly, coy, flaunting it all," while later in the piece he professed to be insulted by the charges aimed at him: "I'm not stupid enough to have done the things they accuse me of! God gave me a good brain. What I have done nobody knows about because I don't get caught."

And yet, less than two weeks after the *Times* profile ran, the news broke that Barry had been caught, on film, smoking crack cocaine at a downtown D.C. hotel in the company of his mistress, Hazel Diane "Rasheeda" Moore. The Night Owl was outraged at Moore's apparent cooperation in what turned out to be an FBI sting operation. "I'll be goddam," he muttered over and over as he was arrested. "Bitch set me up." He was arraigned the next day, on January 19, 1990—exactly one year after the mayor swore before a grand jury that he had never smoked crack with his associate Charles Lewis, who testified that indeed he had. A month later, Barry was indicted on three counts of perjury.

Such an epic disgrace would have been more than enough to ruin most politicians. But for the man dubbed "Mayor for Life" by the *Washington City Paper,* it was simply a bad blip. After Barry served his six-month sentence, his loyal constituents—quite a few of them on the city's payroll—elected him to the city council and then, astonishingly, made him mayor again—twice!

"I'm gonna be like that lion the Romans had," Barry told the *Times* before his ignominious (but temporary) fall. "They can just keep throwin' stuff at me, you know? But I'll be kickin' their asses, every time! In the end, I be sittin' there, lickin' my paws!"

JANUARY 20, 1953

Harry Didn't Like Ike:
A Bitter Exchange

The essence of democracy requires ceding power, but few presidents have relished the prospect of abdicating control to their successors—especially when the incoming and outgoing chief executives really don't like one another. John Adams set a precedent by slipping out of town before his rival Thomas Jefferson's Inauguration. His son John Quincy Adams did the same thing after losing a most virulent election to Andrew Jackson. But few transitions were quite as contentious as when Dwight D. Eisenhower replaced Harry S. Truman on January 20, 1953. As presidential adviser Clark Clifford recalled, "The hatred between the two men that day was like a monsoon."

The relationship between General Eisenhower and his former commander in chief had turned sour during the 1952 presidential campaign, in which the Republican Eisenhower faced off against Democrat Adlai Stevenson. "The general doesn't know any more about politics than a pig knows about Sunday," Truman once snorted, while Eisenhower attacked what he called "Truman's mess in Washington."

Truman was appalled by some of Eisenhower's behavior, particularly his self-appointed peace mission to Korea, which the president dismissed at a press conference as "political demagoguery." And when Eisenhower succumbed to Republican pressure to not defend his mentor Gen. George C. Marshall against scurrilous attacks by Senator Joseph McCarthy, Truman was quick to condemn him. "[It was] one of the most shocking things in the history of this country," the president said. "The trouble with Eisenhower . . . he's just a coward . . . and he ought to be ashamed for what he did."

The bitterness between the two men reached a peak on Inauguration Day, when they were forced to ride side by side to the Capitol. Eisenhower wondered aloud "if I can *stand* sitting next to that guy," and then refused Truman's offer to come inside the White House for coffee. Instead, he waited for the president outside in the car. "It was a shocking moment," recalled CBS correspondent Eric Sevareid, who observed the incident, and a slight that Truman would never forget.

"I'm not one of Mr. Eisenhower's admirers," he later wrote. "I tried so hard to be pleasant and cooperative when I was turning the office over to Eisenhower, but he acted as if I was his enemy instead of the fellow who'd had the job just before him."

Though Eisenhower and Truman differed in their accounts of the conversation that took place along the route to the Capitol, it was most certainly frosty. As White House usher J. B. West put it, "I was glad I wasn't in that car."

JANUARY 21, 1535

Adventures in Unchristian Christianity, Part I: Post No Notices... Violators Will Be Incinerated

There was a particular breed of heretic in Renaissance France for whom burning at the stake was deemed just too light a punishment by King Francis I. In a 16th-century version of viral messaging, a band of naughty Protestants anonymously posted notices all over Paris and beyond, mocking the doctrine that Christ is actually present in the Eucharist. One even made it into the king's own bedroom, which particularly incensed Francis, as did a second round of posters denouncing the pope and Catholic clergy as "a brood of vermin . . . apostates, wolves . . . liars, blasphemers, murderers of souls."

A large reward was offered for the names of those who perpetuated the sacrilege that became known as the Affair of the Placards. Retaliation was swift and severe. On January 21, 1535, the bareheaded king, dressed in black and holding a lighted taper, made a solemn procession through the streets of Paris to the Cathedral of Notre Dame. He was accompanied by his sons, carrying the Eucharist under a canopy; all the other highest ranking nobles and ecclesiastics of France; and an array of sacred relics, like the head of St. Louis and what was believed to be the original crown of thorns. Then, after an expiatory Mass, while the king dined, six of the accused heretics were executed in front of the cathedral—"by a method judged fit to appease the Deity," as historian Will Durant put it.

The condemned were suspended over a roaring fire, like chestnuts, and then repeatedly dipped into the flames to prolong their suffering. And Francis didn't stop there. There were so many subsequent burnings that even the staunchly anti-Reformation pope, Paul III, finally had to order the "Most Christian King"* to cool it.

JANUARY 22, 2010

For Conan, No Tomorrow for *Tonight*

"Hello, kiddo," came the instantly recognizable voice over the phone. Johnny Carson, the esteemed "King of Late Night,"

---

* *The traditional title of France's monarchs, conferred by the papacy.*

was calling to congratulate Conan O'Brien on his announced succession as host of NBC's *The Tonight Show,* the same position Carson famously held for three decades. "For O'Brien," that call in 2004 "was a bit like being blessed into the priesthood by the Pope himself," wrote *New York Times* television reporter Bill Carter, who recounted the conversation in his book *Desperate Networks.* But the inheritance of one of television's most venerable programs, a long-held dream for O'Brien, would have to be deferred for five years until the scheduled retirement of then host Jay Leno. The younger man joked to Carson about the delayed takeover: "If I live to see it," to which the retired host replied, "Yes, it does seem like a long engagement before the marriage." The divorce would happen so much quicker.

On Monday, June 1, 2009, *The Tonight Show With Conan O'Brien* finally made its debut with a brand-new stage set, comedian Will Ferrell as the first guest, and, most important, impressive ratings. O'Brien's dream had at last been fulfilled. But the next day, Tuesday, the ratings slipped, and they continued to slide until at one point in its first month the program reached its smallest audience in the more-than-half-century history of *Tonight,* according to *The New York Times.* Then came another disaster. Instead of retiring, previous host Jay Leno began a prime-time variety show on NBC that September. It was a massive flop, dragging down the ratings of all the programs that followed it on the network—including O'Brien's.

To rectify the problems it had created, NBC executives made what was widely regarded as a colossally stupid decision: Leno would be brought back to late night for a modified version of his variety show beginning at 11:35 p.m., and *The Tonight Show* would be pushed back to 12:05 a.m. O'Brien, who hadn't been told of the plan in advance, balked. "I believe that delaying *The Tonight Show* into the next day to accommodate another comedy program will seriously damage what I consider to be the greatest franchise in the history of broadcasting," he said in a statement. "*The Tonight Show* at 12:05 simply isn't *The Tonight Show.*"

On January 22, 2010—less than eight months after his debut—O'Brien hosted his last *Tonight Show.* Will Ferrell was among his final guests and, in an ironic twist, the ratings soared. As for that fancy new set, Jack McBrayer made an appearance in character as NBC page Kenneth Parcell (from the show *30 Rock*) and noted to an improvised tour group that "NBC spent more time building this studio than using it."

JANUARY 23, 1968

Saluting North Korea— With One Finger

O n January 23, 1968, North Korea captured the U.S.S. *Pueblo,* a small, rickety surveillance vessel on its first intelligence-gathering mission. One crew member, Duane Hodges, was killed in the assault, and 82 others, some grievously wounded, were taken prisoner. To be sure, it was a humiliating Cold War catastrophe for the United States, already deeply mired in the Vietnam War. But it was a propaganda debacle for the diminutive North Korean leader Kim Il Sung as well—thanks to the subversive efforts of the *Pueblo*'s captured crew, who used the only weapons they had to undermine the so-called Great Leader: their agile minds and their middle fingers.

Flexing his mini-muscles, Kim Il Sung made a spectacle of his American prisoners, trotting them out before the cameras and coercing confessions of their evil intent toward the Democratic People's Republic of Korea. Given the savage beatings and other forms of torture the malnourished, ailing crew members had endured throughout their 11-month ordeal, there was little they could do to defy their captors—at least directly—but their subtle resistance ultimately made a mockery of Kim's oppressive tactics.

Subversive messages were embedded into the forced confessions. In one, for example, the men assured the North Koreans that they wished to "paean" (a word that by definition means to offer praise but that happens to sound a lot like "pee-on") not just their country, but their leader as well. In another, the *Pueblo*'s commander, Lloyd M. Bucher, wrote in tiny Morse code "This is a lie." But what really inspired the men was the discovery that their subjugators had no clue what the raised middle finger meant. "We now had a weapon!" wrote crew member Stu Russell. "Back in our rooms we were elated; this was one more thing we could use to discredit the propaganda we were being forced to grind out." From then on, the men incorporated the single-digit salute into all the forced photos of themselves that North Korea sent out to impress the rest of the world with its might.

U.S.S. Pueblo *crew members raise a subtle "salute" to their North Korean captors.*

JANUARY 24, A.D. 41

Kiss *This,* Caligula: The Falsetto Assassin Strikes Back

While the Roman emperor Caligula may have been one of the most depraved rulers in history—a self-proclaimed god who slept with his own sisters and gleefully reveled in the blood-letting of friend and foe alike—it wasn't his cruelest excesses that ultimately did in the half-mad monster. Rather, it was his incessant teasing of a particularly sensitive Praetorian Guard.

By most ancient accounts Cassius Chaerea was a strong and brave soldier, but he was saddled with an unfortunate impairment: an effeminate, high-pitched voice that some attributed to a war wound he sustained in the genital region. Caligula rarely missed an opportunity to mock his guard, assigning him such humiliating watch words as "Venus," which was slang for a castrated man, or "Priapus," for the minor Roman god often depicted with an enormous erection. And, as the ancient chronicler Suetonius reported, whenever the emperor had Chaerea kiss his ring, he would "hold out his hand . . . forming and moving it in an obscene fashion."

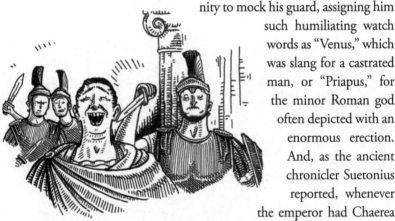

Fed up with the emperor's constant taunts, Chaerea plotted his assassination, attracting other disaffected Romans in the process. And on January 24, A.D. 41, the deed was done, with "Priapus" delivering the first thrust of the knife.

JANUARY 25, 1995

In Norway, the Rocket's Red Scare

A bad day averted can still be a bad day—like those times when the world is just a blink away from nuclear annihilation, just as it was on January 25, 1995. Early that morning, a joint U.S.-Norwegian scientific team launched a four-stage rocket from an island off Norway's northwestern coast to study the aurora borealis. Only problem was, the Russians never got the memo alerting them to the launch, and the rocket's appearance in the sky deeply unnerved them. The rocket bore a resemblance to U.S. Trident missiles and came from a region the Russians had long considered among the most threatening to their defenses. What resulted was "the single most dangerous moment of the nuclear missile age," as Peter Pry, a former CIA official, described it in his book *War Scare*. On red-hot alert, President Boris Yeltsin and the Russian high command—their fingers poised over the button that could lead to Armageddon—had only minutes to decide whether to strike back with the 4,700 strategic warheads at their disposal. Fortunately for the fate of mankind, the rocket fell into the sea and the button remained unpushed.

JANUARY 26, 1998

Bedeviled by a Blue Dress

One of life's certainties is that politicians lie, but perhaps none more brazenly than Bill Clinton did on January 26, 1998, when he vehemently denied having an affair with a certain White House intern. "I want to say one thing to the American people," the president declared, red-faced and finger pointing with indignation. "I want you to listen to me. I'm going to say this again: I did not have sexual relations with that woman, Miss Lewinsky." However, Miss Lewinsky had evidence of her dalliances with the chief executive embedded in a blue dress she had worn during one such encounter, and seven months later, in the face of this evidence, Clinton was forced to tell a different story: "I did have a relationship with Miss Lewinsky that was not appropriate," he admitted on August 27. "In fact, it was wrong."

JANUARY 27, 1595

Oh, Brother!
Why You Wouldn't Want to Be the Sultan's Sibling

"Bear, like the Turk, no brother near the throne."
—Alexander Pope, *Epistle to Dr. Arbuthnot*

Sultan Mehmed II, "the Conqueror," devised a simple solution in the mid-15th century for the fierce sibling quarrels that had long plagued the succession to the Ottoman throne: fratricide. "And to whomsoever of my sons the Sultanate shall pass, it is fitting that for the order of the world he shall kill his brothers," Mehmed II decreed (after having his own infant brother strangled). Nearly a century and a half later, the murderous policy had a particularly devastating effect on Mehmed III's brothers—all 19 of them!—when he came to the throne on January 27, 1595. The young men, some of them still babies, were ritually strangled with a bowstring and then buried with all due solemnity in the same tomb as their recently deceased father.

Costume Drama: The Worst Burning Man Festival Ever

B y 1393, Charles VI of France was already showing worrisome signs of the psychosis that would eventually rob him of all reason. His physician suggested that ways be found to divert and amuse the increasingly unbalanced monarch, and so a masquerade in which he participated was held on the evening of January 28 to celebrate the fourth marriage of one of Queen Isabeau's ladies-in-waiting. As it turned out, though, the event known as the Ball of the Burning Men very well may have been the spark that sent Charles right over the edge.

Traditionally a widow's remarriage was an occasion for mockery and foolishness, characterized by "all sorts of license, disguises, disorders, and loud blaring of discordant music and clanging of cymbals," as historian Barbara Tuchman explained in *A Distant Mirror: The Calamitous 14th Century*. This particular masquerade took on a distinctly pagan flavor, with five high-ranking knights, along with the king, dressed as wildmen from the woods. Their costumes, sewn onto the men, were made of linen soaked with resin to which flax was attached so that, as Tuchman wrote, "they appeared shaggy and hairy from head to foot." The men also wore masks of the same material. It was all fun and festive, but, alas, highly flammable.

As the disguised knights and the king

ran about mimicking savages by howling like wolves and screaming obscenities, the king's younger brother, Louis, Duke of Orléans, arrived late and drunk. He was also carrying a torch, which had been strictly forbidden for the other guests. According to one account, the duke went up to one of the dancers, and in an effort to determine his identity, held the torch up to his face. He got too close, though, and the knight's resin-soaked costume instantly erupted into flames, which quickly spread to the men dancing near him. The contemporary chronicler known as the Monk of St. Denis graphically described what followed: "Four men were burned alive, their flaming genitals dropping to the floor . . . releasing a stream of blood." Only one knight managed to survive the Ball of the Burning Men—by hurling himself into a vat of wine.

King Charles was fortunate enough to be standing away from his fellow dancers, and he was protected from the sudden inferno by the voluminous skirt of his aunt, which she cast over him. Still, the French sovereign was never the same again. Madness eventually enveloped him and rendered him unfit to rule. The poor king was unable to recognize his own wife and spent his remaining years walking around, very gingerly, convinced that he was made entirely of glass.

JANUARY 29, 904

Papal Bully

It was bad news for deposed pontiffs Leo V and his rival Christopher (now considered an "antipope" by the Catholic Church) when Sergius III obtained the papal throne on January 29, 904. Both men, now in prison, were immediately strangled to clear the title. Another former pope fared rather poorly under Sergius, too. According to an account by the 15th-century Italian writer Bartolomeo Platina, the corpse of the long dead Pope

Formosus—having already been once exhumed and put on trial in a grisly spectacle known as the Cadaver Synod—was dug up again, beheaded, and thrown into the Tiber "as unworthy the honor of human burial."*

JANUARY 30, 1649 *and* 1661

Dead and Deader: An Execution and an Exhibition

O n this cold January day in 1649, King Charles I stepped from the Banqueting House of Whitehall Palace and onto a scaffold erected just outside. Behind the king, in the room he'd just departed, was the brilliant fresco celebrating the glories of his Stuart dynasty; before him was the block upon which he was to have his head chopped off—the first and only British monarch to suffer such a fate, having been defeated in a long civil war with Parliament and subsequently convicted of treason. A massive crowd had gathered to witness the unprecedented spectacle but could not hear the king as he spoke his final words. "I go from a corruptible to an incorruptible crown where no disturbance can be," Charles told the Bishop of London before laying his head on the block. Then, with a single blow of the ax, the executioner completed the bloody deed.

Exactly 12 years later, the late king's nemesis and the architect of his demise, Oliver Cromwell (no direct relation to the other

---

* *Some historians dispute Platina's account. What remains certain, though, is that Sergius, who participated in the original Cadaver Synod as a bishop, honored the mad pope (Stephen VI) who had convened it by adding an epitaph to his tomb, lauding Stephen's actions against "the haughty intruder Formosus."*

decapitated Cromwell—see January 6) also faced public execution. But he bore no expression on the occasion and seemed oblivious to the entire proceeding—perhaps because he had already been dead for nearly three years.

Even though he had abolished the monarchy, and despite his own Puritan sensibilities, Cromwell lived like a king while serving as Lord Protector. He occupied the royal palaces and, when he died in 1658, was buried among Britain's deceased monarchs in Westminster Abbey. But he would not rest in peace. After the monarchy was restored under Charles II in 1660, Cromwell's corpse was exhumed from the abbey and, on the anniversary of Charles I's execution, dragged to Tyburn, where common criminals met their end. The body was hanged, and then the head was lopped off, spiked on a pole, and put on gruesome display atop Westminster Hall, where it remained for the next two decades as a grim warning to all who would ever dare threaten a king again.*

Feet Odor: The Stinkiest Sneaker Commercial in History

On January 31, 1999, the giant shoe retailer Just For Feet tripped and fell flat on its face—right in front of an estimated 127 million television viewers. The Birmingham, Alabama–based company, which in recent years had expanded into a retail behemoth with superstores across the United States, was anxious to

---

A severe storm reportedly blew the grisly relic off the roof of Westminster Hall, and after changing hands over several centuries, the head reputed to be Cromwell's was buried in 1960 at Sidney Sussex College in Cambridge.

update its image. And what better way than to run a spectacular commercial during the Super Bowl, when viewers were known to scrutinize product ads for their entertainment value almost as closely as they watched the game. The cost was exorbitant, but the exposure priceless. Just For Feet took the plunge.

"What we were looking to do was to start to build our brand," CEO Harold Ruttenberg told Salon.com in a May 1999 article. "What we wanted was for people to see this and say, 'Boy, that was terrific. Now we're customers of yours. We want to shop with you.'" Rather than coming off as edgy and relevant, though, the spot that ran during the fourth quarter made Just For Feet seem stunningly racist instead.

The ad opened with a shot of what appeared to be four white men (the race and sex of some of them was later disputed) in a military Humvee—"just for feet" on the license plate—tracking the footprints of a barefoot black runner in Kenya as a lion looked on. Catching up with the man, the pursuers offered him water, apparently laced with some kind of tranquilizer. Upon drinking it, the runner immediately collapsed to the ground, after which the men forced a pair of Nikes on his feet. Then, when the helpless man recovered his senses, he saw the shoes on his feet and began to shout, "Noooooo!" The spot closed with him still trying to shake the shoes from his feet as he ran away.

The backlash from the ad was immediate and fierce. "Appallingly insensitive," declared Stuart Elliott in *The New York Times*. Writing in *Advertising Age* magazine, Bob Garfield called the commercial "neo-colonialist . . . culturally imperialist, and probably racist. Have these people lost their minds?" *The Des Moines Register* suggested Just For Feet be renamed "Just For Racists," and in an editorial said that "the ad agency who signed off on the commercial should be required to come up with a campaign that shows the worst about their own cultures."

Obviously this was far from the kind of response Just For Feet desired in its first foray into big-league advertising. Accordingly, it sued the advertising firm of Saatchi and Saatchi, which had created the commercial. "As a direct consequence of Saatchi's appallingly unacceptable and shockingly unprofessional performance," the complaint read, "Just For Feet's favorable reputation has come under attack, its reputation has suffered, and it has been subjected to the entirely unfounded and unintended public perception that it is a racist or racially insensitive company."

Advertising executive Grant Richards, for one, had little sympathy for either side of the dispute. "The agency was a fool for proposing such a thing, and the client was a fool for paying for it," he told *Advertising Age* in 2000. In the end, Just For Feet's complaint became irrelevant; the company went bankrupt in 1999 and collapsed in the midst of a massive accounting fraud.

February

FEBRUARY 1, 2004

Keeping a Breast
in the News

On a day that saw two suicide bombings in previously calm Kurdistan, hundreds of pilgrims crushed to death at the Muslim holy site of Mecca, and continuing genocide in Darfur, media attention in the United States and elsewhere around the world was focused on something else entirely: the brief exposure of Janet Jackson's nipple during a halftime performance at Super Bowl XXXVIII. So riveting was the event, in fact, that it broke all records for Internet searches and inspired the advent of YouTube. Terror and mass starvation, it seems, just couldn't compete.

Doctored to Death

Britain's King Charles II was renowned for his vigor—both in the bedroom, where he sired scads of royal bastards by a number of different mistresses, and in his overall health. But on the night of February 1, 1685, the so-called Merry Monarch went to bed feeling a little less than his hearty self. Then, after a restless sleep, Charles awoke the next morning "looking pale as ashes and ghastly," according to his groom, as well as "unable or unwilling to say a single word . . . his face pale as death . . . speechless." And so began an excruciating, five-day ordeal for the king, provided courtesy of the realm's finest physicians.

After the king fell unconscious, a doctor opened his veins with a penknife and drained 16 ounces of his blood. After the king showed no improvement, many more medical experts were on the scene. "The majority pronounced him apoplectic," wrote Lord Macauley, "and tortured him during some hours like an Indian at a stake." A frenzy of "remedies" were prescribed— nearly 60 in all, including such potions as Oriental bezoar stone from the stomach of a goat and spirits of human skull. Some of the treatments were so toxic that they burned poor Charles's lips and tongue and caused scalding urination. The king's head was shaved and hot irons applied to draw out the bad humors from his brain, while other parts of his body were similarly blistered using heated cups.

Various emetics were forced down his throat. And, of course, there was more bleeding—the ultimate 17th-century cure-all.

Yet despite "every kind of treatment attempted by Physicians of the greatest loyalty and skill," as the subsequent doctor's report read, Charles continued to ail. On February 6, he finally expired, but not before issuing a wry apology, "for being such a time a-dying."

FEBRUARY 3, 1959

Bad News on the Doorstep

Waylon Jennings was lucky enough to have given up his seat on the chartered plane and lived to become a legend of outlaw country music. Bandmate Tommy Allsup also avoided the flight, having fortuitously lost a coin toss with Ritchie Valens. And Dion DiMucci, of Dion and the Belmonts fame, simply decided the plane ticket was too expensive. Alas, there was only so much good fortune to go around that day, and it ran out on rock-and-roll pioneers Buddy Holly and J. P. "the Big Bopper" Richardson, as well as Valens, when their plane crashed into an Iowa cornfield on February 3, 1959—"The Day the Music Died," as Don McLean so memorably put it in his 1971 song "American Pie."

FEBRUARY 4, 1998

Somebody Must Not Have Liked
Windows 98

As if their personal safety isn't enough of a worry for public figures, there's always the lurking danger of assaults on their dignity. Take Elizabeth II, for example. First the queen was pelted with eggs—one of which dripped down her dress—during a 1986 tour of New Zealand. Then, in Australia, a construction worker dropped his trousers and mooned the monarch as her motorcade passed. Poor Tom Cruise was splashed in the face with a squirt gun while answering a question on the red carpet, and President George W. Bush was subjected to the ultimate Arab insult when an Iraqi reporter lobbed a pair of shoes at him during a press conference, shouting, "This is a farewell kiss from the Iraqi people, you dog." (The president successfully dodged each missile.)

Even one of the world's richest men, Bill Gates, was forced to eat humble pie—literally—when on February 4, 1998, a creamy confection was plastered on his face while he was in Belgium for

Bill Gates bears the sweet remnants of a cream pastry attack in Belgium.

a business conference. But at least Gates wasn't alone in enduring such a humiliating assault. Fellow billionaire Rupert Murdoch has also been pied, as have San Francisco mayor Willie Brown, beauty queen turned anti-gay crusader Anita Bryant, conservative commentator William F. Buckley, King Carl XVI Gustaf of Sweden, clothing designer Calvin Klein (with a pie actually intended for fellow designer Karl Lagerfeld), U.S. Senator Daniel Patrick Moynihan, consumer advocate and perennial presidential candidate Ralph Nader, and movie star Sylvester Stallone—to name just a few.

FEBRUARY 5, 1969

Not Ready for Prime Time— or Any Time

On Wednesday, February 5, 1969, ABC premiered *Turn-On,* a sketch show one of its producers described as a "visual, comedic, sensory assault involving animation, videotape, stop-action film, electronic distortion, computer graphics—even people." Mostly, though, it was a garbled program of sophomoric sex jokes no one thought were funny. In fact, WEWS-TV, the ABC affiliate in Cleveland, was so unamused that it yanked *Turn-On* from the air at the first commercial break and sent the network management an angry telegram: "If your naughty little boys have to write dirty words on the walls, please don't use our walls. *Turn-On* is turned off, as far as WEWS is concerned." The affiliate revolt continued. Denver's KBTV didn't even bother to air the episode. KATU in Portland, Oregon, and Seattle's KOMO-TV made the same decision. Within the week, ABC took the affiliates' cue and canceled *Turn-On* after a single, only partially seen episode.

Dim Bulbs: The Foolish Frenzy of the Dutch Tulip Bubble

One of the most spectacular market collapses in history was caused not by frenzied real estate speculation or dangerous derivatives trading, but by the simple tulip. The flower had found great favor in the Netherlands after being introduced from Turkey in the late 16th century. Bulbs became quite pricey as the demand for the limited supply of the slow-growing cultivar increased; tulips became even more desired after a botanical virus caused vividly colorful streaks to run through the petals of certain varieties. In the mania that ensued, it seemed everyone wanted to have at least one precious bulb as the ultimate status symbol. As speculators entered the picture, prices soared even higher—absurdly high, with people selling their land and homes to enter the tulip market. Then, on February 6, 1637, the tulip bubble burst. Apparently no one showed up that day to bid on bulbs at the market in the town of Haarlem, perhaps kept away by an outbreak of the plague. Panic ensued, and, as the tulip's popularity faded, fortunes were lost in an instant. Now, nearly four centuries later, one of the Netherlands' most famous exports can be purchased in bulk—for next to nothing.

Roasted Masterpieces Florentine: The Bonfire of the Vanities

On February 7, 1497, all the fun to be had in Florence went up in flames in a spectacle known as the Bonfire of the Vanities.

In an effort to rid the city-state of its sinful preoccupation with luxury, beauty, and entertainment, the fanatical Dominican friar Girolamo Savonarola—who effectively ruled the republic after the Medici were temporarily driven out—coerced Florentines to submit their most precious objects to a massive pyre erected at the Piazza della Signoria. Heaped onto the multitiered structure were valuable paintings (including, by some reports, works by Botticelli), statuary, books by Petrarch, Dante, and Boccaccio, furniture, tapestries, cosmetics, sumptuous clothing, musical instruments, gaming tables, playing cards, and thousands of other things that added a little zest to life. As the monk's followers danced ecstatically around the colossal pile, everything burned. It was ironic, then, that a little over a year later, after being excommunicated by the pope and condemned as a heretic, Savonarola himself was consigned to the flames at the very same public square—a site that soon enough would be under the watchful eye of Michelangelo's very nude (and, as the monk no doubt would have viewed it, very lewd) statue of David.

FEBRUARY 8, 1587

Random Ax of Incompetence: The Queen's Botched Beheading

Death tends to be a drag, but for Mary Queen of Scots, it was a debacle as well. After fleeing her own rebellious kingdom in 1568, Mary became a prisoner of her cousin Elizabeth I of England for nearly two decades. Then, after being charged in a conspiracy to kill the English queen and replace her on the throne, she was condemned to death.

On February 8, 1587, the doomed monarch was led into the Great Hall of Fotheringhay Castle, where a scaffold had been erected for the occasion and the headsman awaited. The gathered witnesses stood grimly as Mary prepared herself and then laid her head on the block. With that, the executioner took a mighty swing with the ax. He missed. The blow struck the back of her head instead of the neck. Witnesses reported the stunned queen muttering "Sweet Jesus!" before a second strike all but severed her head. The headsman, exasperated by his own incompetence, was forced to saw away the remaining sinew to finally finish the job.

Alas, the ordeal wasn't over. After an execution, it was common practice to hold the head aloft to the witnesses. But when the headsman raised the queen's, it escaped his grasp and plopped on the floor. Mary had been wearing a wig, which was all that was left in the hapless executioner's hand.

As a final indignity, the corpse of the Scottish queen lay moldering in a sealed coffin for months at the castle before finally being given a decent burial.*

FEBRUARY 9, 1973

Good Thing It Was Built by an Insurance Company: The Skyscraper That Didn't Like the Sky

The sky was falling—or at least it seemed to be. Giant 500-pound panels of mirrored glass came crashing down from Boston's John Hancock Tower on February 9, 1973. It was just

---

* Mary was initially buried at Peterborough Cathedral, but her son, King James I, moved her body to Westminster Abbey—her elaborate tomb located just opposite from that of her nemesis, Queen Elizabeth I.

the latest in a long cascade of collapsing panes, which ultimately left more than an acre of the gleaming building pockmarked with black-painted plywood. But the timing that day was particularly unfortunate, coinciding as it did with the building company's denial that the entire glass facade would have to be replaced. That would ultimately become necessary, a result of an epic engineering failure. But, as Robert Campbell reported in *The Boston Globe,* falling windows were actually the least of the now iconic structure's myriad problems.

It all began in the basement, even before the new, rhomboid-shaped skyscraper started to rise from the ground. Three sides of the steel-braced excavation caved in, with a nasty ripple effect on surrounding buildings, especially the 19th-century architectural treasure Trinity Church, which suffered severe damage. "We'll never get it back the way it was," church treasurer Robert Kennard told the *Globe* in 1973. "If they put the Hancock Tower on a helicopter and dropped it into the Atlantic Ocean, most of the parishioners would be happy."*

From there, it only got worse. The completed structure made its occupants seasick. "The tower, in ordinary wind conditions, was accelerating too fast for comfort," Campbell wrote. "It was doing a sort of cobra's dance, swaying a few inches forward and back and, at the same time, twisting." And while that problem was eventually

---

* *The church was ultimately awarded over $4 million in damages.*

fixed, it came after the most daunting prospect of all: The Hancock Tower, its owners were informed in 1975, was in danger of actually tipping over. The unusual length of the structure (almost 300 feet) made it vulnerable, with just the slightest shift in plumb slowly building upon itself until eventually gravity took its course and collapsed the tower on its narrow edge. Fortunately, there was just enough room found in the building's service core to install 1,500 tons of reinforcing steel braces.

But oddly, as the *Globe* reported, absolutely none of the tower's structural deficiencies had anything to do with the most visible sign of distress; the crashing windows. The giant windows fell off, it emerged, only because the reflective chrome applied between the double panes wasn't flexible enough to withstand high winds. The windows have all since been replaced, and the once derided "plywood palace" once again mirrors the sky—intact.

FEBRUARY 10, 1971

I Really Want to Sue You ... George Harrison's "Unconscious Plagiarism"

He was known as the Quiet Beatle, but after the breakup of that legendary band in 1970, George Harrison emerged with a mighty blast of songs—a triple album's worth—that showcased his own musical brilliance. *Rolling Stone* magazine's Ben Gerson deemed Harrison's solo effort, *All Things Must Pass,* "[an] extravaganza of piety and sacrifice and joy, whose sheer magnitude and ambition may dub it the *War and Peace* of rock and roll." Music lovers embraced the album, which shot to number one on music charts across the world. But Harrison would have less than four months to enjoy his multi-platinum success before a lawsuit soured the whole experience.

The first single released from the album was "My Sweet Lord," a catchy spiritual anthem that turned out to be just a tad too catchy, and too derivative of another bouncy tune, "He's So Fine," by the Chiffons—or so a copyright infringement suit filed on February 10, 1971, claimed.

"I wasn't consciously aware of the similarity between 'He's So Fine' and 'My Sweet Lord' when I wrote the song as it was more improvised and not so fixed," Harrison later recalled in his auto-biography, *I Me Mine,* "although when *my* version of the song came out and started to get a lot of airplay people started talking about it and it was then I thought, 'Why didn't I realize?' It would have been very easy to change a note here or there, and not affect the feeling of the record."

After the failure of several rounds of settlement negotiations with Bright Tunes Music Corp., owner of the rights to "He's So Fine," the case finally went to trial in 1976. Harrison, guitar in hand, testified as to how "My Sweet Lord" was inspired and written, while music experts parsed every note. The judge concluded that it was "perfectly obvious the two songs are virtually identical." He did concede, how-ever, that the former Beatle had probably not lifted the Chiffons' song deliberately, but rather was guilty of "subconscious" plagiarism.

The protracted ordeal, including the monstrous expense to defend himself, had a profound effect on Harrison. "It made me so paranoid about writing," he later said. "And I thought, 'God, I don't even want to touch the guitar or the piano, in case I'm touching somebody's note.' Somebody might own that note, so you'd better watch out!"

In the end Harrison, who died of cancer in 2001, was at peace with all that had happened. "I don't feel guilty or bad about it," he said in his autobiography; "in fact ["My Sweet Lord"] saved many a heroin addict's life. I know the *motive* behind writing the song in the first place and its effect far exceeded the legal hassle."

FEBRUARY 11, 2014

Either Way, You End Up With Lots of Gas

A massive natural gas explosion in Greene County, Pennsylvania, literally rocked the earth and caused an intense, five-day inferno. No worries, though. Oil giant Chevron, owner of the fracking well that caused it, found a way to make it right with those neighbors immediately impacted by the blast: Free pizza! One hundred gift certificates—"Special Combo Only"—were mailed with a nice note from Chevron—a gesture, blogger Will Bunch of the *Philadelphia Daily News* noted, that might as well have read: "The Chevron Guarantee: Our well won't explode . . . or your pizza is free."

FEBRUARY 12, 1771

Putting the "S'more" in "Smorgasbord" (and "Morgue," Too)

King Adolf Frederick had the misfortune of ruling Sweden during a period when the monarchy was virtually powerless, so he had a lot of free time on his hands. As a mere figurehead, there was really nothing much for the king to do but decorate snuff boxes (his favorite hobby) and eat. One meal in 1771 proved particularly memorable, as it was Adolf Frederick's last: lobster, caviar, sauerkraut, and kippers, all washed down with champagne. But it was undoubtedly dessert—*14* servings of the extremely rich sweet roll known as *semla*—that caused the king's fatal stroke soon after he finished the feast.

The Painter's Prude Awakening

Although he is now considered one of the greatest American portrait painters, no one paid much attention to Thomas Eakins the artist in 1886. They were too consumed by Eakins the unconventional art instructor—the one who dared expose the nude to his students, both male and female, in a rigidly repressed era when even the exposed ankle of a woman was considered scandalous.

"Where the tendency of the age was to cover up, Eakins' was to strip bare, to get down to the natural and essential," wrote his biographer, Lloyd Goodrich. Eakins himself once wrote, "I see no impropriety in looking at the most beautiful of Nature's works, the naked figure." And that's just what got him stripped of his position as director of the Pennsylvania Academy of Fine Arts.

Eakins had long courted trouble with his introduction of nudity into the academy—including his own on at least one occasion—but never more so than in early 1886, when he removed the loincloth of a male model to demonstrate to a class of women the exact motion of the pelvis.

Hauled before the academy's board of directors and grilled relentlessly about his teaching methods—"the thing was a nightmare," he later said—Eakins was forced to resign on February 13, 1886. And no amount of protest from the majority of students devoted to their instructor would alter the decision. "We will not ask Mr. Eakins to come back," one of the directors announced to the press. "The whole matter is settled, and that is all there is about it."

The loss of his prestigious position was a devastating blow, particularly since he had yet to impress anyone as an artist. "No one collected Eakins but Eakins," a critic later remarked. And though he would return to the classroom—including at a breakaway institution formed by students disaffected by his dismissal from the Pennsylvania Academy of Fine Arts—he was continuously scorned, both as an artist and a man, even by members of his own family, some of whom actively conspired against him.

In 1895, Eakins was dismissed from Drexel Institute, again for his unconventional use of the nude, and within a few years he withdrew from teaching altogether. Sadly, there would be no recognition of his brilliance before he died in 1916; that would have to wait until decades later. "My honors are misunderstanding, persecution & neglect," the artist wrote of himself, "enhanced because unsought."

FEBRUARY 14, 1779

Captain Cooked: A Grisly End in Hawaii

Captain James Cook, widely acclaimed as the greatest sea explorer of all time, once wrote that his ambition led him "not only farther than any man has been before me, but as far as possible for a man to go." Heady words indeed, but certainly true for the time. During his three famed expeditions of the 1770s, Cook and his team of adventurers sailed vast, uncharted distances—from the tropical delights of previously unknown Pacific islands to the forbidding frozen seas of both the Arctic and the Antarctic—recording, mapping, and generally reshaping what Europeans knew of the world. But it was in his quest to find the elusive Northwest Passage that Captain Cook's voyages of discovery came to an abrupt and brutal halt in Hawaii.

The local population welcomed the members of Cook's expedition when they found safe harbor at Kealakekua Bay, along the coast of Hawaii's Big Island. In fact, the natives' treatment of Cook "seemed to approach to Adoration," reported James King, a second lieutenant aboard the ship *Resolution*. What King and the others didn't know was that their arrival coincided almost perfectly with an annual religious observation, during which the god Lono—associated with peace and plenitude—gained a brief period of ascendancy over the warlike deity Ku. Thus, Captain Cook was regarded as the physical incarnation of Lono, and that explained what King observed as "the very Abject & slavish manner, in which the commonality shewd their respect."

After several months spent basking in the Hawaiians' hospitality, Cook departed to continue the expedition north—just as Lono's time of rule was traditionally eclipsed by Ku. The British ships had not sailed very far, however, when one of the masts broke. There was no choice but to return to Kealakekua Bay for repairs. Unfortunately, the Hawaiian people saw Cook/Lono's unexpected return as a threat to Ku, embodied by a native monarch named Kalani'opu'u. The balance of power had now shifted to a dangerous degree.

The previously welcoming Hawaiians now turned hostile. They threw rocks at the interlopers, exposed their backsides, and brazenly stole from them. "Ever since our arrival here upon this our second visit we have observ'd in the Natives a stronger propensity to theft," noted Cook's second-in-command Charles Clerke, as "every day produc'd more numerous and more audacious depredations."

The British attempted to retaliate with firepower, but the lengthy time needed to reload limited their efficacy. Then, on February 14, 1779, hostilities reached a climax when locals seized Captain Cook and four marines accompanying him, repeatedly clubbed them, and held them under water, after which their corpses were dragged away to the interior. The bodies were then subjected to a ghastly postmortem ordeal, albeit one that was supposed to honor them as warriors: being cooked and stripped of flesh, with the pieces distributed among the various local chiefs. After much negotiation, what was left of Cook was returned to his men. King left this account:

"He [the chief] gave us a bundle wrapped very decently, & covered with a spotted cloak of black and white feathers, which we understood to be a mourning colour. On opening it we found the Captain's hands, which were well known from a remarkable cut, the scalp, the skull, wanting thigh bones and arm bones. The hands only had flesh on them, & were cut in holes, & salt crammed in; the leg bones, lower jaw, & feet which were all that remained & had escaped the fire."

FEBRUARY 15, 1942

Slung in Singapore: Britain's WWII Humiliation

"The worst disaster and largest capitulation in British history."
—Prime Minister Winston Churchill, recalling
Britain's unconditional surrender of its colonial power
base in Singapore—the supposedly impregnable
"Gibraltar of the East"—to the rampaging forces
of Japan on February 15, 1942

It was yet another devastating Allied setback in the earliest days of World War II (see December 7 and December 8), and a staggering blow to British prestige in the region.

FEBRUARY 16, 1899

Finis! But What a Way to Go . . .

French president Félix Faure was having a perfectly delightful day dallying with his mistress, Marguerite Steinheil, when at the climactic moment the French euphemistically call *la petite mort* (the little death) something bad happened. Faure suffered a massive stroke, which caused that little death he no doubt enjoyed so much to grow into one significantly less appealing.

Molière: The *Last* Role of a Lifetime

Perhaps life has never mimicked art with quite as much irony as it did on the evening of February 17, 1673, when the famed French actor and playwright Jean-Baptiste Poquelin (better known by his stage name Molière) gave his final performance—ever—playing the role of the hypochondriac Argan in his own farce, *Le Malade Imaginaire (The Imaginary Invalid)*. While acting out Argan's chimerical ailments, Molière succumbed to a very real coughing fit and collapsed on stage. Trouper that he was, the actor managed to complete the performance. But then, just hours later, he died of hemorrhage from a burst blood vessel.

The Spy Who Mugged Me

Bonnie Hanssen was about to drive into an abyss of betrayal so dark and dreadful as to render her almost speechless. Worried that her husband had not yet returned for dinner after dropping his friend off at the airport on the evening of February 18, 2001, she went to see if he might still be there. Instead, she found a swarm of FBI agents who immediately took her into custody and informed her that her husband—one of their own—had just been arrested for espionage. As it emerged, Robert Hanssen wasn't just any ordinary spy, either. Rather, the FBI counterintelligence agent was one of the worst traitors the United States had ever known: a modern-day Benedict Arnold whose treachery in selling vital secrets to the Soviet Union stretched back years, grievously compromised his country, and, inevitably, caused suspicion to fall on his own wife. Yet, for all that, another hideous revelation awaited Bonnie Hanssen: a personal betrayal of the most mortifying and invasive sort.

The friend Robert Hanssen had dropped off at the airport that fateful February afternoon—the best man at their wedding, godfather to one of their six children, and frequent guest in their home—had, unbeknownst to her, been spying on Bonnie while she was having sex with her husband, watching via a hidden camera Robert had set up himself. The churchgoing spy liked to have his friend watch—and always had, ever since 1970, when he

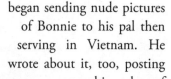

began sending nude pictures of Bonnie to his pal then serving in Vietnam. He wrote about it, too, posting graphic tales of voyeurism on the Internet, including one about Bonnie and his friend that he titled "The 'Unwitting?' Porn Star."

"She reacted with shock and horror," wrote David Wise in his book *Spy: The Inside Story of How the FBI's Robert Hanssen Betrayed America*. "Her remark was buzzing around in the family, and for good reason. What Bonnie had told her sister . . . was brief and unforgettable: 'My husband is a traitor and a pervert.'"

FEBRUARY 19, 1977

Noooo, Not "Best New Artist"! Pop Music's Ticket to Obscurity

The song is instantly recognizable: "Sky rockets in flight . . . afternoon delight"—the performers, on the other hand, not so much. Perhaps that can be chalked up to the Best New Artist Grammy awarded to the Starland Vocal Band on February 19, 1977—"the kiss of death," as band member Taffy Danoff once described it in an interview with VH1. "I feel sorry for everyone who's gotten it since." Hers was a sentiment no doubt shared by many of the other Best New Artist designees whose once promising careers all but evaporated in the wake of their Grammy glory—especially those "one-hit wonders" who received the award in the years immediately following the Starland Vocal Band. What ever happened to Debby Boone (1978)? Or A Taste of Honey (1979)?*

With some very notable exceptions, like the Beatles (1965) or Mariah Carey (1991), the Best New Artist award has often proved to be a one-way ticket to obscurity: "The Curse of Christopher Cross," as *The Washington Post* called it—a reference to the 1981 recipient who, the newspaper noted, "released more than a dozen albums after his win, yet his own parents probably could not pick him out of a lineup."

Perhaps there is no better evidence of a Best New Artist jinx than the fate of 1990 winners Milli Vanilli, who were stripped of

* As for the Starland Vocal Band, its four subsequent albums flopped, after which the group (and the marriages of the quartet's two couples) disintegrated.

their Grammy when it was revealed that they hadn't actually sung one note on their multi-platinum album *Girl You Know It's True.* Fortunately for the other Best New Artist nominees that year, the Grammy committee decided not to bestow the award on the runner-up—"perhaps figuring," as the *Post* noted, "everyone had suffered enough."

FEBRUARY 20, 1939

George Washington Hitler?

George Washington would have seethed with disgust had he still been alive for the birthday party held in his honor on February 20, 1939, at Madison Square Garden. Sure, there was a great turn-out—about 20,000 people—and spirits were high. But the organizers of the evening, the German American Bund, seemed much more intent on honoring Adolf Hitler than the actual birthday

The German American Bund celebrates George Washington and Adolf Hitler.

boy. Under a giant banner of the nation's first president, flanked by Nazi swastikas, a succession of speakers spewed enough anti-Semitic venom to make the event in the heart of New York City worthy of a Nuremberg rally.

With the audience whipped into a full frenzy, Fritz Kuhn, president of the Bund and host of the night's activities, at last made his appearance. To howls of appreciation, he made repeated references to President Franklin D. Roosevelt as "Frank D. Rosenfeld" and his New Deal as the "Jew Deal." Mercifully, it was Kuhn's last moment in the spotlight. Soon after the rally, he was arrested on a variety of criminal charges—including embezzlement from the very same Madison Square Garden event his group had sponsored—and eventually deported back to Germany.*

FEBRUARY 21, 1848

The Communist Manifesto: An Idea That Should Have Remained One

P lato presented his idea of the ideal society in *The Republic.* Thomas More did the same thing in *Utopia,* as did Voltaire in *Candide.* These were mere philosophical musings, interesting but entirely impractical. Karl Marx and Friedrich Engels followed in

---

* *If Kuhn expected a hero's homecoming, he was sadly disappointed. The Nazis considered him an embarrassment— "stupid, noisy and absurd," as Hans Dieckhoff, Germany's ambassador to the United States, described him. He died on December 14, 1951, in Munich—"a poor and obscure chemist,"The New* York Times *reported, "unheralded and unsung."*

the same vein, but when their *Communist Manifesto* was first published on February 21, 1848, people actually tried to apply—or rather *impose*—this half-baked blueprint for a worker's paradise. Thus, what really should have been left as an academic exercise on political theory instead became the most malignant force of the 20th century.

The lethal tract empowered monsters like Mao and Stalin, metastasized in totalitarian regimes across the globe, and ultimately caused the deaths of an estimated 100 million people through murder and mass starvation. And though the misery continues in North Korea and elsewhere, the socialist system so earnestly advocated by Marx and Engels in 1848 eventually crumbled under the weight of its essential infeasibility.

"Let's not talk about communism," Russian president Boris Yeltsin declared after the collapse of the Soviet Union. "Communism was just an idea, just pie in the sky."

FEBRUARY 22, 1983

Broadway's Bombiest Bomb

On February 22, 1983, Arthur Bicknell's *Moose Murders: A Mystery Farce in Two Acts* opened on Broadway. Then it closed the very same night—a legendary bomb that *The New York Times* later described as "the standard of awfulness against which all Broadway flops are judged." The critics were brilliantly savage in their reviews of what Frank Rich later called "the worst play I've ever seen on a Broadway stage":

- "If your name is Arthur Bicknell, change it." —Dennis Cunningham, WCBS
- "So indescribably bad that I do not intend to waste anyone's time by describing it." —Clive Barnes, *New York Post*

- "I will not identify the cast pending notification of next of kin." —Jay Sharbutt, Associated Press
- "A visit to 'Moose Murders' will separate the connoisseurs of Broadway disaster from mere dilettantes for many moons to come." —Frank Rich, *The New York Times*
- "[It] would insult the intelligence of an audience consisting entirely of amoebas." —Brendan Gill, *The New Yorker*
- "There are bad plays, terrible plays and plays like *Moose Murders*." —*Variety*

Clive Barnes did at least commend actress Eve Arden for having the sense to leave the play before it opened. "Some people have all the luck," he wrote. Holland Taylor, however, had the misfortune of replacing her. "There were things that I put my foot down about and changed," she told *The New York Times*. "But there were things I couldn't change. Like the play."

"Was it really that bad?" asked the playwright, Bicknell, who recalled his friends and family, as well as the cast, slinking out of a party at Sardi's restaurant on opening night. "The simple answer is yes."

FEBRUARY 23, 1669

To Kiss (A Very Dead) Queen

As the daughter, wife, mother, and grandmother of kings, Queen Katherine of Valois might have expected to be treated with a little dignity after her death in 1437. Ah, but it was not to be. Katherine's tomb in Westminster Abbey was destroyed during the reign of her grandson Henry VII to make way for his magnificent new chapel. And for centuries thereafter, the queen's corpse—her bones "firmly united, and thinly cloth'd with flesh, like scrappings of tann'd leather"—lay exposed as a ghoulish tourist attraction.

"Katherine, Queen of England, lieth here," John Weever wrote in 1631, "in a chest or coffin with a loose cover, to be seen and handled of any who will much desire it."

Poor Katherine lay helpless as she was ogled by the masses and had bits of her desiccated skin snatched away by mischievous schoolboys. But the ultimate impiety came on February 23, 1669, when the famed diarist Samuel Pepys celebrated his 36th birthday by essentially molesting the dead queen.

"Here we did see, by particular favour, the body of Queen Katherine of Valois," Pepys wrote of the occasion, "and I had the upper part of her body in my hands, and I did kiss her mouth, reflecting upon it that I did kiss a queen."

It wasn't until 1878—nearly four and a half centuries after her death—that Katherine of Valois was finally given a proper resting place in the abbey, next to her husband, King Henry V. But part of Katherine may still be seen. Her funeral effigy, minus hair and various body parts, is on display at the Abbey Museum.

FEBRUARY 24, 1868

Andrew Johnson: Slurring With Disaster

Andrew Johnson downed three shots of whiskey right before he was sworn in as Abraham Lincoln's second-term vice president. Throughly soused, with his face a vivid red, Johnson teetered to the podium in the Senate chamber to deliver what should have been the most triumphant speech of the onetime tailor's political career. Instead, it was rambling, incoherent tirade about his "plebeian roots"—delivered "in the language of a clown," as the London *Times* reported, "with wild gesticulations and shrieks," by a man whose "behavior was that of an illiterate, vulgar, and drunken rowdy." Senator Zachariah Chandler was among the horrified witnesses of the spectacle. "I was never so mortified in my life," he wrote to his wife. "Had I been able to find a hole I would have dropped through it out of sight."

Having delivered his own second Inaugural speech—widely considered to be one of the most impressive in history—Abraham Lincoln was forced to defend the behavior of his chosen vice president. "I have known Andy Johnson for many years," he said. "He made a bad slip the other day, but you need not be scared; Andy ain't a drunkard." A month later, the president was dead, and the delicate task of reuniting the shredded Union fell to his bullheaded, self-important successor. That wicked hangover Andrew Johnson endured after his appalling Inauguration performance would come to symbolize the rest of his ill-fated presidency—culminating in his impeachment on February 24, 1868.

The new president, a southern Democrat, had one overriding aim, which was to bring the rebellious states back into the Union as swiftly and gently as possible. The plight of freed blacks, many of whom suffered brutal servitude only a notch above slavery, was of virtually no consequence to him. "Whatever Andrew Johnson may be, he certainly is no friend of our race," Frederick Douglass had presciently remarked upon encountering Johnson at his vice presidential inauguration.

Virtually every bit of legislation benefiting the freedmen—from enfranchisement to full citizenship—the president vetoed. This earned him the deep enmity of congressional Republicans and led indirectly to his impeachment. "Andrew Johnson is the impersonation of the tyrannical Slave Power," declared Senator Charles Sumner. "In him it lives again."

The immediate cause of impeachment, however, was the president's attempted dismissal of Secretary of War Edwin Stanton, a holdover from the Lincoln Administration and a staunch Republican ally, who Johnson feared would have too much power when

Congress put the South under military rule. The firing of the secretary (who actually refused to step down and instead barricaded himself in his office) was a direct violation of the Tenure of Office Act, which prohibited the president from removing any member of his Cabinet without Senate approval. Warned of the consequences of tangling with Stanton, the president remained obdurate. "Impeach and be damned," he snorted. Congress responded accordingly.

"I am in favor of the official death of Andrew Johnson," an Indiana congressman declared during the House debate on impeachment. "I am not surprised that one who began his presidential career in drunkenness should end it in crime."

All manner of invective followed. One congressman described Johnson as a "despicable, besotted, traitorous man . . . this accidental president made so by the assassin's bullet." Another said, "He has dragged, as a demagogue, the robes of his high official position in the purlieus and filth of treason." There was even a comparison made between the president and the demented Roman emperor Nero.

A highly sought after ticket to Andrew Johnson's impeachment trial

The venomous orations throughout the impeachment trial—what Johnson contemptuously called "the show" and declined to attend—prompted future president James A. Garfield to remark upon "the insane love of speaking among public men . . . We are wading knee deep in words, words, words . . . and are but little more than half across the turbid stream."

In the end, though, words were not enough. Andrew Johnson survived in office, squeaking by with just one vote.

FEBRUARY 25, 1836

P. T. Barnum:
Dissecting the Truth

Joice Heth had already served P. T. Barnum quite well as the showman's first sideshow attraction—posing for amazed audiences across the Northwest as the infant George Washington's 161-year-old nursing "mammy." So when the nearly blind, almost completely paralyzed old slave died, Barnum saw an opportunity to exploit further the woman he had touted as "The Greatest Natural and National Curiosity in the World" by staging a public autopsy of her at New York's City Saloon on February 25, 1836. Well over a thousand people, each paying 50 cents a ticket, gathered to watch the gory spectacle performed by surgeon David L. Rogers, who concluded that at a mere 80 years old, Heth had been a fraud. Barnum, however, was unfazed by the exposure of what the New York *Sun* called at the time "one of the most precious humbugs that ever was imposed upon a credulous community." Indeed, he wallowed in the free publicity generated by the media frenzy surrounding the autopsy. He even fed it, suggesting to one unsuspecting editor that Heth was actually alive and well and living in Connecticut.

A Second Date of Infamy

President Franklin D. Roosevelt once declared December 7, 1941, "a date that will live in infamy." February 26 holds no such distinction—in any year—but considering what a rotten day it was throughout history, perhaps it should be given some recognition. Consider:

- 1577: Eric XIV, the insane and deposed king of Sweden, ate his last meal in prison—a bowl of poisoned pea soup.
- 1616: Two days after the Roman Inquisition unanimously declared the Copernican discovery of a stationary sun orbited by Earth "foolish and absurd in philosophy, and formally heretical since it explicitly contradicts in many places the sense of Holy Scripture," Pope Paul V ordered that Galileo be informed of the decision and instructed "to abstain completely from teaching or defending this doctrine and opinion or from discussing it."
- 1815: Napoleon Bonaparte, the scourge of Europe and terror of kings, escaped from exile on the small Mediterranean island of Elba to wreak 100 more days of havoc—until his final defeat at Waterloo.
- 1860: On what is now known as Indian Island, near Eureka, California, approximately 100 members of the peaceful Wiyot tribe were slaughtered as they slept by white settlers of the region. The *Northern Californian* reported the massacre: "Blood stood in pools on all sides; the walls of the huts were stained and the grass colored red. Lying around were dead bodies of both sexes and all ages from the old man to the infant at the breast. Some had their heads split in twain by axes, others beaten into jelly with clubs, others pierced or cut to pieces with

bowie knives. Some struck down as they mired; others had almost reached the water when overtaken and butchered."

- 1918: In one of the worst sports disasters of all time, more than 600 people were killed when stands collapsed and caught fire during a horse race at the Hong Kong Jockey Club.

- 1936: Japan faced the largest revolt in its modern history when a group of young radical army officers led some 1,400 troops under their command in an attack on the prime minister's residence and other government and military buildings in Tokyo, killing Home Minister Saito Makoto, Finance Minister Takahashi Korekiyo, and Army Inspector General of Military Training Watanabe Jotaro.

- 1965: President Lyndon Johnson approved the introduction of American ground forces into Vietnam, disregarding the sharply worded warning of Ambassador Maxwell Taylor: "White-faced soldier armed, equipped and trained as he is [is] not [a] suitable guerrilla fighter for Asian forests and jungles. French tried . . . and failed. I doubt that US forces could do much better." Upon learning that two Marine battalions had been successfully deployed, the president gloated about the North Vietnamese leader—a bit prematurely, as it turned out—"Now I have Ho Chi Minh's pecker in my pocket."

- 1987: President Ronald Reagan received a withering rebuke in the final report of the Tower Commission, which was formed to investigate the so-called Iran-Contra scandal—a complicated scheme in which arms had been sold to Iran in exchange for American hostages held in Lebanon, with proceeds diverted to fund Nicaraguan rebels fighting against that nation's leftist government. Rather than being seen as a maniacal schemer bent on undermining the law, Reagan was portrayed by the commission as something almost as bad: in essence, a doddering old coot who remained clueless as members of his administration ran amok, dealing with terrorists and illegally funding a foreign war.

- 1993: An al Qaeda–planted truck bomb was detonated in the parking garage of the North Tower of New York's World Trade Center. Although the terrorist attack failed in its aim to bring down the building, and the South Tower with it, six people were killed and more than a thousand injured.
- 1995: Barings, Britain's oldest bank, the place where Queen Elizabeth II kept her money, collapsed. Incredibly, the catastrophe was caused largely by a single rogue derivatives broker, Nick Leeson, whose fraudulent and unauthorized speculative trades led to losses totaling $1.3 billion.

FEBRUARY 27, 1859

Francis Scott Key's Son Should Have Watched His Ram Parts

The nation's capital has been witness to so many sex scandals that an entire calendar could be filled commemorating the most salacious highlights. But one Washington romp in particular emerged as perhaps the most luridly entertaining of them all—except, of course, for the key player, who ended up dead.

Philip Barton Key II, son of "The Star-Spangled Banner" author Francis Scott Key, had been conducting a torrid, most indiscreet affair with the young wife of his friend Representative Daniel Sickles, himself a bit of a scamp who once introduced his mistress, a brothel owner named Fanny White, to Queen Victoria at a Buckingham Palace reception. Although most of Washington buzzed about the flagrant encounters that occurred right in Sickles's home on Lafayette Square, the cuckolded congressman hadn't a clue. Then, one day, he received an anonymous letter detailing the whole sordid affair. "I do assure you," the letter read, "[Key] has as much use of your wife as you have."

The next day, February 27, 1859, an unsuspecting Key showed up outside the Sickles home, signaling his mistress that he was ready for action. This time, however, it was the enraged husband who ran out of the house, armed with two derringers. "Key, you scoundrel!" Sickles shouted as he chased his former friend through Lafayette Park in broad daylight. "You have dishonored my house—you must die!" With that he fired at Key, but the bullet merely grazed its mark. "Murder! Murder!" Key screamed. Several more shots hit Key in the groin and the chest as he continued to scream for mercy. Then he fell. "Is the scoundrel dead?" Sickles asked a witness to the murder. "He violated my bed!"

Meanwhile, a young page named Bonitz ran to the nearby White House to inform President James Buchanan what his old friend Sickles had just done. Buchanan responded by launching a cover-up by trying to silence Bonitz, who he believed was the only witness to the killing. The president warned the naive page of the ordeal he would face as a trial witness—including being locked up without bail during the proceedings—and urged the young man to flee back home to South Carolina to avoid such a calamity.

President Buchanan's efforts on behalf of his friend proved unnecessary, because an unrepentant

Sickles immediately turned himself in. "Of course I intended to kill him," the congressman told friends. "He deserved it." The three-week trial that followed was a sensation, especially with the then novel defense of temporary insanity, concocted by the lawyers representing Sickles. The jury acquitted the killer after deliberating for little more than an hour.

The capital erupted in celebration at the news. But then the freed murderer did the unthinkable: He reconciled with his wife. All the goodwill he generated after the act of revenge suddenly evaporated. "If Mrs. Sickles was herself guilty before the death of Key she is guilty still, and if one can be forgiven now, Key ought to have been forgiven in February," wrote the Washington correspondent for the Philadelphia *Press,* reflecting widespread public sentiment.

Sickles failed to gain reelection to Congress and was essentially drummed out of town. A part of him remains in the nation's capital, however. The leg he lost during the Civil War is now on display at the National Museum of Health and Medicine.

FEBRUARY 28, 1927

The "Scientist's" Ape Rape

Science took a grotesque step backward in 1927, when Ilya Ivanovich Ivanov, backed by the Soviet government, first attempted to create an entirely new creature from existing representatives of both ends of the human evolutionary spectrum: a hybrid of man and ape. After years of frustration in pursuit of his "humanzee," Ivanov finally got his chance when the governor of French Guinea gave him free rein to conduct a monstrous breeding program at the botanical gardens near the capital of Conakry.

On February 28, the pseudoscientist and his son took two captured female chimpanzees, named Babette and Syvette, held them down with nets and squirted into them human sperm taken from an unidentified local man. "The experiment was carried out by the two of them in a particularly brutal and hurried way," wrote Russian scholar Kirill Rossiianov, "which made the description of it read like it was rape."

Fortunately for the fate of mankind, neither chimp became pregnant—nor did a third chimp, Black, who was knocked out with chloroform and inseminated the following June. So Ivanov decided to switch tactics. He approached the governor with the idea of introducing chimpanzee sperm into hospitalized women, without their knowledge. As Ivanov recorded in his diary, it was a "bolt from the blue" when the governor said no, "a terrible blow."

Discouraged, Ivanov returned to the Soviet Union and obtained permission to impregnate women there—provided they were willing and kept in isolation for a year. Incredibly, he found a volunteer. "With my private life in ruins, I don't see any purpose in my further existence," a woman, identified only as "G," wrote to Ivanov. "But when I think that I could do a service for science, I feel enough courage to contact you. I beg you, don't refuse me."

Ivanov was stuck with only one potential mate for "G," an orangutan named Tarzan. But when Tarzan died suddenly of a brain hemorrhage, the man-ape project died with him. After that, government officials reconsidered their support of Ivanov's ghastly experiments; indeed, they slapped him into prison for alleged counterrevolutionary activities. Soon after his release in 1930, Ivanov died—mercifully without leaving a humanzee, or a hurangutan, as his legacy.

March

———◆———

*"March is the month that God designed to show
those who don't drink what a hangover is like."*
—GARRISON KEILLOR

MARCH 1, 1938

Superman's Creators, Turned Into Chumps in a Single Bound

Jerry Siegel and Joe Shuster created one of the world's most iconic superheroes—Superman. Then they sold him for the paltry sum of $130, which they then had to split between themselves. And while the Man of Steel went on to earn billions for his new owners, Siegel and Shuster died nearly broke. It was either an act of corporate malfeasance worthy of Lex Luthor, to snatch away the rights to the man from planet Krypton, or the result of astonishing naïveté on the part of two young men desperate to introduce their creation to the world.

Superman had long languished in the imagination of Siegel, a lonely outcast from Cleveland, before he met Shuster, his equally alienated fellow dreamer whose vivid illustrations gave dimension to that otherworldly paragon of strength and virtue (as well as his dorky alter ego, Clark Kent, and Lois Lane, who wanted one but not the other).

"When Joe and I first met, it was like the right chemicals coming together," Siegel once recalled. Only problem was, no one else cared. For six years Superman was rejected by a succession of publishers until finally Vin Sullivan, editor of National Allied Publications (precursor of DC Comics), agreed to put him on the June 1938 cover of National's *Action Comics* #1. Superman had at last taken flight, but without Siegel and Shuster along to enjoy the ride.

On March 1, 1938, just before their superhero hit the stands, the young men signed away all rights to their creation—with their names spelled wrong on the accompanying $130 check*—but agreed to give him continuous life as employees of the publisher for ten years. It was a colossal mistake—decision-making kryptonite, which would result in Siegel and Shuster spending decades of their lives wrangling in court to reclaim the rights to their signature character. Finally in the 1970s Warner Communications, the eventual owner of the Superman franchise, gave pensions of $20,000 per year, as well as health benefits, to each of the men, both of whom had fallen on hard economic times.

"There is no legal obligation," Jay Emmett, then executive vice president of Warner, told *The New York Times,* "but I sure feel there is a moral obligation on our part."

Joe Shuster died in 1992, and Jerry Siegel in 1996. Their heirs, however, continued the legal battle long after. Superman, meanwhile, kept well above the fray, continuing the very lucrative pursuit of truth, justice, and the American way.

---

* *The canceled check was purchased at a 2012 auction for $160,000. Meanwhile, copies of the first Superman comic are extremely rare and coveted by collectors, one of whom paid more than $2 million for the issue in 2011.*

March

MARCH 2, 2001

Desecration Takes Effort:
The Taliban's Buddha Butchers

Maya temples bulldozed for road fill in Belize . . . Ancient mummies violated by thieves in Egypt . . . Irreplaceable antiquities plundered in Iraq. The instances of cultural desecration in modern times seem to belie the very concept of civilized society—perhaps nowhere more egregiously than in Afghanistan, where, on March 2, 2001, the Taliban regime launched an assault on two of the world's most splendid treasures, the monumental Buddhas of Bamiyan.

Carved into the mountainside surrounding what had once been a Buddhist pilgrimage site, the statues (one reaching nearly 175 feet high, and the other nearly 120 feet) stood over the region for at least 15 centuries. The Taliban destroyed them in a matter of weeks. "These idols have been gods of the infidels," declared Mullah Mohammed Omar, the Taliban's supreme leader, who ordered their destruction. "The real God is Allah."

After international pleas for the preservation of the colossal statues were ignored, the world looked on in horror as the attack began with antiaircraft guns and artillery. But the Buddhas still stood after the barrage. "This work of destruction is not as simple as people might think," lamented Taliban information minister Qudratullah Jamal. "You can't knock down the statues by shelling as both are carved into a cliff; they are firmly attached to the mountain." In the end, it took strategically placed explosives to complete the ruin. All that remained were the two empty niches that once sheltered the Buddhas. "Muslims should be proud of smashing idols," Mullah Omar said at the time. "It has given praise to God that we have destroyed them."

However, Koichiro Matsuura, director general of the UN Educational, Scientific and Cultural Organization (UNESCO), better reflected universal sentiment when he called the destruction a "crime against culture. It is abominable to witness the cold and calculated destruction of cultural properties which were the heritage of the Afghan people, and, indeed, of the whole of humanity."

Still intact, one of the sacred statues rivals its mountain backdrop in height.

MARCH 3, 2006

Governor Schwarzenegger's Pro-Hispanic Policy: They're Hot

"She's either Puerto Rican, or the same thing as Cuban, I mean they are all very hot. They have the, you know, part of the black blood in them and part of the Latino blood in them that together makes it."

> —*Governor Arnold Schwarzenegger, referring* not *to Mildred Patricia Baena, later revealed to be the mother of his love child, but to California assembly-woman Bonnie Garcia, in a quote later released from a tape of a closed-door meeting on March 3, 2006*

MARCH 4, 1841

Deadly Dull: The Fatal Inaugural Address

He was America's first manufactured candidate: a Virginia aristocrat transformed by the Whig Party into a hard cider–swillin', log cabin–livin' everyman. Certainly William Henry Harrison had served ably as a general in the War of 1812, as well as against Tecumseh's Indian Confederation, but there had been very little to distinguish him in the decades since. It was that very blandness, in fact, that made him the perfect choice for presidential contender—a blank canvas upon which the Whigs could create their own image. Thus, Harrison became a frontier legend and hero of the previously obscure Battle of Tippecanoe. And all he had to do during the campaign against the incumbent, Martin Van Buren, was to avoid any controversial issues and keep his mouth shut.

Harrison complied so thoroughly with the gag order that the Democrats took to calling him "General Mum." Alas, the epithet wouldn't endure. Harrison and his running mate, John Tyler, (popularized together in the ditty "Tippecanoe and Tyler, Too") defeated Van Buren handily, after which the torrent of words that must have been building in the silenced candidate burst forth in the longest, most excruciatingly boring Inaugural Address ever delivered.

The crowds gathered at the U.S. Capitol in the freezing cold of that early March day* must have gained some intimation of the torture that was to follow when Harrison began his address with this laboriously overwrought sentence:

"Called from a retirement which I had supposed was to continue for the residue of my life to fill the chief executive office of this great and free nation, I appear before you, fellow-citizens, to take the oath which the Constitution prescribes as a necessary qualification for the performance of its duties; and in obedience to a custom coeval with our Government and what I believe to be your expectations I proceed to present to you a summary of the principles which will govern me in the discharge of the duties which I shall be called upon to perform."

For over two hours Harrison blathered on, his address peppered throughout with odd references to ancient Rome. But it could have been worse. The president-elect had allowed Daniel Webster to edit the speech, which at least shortened it a bit. Indeed Webster

---

* *Presidential Inaugurations were held on March 4 until the ratification of the 20th Amendment to the Constitution in 1933, which changed the beginning of a presidential term to January 20.*

later boasted that he had killed "seventeen Roman proconsuls as dead as smelts, every one of them."

As much of an ordeal the never ending address was to the audience, it proved fatal to Harrison. He had delivered it without a coat and developed a cold as a result. That turned to pneumonia, and within a month Harrison became the first U.S. president to die in office—quite literally bored to death.

MARCH 5, 1854

Monumental Prejudice:
A Bad Day With Black Rock

The magnificent stone obelisk that is the Washington Monument today was still just a stump in 1854. And thanks to the actions of a group of anti-Catholic, anti-immigrant political agitators called the American Party, or "Know-Nothings," it remained that way for more than two decades.

The trouble began when Pope Pius IX donated a black marble stone for the memorial, one taken from the ruins of the Temple of Concord in the Roman Forum. Though many other states and organizations had also given inscribed slabs to the construction effort, the Know-Nothings saw the papal gift as a loathsome declaration of the Vatican's intent to control the United States through the mass influx of Catholic immigrants.

Outraged by the Holy Father's supposed insult, a band of Know-Nothing Party thugs appeared at the construction site during the late hours of March 5, 1854, overpowered the guard, and snatched away the Vatican stone. By some accounts they then chipped away souvenir shards and tossed the rest into the Potomac River. But whatever happened, the pope's gift was never seen again. Not content with this brazen act of thievery, the Know-Nothings next seized control of the Washington National Monument Society through a rigged election and took over construction. They didn't get very far, though—installing only a few layers of inferior marble (which later had to be replaced) before an appalled Congress stopped funding the project altogether.

More than a decade after construction was abandoned, Mark Twain described the unfinished monument as an "ungainly old chimney that . . . is of no earthly use to anybody else, and certainly is not in the least ornamental. It is just the general size and shape, and possesses about the dignity, of a sugar-mill chimney . . . It is an eyesore to the people. It ought to be either pulled down or built up and finished."

It was not until 1877, with the Know-Nothings having long since dissipated, that work on the Washington Monument resumed. It was finally completed in 1884, and stands as the tallest freestanding stone structure in the world. Evidence of the Know-Nothings' legacy is still clearly visible, however: The exterior of the obelisk is of two distinct shades of marble. The stone used in the first stage of construction was unavailable when the job was resumed so many years later.

MARCH 6, 1835

A Friendship Tested by Fire

The English philosopher John Stuart Mill faced an excruciating task on the evening of March 6, 1835. He had devastating news to deliver to a friend, an admission of personal fault so grievous that only the most magnanimous of men might—just *might*—be able to forgive it. Clutching the charred remnants of a burned manuscript—the only copy of the magisterial history of the French Revolution that Thomas Carlyle had entrusted to him—he arrived at the historian's London home, looking, as Carlyle later wrote, "pale as Hector's ghost."

Trembling and in despair, Mill explained that the manuscript had accidentally been burned as kindling by a maid. Yet while the loss represented countless hours of agonizing labor for Carlyle, it was left to him to comfort his friend long into the night. "Mill, poor fellow, is terribly cut up," Carlyle said to his wife after the shamed philosopher finally left. "We must endeavour to hide from him how very serious this business is for us."

Sure enough, the next day Carlyle sent Mill a most gracious note. "You left me last night with a look which I shall not soon forget," he wrote. "Is there anything that I could do or suffer or say to alleviate you? For I feel that your sorrow must be far sharper than mine . . . Courage, my Friend!"

A note from Mill offering generous compensation for the lost labor crossed Carlyle's. And though the historian gratefully accepted, there still remained the unimaginable task of rewriting. The author was convinced he couldn't do it. "I remember and can still remember less of it than of anything I ever wrote with such toil," he lamented. "It is gone." And so were his notes, which he had already destroyed.

Nevertheless, he forged through; "surely the most leaden, discouraging, all but intolerable task I ever had to do," as he related to his brother. And, as inspiration eventually came "direct and flamingly from the heart," Thomas Carlyle completed one of the greatest works in English literature. As might be expected, John Stuart Mill gave it a glowing review.

MARCH 7, 1997

Wiener-Take-All?
The Case of the Pilfered Penises

Maybe Heinrich Kramer wasn't so crazy after all. In his authoritative guide to the world of witches, *Malleus maleficarum* (see December 5), the 15th-century inquisitor warned that evildoers in league with Satan could make men's private parts disappear. Then, five centuries later, an epidemic of "penis snatching" swept through a number of West African nations, where belief in magic was still very much alive. Fortunately, the people of the Ivory Coast were alerted to the danger by what (they heard) had been a rash of disappearing penises in Ghana, and they took appropriate action. On March 7, 1997, one sorcerer was burned to death in Koumassi, and another beaten to death in Port Bouet. Alas, the reprisals weren't enough to stop the rumored spread of genital theft to nearby Benin. But at least the panicked locals there were armed with gasoline and machetes, along with magical elixirs, to address the threat. More thieving sorcerers were destroyed, and countless penises preserved as a result—at least until that summer, when the problem popped up again in Senegal.*

---

* *There is an actual psychological syndrome, called* koro, *in which men, in a contagious panic, believe their penises have shriveled up or disappeared.*

MARCH 8, 1702

The Enemy Underfoot:
Done In by a Mole

William III was one historical figure for whom a molehill actually had far more significance than any mountain. Indeed, the English king died on this date from injuries sustained after his horse tripped on one. And for that, the unassuming rodent responsible for the lethal mound—"the little gentleman in velvet"—was toasted by William's political enemies for being the agent of his demise.

MARCH 9, 1974

We Lost 29 Years Ago—
Now Come Home
and Get Your Color TV

The abject humiliation that struck most Japanese people on August 15, 1945—when the thin voice of their emperor, never before broadcast, enjoined them to "endure the unendurable and bear the unbearable" in the wake of agonizing defeat—didn't hit Hiroo Onoda right away. In fact, the loyal soldier, unaware of Japan's unconditional surrender in World War II, continued to wage guerrilla warfare in the Philippines for almost three decades before that horrible day of reckoning finally arrived for him on March 9, 1974, when his former commanding officer showed up to assure him that the war was really over. "Suddenly everything went black," Onoda recalled in his book, *No Surrender*. "A storm raged inside me. I felt like a fool for having been so tense and cautious on the way here [to meet the former commander] . . . Worse than that, what had I been doing for all these years?"

Eddie Fisher Gets Some Karma From "Cleopatra"

The sizzling affair between Elizabeth Taylor and her future fifth (and sixth) husband, Richard Burton—launched on location in Rome during the filming of the bloated epic *Cleopatra*—was hot enough to fry the egg on fourth husband Eddie Fisher's face. The fading heartthrob had discovered his wife's infidelity when he made an unannounced visit to the movie set in the winter of 1962.

"It wouldn't have mattered if I had sent them an engraved announcement telling them the time I was coming," Fisher recalled. "They couldn't keep their eyes, not to mention their hands, off each other."

It was a humiliating betrayal—not unlike the one Fisher's former wife, Debbie Reynolds, felt when he left her for Taylor—but there was nothing the cuckolded crooner could do about it. The diamonds he bought Elizabeth for her birthday didn't help, nor did the gun he held to her head. All that was left to do was maintain some semblance of dignity by keeping the torrid affair, which Burton gleefully rubbed in his face, a secret. Alas, Fisher failed in that respect, too.

"It's true," Hollywood gossip columnist Louella Parsons reported on March 10. "Elizabeth Taylor has fallen madly in love with Richard Burton. It's the end of the road for Liz and Eddie Fisher."

Fisher denied the report that same day, but soon after leaving Rome for New York, he was promptly hospitalized after overdosing on amphetamines. Upon his release, the singer made one last public effort to deny what Burton had taken to calling *Le Scandale*.

"The only romance between Elizabeth Taylor and Richard Burton is Mark Antony and Cleopatra," he told a gathering of reporters, "and I might say a mighty good one." Then, as the press conference continued, Fisher took a call from Taylor in Rome. He had placed it earlier with the request that she confirm his denial. But Liz refused to quell rumors.

"You know," the embarrassed singer said, "you can ask a woman to do something and she doesn't always do it."

MARCH 11, 222

The Brattiest Kid in Human History

With predecessors as infamous as Nero and Caligula, it seems ludicrous that a mere boy might equal them in depravity. But during a four-year reign that began in 218—when he was just 14—the Roman emperor Elagabalus managed to do just that.

Perhaps it was the teenager's *five* marriages—including one forcibly imposed on a sacred Vestal Virgin—that alienated him from his subjects. Or his numerous boyfriends. Or his penchant for cross-dressing as a prostitute, and behaving like one, too. Or maybe people just didn't appreciate his "subtle" sense of humor—especially when they woke up with wild animals roaming their bedrooms, or sat on the prototype whoopee cushions the emperor had placed on their seats. Whatever the case, Elagabalus was doomed. He was so unpopular, in fact, that even his own grandmother turned against the young emperor and helped to arrange his assassination.

On March 11, 222, the 18-year-old appeared in public with his cousin Alexander, whom he suspected of being more highly regarded than he was. This was confirmed when a crowd of soldiers began cheering for Alexander while ignoring Elagabalus entirely.

Furious at their act of brazen insubordination, the emperor ordered them all executed. But it was he who was slain instead. The ancient writer Cassius Dio left a vivid account of Elagabalus's violent reckoning:

"His mother, who embraced him and clung tightly to him, perished with him; their heads were cut off and their bodies, after being stripped naked, were first dragged all over the city, then the mother's body was cast aside somewhere or other while his was thrown into the [Tiber River]."

MARCH 12, 1951

Not Just a Rat, but a Lying Rat: Ethel Rosenberg's Brother

Ethel Rosenberg very well may have conspired with her husband, Julius, in selling out her country to the Soviets in the 1940s. But the government had precious little evidence to prove it. Not, that is, until her brother and confessed atomic spy, David Greenglass, perjured himself at the trial that sent his sister straight to Sing Sing's electric chair.

Having admittedly slipped secrets out of Los Alamos, New Mexico, where he worked as a relatively lowly Army mechanic on the Manhattan Project (the U.S. development of the nuclear bomb during World War II), Greenglass had a lot at stake when he testified against his sister. He had been indicted for his crimes, but not yet convicted. Leniency had been dangled before him, and for his wife and co-conspirator, Ruth, as well. She still remained free, in fact; his cooperation assured that. But the authorities wanted something big in return: Ethel Rosenberg. And on March 12, 1951, during his second day of testimony, David Greenglass served his sister up to them on a platter.

Until that time, there was little to indicate Ethel had done anything illegal. Yes, she had been an active member of the Communist Party, and logic dictated that at least she had to be aware of her husband Julius's espionage activities. But not even secretly intercepted and deciphered Soviet cables—later revealed as the Venona project—offered any trace of her overt cooperation. "The [Justice] Department has advised that they do not believe there is sufficient evidence to charge Ethel Rosenberg," noted William Whelan of the FBI. Yet she was arrested anyway, as a hostage to be held in order to force Julius Rosenberg—the main Soviet mole—to reveal the names of more spies.

But neither Rosenberg cooperated, and so now it was vital to get Ethel convicted. Fortunately for the authorities, Ruth Greenglass, still walking free, suddenly recalled a detail before the trial she had neglected to mention before. It was her sister-in-law Ethel, she said, who typed up the notes and summations of what David Greenglass had learned at Los Alamos. The prosecution now had its so-called smoking gun, which David dutifully regurgitated on the stand, with a sickening smile across his face. Alas, it was a lie.

Chief prosecutor Irving Saypol dramatically played up Greenglass's false revelation during his trial summation: "This description of the atom bomb, destined for delivery to the Soviet Union, was typed up by the defendant Ethel Rosenberg . . . Just so had she, on countless other occasions, sat at that typewriter and struck the keys, blow by blow, against her own country in the interests of the Soviets."

Two years later, with all appeals exhausted and presidential clemency denied, Ethel Rosenberg, along with her husband, was executed at Sing Sing on June 19, 1953. The brother who sent her to the electric chair was chagrined by the 15-year sentence he received, although also gratified that his wife and fellow traitor never served a moment behind bars. He was released after a decade and slipped into anonymity, his legacy as a rat cemented.

"You know, I seldom use the word 'sister' anymore," Greenglass told journalist Sam Roberts years later, admitting at the same time that he had lied about Ethel. "I've just wiped it out of my mind."

MARCH 13, 1881

The Tsar Runs Out— and So Does His Luck

They shot at him repeatedly, planted a bomb under his train, and even blew up his dining room at the Winter Palace. But the terrorists just couldn't kill Russia's Alexander II—even if their merciless pursuit did take a terrible toll on his nerves. "Am I such a wild beast that they should hound me to death?" the shaken tsar cried out after yet another failed assassination attempt. Alas, the answer was yes. On March 13, 1881, the killers' luck would change. As Alexander was traveling on a St. Petersburg street, a young man hurled a bomb at his carriage. It exploded, killing and maiming several bystanders, but the tsar was unharmed. Yet after he emerged from the mangled carriage to confront his would-be killer and inspect the damage, a second assassin threw another bomb. This time, it hit its mark. Alexander II—known as the Tsar-Liberator for having freed Russia's long-suffering serfs—was carried back to the Winter Palace, his legs shattered. And there he bled to death.

The Owner Who Sent His Own Team to the Showers

Chris von der Ahe was one of baseball's true originals—the interfering owner of the St. Louis Browns (later Cardinals) who knew next to nothing of the game and came with a flamboyant showman's personality as outsize as the statue of himself he erected outside his ballpark. "I am der poss bresident of der Prowns!" he proclaimed proudly in his thick German accent. Sadly, von der Ahe lost his beloved "Prowns" on March 14, 1899, when his numerous creditors forced an auction of the team on the steps of the St. Louis Courthouse. The affable owner—later eulogized by Charles Comiskey as "the grandest figure baseball has ever known"—was inconsolable. Yet the sale of the Browns wasn't half as devastating for him as it would prove to be for the rival Cleveland Spiders.

In a monopolistic move—perfectly legal at the time—the Browns were purchased by Frank DeHaas Robison, who also happened to own the Spiders—a fairly decent team with a roster of several brilliant players, including future Hall of Famer Cy Young. The only problem with the Spiders was the halfhearted Cleveland fans and their sporadic game attendance. They hated Robison, and he loathed them right back. The situation with the Browns was the exact opposite: an enthusiastic baseball city with a losing team. Robison solved the problem by gutting the Spiders of their best players, including Young, and moving them to St. Louis, a maneuver from which Cleveland would never recover. Indeed, the Spiders emerged from the 1899 season as the worst performing team in baseball history.*

MARCH 15, 44 B.C. *and* 1917

Beware Indeed: 2 Ides, 2 Emperors

"Beware the Ides of March."
—Julius Caesar, *Act 1, Scene 2*

Thanks to Shakespeare's immortal line, Caesar usually gets all the attention for his bad day in 44 B.C. Sure he was betrayed by Brutus and stabbed to death in the Roman Senate, but the Ides of March was no picnic for Nicholas II of Russia either. After a tumultuous reign of over two decades, culminating in a massive revolution sparked by bread shortages and widespread discontent over Russian defeats in World War I, the tsar was forced to abdicate his throne on March 15, 1917. Thus, Nicholas became the last of an imperial line that stretched back centuries.**

So pathetic were the Spiders that they spent the last half of the season on the road, far away from their merciless "fans," which earned the team any number of withering monikers from the press corps: Misfits, Exiles, Discards, Remnants, Outcasts, Cast Adrifts, Wandering Willies, Tramps, Caudal Appendages, Homeless Ones.

**The following year, on July 17, 1918, the deposed sovereign—who as a young man had watched his grandfather Alexander II bleed to death after a bomb blew up beneath him (see March 13)—was murdered by the Bolsheviks, along with his entire family, just outside the Siberian city of Ekaterinburg.*

MARCH 16, 1861

Whittle Big Man: Sam Houston's Last Stand Against Secession

S am Houston fought valiantly for the independence of Texas from Mexico, served twice as the president of the Republic of Texas, maneuvered Texas into the Union, represented Texas in the U.S. Senate, and then became governor of Texas. In many ways, Sam Houston *was* Texas. But on March 16, 1861, the people of Texas turned on him.

Secessionist fervor had been festering in the state since the election of Abraham Lincoln in 1860. Houston vigorously opposed the movement—not because of any abolitionist sentiment (he was a slave owner) or ambivalence about state rights, but simply because he believed it would prove a crippling disaster. No one listened.

In fact, the governor's opposition was not only ignored but also actively circumvented by forces even more powerful than he. On February 1, 1861, a convention of delegates, illegally convened, declared Texas' secession from the Union—a position later backed by popular referendum. Now it remained for Houston to either officially approve the decision and swear fealty to the Confederacy, or face the consequences.

On the morning of March 16, after an agonizing struggle the night before, the governor made up his mind. "Margaret," he said to his wife, "I will never do it." He then went to the State Capitol, took a seat in his office, whittling to occupy himself, and awaited his inevitable exile and disgrace.

Before he was unceremoniously driven out of office that March day, Houston had prepared a message to the people of Texas: "Fellow Citizens, in the name of your rights and liberty, which I believe have been trampled upon, I refuse to take this [secession] oath . . . [But] I love Texas too well to bring civil strife and bloodshed upon her. I shall make no endeavor to maintain my authority as Chief Executive of this state . . . I am . . . stricken down because I will not yield those principles which I have fought for . . . The severest pang is that the blow comes in the name of the state of Texas."

MARCH 17, 1990

Stopping Lightning in Its Path: The Referee's Low Blow

The fight was billed "Thunder and Lightning"—the ultimate light welterweight showdown between two evenly matched, undefeated world champions, Julio César Chávez and Meldrick Taylor. Round after round, the clash lived up to every bit of hype it had generated as Chávez delivered his thunder-packed punches and Taylor retaliated with his own dazzling, lightning-fast blows. It was

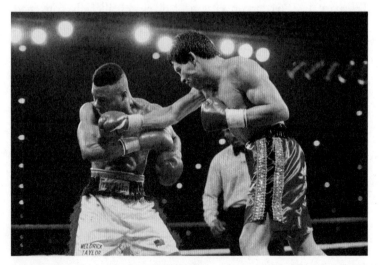

Taylor takes a fierce right from Chávez before an even worse blow from the referee.

Taylor who dominated on the scorecards, but Chávez's relentless pounding was taking a pulverizing toll. Then, in the 12th round, the already thrilling match became historic—not due as much to either Thunder or Lightning, but to Steele—Richard Steele, the referee with what many consider the worst sense of timing ever.

While Chávez would need a knockout to win, Taylor merely had to survive the round. But his corner urged him not to play it safe. Battered and bloody, Taylor nevertheless listened and went in hard. And that's when Chávez nailed him with a right that floored him in a corner. Taylor got right back up, but he was either too dazed or too distracted to respond to a question Steele asked him. It was then that the referee made one of the most controversial decisions in boxing history, one that many still say robbed Taylor of his just glory. Steele stopped the fight—with only two seconds remaining.

MARCH 18, 1990

Heist Almighty: The Boston Museum Caper

Yes, it was bad when the "Mona Lisa" was stolen from the Louvre in 1911. But after two years spent stashed away in a trunk by the thief (a museum employee, as it turned out), Leonardo da Vinci's enigmatic lady was returned to her rightful place in the Paris museum. There have been no such happy endings (yet?) for the priceless paintings and other works of art snatched from the Isabella Stewart Gardner Museum in Boston—the largest theft of private property in American history.

Shortly after midnight on March 18, 1990, two thieves disguised as Boston police officers showed up at the museum and, speaking through the intercom system, claimed to be responding to a disturbance. A habitually stoned security guard buzzed them right in. Then, having successfully breached the first line of defense, the thieves efficiently disabled the second when they confronted the guard and, pretending to recognize him on an old arrest warrant, told him to step away from the desk. He obeyed, without ever thinking to ring the silent alarm. Now there was no stopping the intruders.

After binding the guard and his partner and handcuffing them to a basement pipe, the pair began their rampage through the museum's treasured-filled rooms, ripping works by Rembrandt, Vermeer, Manet, and Degas right out of their frames. They also swiped a magnificent Chinese vase and a finial from the top of a pole support for a Napoleonic silk flag. And though the FBI has followed a number of promising leads, the great works haven't been seen since.

"Think of how bored they get," wrote novelist John Updike in a poem about the stolen paintings, "stacked in the warehouse somewhere, say in Mattapan, gazing at the back of the butcher paper they are wrapped in, instead of at the rapt, glad faces of those who love art." Empty frames that once held masterpieces now hang in their original display places as poignant reminders of the devastating loss—and the hope for their eventual return.

MARCH 19, 1919

Uncle Sam *Wants* You!

It seemed like such a swell idea at the time—at least to the U.S. Navy brass. Rumors were rife around the naval base at Newport, Rhode Island, that certain sailors were consorting inappropriately, not with the ladies of the town, but with each other. A court of inquiry was held, and on March 19, 1919, it concluded that the government must devote "any expense and time necessary" to conduct a "most thorough and searching investigation . . . made by a corps of highly experienced investigators." And who would these intrepid fact finders be? Why, other sailors, of course. As the head of the investigation noted, a "good looking man," somewhere between 19 and 24, would be best suited for "this class of work, with reference to perverts."

But it wouldn't be enough for the young men recruited for the sting operation to simply infiltrate the gay underground and identify their wayward fellows; they were instructed to provide positive proof by actually engaging with the targeted men—intimately. After Assistant Secretary of the Navy (and future U.S. president) Franklin D. Roosevelt signed off on the scheme, the young operatives took to their task with patriotic zeal. The sailors they netted were then court-martialed, with the secret agents providing lurid testimony of their encounters.

So successful was the sting that the Navy expanded the trap to nab Newport civilians as well. And that's when they ran into trouble. A popular local minister was arrested, which prompted his friends and supporters to send an outraged letter to President Woodrow Wilson that was also printed in the *Providence Journal:*

"It must be evident to every thoughtful mind that the use of such vile methods cannot fail to undermine the character and ruin the morals of the unfortunate youths detailed for this duty, render no citizen of the community safe from suspicion and calumny, bring the city into unwarranted reproach, and shake the faith of the people in the wisdom and integrity of the naval administration."

A series of official hearings followed, culminating in a Senate investigation. This time it wasn't homosexual sailors in the crosshairs, but the methods their superiors used to root them out. Roosevelt was sharply rebuked for his part in what the investigating committee called "a most deplorable, disgraceful and unnatural proceeding"—a conclusion that *The New York Times* reported with the blaring headline: LAY NAVY SCANDAL TO F. D. ROOSEVELT . . . DETAILS ARE UNPRINTABLE.

When Britain Almost Didn't Have a World Cup to Win

B ritain's national pride took a severe beating on March 20, 1966—not quite as bad as its steady loss of empire, but almost. Sometime between 11 a.m. and noon that day, thieves managed to swipe the precious Jules Rimet Trophy, the original prize awarded to winners of the World Cup, from its supposedly secure display case in London's Westminster Central Hall. The football (i.e., soccer) world was aghast at the sheer carelessness that Britain, which was to host the World Cup later that summer, demonstrated in caring for the esteemed trophy.

"It would never have happened in Brazil," declared Abrain Tebel of the champion Brazilian federation. "Even Brazilian thieves love football and would never commit this sacrilege."

Fortunately, the trophy was found a week later when a dog named Pickles happened to sniff it out while on a walk with its master. With Britain's battered image

fortuitously salvaged, Pickles became a national hero. But the Jules Rimet Trophy didn't fare quite as well. It was sent to Brazil, where, despite Tebel's grandiose pronouncement about the sanctity of football in that country, it was stolen in 1983—and never recovered.

MARCH 21, 1349, 1556, 1861,
1925, 1933, *and* 1960

Happy Intolerance Day to You

If ever an International Day of Ignorance and Intolerance is established, March 21 might well be the perfect choice. After all, that woeful date has been witness to so many assaults on reason, justice, and basic human decency over the centuries that it should at the very least qualify for recognition.

- 1349: Thousands of Jews were slaughtered in the German town of Erfurt after being accused of causing the devastating plague known as the Black Death.
- 1556: Archbishop Thomas Cranmer, a leader of the English Reformation and compiler of the *Book of Common Prayer,* was burned at the stake for heresy by Queen "Bloody" Mary I.
- 1861: Confederate vice president Alexander Stephens declared in his "Cornerstone Address" that "Our new Government is founded upon exactly the opposite ideas [of the United States Constitution]; its foundations are laid, its cornerstone rests, upon the great truth that the negro is not equal to the white man; that slavery, subordination to the superior race, is his natural and normal condition."
- 1925: Tennessee governor Austin Peay signed into law the Butler Act, which made it illegal to teach in public schools "any theory that denies the Story of the Divine Creation of man as taught in the Bible, and to teach instead that man has descended from a lower order of animals." In other words: Darwin's theory of evolution was kicked out of class.
- 1933: The Nazis announced the opening of their first concentration camp, Dachau.
- 1960: Police in the South African township of Sharpeville opened fire on a large group of protesters who objected to the

severe segregation policies of the white-run government. As a result, 69 people were killed, and 180 injured—a terrible toll that one police commander later tried to justify. "The native mentality does not allow them to gather for a peaceful demonstration," insisted Lt. Col. D. H. Pienaar. "For them to gather means violence."

Yet if March 21 doesn't quite cut it for the commemoration date of sheer human lunacy . . . well, there's always March 22.

MARCH 22, 1144, 1630, 1692, 1871, 1943, *and* 1984

Wait, There's More!

Maybe March 21 could serve as International Day of Ignorance and Intolerance *Eve,* which would then allow for recognition of all the human abominations of March 22 as well. After all, there have been too many to overlook:

- 1144: The body of a 12-year-old boy named William was found in a forest just outside Norwich, England, an ordinary enough event in those dark and brutal times—until a zealous monk by the name of Thomas of Monmouth came along and made him a martyr. In his epic biography, *The Life and Passion of William of Norwich,* the monk stated that the child had been sacrificed by Jews in a gruesome ritual mocking the crucifixion of Jesus—a fantastical tale with devastating implications. Many experts consider the book to be the origin of what historian Alan Dundes called "one of the most bizarre and dangerous legends ever created by the human imagination," the Blood Libel. This widespread belief that Jews routinely killed Christian children in secret rituals has endured for nearly nine centuries, influenced anti-Semites from Martin Luther to Adolf Hitler, and caused untold misery to millions of innocent people over the centuries.

- 1630: Anne Hutchinson—"the instrument of Satan," as Governor John Winthrop called her—was banished from Massachusetts for having dared to challenge the colony's theocratic establishment. Hutchinson believed that a person could reach God through personal intuition, rather than through the observance of institutionalized laws and the precepts of ministers. "As I do understand it," she wrote, "laws, commands, rules, and edicts are for those who have not the light which makes plain the pathway."

- 1692: More enlightenment from Massachusetts, Governor Winthrop's "Shining City Upon a Hill": A contingent of Salem residents came to Rebecca Nurse's home to inform her that she had been accused of witchcraft. Meanwhile, that same day, Rebecca Nurse's specter popped in to see Ann Carr Putnam and, according to Putnam, threatened "to tear my soul out of my body" if she refused to serve Satan.

- 1871: North Carolina's William Woods Holden became the first U.S. governor ever removed from office. His crime: coming down a little too hard on the Ku Klux Klan.

- 1943: The Nazis herded the entire population of the village of Khatyn, Belarus, into a shed, covered the structure with straw, and set it on fire. Those who managed to escape the inferno were immediately shot.

- 1984: Mass hysteria in Manhattan Beach, California, culminated with the indictment of seven teachers and administrators at the McMartin preschool, charged with hundreds of counts of child abuse. Coaxed by "experts" from Children's Institute International, the little ones reported not only sexual abuse but also satanic rituals involving the dismemberment of babies and the exhumation of corpses. The trial of the "McMartin Seven," one of the longest and most expensive in history, ended with total vindication for the defendants. But given the lives ruined, it was a shallow victory.

Massive Con-Fusion: The "Discovery" That Left Scientists Cold

It was the scientific breakthrough of the century, or certainly appeared to be. On March 23, 1989, two respected chemists, B. Stanley Pons, professor of chemistry at the University of Utah, and his colleague Martin Fleischmann of the University of Southampton in England, announced in a press conference that they had achieved a positively Promethean feat by replicating the energy of the sun in a process they called "cold fusion." And, all the more astonishing, they did it at room temperature in a simple glass jar of water.

"We've established a sustained fusion reaction by means that are considerably simpler than conventional techniques," Professor Pons declared.

The implications of such an achievement were staggering: Rather than producing energy by smashing atoms apart, as with conventional nuclear reactors, cold fusion essentially forced them together in a relatively simple process that would give the world an endless supply of cheap, clean energy.

The *Wall Street Journal* and other major news outlets trumpeted the discovery on their front pages, but other scientists were skeptical . . . *very* skeptical. Dr. Steven E. Koonin of Caltech, for one, bluntly insisted that the cold fusion report was merely a reflection of "the incompetence and delusion of Pons and Fleischmann."

The controversy began immediately after the scientists gave their news conference. Mass media was most definitely not the way the scientific community was used to receiving information of important discoveries. Usually such matters were first published for review in scholarly journals, something Pons and Fleischmann's sponsors at the University of Utah neglected to do. Worse, they refused to address specific questions or provide details about the cold fusion process.

"This was no mere breach of etiquette," wrote Robert L. Park, author of *Voodoo Science: The Road From Foolishness to Fraud.* "The integrity of science is anchored in the willingness of scientists to test their ideas and results in direct confrontation with their scientific peers. That standard of scientific conduct was being flagrantly violated by the University of Utah." Then there was the small matter of nuclear radiation. If what Pons and Fleischmann were claiming was true, noted nuclear physicist Frank Close, their lab should have been "the hottest source of radiation west of Chernobyl." Even the physicists at the University of Utah joked among themselves about their colleague's suspicious findings: "Have you heard the bad news about the research assistant in Pons's lab? He's in perfect health."

Yet despite all the scientific sneering, there was nevertheless a mad rush at labs across the world to somehow replicate the cold fusion experiments from what little information could be gleaned. All were unsuccessful. But the question remained: Had Pons and Fleischmann perpetuated a massive hoax, or had they simply misinterpreted important data? "I was convinced for a while it was absolute fraud," Richard D. Petrasso, a fusion scientist at MIT, said in an interview with *The New York Times* in 1991. "Now I've softened. They probably believed in what they were doing."

MARCH 24, 1603

Sir Walter, Treated Rawly Indeed

Elizabeth I adored her dashing courtier, the man perhaps most responsible for launching the British Empire, Sir Walter

Raleigh.* As for the queen's successor, James I: Well, simply put, the sovereign's esteem died with Elizabeth. "Raleigh, Raleigh, I have heard but rawly of thee," the new king remarked upon first meeting the great poet and explorer—the negative pun on his name glaringly apparent. Indeed, Raleigh's numerous enemies in Elizabeth's backbiting court—resentful of his power and influence with the queen—had already thoroughly poisoned the next monarch against him. And so it was that upon Elizabeth's death and James's accession on March 24, 1603, Raleigh's fortunes began their precipitous slide. Still, it would take another 15 years for him to actually lose his head.

King James began his reign with a petty assault on Raleigh's privileges, snatching away his lucrative monopolies—the main source of his income—and insisting upon the return of his London home, Durham House. Four months later, the "damnably proud" Raleigh would be on trial for his life—charged with treason for allegedly conspiring with Spain to dethrone James I and replace him with his cousin Arbella Stuart. It was a sham of a proceeding, about which one of the judges involved later said, "The justice of England has never been so degraded and injured."

Prosecutor Sir Edward Coke, determined to get the verdict King James desired, spewed every manner of invective at the very symbol of the golden Elizabethan era: "a viper . . . the rankest traitor in all England . . . a spider of hell . . . a monster . . . [author of] the most horrible practices that ever came out of the bottomless pit of the lowest hell." But, for all that, Coke didn't have a case—only hearsay produced by Raleigh's enemies. The defendant's pleas to confront his main accuser were abruptly denied. "There must

---

* *That's not to say Elizabeth didn't clash with Raleigh—especially when he secretly married the queen's lady-in-waiting without her permission in 1591 and found himself (along with his bride) clapped into the Tower as a wedding gift.*

not such a gap be opened for the destruction of the King [i.e., the state's case] as would be if we should grant this," declared the Lord Chief Justice.

Despite the preordained guilty verdict, Raleigh acquitted himself well throughout the rigged trial. "Never man spoke better for himself," recalled one contemporary observer. "So worthily, so wisely, so temperately he behaved himself that in half a day the

Poet and explorer Sir Walter Raleigh, imprisoned in the Tower of London

mind of all the company was changed from the extremest hate to the extremest pity." The day before his scheduled execution, King James granted Raleigh a reprieve, of sorts. Instead of the scaffold, he was sent to the Tower of London, where he would remain a prisoner for the next 13 years and write his magisterial *History of the World*. Then, in 1616, Raleigh was released and sent on a voyage to the New World to try, once again, to find the fabled, gold-laden city of El Dorado. The lure of gold in that mythical city apparently trumped the king's long-standing grudge. But there were to be no riches, only revenge.

During the disastrous expedition, the English adventurers came into conflict with the Spanish in South America. Raleigh had been far away from the fighting, during which his son had been killed, but the Spanish ambassador nevertheless demanded retribution. King James was only too happy to oblige. There would be no open trial this time, for James remembered well how "by his wit [Raleigh] turned the hatred of men into compassion." Essentially, he would be summarily executed on the old charge of treason.

On October 29, 1618, the deed was done—despite even the pleas of the king's own wife. Observing the ax that would in moments decapitate him, Raleigh was heard to muse, "This is a sharp medicine, but it is a physician for all diseases and miseries."

MARCH 25, 1988

...And Ebola Is a Bunny-Wunny

"That virus is a pussycat."
—*Peter Duesberg, professor of molecular biology, University of California, Berkeley, in the March 25, 1988, edition of the journal* Science, *rejecting the data that established the human immunodeficiency virus, known as HIV, as the cause of AIDS*

MARCH 26, 1953

For Jonas Salk,
No Vaccine Against the Critics

"He's a folk hero, even though he is . . . not very bright."

—*Renowned scientist Roger Revelle*
on polio vaccine developer Jonas Salk

The panic was intense and widespread as the polio virus continued to render thousands of youngsters paralyzed and, in some cases, unable to breathe without being encased in a so-called iron lung. But in the winter of 1953—the same year 35,000 additional cases of polio were reported in the United States—salvation from the dread scourge seemed imminent as news reports of a potential vaccine began to trickle out of Pittsburgh. That worried Jonas Salk—or, as his numerous critics in the scientific community maintained, excited him with visions of celebrity. The young researcher had indeed obtained some positive results from his trials, but the vaccine had yet to be perfected.

So Salk went to his patron, Basil O'Connor, co-founder (with polio sufferer President Franklin D. Roosevelt) of what became known as the March of Dimes, and obtained radio time either to temper public expectations, as Salk claimed, or, as his enemies insisted, to reap premature acclaim.

The response to the national radio program that aired on March 26, 1953, was predictably divided.

"Salk became the embodiment of a vaccine that would soon save the world from polio," wrote author Paul A. Offit. "To the public, he was an immediate hero. But members of the scientific community criticized Salk for talking about unpublished data and for pandering to the media. The radio address marked the beginning of an animosity that Salk would suffer for the rest of his life."

Indeed, Salk's fellow scientists were left seething with resentment and professional jealousy. "Whether he believes it or not, Jonas went on the air that night to take a bow and become a public hero," observed one critic. "And that's what he became." Albert Sabin, Salk's rival in polio vaccine research,* was particularly venomous. "It was pure kitchen chemistry," Sabin later said. "Salk didn't discover anything."

Salk's reputation among his peers as an inconsequential showboat was such that little of his subsequent research was ever taken seriously. He never won a Nobel Prize, nor was he welcomed into the prestigious National Academy of Sciences. The snubs rankled, but several years before his death in 1995, Salk seemed philosophical.

"I received an inordinate amount of attention and recognition, out of proportion to what was contributed scientifically," he said in a 1991 interview. "It came about altogether because of the relief from fear. It was a human response on the part of the public. But from the point of view of the scientific community, they would see it differently. That was an adverse side effect. But it also provided opportunities in other ways. These are the prices; one has to pay for the pluses as well as the minuses."

---

* *Sabin developed an oral polio vaccine that contained weakened forms of the virus, which eventually supplanted for a time Salk's "killed" vaccine.*

MARCH 27, 1908

Talk About
Intemperance!

If there were two things Representative James Thomas "Cotton Tom" Heflin couldn't stand (besides women voting—see January 12) they were blacks sharing public transportation with whites and the consumption of alcoholic beverages. So of course the prohibitionist congressman from Alabama, who had just unsuccessfully introduced a measure that would segregate the streetcars of Washington, D.C.,* was a bit perturbed when he boarded a trolley near the Capitol on the evening of March 27, 1908—on his way to a temperance meeting—and found Lewis (or Thomas) Lumby not only sitting there but drinking whiskey as well.

When his remonstrations to put away the bottle were met with "vile epithets" from "the negro," as *The New York Times* reported at the time, the enraged Heflin tossed Lumby off the streetcar. Then, when his adversary continued to sass him from the street, the congressman naturally shot at him. The bullet missed, though, and hit a bystander in the toe. Undeterred, Heflin fired again, this time wounding Lumby in the head. He was arrested and charged with assault with intent to kill, and, after being accorded all due courtesy at the police station, released on bail. Cotton Tom was never tried for the shooting, which he later cited as one of the greatest accomplishments of his career. After serving 12 more years in the House, he was elected to the Senate, all the while keeping busy as a member of the Ku Klux Klan.

And he once proudly proclaimed, "God Almighty intended the Negro to be the servant of the white man."

MARCH 28, 193

Going, Going, Gone!

After a century or so of frequent royal assassinations, the Roman Empire hit a new low on March 28, 193, when the elite and swaggering Praetorian Guard slaughtered Emperor Pertinax—ruler of just three months—for having dared try to restore order and discipline among their ranks. Then, later the same day, the Guard did something even more infamous when they offered the imperial throne to the highest bidder at auction.

"When this proclamation was known," the ancient historian Herodian of Syria wrote, "the more honorable and weighty Senators, and all persons of noble origin and property, would not approach the [Guard] barracks to offer money in so vile a manner for a besmirched sovereignty."

But there was one wealthy senator, Didius Julianus, who was not particularly honorable or weighty (in the consequential sense)—in fact, he was notoriously debauched. Prodded by his ambitious wife and daughter, Julianus rushed over to the barracks to make his bid. The Guard, however, wouldn't let him inside. So, standing outside the walls, Julianus shouted his offers against a competing bidder inside the compound, who just happened to be the slain emperor Pertinax's father-in-law.

Having offered a fortune, Julianus eventually won the bidding—although, in this case, winning was relative. The people of Rome were disgusted by the charade. Rather than obeisance, they threw rocks at the new emperor, and, as Herodian reported, "hooted and reviled him as having bought the throne with lucre at an auction." Two months later, Septimius Severus deposed him. "But what evil have I done?" Julianus reportedly cried as he was dragged away to be beheaded. "Whom have I killed?"

MARCH 29, 1683

Burning Love:
Tokyo's Little Match Girl

There was nothing particularly special about Yaoya Oshichi, a grocer's daughter living in 17th-century Japan. Indeed, her memory undoubtedly would have been lost to history had it not been for the extraordinary circumstances of her death—a tale of romance so tragic that it enshrined the 16-year-old girl forever in Japanese literature and theater.

In 1682, a great fire erupted in Edo (now Tokyo), forcing Yaoya and her family to seek refuge in a local temple. There she met Ikuta Shōnosuke, a temple page with whom she soon found herself in love. Sadly, though, the budding romance was destined to last only as long as the family found shelter in the temple. After Yaoya and her family returned home, the young couple was separated. Desperate to reconnect, the girl did something that would have made sense only to a lovelorn teenager: She started a fire in her own home, hoping to re-create the circumstances under which she first met Ikuta.

The penalty for arson in Japan at the time was burning at the stake, but only those above the age of 15 were allowed to be executed. The magistrate hearing Yaoya's case was inclined to mercy and intended to spare the girl from the fearsome penalty. "You must be *15* years old, aren't you?" he said. Alas, Yaoya mistook his meaning and responded that she was actually 16. Exasperated, the judge tried again. "You must be *15* years old, are you not?" he repeated firmly. Again, the frightened Yaoya gave her true age. It was enough to doom her, and on March 29, 1683, the girl who couldn't take a hint was consumed by the flames.

MARCH 30, 1750

The "Surgeon" Who Cut the Daylights Out of Two Great Composers

He was the eye surgeon to the stars, with such luminaries as Britain's King George II and the pope as satisfied clients—or so he claimed. In reality, though, John Taylor was little more than a self-promoting quack—"an instance of how far impudence will carry ignorance," as the famed writer Samuel Johnson described him. With the adopted titles "Chevalier" or "Ophthalmiater Royal," Taylor rode from town to town in a carriage emblazoned with painted eyeballs, made grandiose speeches before gathered crowds at each surgery, and left a long trail of blinded people in his wake. One of them was Johann Sebastian Bach.

The great composer had long suffered poor eyesight, but as his condition worsened, he had the misfortune of meeting the itinerant Taylor, who had just arrived in Leipzig to great fanfare. On March 30, 1750, the celebrity oculist plunged his sharpened instruments into the musical genius's eyes. Then he applied a healing poultice of pigeon's blood, pulverized salt, and just a dash of mercury. After several days, the procedure was repeated—to no avail. Bach was left entirely sightless and in excruciating pain. Four months later, he was dead. But "Chevalier" Taylor was by no means finished with the world's greatest composers. Eight years later he permanently blinded Handel as well.

The Ughscars: Celebrating the Worst of Hollywood With the Golden Raspberries

There once was a time when awful films, with equally awful acting, quietly slipped away—ideally with few taking much notice. But then along came the Golden Raspberry Awards, or the Razzies, to cast a harsh spotlight on these cinematic embarrassments and celebrate the very worst of Hollywood. The ceremony of shame, first held on March 31, 1981, always takes place on the eve of the Oscars, as if to accentuate the contrast between the brilliant and the truly execrable, and has become the bane of many a bad actor.

Madonna and Sylvester Stallone have been particularly notable for their wooden work, and each has been awarded a record number of Razzies as a result. The Material Girl, who probably should have stuck with music, has garnered an impressive 15 nominations, and won 9 for her "acting" in such gems as *Swept Away* and *Body of Evidence*. She even scored a nod playing herself in *Truth or Dare*. Stallone's work has been similarly well received by the Raspberry Academy: 30 nominations and 10 awards for such nuanced roles as Rocky/Rambo. To cap their spectacularly successful Razzie run, the two were given special awards in 2000, honoring them as the worst actor and worst actress of the entire 20th century. Neither showed up to accept.

April

"April is the cruellest month."
—T. S. ELIOT,
"The Waste Land"

APRIL 1, 1998

April Cruel's Day

Who knew Uday Hussein was such a hoot? When he wasn't getting his kicks torturing people to death, or plundering the state to fund his lavish lifestyle, the maniacal son of Iraqi dictator Saddam Hussein apparently loved a good gag. And what better occasion for uproarious despotic antics than April Fools' Day—or, as they call it in Iraq, Kithbet Neesan, April Lie.

On that special day in 1998, the Uday-owned newspaper *Babil* published a front-page article declaring that the punishing sanctions imposed by the United Nations after Iraq's invasion of Kuwait would be lifted. Then, on the second page, readers were let in on the joke, which no doubt left thousands of deprived and malnourished Iraqis howling with laughter.

It would be hard to top himself after that clever prank on the people, but Uday managed it the next year with the announcement

in *Babil* that meager food rations would henceforth be supplemented with bananas, chocolate, and soft drinks. Ha!

Hilarious though he was, Uday seemed to be running out of inspiration when he repeated the same jokes on the next two Kithbet Neesans. Thankfully, the spirit of the day was not entirely lost when Abbas Khalaf Kunfuth, Iraq's ambassador to Russia, apparently channeled Uday's zaniness at a press conference he gave on April 1, 2003—just weeks after a U.S.-led coalition force invaded his homeland. Holding up a piece of paper he identified as a Reuters news report, the ambassador read, "The Americans have accidentally fired a nuclear missile into British forces, killing seven."

Then, after pausing to allow the shock of the news sink in with the gathered media, he shouted, "APRIL FOOLS!"

APRIL 2, 1992

John Gotti: Scratching Out the Teflon Don

He was the rock star mobster—the "Dapper Don," as he was dubbed by the adoring tabloid media for his expensive suits and engaging demeanor. But John Gotti, boss of the Gambino crime family, was also a ruthless murderer who, for years, seemed entirely above the law. Three acquittals in as many high-profile trials only added to his swaggering luster and earned him another moniker: the "Teflon Don," a name that stuck until April 2, 1992, when a jury verdict in a fourth trial proved that Gotti wasn't untouchable after all. Devastating testimony from Gambino underboss turned FBI snitch Salvatore "Sammy the Bull" Gravano, as well as incriminating taped conversations, scratched right through the Teflon surface, resulting in Gotti's conviction on 13 counts, including murder and racketeering, and a life sentence.* "The Don is covered in Velcro," James Fox, assistant director of the FBI's New York office, said after the trial, "and every charge stuck."

APRIL 3, 1895

Wit's End: Bringing Down Oscar Wilde

The late Victorian social mores that author and playwright Oscar Wilde so often satirized reared up and destroyed him almost immediately after his greatest artistic triumph. And all because of what Wilde's intimate companion, Lord Alfred Douglas, once described in a poem as "the Love that dare not speak its name."

Lord Douglas's father, the Marquess of Queensberry, initiated Wilde's rapid downfall—inaugurating a vicious campaign in June 1894, when he went to the writer's home and angrily confronted him about rumored romantic liaisons with his son. He and Wilde quarreled, each threatening the other with bodily harm, before Wilde threw the marquess out of his house and barred him from ever returning.

Just over seven and a half months after the encounter at Wilde's home, the playwright's masterpiece, *The Importance of Being Earnest,* debuted in London on February 14, 1895, and was an instant success. Queensberry had planned to darken the premiere by

---

* *Gotti died in prison a decade after his conviction.*

tossing a bouquet of rotten vegetables onto the stage, but Wilde learned of his plan and had him barred from the theater. Nevertheless, Queensberry lobbed something far more inflammatory four days later when he dropped a calling card at Wilde's club that read, "For Oscar Wilde, posing somdomite [*sic*]." As sodomy was then illegal in England, Queensberry was in fact publicly accusing Wilde of having committed a crime. Encouraged by Lord Douglas, who had his own issues with his dad, the playwright filed a libel suit against Queensberry.

The trial that opened on April 3, 1895, was the first in a rapid succession of events that ultimately ended with Wilde's imprisonment under a sentence of hard labor. To successfully defend himself against a libel charge, Queensberry had to prove that his allegations against Wilde were true and that exposing him was for the greater benefit of society. His attorneys pursued this end vigorously and produced a mountain of salacious evidence that purported to prove Wilde was a homosexual predator determined to corrupt the youth of London. No matter how persuasive Wilde was in the courtroom, the evidence was damning enough to prompt him to drop the charges midway through the trial. Then, with the evidence that had emerged in the libel case, Wilde was promptly arrested and charged with "gross indecency."

Amid a frenzy of press sensationalism, the prosecution opened on April 26, 1895. Wilde was eloquent enough in his own defense that the jury was unable to reach a verdict. However, after a second trial the following month, Wilde was convicted and sentenced to two years of hard labor. The subsequent prison ordeal broke him physically, but somehow advanced him spiritually. He celebrated the experience in a letter to Lord Douglas that was later published with the title *De Profundis*:

> I wanted to eat of the fruit of all the trees in the garden of the world . . . And so, indeed, I went out, and so I lived. My only mistake was that I confined myself

so exclusively to the trees of what seemed to me the sun-lit side of the garden, and shunned the other side for its shadow and its gloom.

Wilde lived another three years in self-exile after his release from prison in May 1897—scorned and penniless. Just before his death in 1900, he reported a terrible dream to Reginald Turner, one of his few remaining friends. "I dreamt that I had died, and was supping with the dead!" Wilde said.

"I am sure," Turner replied, "that you must have been the life and soul of the party."

APRIL 4, 1868

A Slight at the Opera:
The Architect's Fatal Review

In his 1969 book *The Vienna Opera,* historian Marcel Prawy was lavish in his praise of the architects Eduard van der Nüll and August Sicard von Sicardsburg. "Between them," Prawy wrote, "[they] had designed a superb opera house [in Vienna], a perfect blend of beauty and absolute functionalism." Yet the reviews for the now iconic structure were significantly less glowing when it was built a century earlier—with tragic consequences for the design team. People criticized the Vienna State Opera for standing too low amid its opulent surroundings; "a buried treasure box," some called it—a verdict with which Austrian emperor Franz Josef was heard to agree. The criticism, especially the emperor's, proved too much for van der Nüll, who, in the ultimate operatic act, hanged himself on April 4, 1868. Ten weeks later, his personal and professional partner Sicardsburg was dead from what many believed was a broken heart. The emperor was so traumatized by the devastating

Vienna State Opera, object of harsh scrutiny in its early days

effect his words had on van der Null that from then on he reportedly praised everything he saw with a pat declaration: "It was very
beautiful, I liked it a lot."

APRIL 5, 1993

A Hard Day's Night for the University
of Michigan's "Fab Five"

They were Wolverine rock stars: five dazzling players—all sopho-
mores at the University of Michigan—ready to pounce in their
much imitated saggy shorts, black Nikes, and black socks pulled way
up high. The "Fab Five," as they were known, had already shot to
fame the year before when they became the first all-freshman starters
to reach the NCAA Championship. They lost to Duke, but now
they were back—cocksure and predatory as they sauntered onto the
court to face the University of North Carolina Tar Heels for the title.
"Y'all are going to lose this game," pronounced Wolverine forward
Chris Webber, the NCAA Men's Basketball first team All-American.

Before the night was over, though, the arrogant boast would bite Webber right in the behind—reduced as he was to mortifying shame.

With less than 30 seconds remaining in the game, and Michigan trailing by two points, Webber grabbed a defensive rebound. With the rest of the Wolverines' primary ball handlers already upcourt, Webber headed up the court and took the ball to the baseline. But he was double-teamed, which prompted him to make one of the biggest blunders in basketball history: With no timeouts remaining, Webber called a timeout.

The Tar Heels gained two more points from the resulting technical foul, immediately after which they cinched the game (77-71) with two more successful foul shots. As the rest of the Fab Five stood stunned, Webber cried out, "I cost our team the game."*

APRIL 6, 1199

All Is Forgiven . . . Well, Not All

The warrior king Richard I, "the Lionheart," didn't meet his end in battle, as might have been expected, but on a day relatively free of hostilities, as he casually walked around the perimeter of a castle

---

* *As it turned out, Webber cost his team a lot more than the championship; he cost them their place in history. After a massive scandal involving payoffs to Webber and several other Wolverines over the years was revealed, the University of Michigan suffered steep penalties—some of them self-imposed. Among them: All the accomplishments of the Fab Five were erased from the record books, and the banners commemorating their two appearances in the Final Four were removed from the rafters of Crisler Arena. As Pete Thamel later wrote in* The New York Times, *"The Fab Five's legacy has gone from black socks to black marks, their swagger replaced by the shame of bequeathing the Michigan basketball program a generation of chaos."*

in Châlus, France, without armor. Suddenly, a young man fired his crossbow from a parapet above, striking the king in the shoulder with the bolt. Though the shot wasn't immediately fatal, the wound became gangrenous and Richard soon realized he was dying. It was then, according to a number of contemporary chronicles, that the king did something entirely unexpected: He had the young man who had shot the arrow brought before him, and—in an act far more reminiscent of the benevolent monarch of the Robin Hood tales than the ruthless king Richard really was—forgave his killer and ordered him released. There the beautiful story of reconciliation might have ended—had it been in another day and time. But this was the tail end of the Dark Ages, where such tender mercies had little place. Disregarding the king's dying wish, his entourage seized the young man after Richard's last breath and had him flayed alive.

APRIL 7, 1990

Roughed Up by the Art Police

It was an exhibit opening like none other—at least in the United States. On April 7, 1990, at 9:25 a.m., the Contemporary Arts Center of Cincinnati opened its doors to a traveling retrospective of artist Robert Mapplethorpe's work, titled "The Perfect Moment." Later that afternoon, Cincinnati authorities, armed with grand jury indictments, temporarily shut it down. The issue wasn't Mapplethorpe's photographic images of flowers, but those of a more homoerotic nature—some of them quite graphic, or, as some in the conservative city that had successfully banned pornography saw it, downright obscene.

"These photographs are just not welcome in this community," said Chief of Police Lawrence Whalen amid the whirl of controversy that preceded the exhibit opening. "The people of this community do not cater to what others depict as art."

To some concerned citizens, the Mapplethorpe exhibit was a direct assault on their values. To others, though, the police raid was an assault on artistic freedom and expression. Museum director Dennis Barrie, who was later tried and acquitted on obscenity charges associated with the show, later argued that when they burst into the Contemporary Arts Center "the police had symbolically walked into every arts institution in the country."

APRIL 8, 1991

Kitty's Claws: The Gossipmonger Pounces Again

Having already thoroughly shredded Jackie O and Liz Taylor, celebrity biographer Kitty Kelley's claws came out sharper and more lethal than ever when, on April 8, 1991, Simon & Schuster released her ferocious, 603-page mauling of former first lady Nancy Reagan. Among Kelley's more salacious revelations: a dalliance with Frank Sinatra (another of Kelley's biographical subjects), her renowned skills as an actress on the casting couch, *Mommie Dearest*–like thrashings of daughter Patti, and bitchy backbiting about Ronald Reagan's vice president, George H. W. Bush.

The meaty morsels Kelley had dished out in the book proved irresistible to the press. Even PBS's staid *MacNeil/Lehrer NewsHour* gobbled them right up, as did *The New York Times,* which published her tidbits right on the front page.

Needless to say, the Reagans were not pleased. "Nancy and I are truly upset and angry over the total dishonesty of Kitty Kelley and her book," Ronnie wrote to his fellow ex-president Richard Nixon, who had sent a message of sympathy. "Your letter will help me keep Nancy from worrying herself sick. She is Kelley's main victim and is very upset."

More condolences poured into the Reagan home from other friends and associates—including some whom Kelley listed as sources. A flurry of public denouncements of the book followed. "I'm listed in the acknowledgments as a contributor," Lou Cannon, author of *President Reagan: The Role of a Lifetime,* complained to *Entertainment Weekly.* "But she never talked to me. Never."

Kelley swatted away at least some of the aggrieved sources by gleefully producing their taped interviews. Others she simply ignored. Journalistic integrity aside, what did Kelley care anyway? She had a massive best seller on her hands, with a $3-million-plus royalty advance to spend. Plus, there were other celebrities to feast upon. Next up: Britain's royal family, the Bushes, and almighty Oprah.

APRIL 9, 1483

Richard III, the Original Tricky Dick

Richard III may not have been the wickedest uncle in English royal history.* But, thanks to the titular play by Shakespeare, King Richard certainly takes the crown of notoriety for his avuncular misdeeds.

The Bard's portrait of a scheming spider crawling over corpses in his quest for the crown—including those of his brother's two sons, Edward V and Richard, Duke of York—has been often been challenged, particularly by members of the Richard III Society, who like to think of the medieval monarch as a paragon of princely virtue smeared by Shakespeare and by history. "I just know that if I were

---

* *That distinction should probably be reserved for his ancestor King John, who reportedly killed his nephew and rival Arthur of Brittany in a drunken rage— after his reputed order to blind and castrate the young man was disobeyed— and tossed the body weighted with stones into the Seine River.*

alive in the 15th century I could borrow a cup of sugar from Richard," gushed Carol Rike, editor of the society's quarterly newsletter.

Yet while there's no definitive proof that Richard III actually ordered the deaths of his young nephews, it's indisputable that he made life really rotten for the boys after the death of their father, King Edward IV, on April 9, 1483. It was Richard who intercepted the new king Edward V as he made his progress toward the capital. It was Richard who installed the 12-year-old sovereign in the Tower of London, where he was joined by his younger brother. It was Richard who managed to have both young men declared bastards, ineligible for the throne. And it was Richard who ended up wearing the crown. What happened to the young princes can only be guessed. The only thing that's known for certain is they were never seen again.

In 1674, the bones of two young men, believed to be those of Edward V and his brother, Richard, Duke of York, were uncovered beneath a stairway as the Tower of London was being renovated and interred with all due ceremony in Westminster Abbey. Had their uncle ordered their deaths, as many historians believe? Perhaps the mystery will never be solved. But Carol Rike would probably have done well to avoid that cup of sugar offered by Richard.

APRIL 10, 1917

Germany's Secret Weapon: Lenin

Revolution in Russia had already toppled Tsar Nicholas II, but when it came to the savage war he waged against Germany, nothing changed. The leaders of the Provisional Government that had replaced Nicholas still pursued that fallen monarch's hawkish policies. Germany, however, had a secret weapon stashed away in Switzerland, one ferocious enough to end once and for all the conflict that had been raging since 1914. The weapon's name: Vladimir Ilyich Lenin—the fiery Bolshevist agitator whose avowed aim was to turn Russia red while ceasing that turbulent nation's involvement in World War I.

On April 10, 1917, Lenin boarded a train in Zurich that would secretly cross Germany and deposit him back in Russia, from where he had been exiled, to launch the violent upheavals that made history. Recalling the event several years later, Winston Churchill said in a speech:

> Lenin was sent into Russia by the Germans in the same way that you might send a phial containing a culture of typhoid or cholera to be poured into the water supply of a great city, and it worked with amazing accuracy.

APRIL 11, 2003

Stuff Happens—and Sometimes It Doesn't

"Stuff happens."
>   —*Secretary of Defense Donald Rumsfeld's*
> *astonishingly cavalier response at an April 11, 2003,*
> *press conference in response to the chaos and looting*
> *that erupted in Baghdad after the U.S. invasion of*
> *Iraq and the fall of Saddam Hussein**

---

* As a side note, nothing *happened on the same day 49 years earlier—at* least according to a computer analysis completed by British computer scientist

Eleanor Roosevelt's Triply Tragic Day

Eleanor Roosevelt was in for a tremendous shock on April 12, 1945. Actually, there were to be three shocks. The first lady was attending a meeting in Washington that afternoon when she received an urgent call to return home. "I got into the car and sat with clenched hands all the way to the White House," she later recalled. "In my heart of hearts, I knew what had happened." Earlier that day, while recovering from exhaustion at his retreat in Warm Springs, Georgia, President Franklin D. Roosevelt had succumbed to a massive stroke.

Mrs. Roosevelt arrived at Warm Springs late that night, only to be hit with more staggering news. Her husband had not died alone, but in the company of Lucy Mercer Rutherford. The first lady had first learned of her husband's affair with Lucy nearly three decades before, when she found their love letters. It had been a severe blow to the marriage, which survived only because of Franklin's promise never to see her again. Now Eleanor's grief was mingled with a profound sense of betrayal. And it only got worse.

The president's cousin Laura Delano had also accompanied him to Warm Springs, and it was she who delivered the news—some

---

William Tunstall-Pedoe in 2010. "Nobody significant died that day [April 11, 1954]," Tunstall-Pedoe observed, "no major events apparently occurred and, although a typical day in the 20th century has many notable people being born, for some reason that day had only one who might make that claim—Abdullah Atalar, a Turkish academic." So, for any reader whose birthday fell on this most boring day, now you know why everyone avoids you at a party.

said with malicious glee—that Lucy had just been there. Then, with a twist of the knife, she told Eleanor that the president had been seeing his onetime mistress for years—and that their meetings, including the one at Warm Springs, had been arranged by Eleanor's own daughter, Anna.

"Mother was so upset about everything and now so upset with me," Anna recalled. Her face was "as stern as it could get when she was angry." To Anna's son Curtis, this was entirely understandable: "He was her husband. She was his wife. He was president. She was first lady. And now Anna had walked into the picture and made it possible for Lucy to return to the president's life. It must have seemed an unforgivable act."

APRIL 13, 1981

Problem Was, It Didn't Win the Pulitzer Prize for Fiction

There is no award in journalism more impressive than the Pulitzer, so naturally *The Washington Post* newsroom celebrated when it was announced on April 13, 1981, that "Jimmy's World," reporter Janet Cooke's astonishing front-page story of an eight-year-old heroin addict, had won the prestigious prize. Yet within days it became apparent that this special recognition was about the worst thing ever to happen to the *Post*.

"Jimmy's World" had caused an immediate sensation when it was published on September 28, 1980. Readers were both mesmerized and incensed by Cooke's account, which began: "Jimmy is 8 years old and a third-generation heroin addict, a precocious little boy with sandy hair, velvety brown eyes and needle marks freckling the baby-smooth skin of his thin brown arms." It was a journalistic bonanza, which the *Post* proudly submitted to the Pulitzer board.

Almost as soon as it won, though, Janet Cooke's story started to unravel. The beautiful young reporter had been a dream hire for the *Post* as it strove to diversify its newsroom: bright, ambitious, and black, with impeccable credentials and a remarkable talent for writing. She was also "a one-in-a-million liar," as Executive Editor Benjamin C. Bradlee later put it—a devastating truth that began to emerge as other news organizations prepared their features on Cooke's Pulitzer win and found numerous discrepancies in what had seemed to be the perfect résumé, all of which were immediately reported to the *Post*.

Cooke had never attended the Sorbonne, as she had claimed, nor did she receive a master's degree from the University of Toledo. And far from graduating from Vassar magna cum laude, she had left that institution after one year. Then, after Bradlee began peppering her with questions in French, he discovered that Cooke had also lied about her fluency in four languages.

It didn't take long for editors to discern that, like her résumé, Cooke had fabricated "Jimmy" as well. "In a way, both she and

Reporter Janet Cooke dreams up another great story.

the story were almost too good to be true," said *Post* editor Bob Woodward, who had earlier gained fame with Carl Bernstein for his Watergate reporting. "I had seen her go out on a complicated story and an hour later turn in a beautifully written piece. This story was so well-written and tied together so well that my alarm bells simply didn't go off. My skepticism left me. I was personally negligent."

Woodward wasn't alone. Although several members of the newsroom staff had expressed concern over the veracity of Cooke's story all along, "Jimmy's World" nevertheless made its way up through the editorial chain of command—all the way to the executive editor. With Bradlee, as the paper's independent ombudsman Bill Green reported, "the story, colors flying, had passed its last and most powerful filter."

Thus began what Bradlee described in his autobiography as "the darkest chapter in my newspaper life." The Pulitzer Prize was ultimately returned, the reputation of a great newspaper battered. "In truth," read a *Post* editorial, "just as readers may feel maltreated by publication of the 'Jimmy' tale and all the subsequent hullabaloo it created, so we at this newspaper feel at once angry, chagrined, misused ourselves, determined to continue the kind of aggressive reporting Miss Cooke's story purported to be and determined also to maintain and honor the highest standards of straight and fair reporting."

APRIL 14, 1865

The Other Attack the Night Lincoln Was Shot

The nation's capital was in a frightful state on the night of April 14, 1865. But the horror wasn't entirely centered on Ford's Theatre, where John Wilkes Booth fired a shot at close range into the head of President Abraham Lincoln. Indeed, just a short distance away, Secretary of State William H. Seward was savagely attacked in his own home by Lewis Powell (aka Lewis Paine), one of Booth's associates.

The assassins' plan had been to essentially decapitate the government by killing the president, the vice president, and the secretary of state. To that end, Powell was sent to Seward's house on Lafayette Square, where the secretary was in bed recovering from a near-fatal carriage accident nine days before. Shortly after 10 p.m., the would-be killer presented himself at the door as a messenger with a prescription delivery from Seward's doctor. The servant wouldn't let him in, however, explaining that the secretary was asleep. Powell barged past anyway and began to march up the stairs, where he encountered the secretary's son Frederick, who also told the hulking, red-faced Powell that his father could not be disturbed.

"Very well, sir," Powell responded, feigning resignation. "I will go." But then he suddenly spun around, aimed his hidden pistol at Frederick's head, and pulled the trigger. It misfired. Enraged, Powell began to pistol-whip Frederick, cracking open his skull, as the son helplessly grappled with him in an effort to stop the much stronger man's murderous progress.

Bursting through Seward's bedroom door, Powell stabbed wildly at Private Robinson, a soldier stationed on guard there, slashing the man's forehead and sending him reeling. He then shoved aside Seward's daughter Fanny and leapt upon the prone secretary's bed, holding him down with one hand while stabbing him over and over in the head and neck, nearly severing his cheek. By this time, Robinson had recovered from the knife blow, and he and another of Seward's sons, Augustus, thrust themselves upon the attacker. Powell stabbed Robinson twice in the shoulder and Augustus in the head before racing out of the house, nearly killing a State Department messenger who had just arrived.

Incredibly, all five men who had been so grievously attacked that night survived their encounter with Lewis Powell, although the secretary of state was left permanently disfigured. "He looked like an exsanguinated corpse," recounted Seward's doctor upon encountering the stricken secretary immediately after the assassination attempt. "In approaching him my feet were deep in blood. Blood was streaming from an extensive gash in his swollen cheek; the cheek was now laid open." As it turned out, a metal splint used to stabilize Seward's jaw after the carriage accident may very well have saved his life.*

Yet while Seward eventually walked away from his near-fatal encounter, and famously purchased Alaska for the United States, his wife, Frances, found the whole ordeal too much to bear. "The wearing anxiety I feel about Mr. Seward and Frederick [who remained in critical condition after Powell fractured his skull] consumes my strength," she wrote to a friend. Then, two months after the attack, she died—perhaps making her the only fatality of Lewis Powell's ferocious rampage.

Death and Taxes and Death

What's done is done on this truly dreadful day: Abraham Lincoln succumbed to the wounds inflicted by his assassin in 1865; the *Titanic* sank in 1912; the Great Mississippi Flood of 1927, the worst in U.S. history, began; and the Boston Marathon bombers committed their dastardly act of terror in 2013. But just to keep the spirit of April 15 alive and relevant, the government would like to remind you that taxes are due in the mail by midnight.

---

* *Even luckier was Vice President Andrew Johnson. His appointed killer, George Atzerodt, was apparently too frightened even to attempt his lethal mission. Nevertheless, Atzerodt joined Lewis Powell on the gallows three months later.*

APRIL 16, 1865

With Malice Toward Many

The assassination of Abraham Lincoln on April 14, 1865, had a ricochet effect on two of his predecessors several days later. Roving mobs gave vent to their grief over the president's shocking murder—the first in American history—by attacking anyone they suspected of having southern sympathies or who failed to demonstrate what they deemed to be proper respect. Across the country people were beaten, stabbed, and in some cases, even lynched by the marauders—some of whom showed up at the home of former president Franklin Pierce in Concord, New Hampshire, on April 16.

Pierce had been a fierce critic of Lincoln, calling him the "instrument for all the evil" in the nation, and describing the Emancipation Proclamation as "the climax of folly & wickedness" because it invited blacks "to slay & devastate without regard to age or sex." Now that the president was dead, the threatening mob demanded to know why Pierce's home wasn't draped in black as thousands of others were, and why there was no flag flying. The former president came outside and confronted the agitators. He, too, mourned for Lincoln, he told them. Then he firmly admonished them that he needed no flag to prove his patriotism. Disarmed by his show of strength, the crowd dispersed.

That same day, former president Millard Fillmore found himself in a similarly precarious position in Buffalo. Like

Pierce, Fillmore had been sharply critical of Lincoln, whom he denounced as a "tyrant . . . who makes my blood boil." And he, too, failed to adorn his house in black. Incensed by this effrontery, a crowd slathered the residence in black paint. Fillmore avoided further violence only when he apologized and explained that he had been preoccupied tending to his ailing wife.

Even Julia Tyler came under assault. Her late husband, former president John Tyler, had advocated secession and was eventually elected to the Confederate Congress (although he died before he was able to take his seat). When word spread that the tenth president's widow had a Confederate flag displayed in her Staten Island home, a gang of club-wielding thugs stormed the residence and snatched what they believed to be the offending Rebel banner.

"The flag so rudely taken away was a fancy tri-color, made some ten years ago," Mrs. Tyler wrote shortly after. "It hung as an ornament above a picture. There was no other flag in the house but a large United States one."

APRIL 17, 1961

The Alamo? Forget It!

The very day that President John F. Kennedy launched the disastrous Bay of Pigs invasion of Cuba, John "Duke" Wayne was contending with a fiasco of his own. His epic film *The Alamo* —a project for which he had poured out his heart and soul, along with most of his personal assets, as producer, director, and star— failed in every Oscar category for which it had been nominated, seven in all, except sound. "Sonofabitch," Wayne lamented to a friend over drinks on that dreary night. "After all this work I thought we'd win something."

Duke had his own theory as to why his somewhat bloated and preachy, yet undeniably earnest, labor of love had been critically savaged and all but shut out at the April 17, 1961, Academy Awards ceremony. "The left-wing critics on the East Coast—they still had it in for me, and they didn't like the idea I was saying that freedom from dictatorship was bought with blood," he told biographer Michael Munn. "They didn't like it that I was using the Alamo as a metaphor for America, and although I wanted to show the Mexicans with dignity, it was a warning against *anything* that stole our freedom, and, yes, that included Communism. They didn't like that. They criticized my politics, not my film."

The critics had indeed been merciless when *The Alamo* was released in the fall of 1960. *Newsweek* called it "the most lavish B movie ever made . . . B for banal," while *The New Yorker* said that Wayne had "turned a splendid chapter of our past into sentimental and preposterous flapdoodle . . . Nothing in *The Alamo* is serious . . . nothing in it is true. *The Alamo* is a model of distortion and vulgarization." But there was something else besides the debatable merits of the movie that many film historians believe contributed to *The Alamo*'s ultimate rejection by the academy: a campaign for votes that proved to be one of the most over-the-top in Oscar history.

To sell *The Alamo* to the academy, Wayne retained Russell Birdwell, whose most notable previous publicity campaign had been to make Jane Russell's breasts the focus of Howard Hughes's film *The Outlaw*. Now it was pure patriotism Birdwell was pitching, aggressively, both to the public and to the academy. Essentially, it was every American's duty to see *The Alamo,* and every academy member's responsibility to vote for it—democracy depended upon it. "What Will Oscar Say to the World This Year?" screamed a banner caption above a picture of the battered Alamo. Another ad read, "It's Up to Oscar!" Duke himself was quoted in Birdwell's flag-waving campaign:

"These are perilous times. The eyes of the world are on us. We must sell America to countries threatened with Communist domination. Our picture is also important to Americans who would appreciate the struggle our ancestors made for the precious freedom we now enjoy."

All this forced apple pie proved too much for Dick Williams, a columnist for the Los Angeles *Mirror,* who objected to the campaign's overt patriotic challenge and the implication that one's "Americanism may be suspected if one does not vote for *The Alamo.* This is grossly unfair. Obviously one can be the most ardent of American patriots and still think *The Alamo* was a mediocre movie."

Yet Birdwell's rah-rah campaign was subtle compared with the one launched by Chill Wills, who played hard-drinkin' Beekeeper in *The Alamo,* after he was nominated for an Oscar as best supporting actor. In one film industry publication, Wills's publicist took out an ad that listed all the academy members. "Win, lose or draw," the copy read, "you're still my cousins and I love you all." (Groucho Marx wryly responded in another ad in *Variety:* "Dear Mr. Chill Wills, I am delighted to be your cousin, but I'm voting for [Wills's competitor] Sal Mineo.")

Another ad featured a picture of the entire *Alamo* cast on the set, with a large inset of Chill. The copy, which some, in Texas particularly, found monstrously offensive, read: "We of the Alamo cast are praying harder—than the real Texans prayed for their lives in the Alamo—for Chill Wills to win the Oscar as the Best Supporting Actor—Cousin Chill's acting was great. Your Alamo Cousins."

So intense was the reaction to the self-aggrandizing (and sacrilegious) ad that John Wayne was forced to issue a response: "I wish to state that the Chill Wills ad . . . is an untrue and reprehensible claim. No one in the Batjac organization [Wayne's production company] or in the Russell Birdwell office has been a party to his trade paper advertising. I refrain from using stronger language because I am sure his intentions were not as bad as his taste. John Wayne."

Despite Duke's attempt at damage control, Oscar still frowned. And for that, Wayne remained bitter. "There was a lot of jostling for the Oscars," he told Michael Munn. "There always has been, and there always will be. But the only film that gets criticized for its

Oscar campaign is *The Alamo*. Why is that? And which film won the Best Picture that year? *The Apartment*. A comedy about how funny it is to let your boss use your apartment to commit adultery. *The Alamo* was about courage, justice, and freedom. Sour grapes? You bet."

APRIL 18, 1912

Titanic's Manager: No Lifeboat Could Save His Name

J. Bruce Ismay may have survived the sinking of the *Titanic*, but his reputation went down with the ship. Almost as soon as he stepped off the rescue liner *Carpathia* with the other 705 passengers, mostly women and children who had managed to escape the doomed *Titanic* four days earlier, the press assault began. The chairman and managing director of the White Star Line was instantly transformed into the most reviled man in the world—excoriated not only as a coward but also as the architect of the disaster for failing to furnish the ship with enough lifeboats and for having allegedly ordered the *Titanic's* captain to accelerate the ship's speed to reach New York faster.

"Regardless of the fact that brave

men, noble women and helpless children all around him were doomed to death because the liner upon which they were prisoners had not furnished enough life boats to save them, there was enough room for this one MAN," thundered *The Denver Post* on April 18. The front-page feature then concluded with this indictment: **"J. Bruce Ismay—Remember the Name—the Benedict Arnold of the Sea."**

Over the next few days, the attacks grew even more vitriolic. The Hearst syndicate published a full-page cartoon depicting Ismay in a lifeboat watching the sinking *Titanic* with the caption: "This is J. Brute Ismay" and "We respectfully suggest that the emblem of the White Star be changed to that of a yellow liver."

Subsequent inquiries in New York and London proved inconclusive as to Ismay's actual role in the disaster. There was no proof, for example, that he had recklessly ordered the *Titanic* full steam ahead, and the limited number of lifeboats actually exceeded the maritime requirements of the time. Still, Ismay's very survival served to condemn him—even if it was true, as he claimed, that there were no other women and children around at the time he boarded the lifeboat. With stories abounding of brave men meeting their frozen fate with dignity, the image of this one man skulking to safety was inescapable. Indeed, he spent the remaining decades of his life suffocating under a toxic yellow cloud of dishonor—and there was no lifeboat to save him from that.

APRIL 19, 1912

A Snub Is a Snub Is a Snub

The acclaimed but often impenetrable author Gertrude Stein received the following rejection letter—cruelly mocking her eclectic writing style—from London publisher Arthur C. Field, dated April 19, 1912:

Dear Madam,

I am only one, only one, only one. Only one being, one at the same time. Not two, not three, only one. Only one life to live, only sixty minutes in one hour. Only one pair of eyes. Only one brain. Only one being. Being only one, having only one pair of eyes, having only one time, having only one life, I cannot read your M.S. three or four times. Not even one time. Only one look, only one look is enough. Hardly one copy would sell here. Hardly one. Hardly one.

Many thanks. I am returning the M.S. by registered post. Only one M.S. by one post.

APRIL 20, 1889

The Day Hitler Was Hatched

Adolf Hitler was born in Braunau am Inn, Austria, on this day. Would that he had shared the fate of his siblings Gustav, Ida, Otto, and Edmund—all of whom died before the age of six. Instead, the little Nazi in knickers survived not only childhood but also two significant injuries during World War I and at least six assassination attempts *before* his rise to power in 1933. Bolstered by this cockroach-like resilience, the second-rate painter foisted himself on the world as a first-rate monster.

An Englishman by the name of Henry Tandey was one individual who may have unwittingly assisted the future führer when both were soldiers fighting on opposite sides during the Battle of Marcoing in 1918. An injured Hitler passed through Tandey's line of fire. "I took aim," he recalled years later, "but couldn't shoot a wounded man, so let him go." It was a humanitarian decision that would haunt the young private for the rest of his life. "If only I had known what he would turn out to be," said Tandey. "When I saw all the people, women and children, he had killed and wounded, I was sorry to God I let him go."*

#%*ing It Up Big Time

In what could qualify as one the worst first days on the job ever, rookie news anchor A. J. Clemente blew his nascent broadcasting career within moments of his April 21, 2013, debut on NBC affiliate KFYR in Bismarck, North Dakota. "F#%*ing S#&t," the jittery anchorman muttered, apparently unaware that the news program—his last, as it turned out—had begun seconds before his outburst. "That couldn't have gone any worse!" tweeted Clemente, who, after what was perhaps the briefest career in the history of television journalism, became a bartender—a job that presumably offered a little more latitude for his foul mouth.

In contrast to Clemente's broadcast implosion, "newsman" Geraldo Rivera's career blossomed gloriously after one of the greatest television debacles of all time. On the same date as Clemente's ill-fated debut 17 years earlier, Rivera breathlessly presided over a special two-hour prime-time broadcast of the opening of gangster Al Capone's secret vault, which, in the end, contained *nothing*. Unlike Clemente, though, Rivera thrived in the aftermath of the disaster—even when in a sensationalistic cesspool (see November 3). "My career was not over, I knew, but had just begun," Rivera wrote in his autobiography. "And all because of a silly, high-concept stunt that failed to deliver on its titillating promise."

---

* *It should be noted that questions about some aspects of this classic World War I story linger, although no part of it has been definitively disproved.*

APRIL 22, 2009

Right, Unless There's Too Much of It and It Bakes the Planet

" As a matter of fact, carbon dioxide is portrayed as harmful! But there isn't one study that can be produced that shows carbon dioxide is a harmful gas. There isn't one study because carbon dioxide is not a harmful gas—it is a harmless gas. Carbon dioxide is natural. It is not harmful. It is part of earth's life cycle."

—*Representative Michele Bachmann's
Earth Day message, delivered on the floor of the
U.S. House of Representatives, April 22, 2009*

APRIL 23, 1014

Brian Boru: Harping on His Defeat

There was good news and bad news for Brian Boru on April 23, 1014. The good news: The mighty Irish king vanquished his enemies—including the invading Vikings—at the fiercely fought Battle of Clontarf. The bad news: He was killed in the process, as were his son and grandson. Such was the dichotomy of the day that it prompted a Norse poet to write, *"Brjánn fell ok helt velli*—Brian fell and was victorious."

Still worse news came much later. While Boru has stood for centuries as an Irish hero, revisionist historians of the modern era began chipping away at his reputation. The clash at Clontarf wasn't so much a massive defeat of the Danish hordes, they insisted, but rather another in a series of squabbles with a rival king from the home turf. Boru's biographer Sean Duffy rejects this account. In his opinion, the king deserves most of the laurels that legend has bequeathed.

"Let us hope that, in the flurry of commemorations to take place this year [2014], sight is not lost of the real Brian Boru and of his real achievements," Duffy wrote in *The Irish Times*. "He is so intrinsic to the Irish imagination that the emblem of the nation, displayed on everything from our coinage and the presidential standard to Mr. Guinness's pint of plain—and on display in Trinity College—is the Brian Boru harp. You could hardly imagine it being called anything else."

APRIL 24, 1975

Badfinger's Manager Came and Got It

Few bands in the history of rock began as auspiciously as Badfinger. The Beatles adored them, and signed them to their record label in 1968. Paul McCartney wrote and produced their first smash single, "Come and Get It," while singer-guitarist Pete Ham displayed his own impressive songwriting abilities with the follow-up hits "No Matter What," "Day After Day" (produced by George Harrison), and "Baby Blue." With bandmate Tom Evans, Ham also wrote "Without You," described by McCartney as "the killer song of all time," and one of the most successful ever written.* But, in 1970, with an apparently

---

* *Although Badfinger recorded "Without You" on its 1970 album,* No Dice, *singer Harry Nilsson made the song a huge international hit with his cover*

glowing future ahead of them, Badfinger signed a management contract with a shyster by the name of Stan Polley. It was a devil's pact
that within five years would financially ruin the band and lead to the
tragic deaths of Badfinger's two most talented members.

Pete Ham "was very excited when they signed with the manager
[Polley] from New York," Brian Slater, the band's road manager, told
biographer Dan Matovina. "He felt he wouldn't have to worry about
money; that this fellow was going to take care of it all." Sure enough,
Polley did take care of it all—for himself—embezzling money not
only from the band but also from their record label (the one after
Apple). Embroiled in a sea of financial and legal chaos as a result, Badfinger ceased to function. Broke, despondent, and abandoned, Ham
went to his garage on April 24, 1975, and hanged himself—three days
before his 28th birthday. "I will not be allowed to love and trust everybody," he wrote in a suicide note. "This is better." There was also a
postscript: "Stan Polley is a soulless bastard. I will take him with me."*

The School of Hard Knockouts?

Just one year after awarding the thoroughly loathsome boxing
promoter Don King an honorary doctorate in humane letters,
Ohio's Central State University decided to bestow the same honor
on King's then client Mike Tyson, a high school dropout with a
most impressive rap sheet. In granting the degree, university president Arthur Thomas cited the world heavyweight champion's
positive influence on young people while eagerly awaiting the hefty

---

*the following year. Mariah Carey did the same thing with another version
(one of 180, according to ASCAP) in 1994.*

* *Eight years later, Ham's bandmate Tom Evans killed himself too.*

$25,000 donation promised by the anger-prone pugilist. So, on April 25, 1989—during what President Thomas's assistant Walter Sellers called this "solemn and historic occasion"—Dr. Tyson stood in his burgundy and gold cap and gown and delivered a stirring oration to the university's graduates. "I don't know what kind of doctor I am," he declared, "but watching all these beautiful sisters here, I'm debating whether I should be a gynecologist."

APRIL 26, 2007

Richard Gere Gets
a Bit Too Cheeky in India

A kiss is just a kiss—except in India, where such displays of affection, made in public, are often frowned upon. So when

Richard Gere's very public display of affection ignites ire in several Indian cities.

American actor Richard Gere planted a big wet one on Indian actress Shilpa Shetty during an HIV/AIDS-awareness event in the capital of New Delhi, some people went a little nuts. Gere was burned in effigy by crowds in a number of Indian cities, and on April 26, 2007, a judge in the northwestern state of Rajasthan issued arrest warrants for both him and Shetty. The kiss was "highly sexually erotic," the judge pronounced, and "transgressed all limits of vulgarity." Fortunately for all concerned, the Indian Supreme Court suspended the warrants the following year.

APRIL 27, 1578

Fop Pas: Duel of the Dainty Lads

Henri III of France loved the ladies—or, more precisely, a coterie of foppish young lads who looked and acted an awful lot *like* ladies. These close companions of the king's, known derisively as the *mignons* ("the darling ones" or "the dainty ones"), went to extravagant lengths to look pretty.

"They wear their hair long," reported the contemporary chronicler Pierre de L'Estoile, "curled and re-curled by artifice, with little bonnets of velvet on top of it like whores in the brothels, and the ruffles on their linen shirts are of starched finery and one half foot long so that their heads look like St. John's on a platter."

The mignons' access to the king and their influence on him caused deep resentment among France's oldest and most powerful families. These toxic feelings tended to trickle down to the population at large. As L'Estoile wrote:

"The name *Mignons* began . . . to travel by word of mouth through the people, to whom they were very odious, as much for their ways which were jesting and haughty as for their paint [makeup] and effeminate and unchaste apparel . . . Their occupations are gambling, blaspheming . . . fornicating and following the King everywhere . . .

seeking to please him in everything they do and say, caring little for God or virtue, contenting themselves to be in the good graces of their master, whom they fear and honor more than God."

The rise of the mignons coincided with an era of intense religious strife in France, which at the highest levels of society pitted Henri III and his posse against an ultra-Catholic faction headed by the mighty Dukes of Guise.

And on April 27, 1578, the simmering conflict erupted in a violent episode known as the Duel of the Mignons. What precipitated the duel is unclear, but the result was lethal to four of the six participants. One mignon, Louis de Maugiron, died in the battle, while another, Jacques de Caylus, lingered in agony for over a month before succumbing to his wounds. Henri III was inconsolable at the loss of his two dear companions.

"The king had a wondrous friendship for Maugiron and [Caylus]," wrote L'Estoile, "for he kissed them both when they were dead, had their heads shorn and their blond hair taken and locked away; he removed from Caylus the earrings which he himself had previously given to him and put on with his own hands."

APRIL 28, 1983

Rambo: First Puff—
Stallone Pimps Big Tobacco

There they were, cartoon icons Fred Flintstone and Barney Rubble—and Wilma, too—puffing away on cigarettes and extolling the virtues of the tobacco brand sponsoring their show: "Winstons taste good," said a satisfied Fred, "like a cigarette should." Baseball hero Mickey Mantle didn't pitch just Viceroy cigarettes, but Camel as well. Even Santa loved to smoke, or so the hundreds of cigarette print ads featuring his jolly self would have kids believe. Then, on April 28, 1983, Sylvester "Rocky/Rambo" Stallone signaled his willingness to contribute to the tobacco industry's decades-long infiltration of the youth market with the following memo, addressed to Bob Kovoloff of Associated Film Promotion:

> Dear Bob:
>
> As discussed, I guarantee that I will use Brown & Williamson tobacco products in no less than five feature films.
>
> It is my understanding that Brown & Williamson will pay a fee of $500,000.00.
>
> Hoping to hear from you soon;
>
> Sincerely,
> Sylvester Stallone

APRIL 29, 1996

FDA: Fatal Diet Apathy?

> "I had said, 'Well, you can try. It's never going to get in this country. The FDA would never permit a drug that had little benefit, terrible risk, on the American marketplace. The FDA is your watchdog that looks out for your safety. Their main charge is safety.'"
>
> —*Stuart Rich, M.D., independent consultant to the Food and Drug Administration, on his response to efforts by the drug company American Home Products (now Wyeth) to manufacture and market the diet drug Redux, commonly known as Fen-Phen*

On April 29, 1996, after much internal debate, the FDA approved Redux. And just as Dr. Rich and others had warned, a number of users of the widely prescribed drug developed severe heart valve defects, as well as the inevitably fatal condition pulmonary arterial hypertension. "My reaction [to the FDA decision] was despair," Dr. Rich told *Frontline*. "Why despair? My specialty is I treat patients with pulmonary hypertension. These are the sickest cardiovascular patients that exist . . . It's a death sentence, and it's a slow death, like drowning over months to years, if you can envision what that's like."

APRIL 30, 1978

We Still Wouldn't Cast Her as Catwoman

On April 30, 1978, Alec Wildenstein, scion of a fabulously wealthy family of art dealers, married Jocelyne Périsset, who would later gain notoriety for her efforts to surgically transform her face into that of a feline. The union would cost Wildenstein $2.5 *billion* when the couple's divorce was finalized in 1999, which, it must be said, was more than enough to keep Jocelyne—known derisively as the Bride of Wildenstein—happily licking her whiskers.

May

"*Rough winds do shake
the darling buds of May.*"
—WILLIAM SHAKESPEARE,
"*Sonnet 18*"

MAY 1, 1948 *and* MAY 14, 1961
and 1963

Raging Bull Connor

There must have been something about the merry, merry month of May that got Theophilus Eugene "Bull" Connor's blood boiling. With spring in the air, and racial inequality to be maintained at all costs, the super-segregationist public safety commissioner of Birmingham, Alabama, seemed extra-energized by the season.

Start with May 1, 1948, when Glen H. Taylor, U.S. senator from Idaho, came to Birmingham—"the most segregated city in America," as Dr. Martin Luther King later called it—and tried to enter a meeting of the Southern Negro Youth Congress through a door reserved for blacks, rather than the "Whites Only" entrance. The senator, then running for vice president on the Progressive Party

Bull Connor's bullies assault civil rights demonstrators in Birmingham.

ticket, was promptly seized by the police under Connor's control. "Keep your mouth shut, buddy," they ordered, before hauling Taylor away to jail.*

Then came more invigorating May days in the early 1960s, when Connor's bigotry blossomed furiously in the face of new challenges to white supremacy. The Freedom Riders were coming to town, and Connor was good and ready for them. He had arranged with the Ku Klux Klan a memorable greeting party for May 14, 1961—Mother's Day. According to one Klan informant, the terrorists had

---

* Connor had already given vent to his feelings about racial mixing a decade before, when he halted the integrated meeting of the newly formed Southern Conference for Human Welfare with this delightfully oxymoronic declaration: "I ain't gonna let no darkies and white folk segregate together in this town."

been assured by Connor's Birmingham Police Department that they would be given 15 minutes "to burn, bomb, kill, maim, I don't give a goddamn . . . I will guarantee your people that not one soul will ever be arrested in that fifteen minutes." The Klansmen used the allotted time well, unleashing a savage assault on the riders with iron pipes, baseball bats, and chains.

Two years later, during the first week of May, Birmingham's children inflamed Bull Connor further when thousands took to the streets in peaceful protest. Mass arrests were followed by a full-on assault on demonstrators with fire hoses and attack dogs—images that were captured on film and sent throughout the world. The media glare and national outrage that accompanied it made Birmingham too blistering hot for Connor that May. Unwelcome change was in the air, change he had inadvertently unleashed. By the end of the month, he was out of a job. Worse, his viciousness had pushed the previously inattentive Kennedy Administration to finally address the gross injustices in the South that Connor so viciously represented in Birmingham.

"The civil rights movement should thank God for Bull Connor," President Kennedy said. "He's helped it as much as Abraham Lincoln."

MAY 2, 2004

Young Gaddafi: A Foul Baller

It was enough of a distinction to be the black sheep of a family as thoroughly loathsome as the Gaddafis. Yet Al-Saadi Gaddafi, the notoriously misbehaved third son of the Libyan dictator, managed to outdo himself even on that dubious score by proving himself one of the worst professional soccer players ever to don a pair of cleats. "Even at twice his current speed he would still be twice as slow as slow itself," observed the Italian newspaper *La Repubblica* after young Gaddafi's first (and only) substitute appearance on the field for Italy's Perugia team on May 2, 2004. Worse still, though, was the junior monster's breathtakingly bad sportsmanship, which he demonstrated perhaps most glaringly four years before his fleeting, entirely superfluous, and no doubt political appearance as a big-league professional.

Despite his total lack of talent, Saadi Gaddafi took his soccer seriously—even if no one else did. Through family connections —which meant, of course, the authority of the nation's dictator—little Gaddafi not only was captain of the Tripoli team, but chaired the Libyan Football Federation as well. Yet Gaddafi wanted more than to simply win; he wanted to be a star—the David Beckham of Libya. So, to keep his as the only marquee name, other players were forbidden to have theirs emblazoned on their uniform shirts. Instead, announcers simply identified them by their numbers.

Yet despite Gaddafi's tyrannical control of Libyan soccer, the fans and players of one team—Benghazi's Al-Ahly—undermined him with galling frequency and, in the summer of 2000, drove him into a frenzy of petulant rage. Libya's second largest city had long been the center of seething discontent with the senior Gaddafi's regime (and eventually sparked the revolution that toppled him in 2011), but it held the soccer-obsessed son in particular contempt. After long enduring rigged losses and misplaced penalties, the Benghazi fans finally erupted during one match in which a number of African dignitaries were in the audience. Booing and jeering, they stormed the field and then the town. Then they did something truly memorable: They dressed a donkey in a football jersey just like Saadi's and paraded it around town. Little Gaddafi went ballistic.

"I will destroy your club!" he screeched at Benghazi's then chairman, according to a report in the *Los Angeles Times*. "I will turn it into an owl's nest!" After a series of mass arrests, Gaddafi made good on his threat. As the people of Benghazi were at prayer, bulldozers arrived to carry out his revenge. "Gaddafi's men forced young boys and girls to cheer for them as the stadium was broken down," Ahmed Bashoun, a former Al-Ahly player, told Britain's *Guardian* newspaper. "All our records, our files, our trophies and medals, were destroyed."

Fall of a Rock Star:
The Mountain "Man" Crumbles

It's never easy to lose an old friend. But the people of New Hampshire were particularly saddened when one of their most stalwart and enduring pals collapsed suddenly on May 3, 2003. He was known as the Old Man of the Mountain, a granite crag with uncanny human features that had stood sentinel over the surrounding region for countless millennia and was eventually enshrined on New Hampshire's state quarter. Daniel Webster once wrote of it:

"Men hang out their signs indicative of their respective trades; shoemakers hang out a gigantic shoe; jewelers a monster watch, and the dentist hangs out a gold tooth; but in the mountains of New Hampshire, God Almighty has hung out a sign to show that there He makes men."

The Old Man was already showing worrisome signs of age and decrepitude a century earlier, when efforts began to reinforce its enormous visage with cables and concrete. But the elements eventually had their way.

"With heavy rains and high winds and freezing temperatures, the combination was just right to loosen him up," Mike Pelchat, a state parks official, told the Associated Press. "We always thought it was the hand of God holding him up, and he let go."

Immural Acts?
Rockefeller vs. Rivera

Had it not been for Vladimir Ilyich Lenin, the lobby of New York's RCA building at Rockefeller Center might still be graced by the work of the world-renowned muralist Diego Rivera. The Rockefellers, capitalists to their core, commissioned Rivera, an avowed Communist, to paint a dramatic centerpiece for the new building. The lofty theme: "Man at the Crossroads Looking With Hope and High Vision to the Choosing of a New and Better Future," which, in the midst of the Great Depression, would feature two opposing views of society, with capitalism on one side and socialism on the other. Perhaps some might have thought twice about such a potentially explosive topic, but family matriarch Abby Rockefeller was a big fan of the artist, despite, perhaps, his political views, and the fact that he had already ridiculed John D. Rockefeller in another work. Thus, Rivera set about his creative task—with a great big surprise up his sleeve.

With work on the mural well under way, future New York governor and U.S. vice president Nelson Rockefeller went on one of his frequent visits to check on Rivera's progress. This time, however, he saw something entirely unexpected incorporated into the work: a portrait of Lenin himself. Rockefeller was appalled, and on May 4, 1933, he shared his feelings with the artist in a letter asking him to change Lenin's face to that of an unknown person.

Predictably, Rivera balked at the idea of altering his artistic vision. The same day he received Rockefeller's letter, the artist responded: "Rather than mutilate the conception, I should prefer the physical destruction of the conception in its entirety." With that, what Rivera called the "Battle of Rockefeller Center" was on. The artist was ordered to stop work on the project, and his fee was paid in full.

Amid the ensuing uproar from the art world, Nelson Rockefeller suggested the plywood-covered mural be removed and donated to the Museum of Modern Art. But the museum's timid trustees wouldn't touch it. Then, the following February, Rivera's work was suddenly and unexpectedly smashed to bits and tossed into barrels—an act one critic described as "art murder." The family claimed the destruction was inadvertent, the result of an unsuccessful attempt to remove the artwork intact. But Rivera didn't buy that, nor did many art connoisseurs. In a wire sent from Mexico City—where he eventually reproduced the destroyed mural—the artist seethed: "In destroying my paintings the Rockefellers have committed an act of cultural vandalism. There ought to be, there will yet be, a justice that prevents the assassination of human creation as of human character."

MAY 5, 1806

A Widow in Pyre Straights

Maharani Raj Rajeshwari Devi was one powerful woman, serving not only as Nepal's queen consort but as regent for her young son as well. But then her husband died. Ten days later, on May 5, 1806, she joined him, though not by choice. At a time when women around the world were egregiously undervalued, widows in Nepal and India had it even worse. Such was their sorry state that they were often coerced into the ancient ritual called suttee, where a widow was bound to her husband's funeral pyre and burned along with him. Over the centuries, hundreds of thousands of women met their demise this way—some voluntarily—with the meager compensation of being posthumously honored and declared holy martyrs.

"If the wife has to prove her loyalty and undivided devotion to her husband, so has the husband to prove his allegiance and devotion to his wife," Mahatma Gandhi remarked after a suttee incident in 1931. "Yet we have never heard of a husband mounting the funeral pyre of his deceased wife. It may therefore be taken for granted that the practice of the widow immolating herself at the death of the husband had its origins in superstitions, ignorance, and blind egotism of man."

Lest it be assumed that suttee was merely an aberration of a less enlightened past: Eighteen-year-old Roop Kanwar was burned to death on the pyre of her late husband in the Indian state of Rajasthan on September 4, 1987.

MAY 6, 1983

The Dummkopf "Diaries"

From the diary of a madman: "On Eva's wishes, I am thoroughly examined by my doctors. Because of the new pills I have violent flatulence, and—says Eva—bad breath." Certainly it was a rather bland entry, but a tantalizing tidbit nonetheless—part of what promised to be a historic bonanza of insight into one of the world's most evil men.

On April 22, 1983, the German news magazine *Stern* announced that it had in its possession the personal diary of Adolf Hitler—a long hidden set of some 60 volumes, spanning the years 1932 to 1945, for which the magazine had paid millions. It was a staggering sum, but the prestige that would come from such a scoop was priceless.

Australian media mogul Rupert Murdoch was among those who saw huge profit potential in the diaries and wanted to serialize them in his *Times* of London. To authenticate the documents, he dispatched British historian Hugh Trevor-Roper, a specialist in the 16th and 17th centuries who could barely read German. After hearing *Stern* editors relate the story of how the diaries had been retrieved from a plane crash in 1945 and secretly stashed away by a high-ranking

East German officer, and then reviewing the massive pile of volumes, Trevor-Roper was "satisfied that the documents are authentic."

Even as the world waited anxiously to read the private thoughts of this inscrutable monster, skeptics had reservations. Hitler biographer Werner Maser told Reuters at the time that "everything speaks against it. It smacks of pure sensationalism." The chorus of doubt grew louder when *Stern* published a lavish special issue heralding the diaries on April 25, and held a press conference to crow about it.

Instead of the expected huzzahs, however, editors were confronted with unwelcome questions about the diaries' authenticity. And Trevor-Roper certainly didn't help matters with his sudden and unexpected about-face when asked to address the suspicious press: "As a historian, I regret that the, er, normal method of historical verification, er, has, perhaps necessarily, been to some extent sacrificed to the requirements of a journalistic scoop."

It was a disaster unfolding, the crowning blow of which came on May 6 when the German Federal Archives declared the diaries to be "a crude forgery" and the "grotesquely superficial" concoction of a forger with "limited intellectual capacity."

Stern had been duped by a dope by the name of Konrad Kujau, a "jaunty and farcical figure," as author Robert Harris described him, who apparently expended very little time or effort on his handiwork. The indications of forgery were obvious, from the paper, ink, and glue Kujau used—all of which were manufactured well after Hitler's death in 1945—to the passages lifted directly, albeit often incorrectly, from a book of the führer's speeches and proclamations. Kujau even messed up the Gothic initials embossed on each *imitation* leather volume, some of which read "FH," not "AH."

"We have every reason to be ashamed that something like this could happen to us," announced *Stern* publisher Henri Nannen in the aftermath of the diary fiasco. Indeed, they did. The magazine's editors had allowed their reporter Gerd Heidemann to run amok with the story, without even insisting he name his source. They also ignored the numerous warning signs of fraud that preceded publication. But at least Nannen and his colleagues could take a measure of comfort in knowing that some of what was written in the "diaries" was actually true. The führer really did have what his doctor described as "colossal flatulence . . . on a scale I have seldom encountered before." And horrendously bad breath, too.

MAY 7, 1945

The Harpy in Harry Truman's White House

It was an enchanted honeymoon, and for years afterward all Harry Truman had to do was write "Port Huron" in his letters to remind his wife, Bess, of the blissfully romantic time they had spent together on the Great Lakes. But it ended abruptly when the newlyweds returned to Independence, Missouri, and took up residence with Bess's imperious mother, Margaret (Madge) Gates Wallace. From that day forward, the future president would be stuck under the same roof with a carping mother-in-law who never bothered to conceal her withering contempt for him—even in the White House.

She was known as "the queenliest woman Independence ever produced," as one town native described her, and to Wallace, Truman was nothing but a serf—a filthy farm boy who had the audacity to reach above his station and marry her daughter. Wallace "was a very, very difficult person, and there wasn't anybody in town she didn't look down on," recalled Harry and Bess's schoolteacher, Janey Chiles. "And Harry Truman was not at that time I believe a very promising prospect."

Wallace's low opinion of her son-in-law never wavered, even as his political star began to rise.

She followed the Trumans to Washington when Harry was elected to the U.S. Senate in 1934, which was bad enough. But her irksome presence became near intolerable when she and her scorned son-in-law—having served as vice president—moved into the White House on May 7, 1945, almost a month after the sudden death of President Franklin D. Roosevelt.

Mean Madge was blithely unconcerned about the burdens of the office, and was entirely unsparing in her criticisms of the chief executive. "Why didn't he let General MacArthur run the Korean War in his own way?" she ruminated aloud after Truman famously fired the insubordinate commander of the United Nations forces in Korea. "Imagine a captain from the National Guard telling off a West Point general!"

And when the president's prospects were dismally low in his race against Governor Thomas Dewey in 1948, Madge stood firmly behind his opponent. "Why would Harry run against that nice Mr. Dewey?" she wondered aloud. "I know dozens of men better qualified to be in Mr. Truman's place in the White House."

"Mrs. Wallace always thought Harry Truman wouldn't amount to anything," the president's valet once said. "It galls her to see him in the White House running the country."

MAY 8, 1632

The Holy (Mis)Writ

Some readers of a 1631 edition of the King James Bible were shocked (or at least pleasantly surprised) when they came across the Seventh Commandment in the Book of Exodus: "Thou *shalt* commit adultery." Then there was the apparent blasphemy found in Deuteronomy, chapter 5: "The Lord hath shewed us his glory, and his great asse." (The proper word was "greatnasse.")

With these egregious errors, the 1631 version became known as the Wicked Bible or the Adulterous Bible, and on May 8, 1632, the printers were hauled before the fearsome Star Chamber for their blasphemous mistakes—with the additional charge of printing the Bible on bad paper.

"I knew the time when great care was had about printing, the Bibles especially," declared the appalled Archbishop of Canterbury. "Good compositors and the best correctors were gotten being grave and learned men, the paper and the letter rare, and faire every way of the best, but now the paper is nought, the composers boys, and the correctors unlearned." Worse, he said, even the dreaded Catholics took better care with their "superstitious books."

The printers were heavily fined and banned from their profession, but were lucky enough not to have been mutilated or dealt a similarly gruesome punishment of the day. Meanwhile, history has no record of how many marital beds may have been violated with blessings from the Wicked Bible.

MAY 9, 1914

Smother's Day

Anna Jarvis loved her mother with an intensity that might generously be described as obsessive. While it drove the spinster schoolteacher to relentlessly push for a national day of recognition for mothers—especially her own—it appalled her that Mother's Day devolved into such a crassly commercial monstrosity.

The story began in Grafton, West Virginia, where in May 1908, Jarvis organized a memorial service for her dearly departed mother, who had passed away three years before. She ordered 500 carnations, Mother Jarvis's favorite flower, one for each member of her church congregation. Under the sponsorship of the merchant and philanthropist John Wanamaker, Jarvis soon began to push for a national holiday that would serve as a perpetual tribute to her personal heroine. She lobbied hard—ferociously, some would say—and on May 9, 1914, she triumphed when President Woodrow Wilson signed a joint resolution in Congress and proclaimed the second Sunday in May "a public expression of love and reverence for the mothers of our country."

But that's when things started to turn sour. The tremendous success of Jarvis's mission coincided with the emergence of vile profiteers who began peddling flowers, cards, and candy for the annual occasion. Jarvis went nuts. In one frenzied press release she railed, "WHAT WILL YOU DO to rout charlatans, bandits, pirates, racketeers, kidnappers and other termites that would undermine with their greed one of the finest, noblest and truest movements and celebrations?"

Mother's Day had become for Jarvis a holiday of horrors. But the ultimate insult came in the 1930s, when the U.S. postmaster announced a Mother's Day commemorative stamp bearing the portrait of Whistler's mother. To think the artist's sour-faced old lady was more worthy of the stamp than Mother Jarvis herself! Anna couldn't stand it. She demanded an audience with President Roosevelt and succeeded in having "Mother's Day" stricken from the issue. But the fact that the stamp was still embellished with her mother's favorite carnations was galling.

As the outrages mounted, Jarvis became increasingly unbalanced. On one occasion she stormed into a meeting of the American War Mothers to halt their sale of carnations for Mother's Day and the police had to drag her away kicking and screaming. Eventually Jarvis sealed herself away in her home, with a sign out front that warned strangers away. Inside, she kept an ear close to the radio, utterly convinced her mother was speaking to her through the sound waves.

In the end, there was no place left for the penniless and half-demented old woman but a sanitarium. Fortunately, the mother of Mother's Day never knew her bills were being paid by the hated Florists Exchange.

MAY 10, 1849

Just Speak the Speech …
Skip the Fancy Dance!

It all started with a hiss, when, in 1846, the English actor James Macready decided to spice up his performance as Hamlet with a little dance to accompany his soliloquies. Suddenly, as he pranced onstage in Edinburgh, the unmistakable sound of displeasure came whistling from the audience—delivered by a fellow actor, an American stage idol by the name of Edwin Forrest.

"I do not think that such an action has its parallel in all theatrical history," the appalled Macready scribbled melodramatically in his diary. "The low-minded ruffian! He would commit a murder, if he dare." For his part, Forrest was entirely unapologetic. "The truth is," he wrote in a letter to the London *Times,* "Mr. Macready thought fit to introduce a fancy dance into his performance of 'Hamlet,' which I thought, and still think, a desecration of the scene, and at which I evinced that disapprobation." Thus was launched a petty thespian feud that would ultimately end in a bloody riot.

Three years after the fateful hiss, the by now famously antagonistic actors were in New York—both of them to play Macbeth, at different theaters. American audiences were ready. In an era long before the advent of screen stars, Forrest was their hero; a rugged native son who played his roles with the meaty vigor so lacking in those effete, overly mannered American performers who tried to copy the English, long thought to be superior on the stage. Macready, on the other hand, typified the English old school of acting, and was utterly contemptuous of American audiences. "In this country," he wrote, "the masses, rich and poor, are essentially ignorant or vulgar, utterly deficient in taste and without the modesty to distrust themselves."

The feeling, particularly in light of Macready's known animosity toward the homegrown Forrest, was mutual.

The haughty English actor got an early preview of American ill will on the night his *Macbeth* premiered at New York's Astor Place Opera House, when audiences pelted him with rotten eggs and vegetables and eventually forced the curtain to come down early when they started hurling chairs. Frightened but undeterred, Macready returned to the Astor Place stage on May 10, 1849. And that's when the *real* mayhem commenced.

The audience behaved much as it had at the premiere—that is, demonstrably unappreciative—but outside, a mob that had grown increasingly frenzied suddenly launched an assault on the theater. "As one window after another cracked," the *New York Tribune* reported, "the pieces of bricks and paving-stones rattled in on the terraces and lobbies, the confusion increased, till the [opera house] resembled a fortress besieged by an invading army rather than a place meant for the peaceful amusement of a civilized community." Through it all, the report continued, "the obnoxious actor went through his part with perfect self-possession, and paid no regard to the tumultuous scene before him."

As the riot outside grew more intense, police stationed at the scene had to be reinforced by the military. They were pelted with rocks and stones, and, after several warning shots, finally retaliated by shooting into the mass of people. More than 30 were killed, many more grievously injured. Macready, meanwhile, finished his performance and slipped away unharmed—his impression of boorish American audiences now cemented.

MAY 11, 1846

An American Polk Tale: Stretching Territory... and the Truth

On May 11, 1846, President James K. Polk stood before Congress and declared that Mexico posed an immediate threat to the United States. Foreign troops, he said, had crossed the border and "shed American blood upon the American soil." It wasn't true. Mexico had not invaded, but it had clashed with U.S. troops on disputed land occupied by Mexican civilians. In fact, the only real threat Mexico represented was that it stood in the way of America's Manifest Destiny to grow gloriously westward. Though Polk got his war by deception, his claims were disputed throughout the conflict by a young congressman from Illinois named Abraham Lincoln, who challenged the president to show him the spot on U.S. soil where American blood had been shed. Lincoln was branded a traitor in some circles, but mostly he was ignored. The United States was winning the war—ultimately gaining a huge swath of new territory—and no one was overly eager to question why it had started.

MAY 12, 1937

Throne for a Loop: George VI's Bumbling Coronation

The last thing the shy and reserved Prince Albert wanted was to wear the British crown. Indeed, upon hearing the news that his older, far more charismatic brother, Edward VIII, was determined to abdicate the throne in order to marry his twice-divorced

American mistress—the prince, by his own account, "broke down and sobbed like a child." But duty beckoned, and by the time of his coronation as George VI on May 12, 1937, the reluctant sovereign had, despite widespread concern over his fitness,* rallied his considerable inner strength to answer its call. Only problem was, as the new king retained his regal composure during the sacred ceremony, everyone else around him seemed to fumble.

The day began with an unwelcome wake-up call at 3 a.m., as someone thought that might be a good time to test the loudspeakers outside Buckingham Palace. This was followed by even more noisy disruptions. "Bands and marching troops for lining the streets arrived at 5:00 a.m. so sleep was impossible," the king recorded in his diary. "I could eat no breakfast & had a sinking feeling inside. I knew that I was to spend the most trying day, and to go through the most important ceremony of my life. The hours of waiting before leaving for Westminster Abbey were the most nerve racking."

Inside the abbey, the Bishops of Durham and Wells, whose job by tradition was to stand on either side of the king and support him during the ceremony, were anything but helpful. As George recalled, "When this great moment came neither Bishop could find the words [to the coronation oath], so the Archbishop held his book down for me to read, but horror of horrors his thumb covered the words of the Oath." Worse, when the king stood and tried to move to his throne, he found one of the bungling bishops standing on his robe. "I had to tell him to get off it pretty sharply as I nearly fell down."

Other aides struggled with their tasks as well. The Earl of Ancaster, for example, nearly stabbed the king in the throat as he

---

* *Because of his debilitating stammer (the subject of the 2010 Oscar-winning film* The King's Speech*) and history of illness, many believed the burdens of kingship would be too much for George VI to bear. They were wrong.*

tried to attach his sword, while the Duke of Portland and the Marquess of Salisbury each got their Garter chains tangled with the fringes of the cushions upon which rested the crowns of the king and queen as they tried to pass them to the archbishop.

Yet despite the many coronation mishaps, the king felt spiritually invigorated by the ancient rite; the Archbishop of Canterbury reported him as saying that "he felt throughout that Some One Else was with him." And, as it turned out, George VI became a great king—far better than his woefully self-interested brother would have been—bravely leading his realm through the perils of World War II and the loss of empire in its aftermath.

MAY 13, 1865

An Unfortunate Footnote

Gen. Robert E. Lee had already surrendered at Appomattox Court House a month earlier, prompting his Union counterpart, Ulysses S. Grant, to declare, "The war is over. The Rebels are our countrymen again." Pvt. John Jefferson Williams was fortunate enough to have survived the terrible conflict between the states—during which more than 620,000 men died—up to Lee's surrender. But not all of the fighting stopped: There was to be one final skirmish, a deliberate final stand. On May 12 and 13, 1865, Union and Confederate forces confronted one another along the banks of the Rio Grande near Brownsville, Texas, in what became known as the Battle of Palmito Ranch. It was a small, insignificant clash, with relatively few casualties. Alas, Williams, fighting for the Union, was one of them, earning the distinction of being the last soldier killed in the Civil War that had already ended.

Tarnation!

The process of slathering an opponent in hot tar and covering him with feathers might have seemed a quaint old custom of Colonial America, when British tax collectors were often on the receiving end of this humiliating, often excruciatingly painful ordeal. But a band of vigilantes notoriously revived it in 1912 while confronting labor activists during what was known as the San Diego Free Speech Fight.

The labor movement was viewed by many at the time as dangerously subversive to the established order—particularly in southern California, where in 1910 labor extremists had blown up the headquarters of the *Los Angeles Times*. To curb the recruitment efforts of one organization in particular—the Industrial Workers of the World—the San Diego City Council passed an ordinance prohibiting the soapbox orations that IWW members, or "Wobblies," as they were called, often delivered in the central business district of the city. This restriction of free speech inevitably led to clashes between the Wobblies and their supporters and the conservative residents of San Diego, who were often incited to violence by the local media.

"Hanging is none too good for them," read an editorial in the *San Diego Tribune*. "They would be much better dead, for they are absolutely useless in the human economy; they are the waste material of creation and should be drained off into the sewer of oblivion there to rot in cold obstruction like any other excrement."

So, in addition to the brutal police enforcement of the city's speech restrictions, roving vigilantes viciously attacked those who dared defy the ordinance. On May 14, 1912, the famed anarchist Emma Goldman and her companion Ben Reitman received a most unwelcome taste of this rough justice when they arrived in San Diego to lend their support to the Wobbly protests.

"Give us that anarchist!" screeched the local mob that greeted Goldman; "we will strip her naked; we will tear out her guts!" Goldman avoided being grabbed by the mob, but later that night, Reitman was kidnapped from his hotel room by a band of vigilantes and faced a dreadful ordeal.

Driven to the edge of town, and tormented along the way, Reitman was stripped of all his clothing.

"They knocked me down," he recalled, "and when I lay naked on the ground, they kicked and beat me until I was almost insensible. With a lighted cigar they burned the letters I.W.W. on my buttocks; then they poured a can of tar over my head and, in the absence of feathers, rubbed sage-brush on my body. One of them attempted to push a cane into my rectum. Another twisted my testicles. They forced me to kiss the flag and sing 'The Star Spangled Banner.'" Then, when the fun was over, they let him go—with a few last licks and a one-way rail ticket out of town.

MAY 15, 1998

18 Times a Bridesmaid

S oap opera diva Susan Lucci gave fresh meaning to the word "loser" on May 15, 1998, when she was denied the Daytime Emmy Award as best actress—for the *18th* time.*

---

* *Lucci finally won the following year.*

MAY 16, 1966

Mao's Terror Teens

After nearly starving China to death with his failed "Great Leap Forward," Mao Zedong unleashed a brand-new misery upon his long-suffering people: a purification of communism meant to destroy every last vestige of ancient culture or Western influence. Worse, this so-called Cultural Revolution was enforced by surly teenagers, transformed into Red Guards—millions of whom,

Teenage terrorists in training read from Mao's "Little Red Book."

reporter Robert Elegant wrote, "stalked across the vast nation like hordes of enraged soldier ants."

The traditional respect for elders was turned upside down in this decade-long spiral into insanity that began on May 16, 1966, with mere kids wielding ultimate control over life or death, personal property, and human dignity. With an approving wink from the supreme leader, it was a power sorely abused. Zhang Hongbing, whose denunciation of his own mother led to her summary execution in 1970, was just one of the millions of blindly intoxicated teenagers left with the wreckage of their actions when China finally sobered up after Chairman Mao's death in 1976.

"I see her in my dreams," Zhang said in 2013, "just as young as she was then. I kneel on the floor, clutching her hands, for fear she will disappear. 'Mom,' I cry, 'I beg your forgiveness!' But she doesn't respond. Never once has she answered me. This is my punishment."

MAY 17 *and* 19, 1536

The Boleyns, Doubly Doomed

Thomas Boleyn could not have been soaring higher in the court of Henry VIII. He was the king's father-in-law, after all, and enjoyed all the bounty that accompanied such an exalted position. But in May 1536, ghastly accusations arose charging incest between his children: Queen Anne Boleyn and George, Viscount Rochford. The queen, the salacious indictment against her read, had "tempted her brother with her tongue in the said George's mouth and the said George's tongue in hers, and also with kisses, presents and jewels." Although most historians consider the charges absurd—as did many contemporaries, who even bet on George's acquittal—the siblings were duly condemned in separate trials held on May 15 and found guilty. It was left to their maternal uncle, the Duke of Norfolk, to pronounce the death sentences. Thus, Thomas Boleyn lost his only son to the headsman's ax on May 17, and his daughter Anne to a French swordsman two days later.

MAY 18, 1721

Way Too Old for This S#*t, Part I: The Inquisition Nabs a Nonagenarian

The elderly are usually given a little leeway when it comes to their behavior, but not Maria Barbara Carillo. In 1721, the 96-year-old widow ran afoul of the Tribunal of the Holy Office of the Inquisition, which, two centuries after being established in Spain by the co-monarchs Ferdinand and Isabella, was busier than ever—especially when it came to rooting out those Jews forcibly converted to Catholicism who may have resumed their old religious practices. Poor Maria Barbara Carillo was found to be one of them. After being ritually condemned in a ceremony (known as an auto-da-fé) that was reportedly attended by King Philip V, the old lady was dragged to the outskirts of Madrid and, on May 18, 1721, burned alive at the stake.

MAY 19, 1884

Filet *Mignonette*

When young Richard Parker boarded the yacht *Mignonette* on May 19, 1884, it was if his fate had already been eerily determined. Nearly 50 years before, Edgar Allan Poe published his only novel, *The Narrative of Arthur Gordon Pym*—a tale of maritime adventure and disaster in which the starving survivors of a shipwreck draw straws to determine who among them would be sacrificed and eaten to nourish the others. A character by the name of Richard Parker comes up with the short one and is duly devoured by the rest.

In a remarkable echo of Poe's story, the *Mignonette* was battered by storms while sailing around the Cape of Good Hope en route from Southampton, then England, to Sydney, Australia, and sank. Richard Parker survived the wreck, but not for long. The young man and his three companions drifted for weeks aboard a flimsy dinghy, fending off sharks and sustaining themselves on the two tins of turnips they had managed to salvage. Just as in Poe's tale, the men did capture and eat a sea turtle, but starvation still loomed. Desperate for nourishment, the survivors began to eye one another. A maritime tradition known as the Custom of the Sea provided the solution for such situations: cannibalism. But not until straws were drawn to determine which man would become the meal.

The men of the *Mignonette* neglected this key provision because Richard Parker, dangerously ill from having consumed seawater, appeared very likely to die. Rather than wait for the inevitable, and risk eating corrupted, diseased flesh, the three other survivors instead killed the young man by stabbing him in the neck. Then they ate him.

"I can assure you," one of the survivors recalled, "I shall never forget the sight of my two unfortunate companions over that ghastly meal. We all was like mad wolfs who should get the most and for men fathers of children to commit such a deed we could not have our right reason."

Four or five days after this murderous act of necessity, the three survivors spotted the sails of the German ship *Moctezuma*. Salvation came, one of the men later said, just "as we was having our breakfast, we will call it."

MAY 20, 1875

The Son Sets on Mary Lincoln

Abraham Lincoln tolerated his wife's wild extravagances and occasional fits of fury with benign chagrin; his son Robert, much less so. On May 20, 1875, just over a decade after the president's assassination, the younger Lincoln had his mother committed to an insane asylum. It was an ambush, really, one for which Mary Todd Lincoln was entirely unprepared.

The day before her forced confinement, Leonard Swett, a lawyer and adviser to the late president, arrived unexpectedly at the Chicago hotel where Mrs. Lincoln had taken a room. Accompanied by two guards, Swett escorted her to a packed courtroom where a judge, a previously empaneled jury, and an array of witnesses awaited her. Robert Lincoln was also there, having orchestrated the entire proceeding. The son had been long mortified by the eccentricities of his mother, who had endured the tragic loss of two young sons and witnessed the assassination of her husband. But mostly he was concerned about money—and how much of it she was spending.

The former first lady sat in the courtroom that day, by turns bewildered and infuriated, as a parade of experts—many of whom had never met her—testified as to her unbalanced mind, based solely on reports they had received from Robert. Hotel maids and others were called as well, offering such damning evidence as "Mrs. Lincoln's manner was nervous and excitable."

Then Robert took the stand. "I have

no doubt my mother is insane," he declared before the court. "She has long been a source of great anxiety to me. She has no home and no reason to make these purchases."

The defense rested without ever raising an objection or offering a witness of its own. Robert had his mother's appointed lawyer in his pocket, and he wouldn't have stood for any rebuttal. While the all-male jury retired to determine Mrs. Lincoln's fate, her treacherous son approached and tried to take her hand. Rejecting the transparent gesture, Mary Lincoln made her only statement of the day: "Oh, Robert, to think that my son would do this to me."

Ten minutes later, the verdict of insane was rendered, and the next day Mary Todd Lincoln was locked away.

MAY 21, 1972

Holy Mother of God!
Another Assault on a Michelangelo

St. Peter's Basilica was packed with worshippers and tourists on Pentecost Sunday 1972, when suddenly a madman, yelling "I am Jesus Christ," leapt over a barrier and began attacking with a hammer one of the world's most exquisite works of art, Michelangelo's "Pietà." The damage to the magnificent marble sculpture, the only one ever signed by the artist, was extensive. The 15 hammer blows chipped off the nose of the Madonna holding the body of her crucified son, and they gouged her left eyelid, neck, head, and veil. Her left arm was broken off, with the fingers shattering as it fell to the floor.

Pope Paul VI was understandably appalled by the wanton destruction of such incredible beauty, but, ironically, it was some of his papal predecessors who had led the assault on another of Michelangelo's masterpieces five centuries before. Under the patronage of Pope Paul III, the artist created "The Last Judgment," an enormous fresco behind the altar of the Sistine Chapel. But even as the work was under way, some Vatican prudes objected to the nudity depicted in such a sacred space. Michelangelo retaliated against one such critic, Biagio da Cesena, the pope's master of ceremonies, by painting him into the fresco as a judge in the underworld, with ass's ears and a snake nibbling at his genitalia. When da Cesena complained, the pope jokingly responded by saying he had no jurisdiction in the underworld and so the unflattering depiction would have to remain.

Subsequent popes were not so indulgent, however. Paul IV, the great inquisitor who, as Renaissance writer Michel de Montaigne wrote, "castrated so many beautiful ancient statues in his City so as not to corrupt our gaze," vowed to destroy Michelangelo's fresco as well. But it was Pius IV who actually got the job done. He ordered the artist Daniele da Volterra to cover the offending genitalia of "The Last Judgment," thus earning him the derogatory nickname "the breeches-painter."*

MAY 22, 1856

Sumner's Violent Schooling

In the decades before the Civil War—when sectional differences over slavery and state rights began to intensify to a dangerous degree—edgy lawmakers roamed the halls of Congress armed

---

* *The so-called fig-leaf campaign against "The Last Judgment" continued after Pius IV. In fact, the artist El Greco offered to replace the entire fresco with one "modest and decent" and "no less well painted than the other." Most of these added coverings were removed during the recent restoration of the Sistine Chapel frescoes, but Daniele da Volterra's remained when it was discovered that the plaster upon which Michelangelo painted the privates had been chiseled away and replaced before da Volterra added his infamous breeches.*

with pistols and daggers, practically daring any political opponent to defy them. The House of Representatives "seethed like a boiling caldron," one observer wrote, as "belligerent Southrons glared fiercely at phlegmatic Yankees." Lawmakers challenged one another to duels, took to the floor with scathing orations, and, in one scene reminiscent of a Wild West saloon, reacted like threatened cowboys after one member's gun fell to the ground and accidentally discharged.

There were instantly "fully thirty or forty pistols in the air," Representative William Holman of Indiana reported.

The tension was punctuated by one particularly violent episode in 1856, after Charles Sumner, an abolitionist senator from Massachusetts, delivered his rousing "Crime Against Kansas" speech, in which he argued vehemently against the expansion of slavery into that territory and attacked in particular Andrew Butler of South Carolina, one of the authors of the Kansas-Nebraska Act.

"The senator from South Carolina has read many books of chivalry, and believes himself a chivalrous knight with sentiments of honor and courage," Sumner thundered. "Of course he has chosen a mistress to whom he has made his vows, and who, though ugly to others, is always lovely to him; though polluted in the sight of the world, is chaste in his sight—I mean the harlot slavery."

Representative Preston Brooks, a nephew of Butler's, was infuriated by Sumner's inflammatory, sexually suggestive speech, and retaliated two days later, on May 22. As Sumner quietly worked at his desk in the near-empty Senate chamber, Brooks approached him. "Mr. Sumner," he said, "I have read your speech twice over carefully. It is a libel on South Carolina, and Mr. Butler, who is a relative of mine." Without warning, Brooks then began whacking Sumner over the head with his cane. The assault didn't stop, even after Sumner collapsed on the floor in a bloody heap, and his injuries were so grave that it would take him years to recover and return to his Senate seat.

Northern reaction to Sumner's bludgeoning was one of horror. "The crime is not merely against liberty but civilization," editorialized the Boston *Evening Transcript*. In the South, however, Brooks was hailed as a hero. "Sumner was well and elegantly whipped," gloated the Charleston *Mercury*, "and he richly deserved it." Southerners sent Brooks commemorative canes, with "HIT HIM AGAIN" inscribed on them. Meanwhile, the country careened ever closer to civil war.

MAY 23, 1976

Mistress of the House:
The Call Girl Who Couldn't

"I can't type, I can't file, I can't even answer the phone."

—Liz Ray, "secretary" to Representative Wayne Hays of Ohio, the powerful chairman of the House Administration Committee, first revealing her Capitol Hill office skills in a Washington Post column published on May 23, 1976. Just two months later, the other services Miss Ray rendered her boss, on the taxpayers' dime, cost Hays his job.

MAY 24, 2014

The Minute a Billion Couldn't Buy

Money, it's said, can't buy happiness—or, in the case of one unfortunate billionaire, anything else. On May 24, 2014, Iranian businessman Mahafarid Amir Khosravi was hanged in prison after being convicted as the mastermind behind a massive bank fraud. By some reports, the penalty was carried out so hurriedly that Khosravi couldn't even buy a minute's more time with his lawyer. "I had not been informed about [the] execution of my client," Gholam Ali Riahi was quoted as saying by the news website khabaronline.ir. "All the assets of my client are at the disposal of the prosecutor's office."

MAY 25, 1878

A Post-Grave Encounter

On May 25, 1878, former Ohio congressman John Scott Harrison—son of the ninth U.S. president (William Henry) and father of the twenty-third (Benjamin)—died suddenly at his desk. It was quite a shock to his family, but not nearly as big as the shock when Harrison was found "resurrected" five days later.

During the burial service on May 29, it was noticed that the grave of Augustus Devin, a recently deceased relative, had been disturbed and that the corpse was missing—a not uncommon occurrence in the late 19th century, when body snatchers, or "resurrectionists," as they were sometimes called, dug up freshly interred corpses and sold them to medical schools at a time when anatomical dissections were still illegal.

The next day, several family members accompanied a police officer and a detective to search for Devin's body at the Ohio Medical College. There was no sign of the missing cousin, but just as they were about to give up, the police officer noticed a rope hanging from a chute. When they drew it up they found the corpse of an elderly man hanging from the rope, naked, with a cloth over the head. It wasn't Devin, the men knew, because he died a young man. Still, one of John Scott Harrison's sons lifted away the cloth just to be sure. To his horror he found not his cousin,* but his own father—apparently snatched from his tomb just hours after his burial. Future U.S. president Benjamin Harrison never got over "the taste of hell which comes with the discovery of a father's grave robbed and the body hanging by the neck, like that of a dog, in the pit of a medical college."

MAY 26, 1978

"Accident Park": Thrill Rides Turned Kill Rides

For summer fun—and grievous injury—Action Park in New Jersey's Vernon Valley was *the* place to be. No pesky safety regulations would spoil the fun of the high-risk attractions, which appeared to have been designed by a demented ten-year-old and operated largely by indifferent kids not much older than that. And to dull the pain of broken bones and ferocious skin abrasions, refreshment stands aplenty kept underage patrons well lubricated with imported beer, served by other stoned adolescents. Little wonder "Traction Park," or "Accident Park," or "Class-Action Park," was such a hit—especially with teens. It was a free-for-all, like *Lord of the Flies* with waterslides.

There were literally hundreds of ways to get hurt—or killed—at the perilous amusement park, which opened May 26, 1978, and churned out bombed and bloodied visitors for nearly two decades. A number of them reminisced about their harrowing experiences in a delightful book, *Weird N.J., Vol. 2: Your Travel Guide to New Jersey's Local Legends and Best Kept Secrets.*

---

* *Augustus Devin's body was eventually found at the medical college of the University of Michigan, pickled in a vat of brine.*

Take the concrete and fiberglass monstrosity known as the Alpine Slide, where burns and abrasions were the least of a rider's worries. A picture collage of previously maimed victims greeted patrons as they were disgorged from a ski lift halfway up the mountain. "You'd get on a low plastic seat with wheels and a bar for 'steering,'" recalled Alison Becker in the book. "Then, they'd put you on a long, cracked, downhill racetrack and send you on your way. No helmets. No brakes (none that worked anyway). No warnings about the fact that a misplaced hand could result in a chopped-off finger . . . They actually had the audacity to have a 'slow' lane and a 'fast' lane. They should have been called 'injured' lane and 'dead' lane."

For those who preferred a wetter slide to oblivion, Action Park offered plenty of options. There was the short-lived Cannonball Loop, which had notoriously decapitated a crash dummy during testing. Other high-speed, less-than-smooth waterslides sent mangled, disoriented kids hurtling out over precipices into grimy ponds or shallow pools—with leering attendants on constant lookout for slipped bikinis or amusing injuries.

"Whitewater" kayaking was another popular feature at the park, until some poor patron's boat tipped over (as frequently happened)

Summertime revelers put their lives on the line at "Class-Action Park."

and, while trying to right it, he was electrocuted by a live wire exposed under the surface. Then there was cliff-diving, as Chris Gethard fondly recalled: "I remember this because divers would jump into a pool that was used by anyone, not just those who had previously cliff-dived. So, many people thought they were just going swimming, and had no idea that human bodies would be flying at them from 30 feet high in the sky."

Lifeguards were kept especially busy at the enormous "Tidal Wave Pool," redubbed the "Grave Pool" after several people drowned amid the artificially generated waves. "You know," said a less-than-sympathetic park attendee, "if somebody jumps in and can't swim, that's their problem."

Amid all the mayhem, "First-Aid" carts prowled through the park. "Kind of like a golf cart," remembered Alison Becker, "piloted by two zitty teens wearing oversized EMT shirts, the cart would inevitably be seen looping through the trails, grass, and little forests that surrounded the park. But, when you saw it, you wouldn't see a kid with a scraped knee. You'd see a kid holding a blood-soaked towel on a huge head wound, you'd see a gash the size of a Big Gulp on someone's leg. Blood, blood, blood. All I remember was blood. All for under 25 bucks a person."

MAY 27, 1541

Way Too Old for This S#*t, Part II: The Countess's Inelegant Demise

It would be difficult to surpass the indignity of George, Duke of Clarence's execution—he was drowned in a wine cask in 1478. But the demise of his daughter Margaret Pole, Countess of Salisbury, in 1541 came close. Henry VIII ordered the execution of his once beloved cousin—a plucky survivor of the murderous royal family clash known as the Wars of the Roses of the previous century—mostly in retaliation for the fierce opposition to his policies he faced from her son, Cardinal Reginald Pole. The countess was 67 when she went to the block, which, in Tudor times, made her really old. Nevertheless, according to one story, she was reportedly spry enough to run from her executioner. Around and around the Tower of London courtyard he chased the royal lady, hacking at her all the while, until at last she fell and was duly relieved of her head.*

MAY 28, 1940

The King of Drubs:
Churchill's Wartime Scapegoat

"You can rummage in vain through the black annals of the most reprobate Kings of the earth to find a blacker and more squalid sample of perfidy and poltroonery than that perpetuated by the King of the Belgians."
—*Former British prime minister David Lloyd George on King Leopold III of Belgium*

Belgian resistance was fierce but never stood a chance as the ferocious Nazi war machine stampeded its way through the small, neutral nation. Finally, on May 28, 1940—after 18 days

---

* *According to another equally ghastly account by the imperial ambassador Eustace Chapuys, the countess was confronted with an execution site outside the Tower that consisted only of a low block and no scaffold—a paltry arrangement for a woman of her rank. Worse, Chapuys reported, "a wretched and blundering youth" had been chosen to dispatch her, and "literally hacked her head and shoulders to pieces in the most pitiful manner."*

of valiant yet futile fighting, and as the British and French forces escaped to safety at Dunkirk—King Leopold III, commander of the Belgian Army, was forced into unconditional surrender.

"History will relate that the Army did its duty to the full," the king told his loyal fighting men that day. "Our Honor is safe."

No doubt Leopold believed that, as his own valor was equal to that of his forces as he stood with them until his capture by the Germans. But history would prove most unkind to the unfortunate king. Indeed, the unwarranted assault on Leopold III began immediately after his surrender, launched by the men who made history, and who actually knew better—including that most esteemed of historians, Winston Churchill himself.

With France on the verge of collapse, and Britain's own struggle against Hitler at a dangerous ebb, Prime Minister Churchill stood before the House of Commons on June 4 and—having only recently spoken equitably about the Belgian king—now thoroughly savaged him for "this pitiful episode," as he called Leopold's surrender: "Suddenly, without prior consultation, with the least possible notice, without the advice of his Ministers and upon his own personal act, he sent a plenipotentiary to the German Command, surrendered his Army, and exposed our whole flank and means of retreat."

It was a lie, and Churchill knew it. Both Britain and France had been repeatedly alerted about the Belgian Army's imminent collapse. "We have arrived at the extreme limit of resistance," King Leopold's military adviser, Gen. Raoul van Overstraeten, told the French chief of mission in one such warning. "Our front is frittering away, like a cord which breaks after complete use." In a telegram to Field Marshal Lord Gort—sent just a day before Leopold's capitulation—the British prime minister himself acknowledged Belgium's precarious position: "We are asking them to sacrifice themselves for us."

Yet for all that, Churchill later repeated the calumny against King Leopold in his magisterial history of World War II. Why? Well, as the author acknowledged in *Their Finest Hour,* French prime minister Paul Reynaud had already excoriated King Leopold for what he deemed as his ignoble, treacherous surrender—in essence blaming the Belgian king for France's pending collapse—and he expected his ally, Churchill, to do the same. The British prime minister, as he wrote, acquiesced:

"I thought it my duty, when speaking in the House on June 4, after careful examination of the fuller facts then available, and in justice not only to our French Ally but also to the Belgian Government [in exile] now in London, to state the truth in plain terms."

Churchill's account, however, was far from "the truth in plain terms," and Churchill's son, Randolph, reportedly called him on it. "What you have said and written about this, is nothing else but a heap of lies, as you very well know," the younger man told his father, according to an account by Archduke Otto von Habsburg,* who was present.

"Of course these were lies," Churchill replied provocatively, "but you must not forget that the history of a period is determined by its best author. I am and will remain this author, and therefore whatever I wrote will have to be accepted as being the truth."

MAY 29, 1913

The Riot of Spring:
Berserk at the Ballet

Plenty of rock shows have erupted into riots. Even a Shakespeare play created quite a kerfuffle (see May 10). But a ballet? Well, it happened in Paris on May 29, 1913—during the premiere of Igor Stravinsky's *Rite of Spring*. Most of the audience arrived at the Théâtre des Champs-Élysées expecting something staid and

---

* *In his book* Naissance d'un Continent

traditional, like *Swan Lake* or *Sleeping Beauty*, but instead was exposed to the unconventional music, pagan themes, and novel choreography of the Russian composer's future classic. Almost from the first notes of the bassoon, the booing began and quickly devolved into brawls between the minority in the audience who appreciated Stravinsky's avant-garde approach and the majority who most certainly did not. Even the orchestra was attacked. "Everything available was tossed in our direction," recalled conductor Pierre Monteux, "but we continued to play on." The police were called, and during the intermission they managed to calm the crowd, but no sooner did the second half commence than the fights broke out again.

The composer was so disgusted by the derisive laughter that greeted the first bars of the Introduction that he left the auditorium and watched the rest of the performance from the stage wings as the mayhem grew worse. "I have never again been that angry," Stravinsky later wrote, no doubt taking little comfort from the opinion of some that it was the choreography and not the music that drove the crowd mad.

The critics were as divided as the audience in their reaction to *The Rite of Spring*. Henri Quittard of *Le Figaro* called the work "a

laborious and puerile barbarity" and added, "We are sorry to see an artist such as Mr. Stravinsky involve himself in this disconcerting adventure." Gustav Linor, on the other hand, was enchanted, and noted in the leading theatrical magazine *Comoedia* that the disturbances, while deplorable, were merely "a rowdy debate" between two ill-mannered factions.

Eventually the world came to recognize the merits of Stravinsky's masterpiece, which music commentator Miles Hoffman has said "represents one of the greatest creative leaps in not only the history of music, but in the history of the arts."

MAY 30, 1806

Andrew Jackson:
Breaking the Code Duello

There was a day, especially in the early 19th century, when gentlemen held their personal honor as sacred as scripture. Any perceived insult or affront could easily turn deadly, and often did, as men ferociously confronted one another with pistols in what was called "the court of the last resort." There was a strictly prescribed protocol attached to dueling—these were civilized times, after all, when gentlemen were expected to kill each other with class—and any variance from the so-called Code Duello was considered undignified and contemptible. With his hair-trigger temper and hypersensitivity to the least slight, future U.S. president Andrew Jackson was one of dueling's most ardent enthusiasts. But as one of his adversaries, a Tennessee lawyer named Charles Dickinson, discovered too late, Jackson sometimes neglected to fight by the rules.

The two men came into conflict over some silly spat involving horse racing. Insults were traded until Dickinson took a step no gentleman of honor could afford to ignore: He published a statement in the Nashville *Review,* calling Jackson a "worthless scoundrel . . . a poltroon and a coward." Having thus been "posted," as such public declarations of enmity were called, the future president did what was expected in such circumstances and officially challenged Dickinson to a duel. The men then agreed to settle their differences on May 30, 1806, at a distance of 24 feet.

Jackson recognized that he was at a distinct disadvantage in facing Dickinson, who was well known for his lethal aim. In fact, the lawyer made merry on the journey to the agreed-upon meeting spot, just over the Tennessee border in Logan, Kentucky—convinced that he would make quick work of his opponent. To the delight of his companions, Dickinson at one point shot at a piece of string from 24 paces, severing it, and then left the remnants with a local innkeeper. "If General Jackson comes along this road, show him *that!*" he gloated. By contrast, Jackson was all business as he made his way to Kentucky, plotting strategy with his own companions. It was decided that because Dickinson was by far the superior marksman, it would be better to let him fire first. That way, assuming he survived, Jackson could take careful aim in response, and not have to concern himself with the speed or accuracy of his draw.

Upon arriving at the selected site, both men took their positions. At the order to fire, Dickinson quickly raised his pistol and shot Jackson in the chest. But the general didn't fall. Instead, with teeth clenched he clutched at his chest (where the bullet, only an inch from his heart, would remain for the rest of his life). "Great God!" a horrified Dickinson cried. "Have I missed him?" The stunned lawyer was then ordered back to his mark, as the rules dictated. Jackson was now free to shoot him at his leisure. Slowly and deliberately he raised his pistol, took aim, and squeezed the trigger. The pistol hammer jammed at half cock, however, which should have meant a fair reprieve for Dickinson. It didn't. Disregarding basic dueling etiquette, Jackson again raised his arm and fired. The bullet tore through Dickinson's body and he bled to death. "I'd have hit him," Jackson quipped, dismissing his own injury, "if he had shot me through the brain."

MAY 31, 1990

Imelda Marcos: When's Recess?

Former Philippines first lady Imelda Marcos—she of the thousand pairs of shoes—was fed up. "I get so tired listening to one million dollars here, one million dollars there, it's so petty," the *Times* of London reported her harrumphing after being charged with looting hundreds of millions of dollars from her homeland. And as if to demonstrate how very sick of it all she really was, poor Imelda fainted dead away in the courtroom during her federal racketeering trial on May 31, 1990, forcing a halt to the proceedings as she was carried away on a stretcher. She recovered nicely, though—free to spend her billions after being acquitted a month later. "I was born ostentatious," the shoe fetishist declared in the aftermath. "They will list my name in the dictionary someday. They will use *Imeldific* to mean ostentatious extravagance."*

---

* *Quoted by the Associated Press in 1998*

June

———◆———

"ALL June I bound the rose in sheaves.
Now, rose by rose, I strip the leaves
And strew them where Pauline may pass.
She will not turn aside? Alas!
Let them lie. Suppose they die?
The chance was they might take her eye."

—ROBERT BROWNING,
"One Way of Love"

JUNE 1, 1809

Haydn, the Great (De)composer

Joseph Carl Rosenbaum was appalled by the meager farewell given his musical hero Joseph Haydn on June 1, 1809. With Vienna under siege by Napoleon at the time, the late composer drew few of the honors that might have been accorded him under better circumstances, as many would-be mourners were otherwise engaged.

Yet for all Rosenbaum's outrage over the unceremonious send-off, he was that very day plotting with the cemetery caretaker to desecrate the composer's tomb. His purpose was noble, or so he believed. The disciple wanted the world to understand the great man's genius. And, for that, he needed Haydn's head.

By the time of the composer's death, a relatively new "science" known as phrenology had gained widespread credibility as a means of understanding the human mind through examination of the skull. It was believed that the various shapes and contours of the cranium indicated specific human characteristics. An enlarged region at the back of the head, for example, meant that person had an aggressive propensity for siring children. Rosenbaum's intention was to map musical brilliance using the head of the man who possessed it in such abundance.

He had waited patiently for his trophy during Haydn's final illness, and four days after the burial he was finally rewarded. Alas, the summer heat had already greatly accelerated decomposition, emitting such a foul odor that when Rosenbaum received the putrefying head into his enclosed carriage, he promptly puked. Nevertheless, he was undeterred from his sacred mission.

Having already unsuccessfully experimented in removing the flesh from the severed head of a recently deceased actress, Rosenbaum entrusted the processing of his newly acquired relic to Leopold Eckart, a physician whom he knew and trusted as a friend and fellow phrenologist. In Eckart's expert hands, Haydn's head was methodically stripped of the muscle and ligature that obscured the all-revealing skull.

No one at the time thought anything of the rotting gray mass that been Haydn's brain—of the secrets *it* might contain—and that organ was unceremoniously tossed into the hospital furnace with the rest of the discarded facial flesh.

Meanwhile, Rosenbaum was gratified to see that a far grander memorial service had been arranged on June 15 for his revered idol.*

---

* *Mozart's* Requiem *was played at Haydn's memorial service, which was an*

It was, he wrote, "most solemn and worthy of Haydn"—somehow missing the incongruity of the fact that while the composer was being more appropriately celebrated, his head was "soaking in limewater at a nearby hospital," as author Colin Dickey wrote in *Cranioklepty.*

The corrosive bath did wonders on the skull, transforming it to a gleaming white and ready to be set in the display case Rosenbaum had so lovingly constructed for it. And there it remained for over a decade—an object of reverence and wonder, albeit a secret one—until Haydn's patron, Prince Nicholas II of the House of Esterhazy, decided that the famed composer, whose magnificent music had long filled his court in Eisenstadt, needed a more dignified burial place.

And that's when a most grisly discovery was made. Upon exhumation of the grave—marked with the ironic inscription *Non omnis moriar* (Not all of me shall die)—the prince's agents found a violated corpse in the casket, with only a wig left where the head should have been. Infuriated upon hearing the news, Prince Nicholas ordered a thorough investigation, which seemed not to bother Rosenbaum in the least. "We talked about the Prince sending Haydn's remains, minus the head, to Eisenstadt," he wrote, "and everyone is having a good laugh at the Prince's expense."

Eventually, though, the police did catch up with the head snatcher, who simply gave them a substitute skull. They weren't fooled—that time—but Rosenbaum successfully foisted a second

---

interesting choice, given that composer's head had also been "rescued" several decades before. As the story goes, the sexton of St. Mark's Church in Vienna placed a wire around the neck of Mozart's corpse before it was buried in a mass grave—the better to identify it later. Then, in what biographer Peter J. Davies described as "a moment of animated musical enthusiasm," the sexton dug up the grave, picked through the skeletons until he found the one with the wire, and saved the skull for posterity. Similarly, the remains of Beethoven and Schubert were disturbed in the curious 19th-century obsession with the great composers' skulls.

fake on them, while hiding the real skull in his wife's bed as she pretended to be ill. Thus, "the most valuable relic of Joseph Haydn," as Rosenbaum called it, remained with him for the rest of his life. It was not until 1954—145 years after being detached—that the composer's head, ingloriously passed from owner to owner, was at last reunited with the rest of him.

JUNE 2, 1763

Double-Lacrossed

The ruse was simple, but fatally effective. On the afternoon of June 2, 1763, hundreds of Chippewa and Sauk warriors, under the guise of friendship, gathered in a field outside of Fort Michilimackinac* to play a game of lacrosse. Maj. George Etherington, commandant of the fort the British had recently captured from the French, gave no heed to the warnings he had received that the Indians were far more hostile than they appeared. In fact, he haughtily dismissed the reports, convinced of his military superiority over the so-called savages.

Thus deluded, he and most of his garrison took their places on the sidelines to watch the match between the clay-painted warriors. The Indians' wives, wrapped tightly in blankets, were watching as well. And when, amid the frenzy of the game, the wooden ball was hurled over the fort's wall, they were ready. As the

---

* *In what is now Mackinac City, Michigan*

players rushed in to chase the ball, the women opened their blankets to provide all the concealed weaponry necessary for a massacre.

Alexander Henry, a young fur trader fortunate enough to find a hiding place in the attic, later recalled the ensuing horror he witnessed: "Through an aperture, which afforded me a view of the area of the fort, I beheld, in shapes the foulest and most terrible, the ferocious triumph of barbarian conquerors. The dead were scalped and mangled; the dying were writhing and shrieking under the unsatiated knife and tomahawk; and from the bodies of some, ripped open, their butchers were drinking the blood, scooped in the hollow of joined hands and quaffed amid shouts of rage and victory."

JUNE 3, 1956

Talkin 'Bout Degeneration: That Devil Rock-and-Roll

It was only 1956, with Ike still in office, but already rock-and-roll was becoming dangerous—especially to officials in Santa Cruz, California, where, just past midnight on June 3, police found a dance party at the Civic Auditorium had gotten way out of control. Black kids were dancing with white kids, and, according to Lt. Richard Overton, the crowd was "engaged in suggestive, stimulating and tantalizing motions induced by the provocative rhythms of an all-negro band." The teenagers were sent home, and in response to their outrageous behavior, Police Chief Al Huntsman made it clear that "dances of this type will not be tolerated in the future anywhere in Santa Cruz."

Yet just two days after Huntsman's ban, Elvis Presley took rock to a new low in debauchery—right on national television. During an appearance on *The Milton Berle Show*, the rising King first introduced his lascivious hip swing while singing his hit "Hound Dog."

The press was appalled. "His one specialty is an accented movement of the body that heretofore has been primarily identified with the repertoire of the blonde bombshells of the burlesque runway," wrote critic Jack Gould in the next day's *New York Times*. "The gyration never had anything to do with the world of popular music and still doesn't." Ben Gross in the New York *Daily News* took the critique further, describing Elvis's soon-to-be signature move as "tinged with the kind of animalism that should be confined to dives and bordellos." And to think Madonna hadn't even been born yet.

JUNE 4, 1629

Ship Happens, Part I: The Mutineer's Murder Spree

When it comes to maritime disasters, the wreck of the *Batavia* on June 4, 1629, ranks very low. Most of the men, women, and children aboard survived the catastrophe off the coast of Western Australia and made it to dry land. But for them, the destruction of their ship on a coral reef was just the beginning of a hideous ordeal, stranded as they were with little in the way of food, water, or shelter—and in the hands of a homicidal maniac with delusions of grandeur.

In the aftermath of the wreck, the captain of the *Batavia* and other senior officers sailed off in a longboat in search of rescue. That left under-merchant Jeronimus Cornelisz largely in charge of the survivors—a tyrant, as he turned out to be, of his own tiny, uninhabitable realm. Having already plotted a mutiny aboard the *Batavia,* thwarted only by the shipwreck, Cornelisz now planned to commandeer the rescue ship once it arrived. In the meantime, though, he had to survive. And that posed a problem. There were hundreds of mouths to feed, and only the most meager of rations salvaged from the wreck. For Cornelisz, the solution was simple: murder.

The killings began with a veneer of legality—accusations of theft, say, followed by summary execution. But this false exercise was quickly abandoned as Cornelisz set his murderous cohorts upon the survivors with savage impunity. Dozens of men, women, and children were thus hacked or clubbed to death—eight siblings during one particularly memorable night. And no one knew whose turn would come next.

"So we all of us together expected to be murdered at any moment, and we besought God continuously for merciful relief," recalled the father of the eight slaughtered children. Cornelisz himself didn't participate in the killings; the power over life and death (and seizing women as sex slaves) seemed sufficient—though he did try his hand on one occasion, when he poisoned a baby whose wails were annoying him.

After six weeks Cornelisz's reign of terror came to an end when the *Batavia*'s senior officers returned aboard a rescue ship and joined forces with a band of survivors and defeated him. With little room on the rescue ship—even with the number of survivors so vastly depleted—it was decided to execute Cornelisz and some of his cohorts right on the desert island upon which they had inflicted so much horror. The ringleader, with his hands chopped off and a noose around his neck, remained scornfully impenitent. "Revenge!" he shouted from the gallows. "Revenge!"

JUNE 5, 1888

Widow's Pique: When President Cleveland Pooh-Poohed Her Pension

Take a scorching case of the runs, add a ghastly suicide, top it off with an unsolicitous U.S. president, and—voilà!—all the makings of Johanna Loewinger's most dreadful day. It all started during the Civil War, when Mrs. Loewinger's husband enlisted in June 1861, only to be discharged a little less than a year later. The cause, according to the Army surgeon: chronic diarrhea. Fourteen years later, he slashed his own throat. And that's when matters got a bit messy. A coroner's inquest concluded that the Union veteran had killed himself as a result of his unceasing bowel troubles. Mrs. Loewinger, on the other hand, insisted her husband had been driven insane because of his wartime experiences. She asked, therefore, to receive a widow's pension, which the military had denied her. The U.S. Senate saw fit to grant the request, but on June 5, 1888, President Grover Cleveland vetoed bill number 739, titled "An act granting a pension to Johanna Loewinger." It was diarrhea, not the war, that caused Loewinger to take his own life, the president declared, thus leaving the widow's hopes right in the toilet.

JUNE 6, 1867

Unlucky Strike

The London manufacturing company Bryant & May seized upon the perfect tragedy for promoting its safety matches when, on June 6, 1867, 18-year-old Archduchess Mathilde, a member of the royal Habsburg family of Austria, succumbed to the severe burns she received when her dress caught fire. While most accounts say a cigarette hidden from her father behind her back ignited the dress, others said Mathilde had somehow run afoul of so-called lucifer matches—a type known to be unpredictable when struck, often emitting flying sparks. And that was the angle Bryant & May took with its thoroughly tasteless print advertisement. "PROTECTION FROM FIRE," read the copy at the top of the ad, followed by a newspaper extract detailing Archduchess Mathilde's frightful demise. The advertisement then continued: "The above ACCIDENT could not possibly have occurred with BRYANT AND MAY'S PATENT SAFETY MATCHES."*

JUNE 7, 1999

A Low Profile:
This Kennedy Was No Jack

I t's not uncommon to be an inarticulate dolt in Congress, but it must be particularly galling when one's stupidity is magnified in print by a skilled writer. Take Matt Labash's withering profile of Representative Patrick Kennedy, which appeared in the June 7, 1999, issue of *The Weekly Standard*. With the precision of a surgeon, Labash reduced the young congressman, a scion of the famed political clan, to a blathering, overprivileged, undertalented twit subject to foamy-mouthed tirades—each sentence of his article the journalistic equivalent of death by a thousand

* *Ironically, at the same time Bryant & May was extolling the virtues of its safety matches at the expense of poor Mathilde, its low-paid factory workers in London's East End were succumbing to a hideous ailment known as "phossy jaw," caused by the fumes from the white phosphorus then used in the manufacture of most matches. Symptoms of the disfiguring disease—which came to the public's attention during the famous Bryant & May match girls strike of 1888—began with a sharp toothache and extreme swelling of the gums. The abscessed jawbone was known to glow a greenish white hue in the dark, and then necrotized while emitting a foul odor. The only treatment was surgical removal of the jaw, without which the victim would suffer severe brain damage, organ failure, and eventually a death as arguably dreadful as that of the unfortunate Archduchess Mathilde.*

cuts. But Labash's portrait of the unworthy Camelot prince—"the Kennedy one would be least likely to cheat off of when taking the SAT"—was perhaps most devastating when he allowed Patrick to speak for himself. Here the well-connected whippersnapper, a junior member of the Armed Forces Committee, attempts to grill the secretary of the Navy on how to eradicate racial intolerance from the military:

"So what happens is, things don't get reported because, you know, let's not make much to do about nothing, so to speak. One of the worries I have about, you know, a really zero-defect mentality with respect to defect—I'm not talking now—I mean everyone can acknowledge that if there's a little bit of extremism, I'm not saying that isn't just grounds for you know, expulsion from the military. But how do we address the broader issues . . . Can you answer that in terms of communication?"*

JUNE 8, 1863

Martha Washington's Family Treason

The two men who rode into the fort at Franklin, Tennessee, on the evening of June 8, 1863, shared an impressive pedigree. Both were direct descendants of America's first first lady, Martha Washington,** and close relatives by marriage of Robert

---

* *Patrick's father, Senator Edward M. Kennedy, also demonstrated at times a mortifying lack of articulateness (see November 4).*
** *Through her first marriage, to Daniel Parke Custis. Her second marriage, to George Washington, was childless.*

E. Lee. But neither Col. William (or Lawrence) Orton Williams nor his cousin, Lt. Walter G. "Gip" Peter, Confederate officers both, identified himself as such. In fact, they were spies, disguised as Union officers charged with inspecting military outposts. And that's what got them killed.

Col. John P. Baird, commandant of the Union fort, was deeply impressed by the bearing and dignity of the men, particularly Williams, whose intelligence and manner of speaking he found fascinating. Enthralled as he was, Baird gave but a cursory review to the forged orders they presented. Williams and Peter, using assumed names, claimed they were on their way to Nashville and required passes; they also asked for money, having run into Rebel soldiers who had robbed them. Baird gladly provided both. Then, having declined the commandant's offer to spend the night, the Rebel spies set off again.

It was only after they left that Baird began to have doubts about their story. For one, they had arrived without escorts, which would have been highly unusual for a pair of Army officers on such a mission. Furthermore, they had supposedly survived a Rebel assault, with only their money lost. And, oddest of all, they hadn't even bothered to perform the inspection they claimed they were there to do. Jolted into a panic, Baird ordered the men brought back to the fort.

Williams and Peter returned without resistance to find themselves under arrest. Through a series of telegrams, Baird discovered that no such inspectors existed. He was ordered to court-martial the men immediately and to hang them without delay if they were found guilty. "My bile is stirred," Baird wrote, "and some hanging would do me good."

That very night, in a candlelit tent, Williams and Peter were tried and convicted as spies. The cousins had been on a top secret mission, they admitted, but refused to disclose what it was. The truth was never revealed, as both men were executed the next day.

One Tsarry Excuse for a Tenant

The renowned English diarist John Evelyn complained that he had a lousy tenant for Sayes Court, his beloved home in London upon which he lavished an extraordinary amount of time and money, especially on the gardens. "I have let my house to Captain Benbow," Evelyn recorded in his diary, "and have the mortification of seeing every day much of my former labours and expense there impairing for want of a more polite tenant." The diarist was thrilled, therefore, when the tsar of Russia subleased the home in 1689 during an extended stay in Britain. The poor chap actually thought Peter the Great would be an improvement.

Ominous reports to the contrary soon began to trickle in, however. "There is a house full of people, and right nasty," a servant relayed. It was the tersest of understatements. The colossal tsar, standing nearly seven feet tall, was a prodigious drinker and not particularly prone to observing niceties. (At one point during his incognito tour of Europe to learn about the West, he became annoyed with the squeamishness exhibited by his companions during an anatomical demonstration in Amsterdam and made them each take a bite out of the corpse as punishment.) Peter and his inebriated pals turned Sayes Court into a glorified animal den.

"I went to Deptford to see how miserably the Czar had left my house after three months making it his court," Evelyn wrote on June 9, 1689. What he found was horrifying: Valuable paintings had been used for target practice, furniture was broken, and floors and rugs were stained with grease. Worst of all to Evelyn, though, was the sorry state of his precious garden. A horticulturist detailed the destruction: "Great damages are done to the trees and plants, which cannot be repaired, as the breaking the branches of the wall-fruit trees, spoiling two or three of the finest true phillereas, breaking several hollys and other fine plants." Then there was the fine hedge the writer had cultivated himself—"a glorious and refreshing object," as he described it, "impregnable . . . at any time of the year glittering with its armed and variegated leaves." The tsar and his companions apparently had a blast smashing right through it while riding in wheelbarrows.

JUNE 10, 1994

Genocide, in So Many Words

One of the essential jobs of a spokesperson is to maintain at all costs the message an organization wants conveyed. But as tens of thousands of ethnic Tutsis were being systematically slaughtered by rival Hutus in the African nation of Rwanda, U.S. State Department spokeswoman Christine Shelly demonstrated through awkward bureaucratic doublespeak just how difficult it was to spin genocide. Here is Shelly's exchange with Reuters correspondent Alan Elsner at a press conference held on June 10, 1994:

> Elsner: "How would you describe the events taking place in Rwanda?"
> Shelly: "Based on the evidence we have seen from observations on the ground, we have every reason to believe that acts of genocide have occurred in Rwanda."

Elsner: "What's the difference between 'acts of genocide' and 'genocide'?"

Shelly: "Well, I think the—as you know, there's a legal definition of this . . . Clearly not all of the killings that have taken place in Rwanda are killings to which you might apply that label . . . But as to the distinctions between the words, we're trying to call what we have so far as best as we can; and based, again, on the evidence, we have every reason to believe that acts of genocide have occurred."

Elsner: "How many acts of genocide does it take to make genocide?"

Shelly: "Alan, that's just not a question that I'm in a position to answer."

JUNE 11, 1959

Stamping Out a Classic

"The book is replete with descriptions in minute detail of sexual acts engaged in or discussed by the book's principal characters. These descriptions utilize filthy, offensive and degrading words and terms. Any literary merit the book may have is far outweighed by the pornographic and smutty passages and words, so that the book, taken as a whole, is an obscene and filthy work."

—*U.S. Postmaster General Arthur E. Summerfield's justification for disallowing D. H. Lawrence's classic* Lady Chatterley's Lover *from being sent through the mail. The decision was later overturned by a federal judge who noted, "The Postmaster General has no special competence or*

*technical knowledge on this subject which
qualifies him to render an informed judgment
entitled to special weight in the courts."*

JUNE 12, 1996

When Marge Schott Her Mouth Off

"Hitler was good in the beginning, but he went too far."
—*Cincinnati Reds owner Marge Schott*

After years of unfiltered racial slurs and other grossly insensitive remarks, Marge Schott, baseball's biggest mouth, was finally forced to relinquish daily control of the Cincinnati Reds on June 12, 1996. A few of the more bigoted slams that shot Marge out of the ballpark:

- On star players Eric Davis and Dave Parker: "My million-dollar n*****s."
- "Only fruits wear earrings."
- "I don't like it when they [Asians] come here . . . and stay so long and then outdo our kids."

JUNE 13, 1977

Unspeakably Bad TV:
The Mime Show

Of all the horrors that came out of the 1970s—from shag carpeting to polyester pantsuits—*nothing* could compare to some of the execrable television variety shows that were systematically inflicted on viewers by stoned or stupid network executives. Howard Cosell had one, as did one-hit wonders Starland Vocal Band (see February 19) and apparently everyone else who made the minutest mark on contemporary pop culture. Even the Brady Bunch were resurrected from the dead in 1976 to boogie their way back into the spotlight with ghastly song-and-dance numbers, as well as comedy skits that made their original series seem sublime.

But the very nadir of the decade's faux vaudeville fluff arrived on June 13, 1977, when husband-and-wife mime team Shields and Yarnell were given their own variety show on CBS. That's

Husband-and-wife mime duo Shields and Yarnell: silenced by bad ratings

right, a full-hour prime-time program starring *mimes*—those creepy, voiceless automatons with white-painted faces and exaggerated expressions, always trying to find their way out of imaginary boxes—"entertainers" so thoroughly annoying that even the nutty and depraved Roman emperor Nero had enough decency to banish them.

When the City of Light Went Dark

There was little of the initial terror that usually accompanied a Nazi occupation; indeed, the German soldiers seemed unusually benevolent to the few citizens who remained on the silent streets of Paris. Still, there was no question on the morning of June 14, 1940, that the City of Light had fallen. Giant red banners, the swastika boldly emblazoned upon them, fluttered from the Arc de Triomphe and atop the Eiffel Tower, among other conspicuous places. That same afternoon, the occupiers held a victory parade, goose-stepping their way down the Champs-Élysées, while radios began broadcasting in German. Soon enough, Hitler himself would arrive to tour his newest domain. "In the past I often considered whether we would not have to destroy Paris," the führer told his favorite architect, Albert Speer. "But when we are finished in Berlin, Paris will only be a shadow. So why should we destroy it?"*

---

* *Hitler later changed his mind in 1944, as Paris was about to be liberated, and reportedly issued an order—fortunately ignored—for the city's complete destruction. "Is Paris burning?" the führer was said to have demanded.*

The New Kaiser Rolls off Dead Dad

Frederick III was dying, but not nearly fast enough for his eldest son and heir, Wilhelm, who circled over the deathbed with barely concealed excitement at the prospect of succeeding to the throne. He "fancies himself completely the Emperor and an absolute and autocratic one," his mother contemptuously noted.

When Frederick III finally took his last breath on June 15, 1888, the new emperor immediately set in motion a preplanned military operation that turned the palace into a prison. No one was allowed to leave while Wilhelm rampaged through his parents' possessions—not even his bereaved mother, who was rudely hustled back inside by soldiers when she tried to cut some roses to place on her late husband's bed.

Wilhelm wasted no time disposing of his father's corpse. Even his friend Philip Frederick Alexander, Prince of Eulenburg and Hertefeld, was appalled by the lack of respect. "The dead man was very hastily dressed in his uniform," Eulenburg noted. "No ceremonial . . . no service . . . no thought of the religious aspect."

Hurriedly prepared this way for burial, the dead emperor was dumped into a coffin, which was then hustled away to a nearby chapel being decorated for the next day's expedited funeral. Amid the noise and dust, Emil Ludwig recalled, "the coffin stood among the hammering workmen like a tool-chest."

No foreign leaders were invited to the service, which was conducted with all the solemnity of a pig roast. "The troops were undignified," wrote Eulenburg, "the clergy were laughing and chattering. Field Marshal Blumenthal, with the Standard over his shoulder, reeling about, talking . . . it was horrible."

The unceremonious dispatch was as symbolic as it was unseemly. Though Frederick III had ruled only 99 days—his own father, Wilhelm I, had died earlier in that year of 1888—Wilhelm II was anxious to bury his father's political legacy as a potential liberalizer. Such an approach was anathema to the bombastic and militaristic new emperor—"a mad and conceited ass," as his uncle's wife, the Princess of Wales, called him, and a man who, years later, would play a significant part in the launching of World War I.

"God has not deserted Prussia," Wilhelm declared, "in that he has removed the era of Frederick, husband and wife,* from the annals of history."

JUNE 16, 1871

Dead-icated to His Client

After a colorful career both in Congress and as a leading "Copperhead"—a position that ultimately led to his forced exile to the Confederacy as punishment for his vocal opposition to the Civil War and the policies of "King Lincoln"—Clement L. Vallandigham resumed life as an Ohio lawyer. Eloquent and persuasive, he rarely lost a case. And his defense of Thomas McGehan, charged with murder in a barroom brawl, was no different. Only problem was, in winning an acquittal for his client, Vallandigham lost his life.

The lawyer intended to prove that the victim, Tom Myers, had actually shot himself during the scuffle with McGehan. After court adjourned on the afternoon of June 16, 1871, Vallandigham and a fellow lawyer walked out into the country to determine at what distance and to what degree powder marks were visible when a pistol

---

* *Wilhelm II was equally contemptuous of his mother, Victoria, eldest daughter of Britain's Queen Victoria, who he believed encouraged his father's liberalism and favored Britain's interests over Germany's. It was intolerable, he said, "that our family escutcheon should be bespotted and the Reich brought to the brink of ruin by the English princess who is my mother!"*

was fired at a piece of cloth at close range. They then returned to their hotel, with the pistol used in the experiment still loaded with three bullets.

That evening Vallandigham gathered the defense team to his room to review his planned courtroom demonstration of how Myers accidentally killed himself. Grabbing what he thought was an unloaded pistol, lying right next to the one he had used that afternoon, Vallandigham re-created the scene he wanted the jurors to see, positioning the gun just so. "There, that's the way Myers held it," he said, "only he was getting up, not standing erect." The lawyer then pressed the trigger, but instead of a click there was a flash and the sound of a shot. Vallandigham had used the wrong gun. "My God, I've shot myself," he cried, staggering toward a wall to support himself.

After 12 agonizing hours, the man Lincoln once called the "wily agitator" succumbed to his wound. But with McGehan's eventual acquittal, Vallandigham's winning record at least remained intact.

JUNE 17, 1462

The Real Dracula—Even Scarier

"There seemed a strange stillness over everything. But as I listened, I heard from down below in the valley the howling of many wolves. The Count's eyes gleamed, and he said, 'Listen to them, the children of the night. What music they make!'"

—*Bram Stoker,* Dracula

Four centuries before Bram Stoker published his tale of the famously bloodthirsty count in 1897, Vlad III of Wallachia— the *real* Dracula—created a spectacle of death far more frightening than fiction. It began in darkness, appropriately enough, when on the night of June 17, 1462, Vlad Dracula* suddenly emerged from his deep mountain hideaway and swept down upon a slumbering camp of invading Ottoman Turks, with his howling army behind him. "During the entire night he sped like lightning in every direction and caused great slaughter," a contemporary chronicler reported. Yet in all the mayhem he missed killing his intended quarry, the sultan himself, Mehmed the Conqueror. Still, Vlad had something else in store for his exalted enemy: a horror show that made even the mighty Mehmed II tremble.

Approaching Wallachia's capital of Târgoviște** in pursuit of Vlad, the sultan and his army were confronted with a specially prepared display, Dracula's specialty—a virtual forest of spikes, impaled upon which were the rotting corpses of some 20,000 captured Turks. Stuck on the highest stake, in honor of his rank, was Mehmed's own general, Hamza Pasha. So ghastly was the sight that even the sultan, no pussycat himself when it came to barbarity, was repulsed—yet oddly impressed by his ene-  my's inhumanity. With his army thoroughly demoralized after see- ing the Impaler's cruel

---

* *Vlad's father was given the name "Dracul," for his esteemed membership in the Order of the Dragon. His son, therefore, was called Dracula, or "Son of the Dragon." Bram Stoker is believed to have drawn at least some of the inspiration for his famed Gothic horror novel from this spawn of the Dragon, the historical Vlad Dracula.*

** *Wallachia is part of present-day Romania.*

handiwork, Mehmed led them away—shaking his head in awe, and seeking the respite he needed to fight another day.

JUNE 18, 1959

Louisiana's Most Committed Public Servant: "Plain Crazy" Uncle Earl

It was apparent to almost everyone that Earl K. Long, Governor of Louisiana, was losing it. Though always colorful, he now seemed "plain crazy," as *Time* magazine put it, letting loose an embarrassing stream of obscenities and vituperation in front of a joint session of the state legislature—twice in as many days—drinking excessively, and openly consorting with the stripper Blaze Starr. As one relative noted, "Earl behaved like a kid brought up by strict Baptist parents who had never seen a cigarette, a bottle of whiskey, or a loose woman in his life."

The governor's prim and proper wife, "Miz" Blanche, was obviously mortified by "Uncle" Earl's bizarre behavior and had him sedated and flown to Texas for treatment. But that backfired, badly, when the governor threatened to file federal kidnapping charges against both his wife and his nephew, U.S. senator Russell Long, for taking him across state lines against his will. Acting as his own attorney, he filed a writ of habeas corpus, signing the petition, "Earl K. Long, Governor of Louisiana, in exile by force and kidnapping."

Feisty Uncle Earl eventually got his way by promising to check in to a hospital in New Orleans. He spent only one night there, however, announcing to Miz Blanche the next morning that he would go to his farm and rest there instead. Alarmed, Miz Blanche knew there was no telling what the unbalanced governor on the loose might do, so she arranged to have him legally committed to a state asylum.

Long responded much like a rabid raccoon when police intercepted his car and not-too-delicately dragged the uncooperative governor out of it. Then, after being diagnosed by a court-appointed psychiatrist as a paranoid schizophrenic, Uncle Earl was legally confined at Southeast Louisiana Hospital in Mandeville. He was not happy. "They had to unlock ten doors to reach me," he said. "A dungeon in hell was no worse than Mandeville, and the food is bare as a cupboard in a poor man's house."

After about eight days of forced confinement, Long cleverly secured his release by exercising his still extant powers as governor to dismiss the head of the hospital and replace him with someone more amenable. And though it would seem that his reputation in the aftermath of such ignominy might be permanently destroyed, Earl Long actually got elected to the U.S. House of Representatives the following year.

"You know that I'm not crazy," he said shortly before his death from heart failure, just ten days after the election—"and I've never been crazy, but let me tell you this: If you had done to you what they done to me it would be enough to drive you crazy!"

JUNE 19, 1867

An Offal Way to Treat
the Late Emperor

I t's one thing to kick a man when he's down; quite another to kick him when he's down with no chance of ever getting up again. Such was the treatment received by Maximilian—the Austrian archduke installed and then abandoned by the French as emperor of Mexico—after being executed by firing squad on June 19, 1867. Instead of properly preserving the body so that the emperor's family in Europe might see it one last time before burial, a Mexican physician and a military officer on the scene desecrated it with a combination of gleeful malice and sheer ineptitude.

"What a delight to wash one's hands in the blood of an emperor," exclaimed the embalmer, Dr. Licia, as he plunged in a knife to remove Maximilian's entrails. Then the officer, known as "the Hyena," poured the extracted intestines around the dead emperor's head. "You liked crowns, didn't you," he gloated. "Well, this is your crown now."

There was no embalming fluid on hand, so Dr. Licia improvised with a solution entirely unsuitable for the purpose. Maximilian's corpse quickly turned black. And because no artificial blue eyes could be found to replace the emperor's real ones, which had been removed, the embalmer plucked the black eyes out of a statue of St. Ursula at the local hospital. He also made a little profit for himself by selling off Maximilian's hair and pieces of his heart, conveniently packaged in vials filled with preservative.

The late emperor was now so unrecognizable that even the Republican government that had ordered the execution was embarrassed. Resisting repeated pleas for the return of the body to Europe, President Benito Juárez arranged for the embalming process to be repeated—properly, this time. Maximilian was hung upside down to drain out the inadequate solution Dr. Licia had injected. It was only after Juárez inspected the newly preserved corpse that poor Maximilian was allowed to be sent back home—aboard the same ship that had taken him to Mexico in the first place.

JUNE 20, 1967

Cassius Belli:
Muhammad Ali's Battle

"I ain't got no quarrel with those Vietcong."
—*Muhammad Ali*

On June 20, 1967, boxer Muhammad Ali, who had refused to be inducted into the Army for religious reasons (and was stripped of his world heavyweight championship as a result), was convicted of draft evasion, sentenced to five years in prison, and fined $10,000.*

JUNE 21, 1633

The Day the Earth Stood Still for Galileo

Having been broken by the Roman Inquisition after the publication of his masterpiece, *Dialogue Concerning the Two Chief World Systems*—which Pope Urban VIII believed made a mockery of him in the backward-thinking character Simplicio—Galileo Galilei stood before his judges and abjured everything he believed to be true about the order of the solar system: "I held, as I still hold, as most true and indisputable, the opinion of Ptolemy, that is to say, the stability of the Earth and the motion of the Sun." Galileo's renunciation of Copernicanism ended with these words: "I affirm, therefore, on my conscience, that I do not now hold the condemned opinion [that the sun stands motionless as Earth revolves around it] and have not held it since the decision of authorities [see February 26, 1616] . . . I am here in your hands—do with me what you please." For having been found "vehemently suspect of heresy," the great astronomer would spend the rest of his life under house arrest.

---

* *The conviction was later overturned by the U.S. Supreme Court.*

Eaten Alive by the Public: The Coldest Shoulder for the Arctic Explorers

It was a survival story for the ages. A group of explorers stuck in the farthest reaches of the Arctic—slowly depleted over three years by starvation, frostbite, and despair. "We have been lured here to our destruction," wrote the expedition leader, Adolphus Greely. "We have done all we can to help ourselves, and shall ever struggle on, but it drives me almost insane to face the future. It is not the end that affrights anyone, but the road to be traveled to reach that goal. To die is easy; very easy; it is only hard to strive, to endure, to live."

Incredibly, six men did survive, subsisting on boot soles, bird droppings, and, as it turned out, the corpses of their dead comrades. And yet for all the agony of the ordeal, the rescue of the starving men on June 22, 1884, marked only the beginning of even more suffering.

Greely and his fellows were at first hailed as heroes, rugged and undaunted in the face of overwhelming odds. But then the press caught the whiff of cannibalism. In the frenzy of sensational reporting that ensued, the survivors were left as battered emotionally as they had been physically by the unforgiving frozen wilds.

"The complete history of their experience in that terrible Winter must be told," *The New York Times* declared on August 12, "and the facts hitherto concealed will make the record of the Greely colony . . . the most dreadful and repulsive chapter in the long annals of arctic exploration."

The Rochester Post Express persuaded the family of one of the deceased expedition members, Frederick F. Kislingbury, to allow an exhumation of his body—generously offering to pay the expenses in exchange for exclusive rights to the story. The paper then glee-fully trumpeted its "proof from the grave" that large pieces of flesh had been cut away from the dead officer's thighs and torso.

Not to be outdone, the *Detroit Free Press* added a few more imaginatively macabre details to Kislingbury's autopsy report. The contents of his large intestine, "when placed under a powerful magnifying glass," showed "bits of muscle and tendon," which, the paper asserted, "points very conclusively to the fact that Kisling-bury himself was forced to partake of the flesh of his dead com-rades, as he later became food for the survivors."

Greely was heartbroken as he and his companions were looked upon as nothing more than flesh-eating monsters, and their scientific accomplishments all but ignored in the midst of the ghoulish, press-generated hysteria. "I say that it is news, and terrible news to me," he said after hearing the report from the Kislingbury exhumation. "All these later disclosures and terrible charges come upon me with awful suddenness. I can truthfully say that I have suffered more mental anguish these last few days than I did in all my sojourn in the North."

JUNE 23, 1611

Henry Hudson's Final Passage

Somewhere around the great saltwater bay that famously bears his name rest the remains of Henry Hudson. No one knows where, though, because the fate of the intrepid explorer remains a mystery. Only one thing is certain: On June 23, 1611, Hudson's quest to find the elusive Northwest Passage to the riches of the Indies was abruptly ended by mutiny aboard his ship, *Discovery*. Having spent a brutal winter trapped in the Arctic ice, the expedi-tion leader's starving, scurvy-ridden crew balked at his plan to pro-ceed with the mission as the weather improved, rather than using the opportunity to get back home. Thus, they forced Hudson, his teenage son, and several other loyal crew members onto an open shallop and sailed away—abandoning the doomed men to an unknown fate.

JUNE 24, 1783

The Fleeing Fathers: Congress on the Run

"The grand Sanhedrin of the Nation, with all their solemnity and emptiness, have removed to Princeton and left a state where their wisdom has long been questioned, their virtue suspected, and their dignity a jest."

—*Maj. John Armstrong, in a letter to Gen. Horatio Gates, mocking the Congress* assembled at the Philadelphia State House (now Independence Hall) for its abrupt departure to Princeton, New Jersey, announced on June 24, 1783*

For a new nation, still fresh from its recent victory over the British in the Revolutionary War, it was a bit of an embarrassing flight, prompted by the threat of attack by soldiers demanding back pay for their wartime services. Alexander Hamilton, who supported the move from Philadelphia to Princeton, worried that Congress would be accused of "levity, timidity, and rashness." He was right.

---

* *Formally known as the United States in Congress Assembled, which was convened under the Articles of Confederation*

June

JUNE 25, 1984

Ceaușescu's Palace:
Give It a Bucha-rest

Of all the megalomaniacal building projects with which 20th-century dictators indulged themselves, none came close to the epic size or sheer gaudiness of the presidential palace Nicolae Ceaușescu plopped down for himself right in the heart of Bucharest—"a grotesque Romanian contribution to totalitarian urbanism," as Tony Judt described it in *The New York Times*, "so big (its reception area is the size of a soccer field), so ugly, so heavy and cruel and tasteless, that its only possible value is metaphorical."

Construction of the multitiered monstrosity—the second largest building in the world (after the Pentagon), and once described as a giant Stalinist wedding cake—came at a terrible price, not only in the estimated billion dollars it cost while much of Romania starved, but also in the vast destruction of old Bucharest. Indeed, by the time Ceaușescu laid the cornerstone on June 25, 1984, acre upon acre of historic buildings, churches, and monuments had been bulldozed, marring forever the face of the city once known as "the little Paris of the Balkans."

Ceaușescu merely shrugged at the bourgeois outrage over the lost architectural treasures. After all, he had long pursued a policy of concrete uniformity in construction across Romania—wiping out entire villages and other heritage sites in the interest of what he called "systemization." Unfortunately for him, though, he never got to enjoy the gargantuan monument to his own power. Construction was still incomplete on the kitschy behemoth when the dictator and his wife were summarily executed during the Romanian revolution—exactly five and half years after the cornerstone was laid.

JUNE 26, 1409

Unchristian Christianity, Part II:
A Papal Triple Threat

Catholics of the late 14th century had every reason to be confused, and just a little frightened. Not only were the popes of the era extraordinarily immoral—behaving more like depraved Caesars than spiritual shepherds—but during a period known as the Great Western Schism, the church split in two with two different popes claiming supremacy over the church at the same time. One pope ruled from Rome, the other from Avignon, France— each with his own College of Cardinals and the loyal backing of different European monarchs and learned theologians. Even the future saints of the era took sides. "There are two masters in the vessel who are fencing with and contradicting each other," said Jean Petit at the Council of Paris in 1406.

For three decades the rival papacies clashed until finally the cardinals on both sides had had enough. They deposed both Gregory XII in Rome and Benedict XIII in Avignon, and then, on June 26, 1409, they elected Alexander V to replace them. Only problem was, Gregory and Benedict refused to step aside. So, instead of a unified church under one jurisdiction, there were now *three* duly elected pontiffs—all with bad attitudes.

The death of Alexander V ten months after his accession did nothing to alleviate the untenable situation. It only got worse. John XXIII (not to be confused with the 20th-century pope of the same name) took Alexander's place—just one day after being ordained a priest. Three popes still reigned, with John by far the worst of this unholy trinity. John was charged with all manner of vice, but, as the great historian Edward Gibbon wrote, "The more scandalous charges were suppressed; the Vicar of Christ was accused only of piracy, rape, sodomy, murder and incest."

John was deposed in 1415. Two years later, at the Council of Constance, the other two rival popes were swept aside as well. Martin V was elected in their stead, but the return of one-pope rule by no means meant better times (see January 21, May 21, August 11, November 26, and December 5).

Aching Lies the Head That Wears the Crown

Queen Victoria had already been fired at by four would-be assassins since the beginning of her reign in 1837. But the attack that left her most unamused occurred on June 27, 1850, when an entirely different weapon was used. The young monarch was riding in her carriage, along with three of her children, when

A crazed former army officer attacks Queen Victoria in her carriage.

a deranged former army officer by the name of Robert Pate lunged from the crowd and bopped his sovereign over the head with his steel-tipped cane. Poor Victoria was left dazed and bloody, with a walnut-size welt on her forehead, and a sense of outrage she had not quite felt before:

"Certainly it is very hard & very horrid that I, a woman—a defenceless young woman & surrounded by my children should be exposed to insults of this kind, and be unable to go out for a drive. For a man to strike *any* woman is most brutal, & I, as well as everyone else, thinks this *far* worse than any attempt to shoot which, wicked as it is, is at least more comprehensible & more courageous."

Fortunately for the queen's offended sensibilities, it would be back to traditional firearms for the next three attempts on her life.

JUNE 28, 1914

Franz Ferdinand's Lucky Day—Almost

Call it the Bad Day that almost wasn't. The plot by a band of Serbian nationalists to assassinate Archduke Franz Ferdinand, heir to the Austro-Hungarian throne, had failed. Or so it seemed. As the archduke and his wife, Sophie, traveled through Sarajevo by motorcade, one of six hit men tossed a bomb at their car, but it bounced off the back and detonated under the vehicle behind— severely wounding the occupants and a number of bystanders. The royal couple emerged shaken but unscathed as their motorcade sped away to a previously planned reception at the city's town hall. "Mr. Mayor," said the understandably upset Franz Ferdinand upon his arrival, "I came here on a visit and I get bombs thrown at me. It is outrageous."

Appalling, yes, but at least he was alive.

After the mayor's reception, the archduke decided to cancel the rest of the scheduled events for that day and instead visit those wounded by the failed assassination attempt. The plan was to drive straight to the hospital along a route that would avoid the city center. But the archduke's driver was given the wrong information and took a right turn on Franz Josef Street. It was a fatal error, for it just so happened that one of the assassins, having fled the scene with the others after the failed bombing, was eating at a nearby delicatessen when he spotted the archduke's car reversing after the wrong turn. Unfortunately, the driver put his foot on the brake as he attempted to back up, causing the engine to stall and the gears to lock. A young man named Gavrilo Princip seized this entirely unexpected opportunity.

Princip later testified that he fired indiscriminately. "Where I aimed I do not know," he said, adding that he had raised his gun "against the automobile without aiming. I even turned my head as I shot." Still, it was enough. Remarkably, one of the two random shots hit Franz Ferdinand in the jugular vein; the other bullet tore into Sophie's stomach. The couple remained upright in the car as they were driven from the scene for medical treatment, but their lives were ebbing away. "Sophie, Sophie! Don't die!" the archduke reportedly cried. "Live for our children!"

The rest of the story is all too familiar. The murder of Franz Ferdinand and his wife triggered an inexorable march toward the First World War, one of the bloodiest conflicts in the history of man. And all because of a wrong turn.

JUNE 29, 1796

Unhappy Moo Year

James Dinwiddie, a British professor of mathematics stationed in India, offered a glimpse of just how sacred cows were among the Hindus—and the downside of an accidental bovine death. "A poor man, whose home was lately burned, had a cow burned at the same time," Dinwiddie recorded in his diary. "For this loss to himself, the unfortunate man is condemned by the Brahmins to walk through the streets for one year, bellowing like a cow. He passed where I was this morning [June 29, 1796] bellowing for certain like the animal for the death of which he suffers."

JUNE 30, 1920

No Shot, Sherlock!

Young Frances Griffiths was in a heap of trouble with her mother during the summer of 1917. The ten-year-old had gotten herself muddy and soaked while, she claimed, "playing with the fairies" near a stream behind her home in the tiny English village of Cottingley. Remanded to her room, Frances and her cousin, 16-year-old Elsie Wright, concocted a scheme to convince Mrs. Griffiths that she had been telling the truth about the fairy mishap. They borrowed a camera from Elsie's father, after which Frances posed in front of a group of fairies the girls had clipped out of a children's book and set in place with pins. Elsie then snapped the staged scene that would one day become one of the world's most famous photographs.

It was an amateurish job, all in all, and

Mr. Wright immediately dismissed it as such. But the girls produced more fairy pictures, and someone who should have known better—Sir Arthur Conan Doyle—became entranced by them. The creator of Sherlock Holmes, one of the most brilliant detectives in literature, had in recent years become absorbed in a new form of spiritualism sweeping Britain in the wake of the devastation and loss wrought by World War I. To Doyle, the existence of fairies simply wasn't that far out, and he was thrilled to find evidence of them in Cottingley.

On June 30, 1920, he sent registered letters to both Elsie and her father seeking permission to use the fairy photographs in an article he was writing on the subject for *The Strand* magazine. "I have seen the wonderful pictures of the fairies which you and your cousin Frances have taken," he wrote to Elsie, "and I have not been so interested for a long time." That December, the article was published. "These little folk who appear to be our neighbours, with only some small difference of vibration to separate us, will become familiar," Doyle rhapsodized. "The thought of them, even when unseen, will add charm to every brook and valley and give romantic interest to every country walk."

Doyle's whimsical belief in the wee ones remained undiminished for the rest of his life, while both Elsie and Frances kept their secret close for nearly seven decades. But in 1983, 76-year-old Frances finally broke. "I thought it was a joke," she said at the time, "but everyone else kept it going."

July

———

"Do what we can, summer will have its flies."

—Ralph Waldo Emerson

JULY 1, 1916

No Day at the Beach:
In the Jaws of Death

Charles Epting Vansant became an unwitting American original, in a most horrific way. On July 1, 1916, while swimming off the New Jersey coast, the 25-year-old was mauled to death by a man-eater—the first such fatal shark attack on a recreational bather ever documented in the nontropical waters of the continental United States, and one of the most ferocious ever.

Before entering the ocean that fateful evening, Vansant befriended a Chesapeake Bay retriever on the beach. The new pals then swam out together over the breakers. Some experts believe it was the dog's erratic paddling that may have first attracted the shark. Perhaps the retriever sensed the shark's presence, too, for it suddenly swam back to shore, ignoring Vansant's calls. And that's when witnesses on the beach saw the dark fin break the surface behind the swimmer, headed right toward him. "Watch out!" someone shouted in alarm. But Vansant didn't hear. The warning from the shore then became a chorus, as the sea marauder clamped down on its prey.

Immediately, there came the agonized scream. Charles Vansant was being eaten alive in front of his own family. "Everyone was horrified to see my brother thrashing about in the water as if he were struggling with some monster below the surface," recalled his sister Louise. "He fought desperately, and as we rushed toward him we could see great quantities of blood."

Vansant had somehow managed to make it almost to the shore, and a lifeguard ran into the shallow water to save him. But the shark lingered—chunks of human flesh still in its jagged maw—and resumed its attack. More men rushed into the blood-reddened water, engaged in a life-or-death tug-of-war with a creature they could only describe as "a sea monster." The shark held fast until its belly scraped sand. Only then did it release its victim and swim away—in search of its next meal.* Vansant's father, a physician, desperately tried to save his son, but to no avail. The trauma and blood loss from his all-but-severed leg proved too much for the young man to survive the monstrous encounter.

---

* *Indeed, over the next 11 days, the rogue killer would continue to prey upon New Jersey swimmers—killing three more. Perhaps the most frightening of these attacks occurred in the most unlikely of places—15 miles inland from the ocean, in the narrow tidal estuary of Matawan Creek.*

The Most Costly Soccer Goal Ever

The agony of defeat took on a lethal dimension in 1994 when Andrés Escobar, the once beloved captain of Colombia's national soccer team, was shot dead outside a Medellín nightclub in the early morning hours of July 2. Ten days earlier, he had made a fatal error in a World Cup match against the United States when he scored a goal on his own team. Colombia lost the game and was subsequently knocked out of contention. Devastated fans instantly turned on their onetime hero, as did members of the Colombian drug cartels, who apparently had a lot of money riding on the match. "Nice goooal!" one of their enforcers taunted Escobar each time he fired a shot into him—12 in all—from a .38-caliber pistol. Poignantly, just days before his murder, Escobar's open letter to his countrymen had been published in *El Tiempo,* the nation's most widely read newspaper: "Please, let's maintain respect," he wrote. "A big hug for everyone, and let me say that [playing in the World Cup] was the most rare, phenomenal opportunity and experience I have ever had . . . so see you soon, because life doesn't end here."

Paint It Black: The Death
of Rolling Stone Brian Jones

In 2012, the Rolling Stones celebrated a half century together as "the greatest rock-and-roll band in the world." But one key member was missing from the festivities, having come to a bad end at the bottom of a swimming pool 43 years earlier on July 3, 1969.

Brian Jones was the essential Stone—in the beginning, at least—a multi-instrumentalist with rock star charisma and trend-setting tastes. "He formed the band," wrote Stones bassist Bill Wyman in his autobiography. "He chose the members. He named the band. He chose the music we played. He got us gigs . . . Very influential, very important, and then slowly lost it—highly intelligent—and just kind of wasted it and blew it all away."

The problem was that the band Jones had founded and nurtured was slowly being taken away from him as singer Mick Jagger and guitarist Keith Richards emerged as a formidable songwriting team. And though Jones added his unique musical imprint to such songs as "Paint It Black," with its distinctive sitar, and played the recorder on "Ruby Tuesday," they were ultimately Jagger-Richards tunes. That gave the pair power as the hits kept rolling in.

Always excessive in his use of drugs and alcohol, Jones indulged himself all the more as his role in the band became increasingly marginalized. As The Who's Pete Townshend recalled, he was "on a higher planet of decadence than anyone I would ever meet." And that came with vicious mood swings as well. Jones "could be the sweetest, softest, most considerate man in the world," Wyman wrote, "and the nastiest piece of work you've ever met."

With his burden on the band far exceeding his contributions, Brian Jones was fired from the Stones on June 8, 1969. "We took his one thing away, which was being in a band," drummer Charlie Watts recalled in the documentary *25 X 5*. (He might have added that Keith Richards also took away Jones's girlfriend, Anita Pallenberg.) Less than a month later, Jones was found dead at the bottom of his swimming pool.* He was 27. The coroner's report listed the cause as "death by misadventure," but many believe the ex-Stone

---

At the time Brian Jones died, Jim Morrison of The Doors published a poem titled "Ode to L.A. While Thinking of Brian Jones, Deceased." Morrison would die two years later—on the same date and at the same age.

may have been murdered. "To be honest, he was a bit of a bastard," the always candid Richards told *Rolling Stone*. "And it doesn't surprise me that he came to a sticky end."

JULY 4, 1826 *and* 1831

The Twilight's Last ... Last ... Last Gleaming

T he anniversary of America's Declaration of Independence from Britain proved fatal for three of the first five U.S. presidents: John Adams, Thomas Jefferson, and James Monroe. Each of these Founding Fathers died on July 4—Adams and Jefferson, just hours apart from each other, in 1826, and Monroe five years later.

JULY 5, 1975

Ashe vs. Ass: When Connors Was Blown Off the Court— and Out of Court

F or every victor there must be a loser. And what a loser Jimmy Connors was after Arthur Ashe unexpectedly crushed him—not only in the Wimbledon finals on July 5, 1975, but also in the ultimate battle between decency and total boorishness.

Just before they met on court, Connors had sued Ashe *in* court—for libel. It was merely the latest in a series of lawsuits Connors had filed against Ashe and the various tennis associations of which he was part. The petulant player demanded millions in damages because Ashe had said publicly that Connors's consistent refusal to play for the United States team in the annual Davis Cup tournaments was "seemingly unpatriotic."

In his self-serving autobiography, *The Outsider,* published two decades after Arthur Ashe died, Connors actually blamed his rival for the way he responded to the flurry of lawsuits filed against him. "Arthur didn't have the balls to confront me," Connors wrote, as if somehow his own petty litigiousness made him the epitome of

Arthur Ashe signals victory while Jimmy Connors pouts at Wimbledon.

manliness; "instead, he left a note in my locker at Wimbledon outlining his position. Well, that speaks volumes, doesn't it? All he had to do was come up and talk to me face to face, man to man, but he chose not to."

But what Connors said *really* irked him was when Ashe "walked out on Centre Court wearing his Davis Cup jacket, with U.S.A. emblazoned across his chest." The audacity! Then Ashe proceeded to beat Connors 6-1, 6-1, 5-7, 6-4, becoming the first black man ever to win a title at Wimbledon. He added one more slam in the aftermath by pointing out how Connors had put about 70 percent of his errors "into the middle of the net. He hardly ever put the ball beyond the baseline—that's a sign of choking."

Then, Connors endured one more insult to his already dreary day: His own manager, Bill Riordan, apparently had bet against him in the finals. "I was the heavy favorite, and I understand Bill made out quite well," Connors wrote. "Can you believe it? And he didn't even share his winnings, the cheapskate." Not long after, the chastened Connors dropped Riordan *and* the lawsuits.

JULY 6, 2008

When Jesse Jackson
Went a Little Nuts

"See, Barack's been talking down to black people . . . I want to cut his nuts off."
—*The Reverend Jesse Jackson, whispering to a colleague on television about presidential candidate Barack Obama, unaware that his microphone was recording during a broadcast break. Jackson's crude yet undoubtedly colorful comment was by no means his first unguarded, highly charged utterance. Jackson made a notoriously*

*injudicious remark in 1984, when during his own
presidential campaign he offhandedly referred to Jews as
"Hymies" and New York City as "Hymietown."*

JULY 7, 1456

Oh, Now You Tell Her . . .

The good news for Joan of Arc was that her death sentence was nullified when she was finally acquitted of heresy on July 7, 1456. The bad news: She had already been reduced to ashes at the stake a quarter century before.

JULY 8, 1932

Rock Bottom:
The Depression's Lowest Ebb

"I am convinced we have now passed the worst and with continued unity of effort we shall rapidly recover," Herbert Hoover declared six months after the devastating stock market crash of 1929. "There is one certainty of the future of a people of the resources, intelligence and character of the people of the United States—that is, prosperity!"

The president had every reason to feel optimistic. After all, the market had recovered 30 percent of its value by mid-1930. But the worst, by far, was actually yet to come. On July 8, 1932—a day that made the earlier plummet merely the opening bell to catastrophe—the Dow Jones Industrial Average reached its lowest point of the Great Depression, trading more than 50 percent below the low it had reached on that disastrous October day nearly three years before.

JULY 9, 1640

America's "Peculiar Institution" Begins

Three indentured servants indebted to Virginia planter Hugh Gwyn—two of them of European descent, one African—ran away to Maryland in 1640. All were subsequently captured and sentenced to 30 lashes each. But the equality of the punishment ended there. The servitude of the two white men was extended four years by the court, while the sentence of the other read: "And that the third being a negro named John Punch shall serve his said master or his assigns for the time of his natural life here or elsewhere." Thus, by order of the court on July 9, 1640, John Punch became the first documented slave in the original American Colonies.

JULY 10, 1777

Not Even Clothes: A Rude Awakening for the Redcoat General

It was a Revolutionary-era stealth operation worthy of the Navy Seals—and a mortifying blow to British prestige. In the early morning hours of July 10, 1777, Rhode Island patriot Col. William Barton and a band of about 40 men silently made their way across Narragansett Bay, teeming at the time with British warships. Then, after overcoming a sentry, the men slipped into the house occupied by the British general Richard Prescott and surprised him in his bed. They had come to snatch him away.

"Gentlemen," one of the raiders recorded Prescott exclaiming, "your business requires haste, but do for God's sake let me get my clothes."

"By God, it is no time for clothes," Barton responded, after which the half-naked captive was led away and shoved aboard one of the waiting boats. Miraculously, the kidnappers made it back across the bay without being intercepted.

"He is not much regretted," the British official Ambrose Serle remarked of Prescott's loss.* Nevertheless, the captured general, literally stripped of his dignity, was later exchanged for the American general Charles Lee—who, ironically enough, had been taken by the British the previous December, wearing only his nightgown.

JULY 11, 1804

He Didn't Have a Prayer:
Hamilton's Post-Duel Snub

The story is familiar enough: how the vice president of the United States, having been repeatedly insulted by one of the nation's preeminent Founding Fathers, met his political adversary on a field of honor in Weehawken, New Jersey. And there, having observed the strict decorum of ritualized murder, Aaron Burr shot Alexander Hamilton in a duel to the death. Henry Adams described it as "the most dramatic moment in the early politics of the Union." But for Alexander Hamilton, the ordeal didn't end when he was taken away from Weehawken with a gaping gunshot wound to the stomach. Of that, two fussy, overly pious clergymen made certain.

---

* Even more embarrassing to General Prescott, this was not his first time being taken prisoner; the same thing happened two years earlier in Canada.

Never an overtly religious man, Hamilton nonetheless sought spiritual succor as he lay bleeding and paralyzed. He ended up having to beg for it. The dying man first called for Benjamin Moore, Episcopal bishop of New York and rector of his wife's parish, Trinity Church, to give him Holy Communion. But Moore refused because Hamilton was not only an irregular churchgoer, but also one who had just engaged in the evil practice of dueling.

Having been rejected by one sanctimonious prelate, Hamilton desperately turned to another—his friend the Reverend John M. Mason, pastor of the Scotch Presbyterian Church that stood near his home. Although Mason expressed sympathy for the mortally wounded man's plight, he, too, opted to withhold the sacrament.

Finally, in one last stab at salvation, the Founding Father asked for Dr. Moore to return. "Upon my entering the room and approaching his bed, with the utmost calmness and composure he said, 'My dear sir, you perceive my unfortunate situation, and no doubt have been made acquainted with the circumstances which led to it. It is my desire to receive communion at your hands. I hope you will not conceive there is any impropriety in my request.' " Still, Moore refused.

"I observed to him, that he must be very sensible of the delicate and trying situation in which I was then placed: that however desirous I might be to afford consolation to a fellow mortal in distress; still, it was my duty, as a minister of the Gospel, to hold up the law of God as paramount to all other law: and that, therefore, under the influence of such sentiments, I must unequivocally condemn which had brought him to his present unhappy condition. He acknowledged the propriety of these sentiments, and declared that he viewed the late transaction [the duel] with sorrow and contrition."

Having forced poor Hamilton through several more hoops of religious conciliation, Moore at last relented and *allowed* the penitent

God's mercy. The next day, the rector reported, "He expired without a struggle, and almost without a groan."

Thursday Night Fever: The Night They Drove Old Disco Down

The chants emanating from Comiskey Park, home of the Chicago White Sox, had nothing to do with baseball. "DISCO SUCKS!" the crowd roared, while banners emblazoned with the same message hung from stadium bleachers. In the middle of the playing field, a huge bin filled with disco records was just about to be exploded—all part of an ill-fated promotion on July 12, 1979, dubbed "Disco Demolition Night." As it turned out, records weren't the only thing destroyed during the event.

The anti-disco promotion was the brilliant idea of Mike Veeck, son of White Sox owner Bill Veeck, who was seeking a way to fill seats for the poorly performing team, and local radio station WLUP, "the Loop," whose disc jockey Steve Dahl had an apparently obsessive hatred for the music that had been dominating the late 1970s.

The idea was simple enough. Deeply discounted tickets to Comiskey Park would be given to people who brought along a disco record to be destroyed in the spectacle scheduled for the break in the doubleheader between the White Sox and the Detroit Tigers. Way too many people showed up, however—many of them hopping over turnstiles and climbing fences without tickets. The stadium quickly filled beyond capacity with people and marijuana smoke. Mayhem ensued.

Rowdy spectators—very few of them actually baseball fans—disrupted the first game by tossing firecrackers and empty bottles onto the field. They also threw the vinyl disco albums that had not been collected at the gate.

"They would slice around you and stick in the ground," Tigers outfielder Rusty Staub later told *The New York Times*. "It wasn't just one, it was many. Oh, God almighty, I've never seen anything so dangerous in my life. I begged the guys to put on their batting helmets."

Then, after the Sox lost the first game to the Tigers, 4-1, came the main event. Steve Dahl arrived on the field, driven in a jeep and dressed in camouflage. "This is now officially the world's largest anti-disco rally!" he told the screaming crowd. "Now listen— we took all the disco records you brought tonight, we got 'em in a giant box, and we're gonna blow 'em up *reeeeeeal goooood*."

With that, a massive blast sent fiery shards of vinyl 200 feet in the air. The crowd roared and thousands of people rushed the field. Anything that wasn't destroyed by the explosion, the mob finished—stealing bases (literally), pulling down batting cages, and dancing manically around the burning remnants of disco anthems. And no amount of cajoling could get them back to their seats.

"Holy cow!" the famed sports announcer Harry Caray called out to the crowd over the loudspeaker, asking them to take their seats. When this plea received nothing but a taunting response, Caray and Bill Veeck, accompanied by the Comiskey Park organist, launched into a rousing rendition of "Take Me Out to the Ball Game." Then the riot police were called in, the mob dispersed, and the Sox forfeited the second game against the Tigers.

JULY 13, 1801

Ship Happens, Part II:
The Shelling's Mutual

Just after midnight, on July 13, 1801, the 112-gun Spanish warship *Real Carlos* exploded off Gibraltar. Fifteen minutes later, so did its companion *San Hermenegildo*. Thousands of lives were lost in the twin disasters, but enemy fire wasn't to blame. Rather, thanks to a little British ingenuity and some really bad luck, the two massive ships inadvertently destroyed each other.

The deadly blunder came in the midst of a naval conflict between Britain and the joint forces of France and Spain. Six days before, British ships attacked a French fleet anchored at Algeciras, a fortified port city on the Bay of Gibraltar. But after heavy firing from both sides, the attackers were forced to limp away—and without one of their ships, H.M.S. *Hannibal,* which had been captured by the French. It was humiliating for the British, yet they would be avenged soon enough.

After the first Battle of Algeciras, the French commander requested reinforcements. In response, five Spanish warships sailed through the Strait of Gibraltar and set up a protective block at Algeciras while the French repaired their damaged vessels. Then the nine allied ships set sail together, bound for the Spanish port of Cádiz.

Although he had only half as many warships, the recently thwarted British commander James Saumarez was determined that the allies would not escape. The second Battle of Algeciras was shaping up as the battered and depleted British fleet sailed in dogged pursuit. The relatively new H.M.S. *Superb,* ably captained by Richard Goodwin Keats, had not engaged the French in the first battle and was thus entirely unscathed. Keats sailed ahead of the rest of his fleet to hamper the departing allied convoy as best he could, never imagining how successful he would be.

The massive Spanish warships *Real Carlos* and *San Hermenegildo* trailed the rest of the allied fleet and served as a formidable line of defense. Under cover of darkness, Keats silently ranged the *Superb* beside the *Real Carlos* and opened fire. The damage inflicted was considerable and the huge Spanish ship soon erupted in flames. Worse, though, some of the *Superb*'s missiles catapulted over the *Real Carlos* and struck the *San Hermenegildo,* which was sailing on the other side of its companion. What happened next became an astonishing hallmark in naval history.

Unable to see in the darkness, the captain of the *San Hermene-gildo* thought a British warship had slipped in between him and the *Real Carlos* and began to fire back at the phantom vessel. Of course the only thing he hit was his sister ship, which immediately returned the volley. The *Real Carlos* was now firing at a real enemy from one side and a mistaken one from the other. Seeing this, Keats ceased his assault and retreated behind as the two Spanish behemoths continued to blindly batter each other into oblivion.

JULY 14, 1798

Mr. Adams, Remember That First Amendment Thing?

On July 14, 1798, less than a decade after affixing his signature to what became known as the Bill of Rights, President John Adams affirmed another document with quite the opposite effect on freedom: the Sedition Act, one of a series of highly restrictive laws passed that year. Among its odious provisions, described by Thomas Jefferson as being "so palpably in the teeth of the Consti-tution," the act made it illegal "To write, print, utter or publish, or cause it to be done, or assist in it, any false, scandalous, and malicious writing against the government of the United States, or either House of Congress, or the President, with intent to defame, or bring either into contempt or disrepute."

And that's how Representative Matthew Lyon of Vermont ended up in prison,* having accused the Adams Administration of

---

* *Lyon became infamous a year earlier when, in the midst of a disagreement on the House floor, he spat in the face of his colleague Representative Roger Griswold of Connecticut. But that's another story.*

"ridiculous pomp, foolish adulation, and selfish avarice." Partisan writer James Callender was another who was convicted, fined, and jailed under the Sedition Act. In a particularly virulent tract, *The Prospect Before Us,* Callender called Adams—among other choice epithets—a "repulsive pendant" and a "gross hypocrite . . . hideous hermaphroditical character which has neither the force and firmness of a man, nor the gentleness and sensibility of a woman . . . a hoary-headed incendiary," who "in his private life, [is] one of the most egregious fools upon the continent."*

Given that John Adams had actually signed the sedition law and other extreme measures, which have been, as his biographer David McCullough noted, "rightly judged by history as the most reprehensible acts" of his administration, it could be argued that James Callender had a point about the president he so ferociously attacked.

JULY 15, 1972

This Picture Was Jane Fonda's Biggest Bomb

In the midst of a war that ultimately claimed the lives of more than 58,000 American soldiers—and shattered tens of thousands more—actress Jane Fonda paid a friendly visit to an enemy camp in Hanoi, laughed, sang, and cheerfully posed for a picture straddling a North Vietnamese antiaircraft gun. Americans were appalled by what many perceived as treason, and Fonda was

---

* *Thomas Jefferson delighted in the attacks on his political enemy, Adams—until Callender turned his poison pen against the third president and became the first to accuse him publicly of having sired a child by his slave Sally Hemings. But that, too, is another story.*

Jane Fonda claps and sings during her controversial visit with enemy soldiers.

derisively dubbed "Hanoi Jane" for her behavior. As she said in a televised interview decades later: "I will go to my grave regretting the photograph of me . . . It hurt so many soldiers. It galvanized such hostility. It was the most horrible thing I could possibly have done. It was just thoughtless."

JULY 16, 1858

John Wilkes Booth's Killer Might Have *Been* Nuts, but . . .

Bible literalists over the generations have conveniently overlooked a passage from Matthew 19:12: "And there are also eunuchs who made themselves eunuchs for the sake of the kingdom of heaven. He that is able to receive it, let him receive it." Thomas P. "Boston" Corbett, on the other hand, paid close attention. Seven years before he famously shot and killed Abraham Lincoln's assassin, John Wilkes Booth, in a Virginia tobacco barn, Corbett found a sure way to resist sexual temptation in 1858. With a pair of scissors, and without benefit of anesthesia, he excised his offending instruments of evil.

JULY 17, 1955

The Blunderful World of Disney

There was very little magic to be found on July 17, 1955, when Disneyland made its official debut. In fact, the park's opening was such an epic disaster that not even Snow White's Evil Queen could have conjured it. Fifteen thousand guests had been invited to the opening ceremonies that day, but because of a glut of counterfeited tickets, nearly twice as many showed up—inundating the park and creating massive traffic jams on the Anaheim Freeway. The hordes quickly gobbled up all the available food and, with their sheer mass, nearly capsized Mark Twain's Riverboat. A plumbers' strike had forced Disney to make a choice between working bathrooms or running drinking fountains—thus, toilets flushed, but the lack of water left people parched and cranky in the blistering 101-degree heat. So scorching were the temperatures that the recently paved Main Street became a gurgling tarry mess that sucked off shoes. Rides failed, surly guards intimidated visitors, and a gas leak forced the closure of Fantasyland. No wonder, then, that Walt Disney came to refer to opening day as "Black Sunday."

"Walt's dream is a nightmare," one reporter wrote. "I attended the so-called press premiere of Disneyland, a fiasco the like of which I cannot recall in thirty years of show life. To me it felt like a giant cash register, clicking and clanging, as creatures of Disney magic came tumbling down from their lofty places in my daydreams to peddle and perish their charms with the aggressiveness of so many curbside barkers."

Adding to Uncle Walt's misery was the fact that Disneyland's grand opening was being televised live and viewed by nearly 90 million people. It was a star-studded extravaganza, featuring Ronald Reagan, Bob Cummings, and Art Linkletter as emcees, but various glitches and miscues only made the fiasco more apparent. In one mortifying instance, actor Fess Parker, who played the rugged Davy Crockett in movies and on television, was described as the lovely Cinderella as he led a parade down Main Street.

A lesser man might have been crushed by such a dismal day, but with all the pluck of Mickey Mouse, Walt Disney forged ahead. Just three months later, Disneyland greeted its one millionth guest and went on to become the grandfather of an empire of theme parks, world renowned for their efficiency, cleanliness, and fun—and all with working drinking fountains.

JULY 18, 1877

Pathétique: Tchaikovsky's Marriage That Never Should Have Been

On July 18, 1877, Peter Tchaikovsky stood at the altar with his bride, Antonina Miliukova, and wept. They were not tears of joy, however, for as the great composer recounted, "a kind of pain gripped my heart."

There was nothing really wrong with Tchaikovsky's bride—except for her sex. The fact was, no woman could ever have been a good wife for him; he simply wasn't oriented that way. Nevertheless, there were forces driving him to the altar in 1877: Tchaikovsky called it fate, but more likely it was paternal pressure, as well as the need to conform in a society where homosexuality was reviled. So he settled on Miliukova, a former student whom he didn't really know and who gained his attention only through the lovelorn notes she had sent to him. When he proposed to her, he told her candidly that he did not love her and listed his most disagreeable character traits: "my irritability, volatile temperament, my unsociability, finally my circumstances." Still, Miliukova accepted his proposal knowing that he would never be more than a friend to her.

Tchaikovsky dreaded the arrival of his wedding day, as he related to a friend several days before: "Having lived 37 years with an innate aversion to marriage, it is very distressing to be drawn through force of circumstances into the position *of a bridegroom* who, moreover, is not in the least attracted to his bride . . . In a day or two my marriage with her will take place. What will happen after that I do not know."

While the wedding was horrible, the honeymoon trip was even worse. "When the carriage started I was ready to cry out with choking sobs," Tchaikovsky wrote, and instead of wedding night passion, "I slept the sleep of the dead."

As the loveless, sexless marriage progressed over the next weeks, the composer became increasingly discontented. Not only did he find his wife "physically repugnant," but her company grew tedious as well. Flighty and superficial, as he described her, Antonina shared none of her husband's interests—not even music. Worse, she began to demand more physically than the "brotherly love" he had promised her. The intense pressure of the failing union drove Tchaikovsky to thoughts of suicide. Rather than kill himself, though, he simply left—only six weeks after the ill-fated wedding.

And yet "the Reptile," as Tchaikovsky called his estranged wife with uncharacteristic cruelty, still plagued him. He lived in mortal fear that the scorned woman would expose the secret of his sexuality, and thus any correspondence from her—indeed the mere mention of her name—drove him into nervous fits. At one point he listed her accusations in detail to his brother: "I am a deceiver who married her in order to hide my true nature . . . I insulted her every day, her sufferings at my hands were great . . . she is appalled by my shameful vice, etc., etc."

In the end, Tchaikovsky had only one explanation for his hapless stab at marriage: "There's no doubt that for some months on end I was a bit *insane*."

JULY 19, 1553

Jane Grey's Blues

For nine days, the Tower of London served as the royal palace of England's unwilling queen, Lady Jane Grey. Then, suddenly, it became the prison from which the 16-year-old girl never left. A close relative of the mighty Tudor sovereigns, Protestant Jane had the crown forced on her by her ambitious father-in-law, John Dudley, Duke of Northumberland, who feared that if the throne went to the legitimate successor, Henry VIII's fiercely Catholic daughter Mary, England would be thrust back into papism. Mary triumphed, however, and after less than two weeks of "rule," Jane was formally deposed on July 19, 1553. From that day on, the Tower became a far more menacing place for the "Nine Days Queen"—first as her prison, then as the site of her beheading, and finally as her tomb.

JULY 20, 1846

Using the Wrong Fork:
From Donners to Dinners

Perhaps no left turn has ever been more fateful than the one taken on July 20, 1846, by a group of westbound settlers later known as the Donner party. Had they gone right at the fork they found midway through their journey, and followed the conventional trail to the West like everyone else, the Donners might well have savored the milk and honey of the new Canaan in California and Oregon rather than being forced to devour each other in the frozen hell of the Sierra mountains. But they heeded the siren call of an adventurer named Lansford Hastings—"the Baron Munchausen of travels," as one contemporary called him; a cynic who "evidently regarded the emigrants as fair game."

With grand ambitions to create his own fiefdom in California (which he aimed to snatch away from Mexico), Hastings sought to lure settlers there with the promise of a convenient shortcut along a new trail, one upon which he had never actually stepped foot. He made it sound so simple in his book, *The Emigrants' Guide to Oregon and California*—just a mere waltz to paradise.

The Donner party had been warned of the perils of Hastings's fantasy path by the old mountaineer James Clyman, who had seen some of the obstacles they would face, and, as he recalled, urged them to "take the regular wagon track, and never leave it—it is barely possible to get through if you follow it, and it may be impossible if you don't." But dazzled by the prospect of easy passage, the party leaders ignored Clyman and took that left turn toward their doom.

By the time they realized what a hideous mistake they had made, it was too late. Precious days had been wasted extricating themselves, by which time the weather had closed in and trapped them—just 150 miles from

the safety of Sutter's Fort, California. It was then that the brutal winter ordeal intensified: when the starving party went from eating boiled ox hide to the flesh of their companions. Of the 87 men, women, and children of the Donner party, only 46 emerged alive from the cannibalistic nightmare.

"I have not wrote you half of the trouble we've had, but I have wrote you enough to let you know what trouble is," one of the survivors, Virginia Reed, penned. "But thank God, we are the only family that did not eat human flesh. We have left everything, but I don't care for that. We have got through with our lives. Don't let this letter dishearten anybody. Remember, never take no cutoffs and hurry along as fast as you can."

Sinking Mercury: An Astronaut's Reputation Goes Down the Hatch

It was a halfhearted hero's welcome at best, not because Virgil "Gus" Grissom was merely the second American in space—there was still so much prestige to be had in that—but because he had lost his expensive spacecraft, *Liberty Bell 7,* which sank after splashing down in the Atlantic on July 21, 1961.

"It was especially hard for me, as a professional pilot," he recalled. "In all of my years of flying—including combat in Korea—this was the first time that my aircraft and I had not come back together. In my entire career as a pilot, *Liberty Bell* was the first thing I had ever lost."

But there was much more that Grissom lost in the aftermath, namely his reputation, which sank right along with *Liberty Bell 7.* The astronaut, it was said, had "screwed the pooch," which in aeronautical parlance meant that he had panicked and had prematurely detonated the small explosives that released the spacecraft's hatch. Experts theorized that *Liberty Bell 7* took on water as a result and, as Grissom swam away, became too heavy to be retrieved. The astronaut himself barely survived the ordeal, as he became entangled in lines and his space suit began to drag him under before a rescue helicopter finally plucked him out of the turbulent ocean.

Grissom vehemently maintained that he had not triggered the hatch explosives, that they had blown out spontaneously. "I was just laying there minding my own business when POW! the hatch went," he said at a press conference. "And I looked up and saw nothing but blue sky and water starting to come in over the sill." But at the same time he answered honestly when asked whether he ever felt his life was in danger during the mission. "Well, I was scared a good portion of the time," he said. "I guess this is a pretty good indication."

The media feasted mercilessly on this, portraying the astronaut who had risked his life in space as something of a scaredy-cat. Years later, in his book *The Right Stuff,* author Tom Wolfe cemented Grissom in the public imagination as a bit of a buffoon who had blown the hatch in a blind panic. Moviegoers were given the same impression of the astronaut when *The Right Stuff* was made into a successful film.

Buried in the avalanche of bad press was the fact that Grissom was completely exonerated after an investigation into the hatch detonation. Indeed, so great was NASA's confidence in him that he was chosen to lead two more space missions. Nevertheless, the much maligned astronaut was frustrated by the lack of a technical explanation for the spontaneous release of the hatch.

"We tried for weeks afterwards to find out what had happened and how it had happened," he said. "I even crawled into capsules and tried to duplicate all of my movements, to see if I could make the whole thing happen again. It was impossible. The plunger that detonates the bolts is so far out of the way that I would have had to reach for it on purpose to hit it, and this I did not do. Even when I thrashed about with my elbows, I could not bump against it accidentally."

Grissom eventually became resigned to his bad luck. "It remained a mystery how that hatch blew," he said. "And I am afraid it always will. It was just one of those things."* He even showed a great sense of humor when he commanded the Gemini 3 space mission and dubbed his craft *Molly Brown*—named after the buoyant namesake of the Broadway play *The Unsinkable Molly Brown*. NASA officials objected to the name, but reluctantly backed down when Grissom suggested an alternative: "How about the *Titanic?*"**

JULY 22, 1934

He Got Dillinger, but He Was J. Edgar Hoover's Private Enemy Number One

It was a bad enough day for John Dillinger when that notorious gangster, dubbed "Public Enemy Number One" by the FBI, was gunned down behind Chicago's Biograph Theater on July 22, 1934. But for Melvin Purvis, the G-man who finally nailed him, it was almost worse. His actions that day—and in the subsequent killing of Charles Arthur "Pretty Boy" Floyd—made him a national hero, a status that did not sit well at all with his boss and mentor, J. Edgar Hoover. The megalomaniacal FBI director believed all laurels should rest exclusively on his own head, and he would make Purvis pay for

---

An examination of Liberty Bell 7 after it was recovered from the ocean floor in 1999 failed to resolve the question of how the hatch blew open.

** *The unexpected hatch release of Liberty Bell 7 came with a horrible irony five and a half years later when a flash fire erupted in the command module of Apollo 1 during a preflight test on January 27, 1967. Grissom and fellow astronauts Edward White and Roger Chaffee were killed in the conflagration. The hatch couldn't be opened.*

having snatched his moment of glory: Hoover pursued a vendetta against his former friend for the next quarter century.

Purvis was once the director's golden boy—a southern gentleman, solidly middle class and strikingly handsome. "All power to the Clark Gable of the service," Hoover once wrote to his young protégé in one of many missives that displayed an intimacy few other agents in the Bureau ever enjoyed. As the director told Purvis's father, "He has been one of my closest and dearest friends."

With Hoover's blessing and guidance, Purvis was eventually made special agent in charge (SAC) of the Bureau's Chicago office. There was one overwhelming task at hand: to get the charismatic criminal who was simultaneously terrorizing and enchanting the American Midwest—taunting law enforcement as he did it. "Well, son," the director wrote to Purvis, "keep a stiff upper lip and get Dillinger for me, and the world is yours." He signed it, "Sincerely and affectionately, Jayee."

Purvis had received a tip that Dillinger would be attending a movie at the Biograph on July 22. When the gangster emerged from the theater that night, Purvis spotted him and lit a cigar as a prearranged signal to the other agents and Chicago police officers. Dillinger grew wary and ran into a nearby alley. "Stick 'em up, Johnny," Purvis shouted. "We have you surrounded." The gangster drew his gun, but he was killed before he was able to get off a shot. A near-legendary outlaw was dead and, in the aftermath, a new American hero was born. Alas, that hero wasn't J. Edgar Hoover.

The director dutifully congratulated Purvis, writing that "my appreciation of the success with which your efforts have met in this case is lasting and makes me most proud of you." But he privately seethed as his top agent's star rose.

Hoover "was jealous of him," recalled Purvis's secretary Doris Lockerman. "Unless you continued to please the king, you didn't continue as the favorite very long . . . They saw to it that Purvis got no more assignments that put him in the public eye. He found himself spending months interviewing applicants for jobs as agents. Every effort was made to denigrate him, to embarrass him. He was terribly hurt."

Just one year after his famous takedown of Dillinger, Purvis resigned from the FBI. But "Jayee" was by no means finished with him. Hoover made it his mission to sabotage virtually every endeavor Purvis pursued, and ensured that he was all but erased from the FBI's official history. "It became Bureau policy that Purvis was a nonperson," wrote author Richard Gid Powers. So extreme (and absurd) were some of these measures that Purvis was even written out of the Dillinger story altogether. Indeed, in the Bureau-backed radio series *G-Men,* he was replaced by a marginal, fictionalized character called Nellis. The real star became Hoover, controlling events from his office in Washington, where he famously kept Dillinger's death mask on display.

And so it went until 1960, when Purvis died from a gunshot to the head. Whether it was an accident or deliberate remains uncertain, but, as his son Alston wrote, that didn't matter to Hoover, who immediately announced that Purvis had committed suicide:

"His bulletin made no mention of my father's accomplishments, his sacrifices for the Bureau, his place in history. There were no elegant phrases proffering gratitude, no expressions of sadness or sympathy. The sparseness of the bulletin, as well as its swiftness, suggested a trace of gloating. Hoover simply could not wait to publicize what to him was a long-awaited victory—the final silencing of a man he considered his nemesis."

JULY 23, 1982

On the Set, Tragic Misdirection

Ever since silent film star Buster Keaton fractured his neck performing his own stunts in the 1924 comedy *Sherlock Jr.,* moviemaking has repeatedly proved to be a hazardous profession.* Never more so than on July 23, 1982, when a helicopter crashed on the set of *Twilight Zone: The Movie*. Actor Vic Morrow was decapitated in the accident, as was one of the illegally hired child actors filming with him. A second young performer was crushed to death under the weight of the fallen helicopter. Director John Landis, who many associated with the film insisted had blatantly disregarded safety for the sake of spectacle (although he was acquitted of criminal negligence), seemed oddly unscathed by the tragedy—particularly as he delivered a self-serving eulogy for Morrow. "Tragedy can strike in an instant," Landis declared, "but film is immortal. Vic lives forever. Just before the last take, Vic took me aside to thank me for the opportunity to play this role."

JULY 24, 1684

From Debacle to Debacle:
La Salle's New World Disorder

The French explorer Robert Cavelier, Sieur de La Salle, has long been lauded as "intrepid," "brave," and "capable," but the words "inept," "overbearing," and "obnoxious" would describe

---

* *Other dangers on the set: Margaret Hamilton, who played the Wicked Witch of the West, was severely burned on the set of* The Wizard of Oz *when she made her fiery exit from Munchkinland. Nearly half the cast and crew of* The Conqueror *got cancer after filming downwind from the Yucca Flats nuclear testing site in Nevada. Forty-five eventually died of the disease, including stars John Wayne, Susan Hayward, and Agnes Moorehead, as well as director Dick Powell. Peter O'Toole was nearly crushed to death filming* Lawrence of Arabia *when he was hurled off his camel in the path of an army of stampeding horses.*

him just as well. With overweening ambition, yet lacking basic survival skills, or even a decent sense of direction, the former Jesuit priest stumbled around the Great Lakes seeking glory and riches—chased by creditors, burdened by mutinous companions, and plagued with the kind of misfortune that often accompanies the clueless. Little wonder, then, La Salle named one of his forts Crevecoeur, or Heartbreak—right before his own men plundered the place and burned it down. Yet for all his incompetence, La Salle did manage to navigate the Mississippi River to the Gulf of Mexico, claiming the entire region for the king of France. It was soon after that his troubles *really* began.

King Louis XIV was decidedly unimpressed with La Salle's discovery, which he declared to be useless. In the face of his sovereign's indifference, the explorer was forced to tell him a few lies to get enough men and money to return to Louisiana, set up a colony, and make a profit. Deceit seems to have come naturally to La Salle. For instance, he claimed to be fully fluent in the Iroquois language during his first ventures in North America, when in reality he couldn't speak or understand a word of it. But the lies he now told King Louis were real doozies by comparison, especially the idea that the mouth of the Mississippi was close and convenient enough to launch an invasion to conquer Mexico for France. Not only did he misrepresent the actual distance, but even finding the river's end—from the sea, this time—would prove well beyond La Salle's limited capacities. In fact, it would doom him.

The ill-fated expedition of four ships and three hundred soldiers and colonists left France on July 24, 1684—then turned right back around for repairs. It was a bad start to a journey that only got worse.

Before even reaching the Gulf of Mexico, one ship had been captured by pirates. Then a number of crew members—many of whom found La Salle unbearable—abandoned the voyage during a stop at the French colony of Saint-Domingue; others contracted syphilis as a result of their Caribbean revelries.

And still there was what expedition member Henri Joutel called "that fatal river" to find.

Alas, La Salle sailed right past the mouth of the Mississippi and ended up 400 miles west, at Matagorda Bay, near what is now Corpus Christi, Texas. With all the assurance of an amateur, La Salle insisted they had landed at a branch of the Mississippi and set out on an impossible mission to find the main body of the mighty river. Meanwhile, the expedition's supply ship *Aimable* was wrecked, leaving the colonists without food or weapons to defend themselves. La Salle loudly blamed the ship's captain, Claude Aigron, for deliberately and maliciously destroying the vessel, while Aigron and his crew slipped back to France on the warship *Le Joly*.

The remaining colonists felt "cast away in a savage country," as La Salle's brother wrote, surrounded by poisonous snakes and inhospitable land that became "a perpetual prison." Gradually they succumbed to disease, starvation, and attacks by hostile natives. The final blow came when the last of their ships, *La Belle,* was destroyed in a storm.

By now the surviving colonists despised La Salle. And as he set off to seek help, he was ambushed by some of his companions and shot in the head. The failed explorer's corpse was then stripped naked and tossed in some bushes for the animals to eat. As for La Salle's dream of French domination of the lower Mississippi—well, as Joutel wrote, "Heaven refused him that success."

JULY 25, 1471

Not Exactly Resting in Peace

By all accounts Thomas à Kempis was a saintly man, a humble monk who quietly spent his life in a German monastery translating sacred texts and producing one of Christianity's most popular devotional works, *The Imitation of Christ*. Then, on July 25, 1471, Thomas died at age 91. Or did he? When his tomb was opened years later, scratch marks were found inside the coffin—indicators that a desperate man had futilely tried to escape.

The nightmarish experience of being accidentally buried alive was not uncommon in the centuries before medical technology was capable of assuring death had actually occurred. There are many historical accounts of exhumed coffins that contained corpses contorted in agony and the tell-tale marks of frantic escape attempts.

George Washington so dreaded the possibility of this hideous fate that on his deathbed he pulled his secretary close to him. "I am just going!" the first president whispered. "Have me decently buried; and do not let my body be put into the vault in less than three days after I am dead . . . Do you understand me?" Similarly, the composer Frederic Chopin said as he lay dying, "The earth is suffocating . . . swear to make them cut me open, so that I won't be buried alive." To address this relatively common fear, known as taphephobia, some coffins came equipped with an air pipe to the surface, or an aboveground bell that could be rung from below if the occupant suddenly revived. Other people were buried with weapons to finish the job if necessary.

As to the frightful ordeal of Thomas à Kempis: Legend has it that the holy monk was denied sainthood by the Catholic Church because the evidence of his attempts to free himself from his grave showed that he was insufficiently prepared to accept the will of God. If the story is true, perhaps those judging Thomas's worthiness forgot that his book was focused on imitating Christ and that one of the central tenets of Christianity is that Jesus himself escaped from the tomb.

It's the Economy, Stupid—
Even if You're Churchill

The British people wildly cheered their indomitable wartime leader Winston Churchill on May 8, 1945, V-E (Victory in Europe) Day, hailing him as a singular hero in the defeat of Hitler's Third Reich. Then, a mere two months later, they drove him out of office. It was a stunning reversal of fortune that stung the great man deep in his soul, particularly since he never saw it coming.

The prime minister was in Germany while the election results were tallied, engaged in delicate negotiations with the Soviet Union's increasingly belligerent Stalin over the fate of postwar Europe. It was a crucial moment in history, and Churchill fully expected to return to the table and manage events—right after a brief return home to receive the voters' decision. But he woke up on the morning of July 26, 1945, to learn that he and his fellow Conservatives had been soundly rejected in a Labour Party landslide.

"I've tried them with pep and I've tried them with pap," a bewildered Churchill remarked, "and I still don't know what they want."

Had the election been a referendum on his leadership in confronting tyranny, as Churchill fully expected it would, he undoubtedly would have emerged triumphant. But after years of economic depression, followed by severe wartime austerity, the British people were looking forward to the more comfortable lives Labour promised to deliver. Perhaps if Churchill had recognized this cold political reality, he would not have taken the people's decision so personally. But he was human, after all, and felt keenly the pain of Britain's apparent ingratitude. When his wife, Clementine, suggested consolingly that the defeat may have been a blessing in disguise, the prime minister gruffly replied, "At the moment it seems quite effectively disguised."

JULY 27, 1993

The Vicar of Christ vs.
the *Real* Godfather

The Italian Mafia had a message for John Paul II after that pope passionately condemned "the culture of death" they pursued so savagely. And it wasn't anything like the severed horse head the fictional Corleone family of *The Godfather* put in the bed of one uncooperative character. No, these murderers—members of Sicily's *real* Corleonesi clan—wanted to strike at the outspoken pontiff in a far more demonstrative way. Thus, on July 27, 1993, a massive car bomb exploded (one of three detonated by the Mafia that day)* right in front of St. John Lateran's Basilica, the most significant church of the papacy.** The destruction was extensive, but perhaps in attacking "the Pope's Cathedral," the Mafia forgot about the essential resiliency of that ancient edifice, the first authorized Christian church in Rome. Damaged and revived repeatedly since

---

* Another Mafia-planted bomb exploded in front of Rome's seventh-century Church of San Giorgio in Velabro, which contains the skull of the church's namesake, St. George, known, appropriately enough in this case, as "the dragon slayer." A third bomb in Milan shattered the Pavilion of Contemporary Art and killed five people. These terrorist attacks on July 27 were part of a larger war waged by the Mafia that year—one in which the famed Uffizi Gallery in Florence was also heavily damaged—against the Italian state that would dare try to constrain them.

** The cathedral is the official church of the Bishop of Rome—not St. Peter's Basilica, as is commonly assumed. The importance of this historic structure is inscribed on its facade: "Omnium urbis et orbis ecclesiarum mater et caput," meaning "The mother and head of all the churches of the city and of the world."

it was built in the fourth century, the basilica reliably rose again at the end of the twentieth.

JULY 28, 1835

Not Quite Straight Shooters

Even assassins sometimes have bad days. Take poor Gao Jianli, a wonderfully gifted lute player with an inveterate hatred of Qín Shǐ Huáng, the first Chinese emperor who ruled in the third century B.C. (and hoped to live forever—see September 10). After a failed assassination attempt on the emperor by his associates, Gao Jianli spent years in hiding, struggling as an indentured workman and honing his skills on the lute. Word of his talent eventually reached the emperor, who invited Gao Jianli to play for him. But when he appeared at court he was instantly recognized as one of the men who had earlier plotted against the emperor's life. Nevertheless, Qín Shǐ Huáng was enchanted by the sounds Gao Jianli produced, and could not bring himself to dispatch the source of such beauty. So he blinded the musician to render him harmless. Then, over time, the emperor allowed Gao Jianli to come closer and closer to his person, never failing to praise his skill. The killer lutist was biding his time, however, and having gained the emperor's complete trust, he packed his instrument with lead and took a swing with it at Qín Shǐ Huáng's head. Being blind, though, he missed, and he was summarily executed on the spot.

Another unfortunate assassin was Giuseppe Marco Fieschi, a Corsican crook and forger who thought he had created the perfect weapon to kill King Louis Philippe of France. To ensure maximum effect, Fieschi bound 20 guns together, and as the sovereign and his three sons passed along Paris's Boulevard du Temple on July 28, 1835, he fired the deadly device from an upper-story window. One bullet among the barrage killed the king's horse; another grazed his forehead. But Louis Philippe and his sons emerged relatively unscathed. Others were not so fortunate. Eighteen people were killed, with many others injured—including, most grievously, Fieschi himself. Apparently one of his combined guns had back-fired. No worries, though. French physicians ably restored the failed assassin to health—just in time for him to have his head sliced off by the guillotine.

JULY 29, 1981

With This Ring I Thee Dread

"I felt as though I was a lamb to the slaughter."
—Diana, Princess of Wales, recalling her July 29, 1981,
wedding to Prince Charles—a union millions around the
world watched and believed was a fairy tale come true,
but which ended in bitter divorce 15 years later. Diana
died in a Paris car crash on August 31, 1997.

JULY 30, 1865

No Thanks for the Dirty Truth

Something was terribly wrong at Vienna General Hospital. In one of the institution's two maternity wards, many of the women who delivered there succumbed soon after to puerperal or childbed fever, an often fatal bacterial infection. Strangely, though, the mortality rate in the second ward was almost negligible, prompting many women to beg on their knees for admittance to that section. When invariably denied the choice, some deemed it safer to give birth on the street rather than risk the well-known perils of the first ward. Ignaz Phillipp Semmelweis, the physician in charge, was appalled by the gross statistical discrepancy and determined to discover the cause. "Everything was unexplained," he wrote. "Everything was dubious. Only the great number of victims was an undisputable reality."

Semmelweis was confronted with a most puzzling situation. Conditions at both wards appeared to be almost exactly the same. But through careful observation he eventually realized there was one significant difference. New mothers in the first ward were treated mostly by doctors in training, who often made their rounds right after dissecting cadavers—their smocks still stained with blood and other corpse fluids, hands reeking from the gore. By contrast, the mothers in the second ward were largely cared for by unsullied midwives.

At last it dawned on Semmelweis that the doctors probing the unfortunates in the first ward were actually delivering death with their dirty hands. The obvious solution was a strict hand-washing regimen, using antiseptic chlorinated lime. Mortality rates plummeted as a result. Surprisingly, though, many in the medical profession were skeptical, scornful even, of Semmelweis's solution.

"Doctors are gentlemen, and gentlemen's hands are clean," harrumphed the prominent American obstetrician Charles Meigs. This was in the decades before Pasteur made the connection between microbes and disease, and hygiene was thought to be a silly, inconvenient distraction.

"There was no object in being clean," Sir Frederick Treves (of "Elephant Man" fame) later wrote. "Indeed, cleanliness was out of place. It was considered to be finicking and affected. An executioner might as well manicure his nails before chopping off a head."

Despite the resistance he faced, Semmelweis became fanatical about cleanliness, alienating his superiors at Vienna General in the process. Eventually he was fired. The filthy hands resumed their work, and new mothers once again died in agony. Though he did have a few reputable adherents, Semmelweis's refusal to publish his findings in medical journals or illuminate them in lectures—a failure some historians have attributed to his deep sense of inferiority, or his lack of understanding of just what he had discovered—damaged his cause. So did his increasing stridency, which came in the form of blistering insults lobbed at those in his field who dared to dispute him.

Semmelweis gradually began to show signs of derangement; whether from the systematic rejection of his antiseptic notions, encroaching mental illness, or perhaps both, remains uncertain. On July 30, 1865, a friend lured him to Vienna under the guise of visiting a new medical establishment. There Semmelweis was tossed into an insane asylum, and, as an examination of his corpse would reveal, severely beaten. Two weeks later, the medical pioneer who would one day be revered as the "Savior of Mothers" was dead.

Vindication would come, however, and Semmelweis no doubt would have applauded—with gloves on, of course—the universal adaptation of his sanitation regime.

JULY 31, 1801

Frieze to Death: The Elgins Break Another One

There must have been something in the noble Elgin gene pool that made the destruction of antiquities irresistible. It all began on July 31, 1801, when agents for Thomas Bruce, seventh Earl of Elgin, began hacking away at the ancient marble sculptures adorning the Parthenon in Greece.* It was tough going at times, considering the temple's metopes and other facets had been installed to last, more than 2,000 years earlier. The overseer of the haphazard

---

* *Those that survived the devastating Venetian assault on the Parthenon in 1687 (see September 26)*

dismantling, Giovanni Battista Lusieri, wrote to Lord Elgin about one particularly stubborn sculptured panel: "This piece has caused much trouble in all respects, and I have even been obliged to be a little barbarous."

The English traveler Edward Daniel Clarke was on hand to observe a disastrous episode when one sculpture slipped during removal "and down came the fine masses of Pentelican marble, scattering their white fragments with thundering noise among the ruins . . . Looking up, we saw with regret the gap that had been made; which all the ambassadors of the earth, with all the sovereigns they represent, aided by every resource that wealth and talent can now bestow, will never again repair."

The desecration, deplored by Lord Byron in his epic poem *Childe Harold's Pilgrimage,* continued in stages until 1811, when

A plaster cast stands in for the destroyed sculpture along the Caryatid Portico.

"the last poor plunder from a bleeding land," as Byron called it, was shipped to England and the once glorious Parthenon reduced, as another Englishman wrote, "to a state of shattered desolation."

A generation later, across the globe in China, another Elgin—Thomas Bruce's son James, the eighth Earl of Elgin—was overseeing the destruction of another treasure: the magnificent royal retreat outside Beijing known as the Old Summer Palace. A young British officer named Charles George Gordon described the despoliation that began under Lord Elgin's orders (in retaliation for Chinese aggression in the midst of the Second Opium War) on October 8, 1860:

"We went out, and, after pillaging it, burned the whole place, destroying in a vandal-like manner most valuable property which [could] not be replaced for four millions . . . You can scarcely imagine the beauty and magnificence of the places we burnt. It made one's heart sore to burn them; in fact, these places were so large, and we were so pressed for time, that we could not plunder them carefully. Quantities of gold ornaments were burnt, considered as brass. It was wretchedly demoralising work for an army."

August

*"In August, the large masses of berries, which,
when in flower, had attracted many wild bees,
gradually assumed their bright velvety crimson hue,
and by their weight again bent down
and broke their tender limbs."*

—HENRY DAVID THOREAU

AUGUST 1, 1907

A Boy Scout Can't Be Too Handy

On August 1, 1907, Lt. Gen. Robert Baden-Powell officially founded the Boy Scouts at a camp on England's Brownsea Island. After that, "self-abuse" was never quite the same. Baden-Powell was singularly obsessed with the topic, and, thanks to him, generations of young men were instilled with a terror of that "beastly" vice known as masturbation.

"The result of self-abuse is always—mind you, always—that the boy after a time becomes weak and nervous and shy," Baden-Powell wrote in his famous guide, *Scouting for Boys: A Handbook for Instruction in Good Citizenship*, "he gets headaches and probably palpitations of the heart, and if he carries it on too far he very often goes out of his mind and becomes an idiot. A very large number of the lunatics in our asylums have made themselves mad by indulging in this vice although at one time they were sensible cheery boys like any one of you."

And there was more. If a boy "misused his parts," Baden-Powell warned, he would "not be able to use them when a man; they will not work then. Remember too that several awful diseases come from indulgence—one especially that rots away the insides of men's mouths, their noses, and eyes, etc. . . . The next time you feel a desire coming on, don't give way to it; resist it. If you have the chance, just wash your parts in cold water and cool them down. Wet dreams come from it especially after eating rich food or too much meat, or from sleeping with too warm a blanket over your body or in too soft a bed, or from sleeping on your back. Therefore avoid all these. Avoid listening to stories or reading or thinking about dirty subjects."

In other words: Don't be a boy.

Robert Baden-Powell inspects a Scout troop at Wembley, England, for "misused parts."

AUGUST 2, 1830

Bourbons on Ice

The execution of Louis XVI in January 1793 and, later that year, of Queen Marie-Antoinette brutally ended what was known as the ancien régime in France. But for the remaining members of the Bourbon royal dynasty, the decapitation of the king and queen was only the beginning of their troubles. Bad luck, dashed hopes, and breathtakingly poor decisions kept plaguing the family for the next three decades—until fortune finally turned on them once and for all in 1830.

For the surviving Bourbons, the monarchy didn't end with the guillotine—at least in their own minds. The very second the blade severed Louis XVI's head, his only son automatically became Louis XVII. But there would be no crown for the seven-year-old boy— only isolated imprisonment and vile mistreatment at the hands of his captors. The child was "a victim of the most abject misery and of the greatest abandonment," reported a doctor allowed to see him, "a being who has been brutalized by the cruelest treatments and who it is impossible for me to bring back to life . . . What a crime!"

When the unfortunate child succumbed to disease in 1795, his uncle (Louis XVI's brother) succeeded him—in exile—as Louis XVIII. Yet it was Napoleon Bonaparte who was destined to rule France, and in a less than subtle message to the deposed Bourbons that they had no place there, Bonaparte ordered the kidnapping and summary execution of one of their relatives, the Duc d'Enghien. Still, Louis XVIII bided his time—maintaining his royal dignity as best he could as a near-penniless guest in other kingdoms—until Napoleon finally stumbled by invading Russia and was ultimately driven into exile at Elba.

The Bourbon restoration seemed assured as Louis was invited back to France in 1814 to rule as a constitutional monarch. And, except for another brief exile the following year when Napoleon escaped

Elba and stormed back to France (only to be defeated at Waterloo and sent to permanent imprisonment on the remote island of St. Helena), the obese and gouty king ruled in relative peace until his death in 1824. Louis was then succeeded by his brother, the ultraconservative Charles X, who blew it for the Bourbons once and for all.

The new king was foolish enough to dispense with constitutional restraints his predecessor had adopted and was determined to rule as absolutely as his ancestors had done. It was as if the lessons of the revolution had been lost on him entirely. But Charles X learned the hard way that a people willing to behead one autocratic king were fully prepared to unseat another. Thus, on August 2, 1830, in the midst of a burgeoning second revolution, the last Bourbon of the direct royal line was forced to abdicate.*

AUGUST 3 *and* AUGUST 10, 1943

Old Blood and ... Nuts? General Patton's "Slapshod" Leadership

L t. Gen. George S. Patton strode into a military evacuation hospital on August 3, 1943, in the midst of the fiercely fought Sicily

---

* In an interesting twist, Charles's son Louis Antoine, the Duc d'Angoulême, was married to his niece Marie-Thérèse, the eldest child of guillotine victims Louis XVI and Marie-Antoinette. When the king abdicated, he bypassed his son and daughter-in-law in the succession in favor of a grandson. But for about 20 minutes, Louis Antoine refused to step aside. Thus, in that brief interim, he was actually king of France—at least in theory—and Marie-Thérèse, the abused and discarded orphan of the Terror, became his 20-minute queen. In the end, none of Charles's descendants came to the throne, which was given to a distant relative, Louis-Philippe, the last king of France.

campaign of World War II, and came upon Pvt. Charles H. Kuhl, slouched on a stool, looking too well to be there. Patton demanded to know where he was hurt, to which Private Kuhl reportedly replied with a shrug that he was not wounded, but "nervous," adding. "I guess I can't take it." Indeed, Kuhl had been admitted with what his medical chart described as a "psychoneurosis anxiety state, moderately severe"—a condition now recognized as post-traumatic stress disorder. The hard-bitten Patton was having none of it.

"The General immediately flared up," wrote his biographer Martin Blumenson, "cursed the soldier, called him all types of a coward, then slapped him across the face with his gloves and finally grabbed the soldier by the scruff of his neck and kicked him out of the tent." The enraged general demanded that Kuhl immediately be sent back to the front, adding, "You hear me, you gutless bastard? You're going back to the front."

Still seething that night, Patton vented into his diary: "[I met] the only arrant coward I have ever seen in this Army. Companies should deal with such men, and if they shirk their duty, they should be tried for cowardice and shot." Two days later, he made those feelings official policy in a directive to the Seventh Army.

Then, almost as if to taunt Patton's hard-as-nails sensibilities, he encountered another "malingerer" during a hospital visit seven days later. Against his own wishes, Pvt. Paul G. Bennett had been removed from the front, suffering all the symptoms of what was then known as "battle fatigue." Patton came up to the shivering young man, who also had a high fever, and asked what the trouble was. "It's my nerves," Bennett responded. "I can't stand the shelling anymore."

At that point, the general lost it—again—and slapped the private in the face. "Your nerves, hell!" he screamed. "You are just a goddamned coward. Shut up that goddamned crying. I won't have these brave men who have been shot at seeing this yellow bastard sitting here crying." With that, Patton slapped Bennett again, knocking his helmet liner off.

"You're going back to the front lines and you may get shot and killed, but you're going to fight," the general continued in his verbal assault. "If you don't, I'll stand you up against a wall and have a firing squad kill you on purpose. In fact, I ought to shoot you myself, you goddamned whimpering coward." With that, Patton pulled out his pistol threateningly, prompting the hospital's commander, Col. Donald E. Currier, to physically separate the two. Patton left the tent, yelling to medical officers to send Bennett back to the front lines.

Patton's superior, Gen. Dwight D. Eisenhower, was appalled upon hearing of the slapping incidents, and wrote to the general that "I must . . . seriously question your good judgment and your self-discipline as to raise serious doubts in my mind as to your future usefulness."

In the aftermath of his violent outbursts, Patton was forced to apologize to the men he had abused—which he did most grudgingly—and was effectively sidelined for the next 11 months of the war. Still, Private Kuhl took a relatively benign view of what had happened on August 3. Patton "was pretty well worn out," he said later. "I think he was suffering a little battle fatigue himself."

AUGUST 4, 1983

Murder Mysteries?
The A-Girl and the Seagull

August 4 murder mysteries abound. Did the Kennedys have Marilyn Monroe murdered on that date in 1962 to prevent the troubled actress from revealing the affair she conducted with the president (and, possibly, his brother, the attorney general)? Or was it really just a suicide? Equally riveting: Did New York Yankee Dave Winfield deliberately kill a seagull during a game in Toronto against the Blue Jays? Or was it just an unfortunate mishap? Let's focus on the latter.

It was a hazy summer evening in Toronto, where more than 36,000 people—and a seagull, perched at right-center field—had gathered to watch the game at Exposition Stadium. Suddenly, at the end of the fifth-inning warm-up, a ball hurled from the outfield by Winfield struck the unsuspecting gull with terminal velocity. It collapsed and, after a few twitches, died. As the crowd jeered the killer Yankee, a ball boy covered the victim's corpse with a towel and removed it from the field. (A later autopsy revealed severe trauma to the head and neck.) Then, immediately after the game, which the Yankees won, their star outfielder was arrested for the crime. But was he guilty? Had Winfield taken deliberate aim at the seagull?

"From accounts of eyewitnesses, it would appear that way," Sgt. Murray Lee of the Toronto police department said at the time. The arresting officer, Constable Wayne Hartery, who saw the incident firsthand and made the decision to take Winfield in, agreed. Even 30 years after the killing, Hartery remained convinced of the Yankee's culpability, as he told the Toronto *Star* in 2013. "I'll guarantee you 100 per cent he tried to hit it, he aimed for it."

Nevertheless, Winfield, who was released on bail after about an hour in custody at the same station that held the victim in a freezer, strongly maintained his innocence. "I had finished playing catch with [left fielder] Don Baylor . . . and turned and whipped the ball to the batboy, and the seagull happened to be there and caught it in the neck," he told reporters. "It was unfortunate, but it was an accident."

Some skeptics would point out that's exactly what a killer would say. But Yankees manager Billy Martin provided what was perhaps the most compelling exculpation of his player: "They say he hit the gull on purpose. They wouldn't say that if they'd seen the throws he'd been making all year. It's the first time he's hit the cutoff man. I'll bet you he could throw the ball a thousand times and not be able to hit the bird."

So there it is: One dead actress, still a worldwide star, and one forgotten seagull—forever shrouded in the mysteries of August 4.

AUGUST 5, 2001

The Caddie's Wildly Subpar Performance

Some people just don't get it. Then there are those who *really* don't get it. Take professional golfer Ian Woosnam's caddie, Miles Byrne, who committed a breathtaking blunder during the 2001 British Open at Royal Lytham. Woosnam's game had been in decline for years since he reached the top of the Official World Golf Ranking in 1991. But fortune seemed to be smiling upon the diminutive Welshman once again at the Open, when he nearly holed his opening tee shot. Then the unthinkable happened. "You're going to go ballistic," his caddie Byrne warned him at the second tee. Woosnam's bag, it turned out, contained 15 clubs, one more than the maximum allowed. Byrne had forgotten to remove the extra club after a practice round—a bungle that cost the once great golfer a two-shot penalty, the chance at his first British Open title, and a small fortune in prize money. As Byrne predicted, Woosnam did go ballistic, hurling the offending club into the grass and unprintable curses at his caddie. But, astonishingly, he didn't fire him on the spot.

"It's the biggest mistake he will make in his life," Woosnam told the London *Daily Telegraph*. "He won't do it again. He will have a severe bollocking when I get in but I am not going to sack him. He's a good lad; he just has to watch what he's doing."

It was a miraculous reprieve for Byrne, but somehow the caddie missed the message. Two weeks later, he broke one of the most basic rules of his profession: to show up. Byrne overslept and missed Woosnam's tee time in the Scandinavian Masters on August 5. Club officials had to help the golfer break into his own locker to get his playing shoes, as his sleepy caddie had the only key. Now there would be no mercy for Byrne. "I gave him a chance," Woosnam said. "He had one warning. That was it."

AUGUST 6, 1945

Armageddon Twice Over: The Man Who Got Nuked Twice (and Lived to 93)

The ordeal of Tsutomu Yamaguchi is entirely a matter of perspective: Either he was one of the unluckiest men in history, or truly among the most fortunate. On August 6, 1945, the 29-year-old engineer for Mitsubishi Heavy Industries was on a business trip in Hiroshima, Japan, when the United States dropped the world's first atomic bomb in warfare and incinerated the city. Yamaguchi was about two miles away from the epicenter of the blast, but he was nevertheless temporarily blinded, left with his eardrum destroyed and horrific burns over much of the top half of his body. The next day, he suffered more radiation exposure as he made his way to the city center in an effort to find a way home—to Nagasaki.

Yamaguchi was back at work three days after the nuclear holocaust that nearly killed him. Then, the incredible happened. While detailing the events of the prior few days to his boss, a second atomic bomb was dropped on Nagasaki, killing 70,000 people and devastating the city so thoroughly that, in the words of its mayor, "not even the sound of insects could be heard." While Yamaguchi and his boss spoke, a familiar blinding light suddenly filled the room. "I thought the mushroom cloud had followed me from Hiroshima," he later told Britain's *Independent*. Incredibly, Yamaguchi survived—again—though not without suffering.

"For many years he was wrapped in bandages for his skin wounds, and he went completely bald," his daughter, Toshiko, told the *Independent*. "My mother was also soaked in black rain [the radioactive rain that fell after both bombings] and was poisoned." Still, Tsutomu Yamaguchi lived to be 93, his wife 88.

AUGUST 7, 1974

Nixon Driven to His Knees

Pick a day—any day—and odds are it was a bad one for Richard Nixon. "You won't have Nixon to kick around anymore," the much aggrieved politician once declared to the press after being defeated in the 1962 race for California governor. But the man who would go on to become the 37th president of the United States remained constantly under siege—often by his own demons—and, more frequently, by those external forces of darkness he was convinced were out to destroy him. "President Nixon is so rich in living enemies that he probably doesn't qualify as his own worst," journalist Kenneth Crawford once wrote. Among those who made the brooding, paranoid president perpetually miserable:

- Ivy League presidents: "Why, I'll never let those sons-of-bitches in the White House again. Never, never, never."
- His own Cabinet: "I'm sick of the whole bunch . . . a bunch of goddamned cowards!"

- Blacks: "[T]hese little Negro bastards on the welfare rolls."
- Homosexuals: "Fags," "I can't shake hands with anybody from San Francisco."
- The media: "Never forget the press is the enemy, the press is the enemy . . . Write that on a blackboard 100 times."
- Ted Kennedy: "If he gets shot, it's too damn bad."
- The Supreme Court: "You know, those clowns we got on there, I tell you, I hope I outlive the bastards."
- *Washington Post* publisher Katharine Graham: "[A] terrible old bag."
- The State Department: "Screw State! State's always on the side of the blacks. The hell with them!"
- Mark Felt, associate director of the FBI later revealed to be "Deep Throat": "Everybody is to know that he is a goddamn traitor and just watch him damned carefully."
- *The New York Times:* "I'm gonna fight that son-of-a-bitching paper. They don't know what's gonna hit them now."
- And then there were those most pernicious enemies of all, "the goddamn Jews": "The Jewish cabal is out to get me . . ." "The Jews are irreligious, atheistic, immoral bunch of bastards . . ." "What the Christ is the matter with the Jews . . ." "The Jews are all over the government . . ." "Most Jews are disloyal . . ." "Generally speaking, you can't trust the bastards. They turn on you."

All the president's slurs were faithfully captured on the taping system he had installed in his offices in February 1971, as were his numerous dirty dealings—including the criminal conspiracy to cover up the break-in of the Democratic Party headquarters at the Watergate complex. The revelation of this smoking gun tape in the midst of the Watergate investigations caused whatever remaining support Nixon had in Congress to evaporate, and led to what was perhaps the worst day of his life.

The president had vowed he would never resign from office, but by August 7, 1974, it was clear he had no choice, other than to stand trial and almost certainly be convicted of high crimes. After breaking the news to his tearful family—having already repeatedly lied to them about his own culpability—Nixon retired to the Lincoln Sitting Room, his favorite space in the White House, and summoned Secretary of State Henry Kissinger.

"Will history treat me more kindly than my contemporaries?" the distraught president, well on his way to becoming drunk, asked the secretary. Nixon then invited Kissinger, a Jew, to kneel down and pray with him, after which the president remained on his knees and began sobbing. "What have I done?" he cried. "What has happened?" Helpless in the face of this booze-soaked meltdown, Kissinger did his best to comfort Nixon, now curled up on the floor in emotional agony.

The next day Richard M. Nixon announced his resignation, the only president ever to do so. He would spend the remaining two decades of his life waging what *Washington Post* reporter Bob Woodward described as "a very aggressive war with history, attempting to wipe out the Watergate stain and memory." But as the White House tapes continue to show exactly what kind of man he was, it is clear that history will have Nixon to kick around for a very long time to come.

AUGUST 8, 1588

When God Switched Sides

Apparently God was a fanatically Catholic Spaniard who savored the smell of burning heretics and had a real beef with the queen of England—or so Philip II of Spain fervently believed.

Like many a monarch over the centuries, he was convinced that he was the living instrument of the divine will. As he once told one of his military commanders, "You are engaged in God's service and in mine—which is the same thing." But Philip's notions would be put to the test in an epic sea battle on August 8, 1588.

God and Philip were continually vexed by the shenanigans of the Protestant queen of England, Elizabeth I, the king's former sister-in-law.* The queen, with a wink, gave tacit approval to plundering Spanish ships laden with treasure from Philip's vast New World domains—especially since she got to keep a huge chunk of the proceeds—and, in addition, gave military support to Protestant rebels in the Spanish Netherlands. Perhaps worst of all, though, the English queen was herself a heretic—the spawn of Henry VIII's unholy union with his second wife, Anne Boleyn—who had already been declared by the pope as unfit to rule. Philip and the Almighty were determined to launch an invasion to rid the world of the English Jezebel.

"I am so keen to achieve the consummation of this enterprise," the king declared. "I am so attached to it in my heart, and I am so convinced that God our Savior must embrace it as His own cause, that I cannot be dissuaded. Nor can I accept or believe contrary."

In February 1587, Elizabeth ordered the execution of Mary Queen of Scots (see February 8)—whom many Catholics viewed as the legitimate ruler of England—which gave fresh impetus to Philip's holy crusade against England.

Alonso Pérez de Guzmán, Duke of Medina Sidonia, Philip's choice to lead what was called the Enterprise of England, was not a promising one. "My health is not equal to such a voyage," Medina Sidonia protested when he learned of the king's intention, "for I know by experience of the little I have been at sea that I am always seasick and always catch cold . . . Since I have no experience either

---

* *Philip II had been married to Elizabeth's older half sister, the Catholic monarch known to history as Bloody Mary.*

A lithograph shows Queen Elizabeth's glorious defeat of the Spanish Armada.

of the sea or of war, I cannot feel that I ought to command so important an enterprise."

God had it covered, Philip assured him: "This is a matter guided by His hand and He will help you." At the end of May 1588, the Spanish Armada was launched from newly annexed Portugal: 130 ships (and as many priests), along with nearly 30,000 soldiers and sailors, set sail against England. The enemy would be formidable, one officer admitted to the papal envoy, with "faster and handier ships than ours, and many more long-range guns, and know their advantages as well as we do. [They] will never close with us at all, but stand aloof and knock us to pieces with their culverins [a type of cannon] without our being able to do them any harm. So we are sailing against England in the confident hope of a miracle."

But there would be none. After a series of inconclusive skirmishes, the end of King Philip's divinely inspired mission came on August 8, while the ships of the Armada were anchored at the small Flemish port of Gravelines awaiting a rendezvous with the Duke of Parma's land force. English guns battered the fleet mercilessly, while the launch of burning ships into their midst caused the Spanish to panic and cut anchor. The ultimate defeat of the enterprise came not at the hands of the English, but by what can only be described as an act of God.

A great "Protestant Wind" drove the sundered Armada farther toward the North Sea, and as it attempted to make its way home around Scotland and down the western coast of Ireland, savage storms destroyed much of the remaining fleet. Could it have been that Philip II's God had converted? The English seemed to think so, for inscribed on their victory medallions was this message: "God blew with His winds, and they were scattered."

The Seat of Power: LBJ's, um, Crotchety Pants Order

On August 9, 1964, President Lyndon B. Johnson exercised one of the perks of his high office—to order custom-made Haggar pants directly from the company's chief. Alas, the presidential conversation with Joe Haggar was recorded for posterity—and, in terms of dignity, it fell a little short of, say, the Gettysburg Address.

After giving specifications for waist size and pocket depth, Johnson added, "Now, another thing, the crotch, down where your nuts hang, is always a little too tight. So when you make 'em up, give me an inch that I can let out there, uh, because they cut me. They're just like ridin' a wire fence." Then, with a healthy presidential belch, Johnson continued: "Let's see if you can't leave me about an inch from where the zipper ends, right under, back to my bunghole."

Fortunately, the White House recordings were limited to audio, sparing history the sight of President Johnson's penchant for holding forth while sitting on the toilet, or waving his privates around to make a point.

AUGUST 10, 1628

Ship Happens, Part III: Vasa Matter

Through war and conquest in the early 17th century, King Gustavus Adolphus managed to transform Sweden from an insignificant backwater into a formidable European power. Now he needed warships to reflect his kingdom's glory and might—the biggest and most impressive ever built. The *Vasa* was intended to be the first of this super-fleet, and Gustavus Adolphus spared no expense in its construction. Unfortunately, the king was equally unsparing with his opinions and specifications. He knew exactly what he wanted in his ship, which made it positively grand—just unseaworthy.

Richly ornamented and laden with cannon capable of more firepower than any ship in history, the *Vasa* made its debut on a beautiful, ever-so-slightly-breezy August day in 1628 as thousands gathered to watch its maiden voyage. But almost as soon as the top-heavy ship left the harbor of Stockholm, a wisp of wind tipped it over. The *Vasa* sank quickly, along with Gustavus Adolphus's pride, and between 30 and 50 sailors drowned—less than a nautical mile from shore. The mighty ship that ruled the seas for a few minutes lay submerged and forgotten for nearly four centuries until it was finally recovered in 1961. The *Vasa* has now been restored to glory, only this time safe and sound on dry land.

AUGUST 11, 1492

Partying With the Pope
(and His Mistress and His Kids)

Rodrigo Borgia was ecstatic. Having spent a fortune bribing his fellow cardinals in a tight election, he won the Throne of

St. Peter on August 11, 1492. The new pope, who took the name Alexander VI, now held in his greedy paws all the considerable power and wealth that came with that exalted position. So of course His Holiness—along with his mistress and illegitimate children (one of whom was subsequently made a cardinal before he turned 20)—had to celebrate, which they did with the kind of unbridled pagan pomp not seen in Rome since the days of the ancient emperors.* The world belonged to the Borgias, and though the price was steep, they had what they wanted. "Alexander sells the Keys, the Altar, Christ Himself," went a ubiquitous epigram of the day. "He has a right to for he bought them."

AUGUST 12, 2009

ALS Well After All

Few messages could be worse. In a letter dated August 12, 2009, more than a thousand veterans of the Gulf War were informed by the Department of Veterans Affairs that they had been diagnosed with amyotrophic lateral sclerosis (ALS)—better known as Lou Gehrig's disease—a debilitating, invariably fatal neurological disorder. Then, after a period of agonizing uncertainty, and in some cases utter panic, the veterans were informed that the diagnosis had been a mistake, caused by a glitch in coding. "I can't even describe the intensity of my feelings," former Army sergeant Samuel Hargrove, a father of two from Henderson, North Carolina, told the Associated Press in the aftermath of the debacle. "I didn't know how to approach my family with the news."

---

* During the extravagant coronation procession, the new pope passed under a triumphal arch with a gilded inscription that read, "Rome was great under Caesar, greater far under Alexander. The first was a mortal, the latter is a god."

And This Is for That D Minus!

M ost every teacher dislikes a classroom filled with rude, unruly kids. But poor Cassian of Imola faced a particularly nasty bunch in the fourth century. As a Christian, the now sainted schoolmaster refused to offer sacrifice to the Roman gods, as prescribed by the emperor. So as punishment he was turned over to his own students, who gleefully tied him to a pole and stabbed him to death with their writing implements.

Blew It by Sea:
Paul Revere's Naval Disaster

W hen it comes to patriotism, few Americans enjoy a more glorious reputation than Paul Revere—even if Henry Wadsworth Longfellow embellished a bit in recounting the "Midnight Ride" that made him so famous. But there would be no poetic accolades for a later chapter in Revere's revolutionary career, when in 1779 the heroic alarmist was confronted by a barrage of ruinous charges—including dereliction of duty and even cowardice—that left him disgraced and under house arrest.

The allegations arose from one of the most disastrous military campaigns ever pursued during the American War of Independence. In June 1779, British forces took possession of a peninsula in Maine's Penobscot Bay, intending to establish a colony of Loyalists under their protection there, as well as a base from which to operate against New England. In the face of such aggression, Massachusetts, which had jurisdiction over Maine at that time, decided to mount a naval expedition to dislodge the enemy. What should have been a relatively simple exercise turned into an utter debacle.

The enormous American fleet that sailed up Penobscot Bay on July 25 appeared so formidable that the outgunned, outmanned British, who were defending a still incomplete fort, recognized the inevitability of defeat. But paralyzing indecision and sharp disagreements over how to proceed with the assault quickly squandered the Americans' initial advantage.

On August 13, Paul Revere, a lieutenant colonel serving as head of artillery, recorded the arrival of British reinforcements—five ships—in his diary. The next day, an ignominious retreat was ordered. The ill-trained colonial militia fled, while most of the fleet was destroyed in what has been described as the greatest American naval disaster before Pearl Harbor.

Revere came under direct attack in the blame game that followed the fiasco. Among a flurry of accusations, one commanding officer charged him with disobeying orders, abandoning his troops, and desertion. On September 6, 1779, he was arrested, dismissed from the militia, and ordered to home confinement. Much to his dismay, though, Revere was not court-martialed—the only way he felt he might restore his tarnished honor.

"I beg your Honors, that in a proper time, there may be a strict enquiry into my conduct where I may meet my accusers face to face," he wrote to the Massachusetts Council on September 9. That letter was followed by another, in which Revere again pleaded for an open hearing. "It lays with you in a great measure, from the evidence for and against me, to determine what is more dearer to me than life, my character."

Two and half years later—having lingered "under every disgrace that the malice of my enemies can invent"—Revere was at last formally tried. And though he was exonerated of all charges, it would take Longfellow's poem, written over eight decades after the Penobscot disaster, to enshrine him forever as an untarnished American legend.

AUGUST 15, 1434

If There Were One Person Who Should Have Been Burned at the Stake...

Having served as Joan of Arc's highly decorated comrade-in-arms during the Hundred Years' War, Gilles de Rais retired from the battlefield to pursue other interests—specifically, child molesting and murder. Hundreds of little ones were captured, abused, and killed in the most ghastly ways imaginable.

Perhaps trying to atone somehow for his unspeakable acts, Gilles funded the construction of a magnificent, cathedral-like structure dedicated to children, ironically called the Chapel of the Holy Innocents. No expense was spared on the sanctuary, which was dedicated on August 15, 1434, with Gilles presiding as the self-appointed Canon of Saint-Hilaire de Poitiers.

"The portable candlesticks and those for the altar, the censers, the crosses and chalices, the ciboria, the reliquaries . . . were made of solid gold and silver," family members recalled in *Mémoire des Héritiers,* "adorned with precious stones, finely engraved, set with brilliant enamels, and the perfection of the craftsmanship surpassed the richness of the material."

But where Gilles really lavished his wealth was in the procurement of angelic-voiced choirboys for the chapel. "Music transported Gilles," wrote biographer Leonard Wolf. "Especially the music of boys' voices, singing or in pain."

AUGUST 16, 1962

Pete Best, Future Footnote

After years playing small, dingy clubs and receiving disheartening rejections from major record labels,* the Beatles were poised to burst into musical history by the summer of 1962. But without their drummer, Pete Best, who on August 16 of that year was unceremoniously fired from the soon-to-be legendary quartet—relegated to a footnote in the Beatles' magical journey as Ringo Starr quickly took his place. "The lads don't want you in the band anymore," was reportedly all he was ever told that fateful day. Even now, the reasons for Best's sudden dismissal remain vague.

The group's producer, Sir George Martin, later acknowledged having played a part in Best's firing—however inadvertent—as the Beatles prepared to record their first single. "I decided that the drums, which are really the backbone of a good rock group, didn't give the boys enough support," Martin recalled. He suggested that a new drummer be used in the studio. "I felt guilty because I felt maybe I was the catalyst that had changed his [Best's] life."

Brian Epstein, the band's manager, later wrote in his autobiography that he was "not anxious to change the membership of The Beatles at a time when they were developing as personalities . . . I asked The Beatles to leave the group as it was." But, as it turned out, the other members of the band were more than ready to let their drummer go.

---

* In a now famous rejection from Decca, one executive declared, "We don't like your boys' sound . . . Groups are out; four-piece groups with guitars, particularly, are finished."

Best had shared equally in the Beatles' struggle to succeed, but as some close to the group observed, he was never really one of them. While John Lennon, Paul McCartney, and George Harrison shared similar sensibilities and humor, their drummer remained aloof from all the pill-popping, good-time antics of the others. So, when it came down to a question of their bandmate's musical chops, the Beatles didn't hesitate to, well, drum him out.

"It was a strictly professional decision," McCartney later said. "If he wasn't up to the mark . . . then there was no other choice." Still, they each expressed regret about how the matter was handled. Lennon, for one, admitted that "we were cowards when we sacked him. We made Brian [Epstein] do it."

The subsequent success of the band proved unbearably painful to the scorned ex-member—at least for a time. Best admitted to having tried to commit suicide in the wake of his dismissal, but in the end he became far more philosophical about the experience. "Some people expect me to be bitter and twisted, but I'm not. I feel very fortunate in my life," he told Britain's *Daily Mail* in 2007. "God knows what strains and stresses the Beatles must have been under. They became a public commodity. And John paid for that with his life."

AUGUST 17, 1661

Le Toast, C'est Moi:

Burned by the Sun King

Nicolas Fouquet learned the hard way that it was never a good idea to eclipse the Sun King. Under the patronage of Cardinal Mazarin, who essentially ruled France until Louis XIV came of age, Fouquet had risen to great heights in the French government, ultimately serving as the realm's superintendent of finances. It was an extraordinarily lucrative post, especially under Mazarin, when the lines between graft, class privilege, and the legitimate management of the state's wealth were blurry at best. Fouquet proved to be remarkably adept at providing not only for the steady stream of income Mazarin needed to finance France's war against Spain and other state expenses, but for the Cardinal's vast personal extravagances as well. In the process, the ambitious minister made a nice fortune and was eager to proclaim his status in the most ostentatious way possible.

To that end, Fouquet embarked on a project to build a grandiose baroque château outside Paris, the likes of which had never before been seen in France. No expense was spared in the design, construction, and decoration of Fouquet's grand testament to himself, which he named Vaux-le-Vicomte. Among all the richly appointed rooms, one motif was consistently featured: the Fouquet family herald depicting a squirrel climbing high among the leaves of a tree, and the accompanying motto, *Quo non ascendet?* (To where will he not climb?) Apparently Louis XIV was wondering the same thing himself.

On August 17, 1661, the minister hosted his king at a grand fete to celebrate the completion of Vaux-le-Vicomte. The royal party was treated to a sumptuous meal served on plates of silver, after which Molière (see February 17) debuted a new play outside in the estate's elaborate gardens. The evening was then concluded with a dazzling display of fireworks, including a burst of rockets that seemed to engulf the château's great dome in light and flame.

The entire display was meant to impress the king and launch Fouquet's career to even greater heights as his prime minister. Yet King Louis proved himself to be the ultimate party pooper. Fouquet's grand fete only fueled the king's seething resentment (even if it did inspire him to exceed the grandeur of Vaux with his own palace of Versailles) and confirmed his suspicions that the superintendent of finances had been plundering the state for his own benefit. As a result, the squirrel climbing ever higher was locked in a cage for life.

"I used to think the king held me in greater regard than anyone else in the kingdom," the stunned Fouquet lamented after his sudden arrest. Remarking on this precipitous downfall, Voltaire later quipped, "On 17 August, at six in the evening Fouquet was the King of France: at two in the morning he was nobody."

AUGUST 18, 1644

A Pact With the Devil— and Satan Even Had It Notarized

On August 18, 1644, a French priest named Urbain Grandier was burned alive for sorcery. But this was not a typical case of religious fanaticism run amok, and it had nothing to do with a vendetta the all-powerful Cardinal Richelieu had against the outspoken priest—as silly historians continue to insist. No, as it turned out, the good father really *was* in league with the band of demons who possessed a group of nuns in the town of Loudun and drove them into most unsisterly fits of writhing ecstasy. The authorities had proof of that in the actual pact Father Grandier had signed with Lucifer and his fellow devils—obtained after one demon, Asmodeus, was compelled by priestly powers to snatch it right out of Lucifer's private cabinet in hell. The signed and notarized document produced at Grandier's trial (and now preserved at the Bibliothèque Nationale de France) read:

> We, the influential Lucifer, seconded by Satan, Beelzebub, Leviathan, Elimi, and Astaroth, together with others, have today accepted the covenant pact of Urbain Grandier, who is ours. And him do we

promise the love of women, the flower of virgins, the chastity of nuns, the respect of monarchs, honors, lusts and powers. He will go whoring three days long; intoxication will be dear to him. He offers us once in the year a seal of blood, under the feet he will trample the holy things of the church and he will ask us many questions; with this pact he will live twenty years happy on the earth of men, and will later join us to sin against God.

AUGUST 19, 1692

And Speaking of the Devil...

After making their unholy pact with Urbain Grandier (see August 18), Lucifer and the gang were up to their old tricks again—this time across the Atlantic in New England, where they aligned themselves with a Puritan minister by the name of George Burroughs. As astute authorities in Salem, Massachusetts, discovered, Burroughs was not merely a servant of Satan, as so many women of the town were found to be. Rather, he was the very source of evil—a fact confirmed by one of Salem's hysterical teenagers, who swore that Burroughs's apparition had appeared to her and told her, "He was above a witch; he was a conjurer."

The minister, who had left Salem a decade before in the midst of a salary dispute, was arrested in the town of Wells (in what is now Maine), where he had diabolically convinced the people he served of his goodness. Belying that fraud, evidence was presented at trial that the minister was possessed of demonic strength—as well as other depraved powers. The sentence, of course, was death. But a complication arose at the gallows.

With the noose around his neck, Burroughs loudly proclaimed his innocence, and then, horrors, perfectly recited the Lord's

Prayer. Lucifer's earthly representatives were not supposed to be able to do that! Witnesses at the scene started to become agitated. Was an innocent man about to suffer the ultimate penalty? Fortunately, the esteemed minister Cotton Mather was on hand for the execution and quickly quelled their concerns. "The Devil has often been transformed into an Angel of Light," he declared. And with that, George Burroughs, the devil's ringleader in Salem, was sent straight to hell.

AUGUST 20, 1968

Blanked Czech: The Soviets' Brutal End to the Prague Spring

A liberalizing spirit swept through Communist Czechoslovakia in 1968, during what became known as the Prague Spring. The once oppressed people—stuck helplessly in the Soviet orbit—breathed deeply the newfound freedoms inaugurated by the reformist Czech leader Alexander Dubček. But, later that summer, the Soviet bear took a vicious paw swipe across what Dubček had called "socialism's human face"—and ripped it right off. The Soviet invasion of Czechoslovakia on the night of August 20, 1968, was sudden, swift, and decisive; the largest military deployment in Europe since World War II. Resistance was futile, and as the world stood by, totalitarianism, backed by tanks, was restored. "My problem was not having a crystal ball to foresee the Russian invasion," Dubček recalled. "At no point between January 1 [a few days before he became First Chairman of the Communist Party of Czechoslovakia] and August 20, in fact, did I believe that it would happen."

AUGUST 21, 1745

Mr. Catherine the Great Peters Out

Before her love life became the stuff of legend, Russia's future empress, Catherine the Great, came to her marital bed as a blushing virgin. And thanks to her nincompoop of a husband, the future Peter III, she remained so for the next eight years. The wedding ceremony, held on August 21, 1745, had been a splendid affair befitting a future Russian sovereign, but the honeymoon was a nightmare for Catherine.

"The ladies undressed me and put me to bed," Catherine later wrote of her wedding night. "Everybody left me and I remained alone for more than two hours, not knowing what was expected of me. Should I get up? Should I remain in bed? I truly did not know. At last Mme. Krause, my new maid, came in and told me very cheerfully that the Grand Duke [Peter] was waiting for his supper which would be served shortly. His Imperial Highness came to bed after supper and began to say how amused the servants would be to find us in bed together." Then he promptly passed out.

Night after night, Catherine was neglected by her grossly immature spouse, who far preferred the company of the toy soldiers he brought to bed with them than the caresses of his wife.

The situation only grew more intolerable as the years passed. When he wasn't ignoring his wife, he bored her with his incessant babbling. "Never did two minds resemble each other less," she wrote. "We had nothing in common in our tastes or ways of thinking." Along the way, Peter picked up dog training as a diversion, which, Catherine noted ruefully, was an unwelcome addition to his vain attempt to become a violinist—especially since he decided to keep the hounds in the apartments they shared. "So," she wrote, "from 7 o'clock in the morning until late into the night, either the discordant sound which he drew very forcefully from the violin or the horrible barking and howling of the five or six dogs, which he thrashed throughout the rest of the day, continually grated on my core. I admit that I was driven half mad . . . After the dogs I was the most miserable creature in the world."

Peter's treatment of his poor wife grew increasingly cruel, especially after he succeeded as emperor in 1762 and threatened to discard her in favor of his flaunted mistress. Catherine had the last laugh, though. After six months of Peter III's disastrous rule, during which he managed to alienate his new subjects with his bizarre behavior, Catherine deposed him and took the Russian throne for herself.

AUGUST 22, 1983

The Artist's Negative Impression

New York socialite Cornelia Guest thought she was just going to the movies with Andy Warhol on a Monday night in 1983. The poor thing had no idea that the artist carefully scrutinized her and thought her no smarter than a soup can. Nor did she know that Warhol's impression of her would be recorded for posterity in his diary. "The movie [*Daniel*] is absorbing," he wrote on August 22. "Cornelia got so absorbed. She's strange. I really don't know if she's smart or stupid . . . Cornelia just goes in and out and sometimes she's a moron. But oh, she got so absorbed in this, it was like a history lesson for her, and I made a point of quizzing her on it later and she had understood everything."

AUGUST 23, 1939

A Monster Is Out-Monstered

hat happens when two devils shake hands? Well, pretty much what happened on August 23, 1939, when the Soviet

Union signed a nonaggression pact with Nazi Germany. Stalin and Hitler, monsters both, allowed one another plenty of leeway to devour their neighbors—which they did with gluttonous glee. But, evil being evil, one of the partners was bound to break the pact. Sure enough, Hitler invaded Russia less than two years later. Stalin was stunned and, having already executed most of the top Soviet military leadership, helpless. "Lenin founded our state," he said despondently before going into hiding, "and we've fucked it up."

AUGUST 24, 2006

Dwarf-Tossing:
The Demotion of Pluto

Pluto held so much promise when it made its dazzling debut in 1930 as the ninth planet of the solar system. There was much speculation that the newest addition to the celestial family could very well be the greatest of them all—larger, even, than mighty Jupiter. In the excitement of this amazing new discovery, few then could have imagined the grim future in store for the frozen mass that would be named for the Roman god of the underworld.

As science progressed, Pluto gradually diminished. Far from the massive orb it was first thought to be, the outlying planet was proved to be a relative speck—the runt of the nine orbiting spheres. And it only got worse. Pluto's erratic path and diminutive size led some to conclude that it wasn't really a planet at all, but merely an asteroid. Fiercely debated among astronomers, the concept gained traction. Then, on August 24, 2006, came the crowning blow: The once proud Pluto—enshrined in the Styrofoam of countless science fair projects—was officially demoted to the status of "dwarf planet."

There might have been some compensation in being the largest of the stunted planetoids in orbit past Neptune in what is known as

Mourners decorate Pluto's marker near the Smithsonian Castle Rose Garden.

the Kuiper belt, but, alas, it was not to be. Another dwarf, Eris, was soon found to be more massive. "This was Pluto's last chance to be the biggest thing found so far in the Kuiper belt," said Mike Brown, a professor of planetary astronomy at the California Institute of Technology, who discovered Eris and later confirmed its size. "There was a possibility that Pluto and Eris were roughly the same size, but these new results show that it's second place at best for Pluto."

AUGUST 25, 1830

A Fight at the Opera

Call it the birthday tribute that backfired—spectacularly. On August 25, 1830, in Brussels, Belgium, the Théâtre Royal de la Monnaie staged a production of Daniel Auber's opera *La Muette de Portici (The Mute Girl of Portici)*. It was supposed to honor King William I of the United Kingdom of the Netherlands, whose realm then included Belgium. But the birthday boy was in for quite a surprise that night. Rather than inspire loyalty to the king, as was intended, the opera—with its patriotic tale of a lowly fisherman who started an uprising against the Spanish rulers of Naples in 1647—whipped the audience into a nationalistic riot that quickly spilled out onto the streets of Brussels. As it turned out, no one much liked King William, whose rule was considered oppressive. A revolutionary spark had been ignited that night at the theater, and within a year, William I was no longer king of a newly independent Belgium.

AUGUST 26, 1346

Wartime, No See: The Charge of the Blind King

King John I of Bohemia was a brave warrior, no doubt about it. But he was also blind—a distinct disadvantage in any battle; particularly so on August 26, 1346, when John and his French ally, Philip VI of France, faced the English army of Edward III at Crécy. With the introduction of the lethally efficient English longbow—the medieval version of a nuclear weapon—warfare took a decided turn in this clash of kings. John, however, was undeterred. Eager for action, the sightless (and, at age 50, well past his prime) monarch gathered his most loyal comrades around him. "Sirs," he said to them, according to the contemporary chronicler Jean Froissart, "ye are my men, my companions and friends in this journey: I require you bring me so far forward, that I may strike one stroke with my sword." To accommodate their king, and guide him into the thick of the battle, the men tied all the reins on their horses together and charged. As Froissart concluded his account: "They adventured themselves so forward, that they were there all slain, and the next day they were found in the place about the king, and all their horses tied each to other." Victims, it must be said, of blind ambition.

AUGUST 27, 1896

And Before You Could Say Zanzibar, the War Was Over

Sultan Khalid bin Barghash of Zanzibar, after reigning for just two days, lost not only his throne on August 27, 1896, but also the shortest war in history. The blink of a conflict with Britain began at approximately 9 a.m., and lasted for less than an hour.

The United Kingdom had once recognized the independence of the island nation off the east coast of Africa—until 1890, when in the midst of colonial clashes with Germany, Ali Bin Said put his sultanate under British protection. And therein was the seed of discord, for, as part of the agreement, Britain was given veto power over the accession of Zanzibar's future sultans.

On August 25, 1896, Ali Bin Said's successor, his nephew Hamad bin Thuwaini Al-Busaid, died suddenly—most probably poisoned by his cousin Khalid bin Barghash, who immediately proclaimed himself sultan and occupied the royal palace. The British, however, had a different candidate in mind—a sultan more receptive to their own interests. Accordingly, they insisted Khalid step down. He ignored them. Instead, he mustered a force of palace guards, as well as a contingent of servants, slaves, and civilians. He also commandeered Zanzibar's navy, which consisted of one decrepit wooden sloop, H.H.S. *Glasgow*. Despite repeated warnings, Khalid remained defiantly barricaded in the palace, artillery aimed at the British ships gathering in the adjacent harbor. War now seemed imminent.

Hostilities were set to commence at 9 a.m. on August 27, the last possible moment Khalid was given to haul down his flag and abandon the palace complex. The evening before, British residents of the capital were removed to safety. "The silence which hung over Zanzibar was appalling," reported U.S. consul Richard Dorsey Mohun. "Usually drums were beating or babies cried but that night there was absolutely not a sound."

The next morning, Khalid delivered a message to the British consul Basil Cave. "We have no intention of hauling down our flag," he declared, "and we do not believe you would open fire on us." To this Cave responded, "We do not want to open fire, but unless you do as you are told we shall certainly do so." With no further communication from the usurping sultan, the British bombardment began as scheduled. About 40 minutes later—with the palace destroyed, *Glasgow* sunk, and Khalid on the run—it ceased.

And with this great military triumph, Britannia once again ruled the waves—as well as the puppet sultan installed in Khalid's place.

AUGUST 28, 2013

MLK's Kids: Sharing the Dream— for a Fee

Martin Luther King, Jr.'s "I Have a Dream" speech is one of the most memorable in history, which is a good thing, since his children have ensured that their dad's inspirational words are very rarely read or heard in their entirety without payment of a big fat licensing fee. Yes, the universal message of justice, love, and tolerance King proclaimed may be one for the ages, but it's also a commodity assiduously guarded by his heirs.

While the great civil rights leader now stands permanently enshrined on the National Mall beside Washington, Jefferson, and Lincoln, his is the only legacy among them that came with a price tag. Indeed, it cost the organizers of the King Memorial nearly

$800,000 to license his words and image for fund-raising. That kind of money is out of reach for most educational enterprises or historical documentaries—Congress balked at the $20 million the King children were charging to "donate" their father's papers to the Library of Congress—but corporations like Mercedes-Benz, Alcatel, and Cingular Wireless have ponied up to use King's words in their advertising campaigns (one of which also included quotes from Kermit the Frog and Homer Simpson).

"My father gave away everything," Martin Luther King III said in the book *Children of the Movement.* "He didn't worry about money. People expect us to be like him."

Those foolish enough to maintain such expectations of filial imitation have been summarily disabused of them by the notoriously litigious King family. Both CBS News and *USA Today* were sued for having reproduced the "I Have a Dream" speech, as were the makers of a PBS documentary about the civil rights movement, *Eyes on the Prize,* for using unlicensed film footage. Even close family friends have been targets of the covetous clan. Singer Harry Belafonte—a close family friend—was stopped by the estate from selling memorabilia from his own collection, while Andrew Young, one of King's top aides, has been sued for using footage that features both him and the civil rights hero.

When not distracted by the flurry of lawsuits filed against others, the three surviving King children have kept themselves occupied with legal actions against one another. In 2008, for example, Martin III and his sister, Bernice, charged their brother, Dexter, with misappropriating estate funds. And on August 28, 2013—the 50th anniversary of their father's famous March on Washington—Martin and Dexter joined forces in a suit against Bernice for her alleged misdeeds as director of the Martin Luther King Jr. Center for Nonviolent Social Change.

"If they were to be judged by their character," law professor Jonathan Turley wrote of Martin III, Dexter, and Bernice in the

Los Angeles Times, "the verdict would surely make King's towering granite statue blush."

AUGUST 29, 1533

And Speaking of Greed...

Having been ambushed and imprisoned by the Spanish conquistador Francisco Pizarro, Atahualpa, the last Inca emperor, paid literally a king's ransom to free himself—an entire room filled floor to ceiling with gold, by some accounts. A lot of good it did him, though. Pizarro took the gold and, on August 29, 1533, had Atahualpa executed anyway.

AUGUST 30, 1888

Something to Grouse About...
at Least for a Grouse

Life for the lowly grouse was never secure in the English moors, where tweedy aristocrats of the 19th century vied with one another to bag as many of the birds as possible in a single day of shooting. The competition was intense, but no one managed to outdo Thomas de Grey, sixth Lord Walsingham, who on August 30, 1888, killed an astonishing 1,070 grouse on Yorkshire's Blubberhouses Moor.*

A Thorough Tongue-Slashing

In an age when capital punishment was still a fearsome weapon of state, often brutally applied, Empress Elizabeth of Russia made the relatively enlightened promise to never execute any of her subjects. Maiming, though, was another matter entirely. And on August 31, 1743, one unfortunate woman of the court learned the painful lesson that mercy was relative.

Natalia Lopukhina was once described as "the brightest flower of St. Petersburg court," a dangerous designation in the company of a jealous empress who resented the very idea of any woman shining brighter than she. Worse, Lopukhina had made the grave mistake of snubbing Elizabeth while she was out of favor during the prior reign of Empress Anna. So when the insufferable beauty was accused of joining a conspiracy against the empress, Elizabeth was ready to pounce.

Weeks of torture, however, proved only that the so-called plot "was . . . little more than the ill-considered discourses of a couple

---

* No doubt tired of the same old bird after such a massive, record-breaking slaughter, Lord Walsingham turned his attention elsewhere, and one day the following January he collected "what might be the most varied bag ever recorded," as Outdoor Life magazine described it: "65 coots, 39 pheasants, 23 mallards, 16 rabbits, 9 hares, 7 teal, 6 partridges, 6 gadwalls, 4 pochard ducks, 3 swans, 3 snipe, 2 moorhens, 2 herons, 1 otter, 1 woodcock, 1 wood pigeon, 1 goldeneye, 1 rat, and a pike, shot as it swam through shallow water."

of spiteful passionate women," as the English minister Cyril Wych reported. Still, Lopukhina was found guilty. And though Elizabeth "benevolently" spared her rival the ghastly fate of traitors—slow and tormenting execution—she found another way to exhaust her wrath. Lopukhina was stripped naked in a public spectacle, lashed until her skin was shredded, and then, as the crowd roared, her tongue was torn out of her mouth.

"Who'll take the tongue of the beautiful Mrs. Lopukhina?" the torturer reportedly cried while waving the bloody stump. "It's a lovely piece and I'm selling it cheap. One ruble for the tongue of the beautiful Mrs. Lopukhina!"

September

—✦—

SEPTEMBER 1, 1904

The Pigeon's Swan Song: The Final Passenger Departs

They were once the most abundant birds in North America, teeming among the virgin forests east of the Rockies. Samuel de Champlain reported their "countless numbers" in 1605, while Gabriel Sagard-Théodat wrote of "infinite multitudes." Indeed, it was said that a single flock, spread over a mile, might take several hours to fly overhead. But within three centuries, the passenger pigeon was extinct.

The gradual loss of their forest habitat was only the beginning of the passenger pigeons' demise; mass slaughter ensured it. The birds' natural inclination to roost closely together—when their evening chatter could be heard for miles around and their sheer mass often broke tree branches—made them especially easy to kill. Hunters could net hundreds of thousands at a time, which were then sold cheaply to city markets or even ground into fertilizer.

Toward the end of the 19th century, people finally began to take note of the passenger pigeons' plight, but conservation efforts came too late. To reproduce successfully, the social animals needed to be among their large flock of companions. And since those communities had all been decimated by the end of the century, the few stragglers left in captivity remained essentially sterile.

"Martha," a resident of the Cincinnati Zoo, was the last of this once thriving species. When she died on September 1, 1904, the graceful passenger pigeon was gone forever. All that's left now are Martha's stuffed remains, kept in storage, along with her preserved insides, at the Smithsonian Institution.

SEPTEMBER 2, 1960

A Delay at the Races: Suriname's Olympic-Size Screwup

New Zealand runner Peter Snell's day couldn't have been better when, on September 2, 1960, he won the gold in the

800-meter race during the Summer Olympics in Rome and became a national hero. For Siegfried "Wim" Esajas of Suriname, though, that same day was the absolute worst.

Esajas was the first athlete from the tiny South American country (then a Dutch colony) ever to go to the Olympics. But he never got to race. It wasn't an injury that sidelined him, but extraordinarily bad timing. He showed up for the qualifying race in the afternoon only to discover that it had already taken place that morning. Word quickly spread that Esajas had overslept, and he returned to Suriname in disgrace.

Thus, while Snell was celebrated—and even got his own postage stamp—poor Esajas became a laughingstock. Even as late as 1976, the announcer at the opening ceremony of the Olympics in Montreal introduced the Suriname delegation as the country that slept through its first Olympics.

Redemption for Esajas came late, two weeks before his death at age 70 in 2005. Learning that the much maligned runner was terminally ill, the Suriname Olympic Committee decided to reexamine what had happened in 1960. As it turned out, Esajas had not overslept but had been given the incorrect start time by Fred Glans, then secretary-general of the Suriname committee. Glans recorded the incident, but for some reason the committee never reported it. Because of that, Esajas lived in shame and regret for four and a half decades.

"The events in Rome caused a wound in my father's soul that never healed," his son Werner Esajas said. "He felt he was robbed of what could have been the greatest moment of his life."

The Olympic Committee's belated atonement came in the form of a plaque honoring him for being Suriname's first Olympian, and a letter of apology. Most important, they restored his dignity. "His eyes lit up and he was happy," the younger Esajas told the Australian Associated Press in 2005. "I think it was enough for him to finally have peace."

Neville Chamberlain: Appease for His Time

A jubilant Prime Minister Neville Chamberlain returned home from Germany on September 30, 1938, with a pact he was certain would ensure peace for Britain. The crowd that gathered to greet him at the Heston airfield outside London roared its approval when he read a passage from the document he had just signed with Adolf Hitler, noting the determination "of our two peoples never to go to war with one another again."

Following a rapturous reception at Buckingham Palace with King George VI and Queen Elizabeth, Chamberlain slowly made his way back to Downing Street. From a first-floor window of the prime minister's official residence, Chamberlain shouted his immortal message to the masses: What had been achieved that day was nothing less than "peace for our time."

A crisis with Hitler's aggressive regime had been averted with what became known as the Munich Agreement, which essentially allowed Germany to gobble up most of Czechoslovakia in exchange for the guarantee that the Third Reich's territorial ambitions would end there. For a nation with fresh memories of the carnage of the Great War* two decades earlier, when an entire generation of young men had been senselessly slaughtered, the peace terms made Chamberlain a hero. Yes, he had sacrificed a friendly nation to the Nazis, but, as he said in an address, at least young Englishmen wouldn't have to die "because of a quarrel in a faraway country between people of whom we know nothing."

As World War I was called before the eruption of World War II

Amid all the acclaim, there were some dissenting voices—most notably that of future prime minister Winston Churchill, who abhorred the abandonment of Czechoslovakia as an act not only dishonorable but also futile in achieving real peace. "And do not suppose that this is the end," he declared. "This is only the beginning of the reckoning."

Indeed, Hitler's true greed and ambition quickly revealed themselves. Less than a year after the Munich Agreement was signed, the Nazis invaded Poland. And, on September 3, 1939, Chamberlain had to declare war on Germany. That same day he made an agonizing personal testament before Parliament: "This is a sad day for all of us, and to none is it sadder than to me. Everything that I have worked for, everything that I have hoped for, everything that I believed in during my public life, has crashed into ruins."

All at once, the man hailed for having achieved "peace for our time" was transformed into a foolish appeaser, beguiled by an insatiable monster. "Few men can have known such a tremendous reverse of fortune in so short a time," he said ruefully, three weeks before his death in November 1940. And though some historians have softened in their assessment of Neville Chamberlain, his reputation remains forever stained.

SEPTEMBER 4, 1957

The Edsel:
Ford's Defining Failure

In the great American marketplace, some ultrahyped products are bound to fizzle: Witness Frito-Lay's line of snack foods laden with the fat substitute Olestra (and a federally mandated warning, "may cause abdominal cramping and loose stools"). Then there

Extensive advertising for the Ford Edsel fails to deliver sales.

was "New" Coke, celery-flavored Jell-O, McDonald's McDLT (not to mention McPizza and McLean), the United States Football League, Susan B. Anthony dollar coins, and any number of dot-com busts. But the most spectacular failure of them all—the very Chernobyl of new-product disasters—was without a doubt the Ford Edsel. So colossal was this multibillion-dollar flop that *Edsel* even became a new word in Webster's New World dictionary: "a product, project, etc. that fails to gain public acceptance despite high expectations, costly promotional efforts, etc."

The Ford Motor Company was very clever in the marketing, if not the design, of its new line of cars, oddly named after founder Henry Ford's son. The company's marketing wizards bombarded the public with tantalizing ads touting the Edsel as the car of the future, but they never showed what it actually looked like.

The big reveal was scheduled for September 4, 1957—or "E-Day," as the company called it. Throngs were lured to showrooms by the hype, but with the unveiling came not the expected gasps of awe, but groans and giggles instead. The mysterious Edsel turned out to be a motorized absurdity, its most prominent feature being a vertical instead of a horizontal front grille. Shaped like an elongated O, the chrome grille was enormous—an unfortunate necessity as Ford engineers discovered that the hip vertical "innovation" had to be made larger and larger to suck in enough air to cool the engine. The result, *Time* magazine noted, was that the Edsel looked like "an Olds sucking a lemon."

Worse, there was nothing particularly original in the actual engineering of the car. Instead, the Edsel was plagued with problems like peeling paint, doors that failed to close, and a push-button transmission (cleverly located in the center of the steering wheel) that tended to freeze up. A running joke among car commentators was that Edsel stood for "Every Day Something Else Leaks."

As sales continued to plummet, Ford became desperate enough to offer those willing to take the Edsel for a test drive the chance to win a free pony. Most winners, however, opted for the alternative cash prize, leaving Ford not only with a forsaken automobile line but with thousands of unwanted equines as well. Finally, the Edsel was put out of its misery in 1959—the only bright side being that the enormity of the failure now makes the once spurned automobiles highly sought after collectors' items.

SEPTEMBER 5, 1921

Bad Rappe? The Ruination of Fatty Arbuckle

One of Hollywood's biggest box office draws, this hefty silent-era comedian delighted audiences with his hapless charm and what might best be described as elegant slapstick, stumbling through any number of absurd situations with remarkable dexterity and grace, despite his considerable weight. But Roscoe "Fatty" Arbuckle's flourishing screen career was utterly ruined in just one day.

After completing three pictures and signing a new three-year contract with Paramount Pictures for $1 million—a then unheard-of amount—Arbuckle drove up to San Francisco with a group of friends to celebrate over the Labor Day weekend in 1921. The booze was plentiful and the party nonstop, but on Monday, September 5, something terrible happened to one of the guests, a starlet by the name of Virginia Rappe. She ended up dead from acute peritonitis caused by a ruptured bladder. Accounts differ over exactly what happened.

According to Arbuckle, he found Rappe throwing up in his bathroom when he entered his room to change clothes. After cleaning her up, he put her atop his bed to rest, then rejoined the party. When he came back, though, Rappe was on the floor. Arbuckle claimed to have returned her to the bed, rubbed ice on her to cool her, and then went to get help. A hotel doctor attributed the actress's condition to overimbibing and recommended she sleep it off. Arbuckle then returned to Los Angeles the next day.

Rappe's companion at the party, "Bambina" Maude Delmont, told an entirely different story. The film star, she claimed, had brutally raped the young woman. And in an era of rabid yellow journalism, it was Delmont's story that proved irresistible to a ravenous press—never mind her long history of blackmail and extortion. Newspapers were filled with sensational stories of the helpless starlet being ravaged by the obese and lecherous movie star. It was his weight, they said, that crushed the poor girl, while tossing in salacious accounts of Rappe being violated with a bottle. So hot was the story that press baron William Randolph Hearst bragged to the film comedian Buster Keaton that it sold more newspapers than the sinking of the *Lusitania*.

Arbuckle was arrested on September 11 and charged with manslaughter. But a hung jury (ten to two for acquittal) resulted in a second trial. This, too, ended without a verdict. Finally, after deliberating for only a few minutes, a third jury declared

Arbuckle not guilty. During the course of the proceedings, a number of facts emerged that the press had conveniently overlooked: Delmont's shady history, coerced witnesses, and, perhaps most important, Rappe's recent abortion that very likely caused her ruptured bladder. Indeed, the jury felt Arbuckle had been so maligned that it took the unusual step of issuing him a written apology.

Such benevolence had little effect on an inflamed public, however. Despite his acquittal, the once beloved star was shunned and, aside from a few small roles, never really worked again. "I don't understand it," Arbuckle once said of his precipitous fall from favor. "One minute I'm the guy everybody loved, the next I'm the guy everybody loves to hate."

SEPTEMBER 6, 1657

The Emperor's Rise and Fall: A Hard Road to (Vi)Agra

The great Mogul emperor Shah Jahan erected the magnificent Taj Mahal in Agra, India, as an enduring tribute to his dead wife. But it was with another enduring erection that the emperor created a far less savory legacy. On September 6, 1657, he fell ill with what court records of the time euphemistically called "stangury." Other contemporary chroniclers were a bit more blunt, however. It appears the aging emperor had become enamored of a young woman, and, in order to engage with her, resorted to certain aphrodisiacs with long-lasting effects.

"Shah Jahan brought this illness upon himself," reported Niccolo Mannuci. "He wanted to enjoy himself like a youth, and with this intent took different stimulating drugs. These brought on a retention of urine for three days, and he was almost at death's door."

The mortifying episode might have passed as yet another footnote of imperial overindulgence had it not been for Shah Jahan's four fractious sons who, upon learning of their father's illness, immediately went to war with one another over the succession. What resulted rocked India's Peacock Throne. The ailing emperor was deposed and relegated to a gilded imprisonment for the rest of his life. Two of his sons were defeated in the fratricidal clash; a third managed to flee, while the fourth, Aurangzeb, murdered his two defeated siblings, snatched the throne from his father, and proceeded to launch a bloody religious war in India that eventually killed millions. And all this because one old man felt a little frisky.

Shah Jahan at first rebelled against his confinement and tried to arrange the assassination of his usurping son Aurangzeb, who had been kind enough to send his dad the severed head of one of his brothers. In the end, though, the deposed emperor remained in prison, staring out at the Taj Mahal from his palace in Agra, until he joined his late beloved wife there seven years after losing his throne.

SEPTEMBER 7, 1303

Boniface-Off:
The King vs. the Pope

Pope Boniface VIII was feeling a little full of himself in 1302 when he proclaimed in the bull *Unam sanctam* that he was essentially the boss of the entire world—"that it is absolutely necessary for salvation that every human creature be subject to the Roman Pontiff." And that included kings. In response to this unprecedented assertion of supreme spiritual *and* temporal authority, Philip IV of France, long at odds with the pope, quickly indicated he was having none of it by publicly accusing Boniface of a litany of sins: heresy, blasphemy, murder, sodomy, simony, sorcery—and even failure to observe fast days. Boniface was unamused and began to prepare papers excommunicating the French king. But before he could finish, mercenaries sent by Philip stormed the pope's retreat at Agnani and, on the night of September 7, 1303, took him prisoner. As if this weren't humiliating enough for the pretentious pontiff, the would-be supreme sovereign of the world, one of his captors gave him a good slap across the face*—an act of lèse-majesté that reverberated through Europe. After only three days, Boniface was released from captivity, but the shame of the experience was simply too much to bear. Within a month, the pope was dead—only to be relegated to an infamous afterlife in Dante's eighth circle of hell.

SEPTEMBER 8, 1998

The Artificially Sweetened Smell of Success: When McGwire Shot Past Maris

Although many were disappointed that it was Roger Maris and not Mickey Mantle who surpassed Babe Ruth in single-season home runs (see October 1), at least Maris's performance

---

* *Some sources say it was more of a mauling.*

was considered clean. Not so for Mark McGwire, who broke Maris's record on September 8, 1998. Years later, McGwire admitted having been juiced on steroids.

It Takes Guts (Especially Stinking Ones) to Shut Down a King's Funeral

It had to hurt when William the Conqueror came crashing down on the pommel of his saddle, rupturing himself after his horse reared. But that was nothing, really, compared to the ordeal he faced after succumbing to his injury on September 9, 1087. No sooner had William drawn his last breath than his closest companions sped off to protect their interests elsewhere. That left the servants, who, as the chronicler Orderic Vitalis recounted, "laid hands on the arms, the plate, the linen, and the royal furniture, and hastened away, leaving the corpse almost naked on the floor of the cell."

Then came the funeral. William had grown a bit fat since winning Britain after the Battle of Hastings two decades before—so fat, in fact, that he had to be crammed into his stone coffin, causing his insides to burst. The horrific smell became so intolerable that the funeral services had to be cut short and William hastily buried. But the story didn't end there.

For no apparent reason, Rome ordered the Conqueror's tomb at Caen opened in 1522. The corpse was reportedly so well preserved (minus, of course, the exploded entrails) that a portrait of the king was able to be painted from it. Four decades later, however, French Calvinists ransacked the grave and scattered the remains. All that was left of William the Conqueror after that was a lone thighbone.

September

SEPTEMBER 10, 210 B.C.

Mercury: The Emperor's Element of Demise

He was a mighty emperor, the first to unite China under one rule. But, alas, Qín Shǐ Huáng (see July 28) was also mortal—a pesky inconvenience for a monarch convinced of his superiority over all other men. Still, he had conquered so much. Why not death? The quest for eternal life eventually became Qín Shǐ Huáng's singular obsession, and made him prey to all kinds of quacks and alchemists who foisted upon him every conceivable death-defying elixir. It was one such concoction, mercury-infused pills, that reportedly killed the 49-year-old emperor on September 10, 210 B.C.

Qín Shǐ Huáng had lost his battle to live forever, but at least there was still the afterlife, for which he was extravagantly prepared. An entire city was constructed to serve the late emperor's needs, including an enormous army of terra-cotta warriors to protect him. His tomb, according to one ancient text, "was filled with models of palaces, pavilions and offices as well as fine vessels, precious stones and rarities." And, apparently, mercury. No one at the time seemed to have associated the poisonous effects of that particular element with the emperor's untimely demise. If they had, perhaps they wouldn't have threatened Qín Shǐ Huáng's continued existence by creating the artificial rivers of the toxin that reportedly flowed throughout his underground kingdom.*

---

* *Unlike the army of clay warriors, many of which have been uncovered since their discovery in the early 1970s, Qín Shǐ Huáng's actual tomb remains untouched by archaeologists. However, high concentrations of mercury there have been detected, which some scholars believe lends credence to the ancient accounts of flowing mercury rivers.*

SEPTEMBER 11, 2001

By permission of Marshall Ramsey and Creators Syndicate, Inc.

SEPTEMBER 12, 1876

The King's Stealth:
How Leopold II Slithered
His Way Into Africa

K ing Leopold II of Belgium thought little of his own European
kingdom—"small country, small people," he once remarked.
So with ambitions that extended far beyond his own borders and the
constitutional constraints imposed upon him, Leopold concocted a
fiendish scheme to snatch what is now the Democratic Republic of
the Congo and make it his personal fiefdom. But with neither the
money nor the power, the king could not simply storm into Africa
as a conqueror and take his chunk of the continent. He had to

operate by stealth—to present himself to the world as a humanitarian eager to improve the plight of these uncivilized, impoverished people. In this he was frighteningly successful, laying the groundwork for what has often been called the African Holocaust.

The king took a significant step in buffering his compassionate veneer when, on September 12, 1876, he opened the Brussels Geographical Conference—a convocation of the world's leading African explorers, scientists, and philanthropists, which Leopold had personally arranged and overseen with meticulous attention to every detail.

"I insist," the king wrote in a confidential note to the delegates, "on the completely charitable, completely scientific and philanthropic nature of the aim to be achieved. It is not a question of a business proposition; it is a matter of a completely spontaneous collaboration between all those who wish to engage in introducing civilization to Africa." As for his own agenda, Leopold declared to the gathered delegates that Belgium was happy and "contented with her lot" as a small country with no colonial ambitions, and that he was simply pleased to be able to facilitate such a worthy endeavor for the betterment of the world.

The delegates were enchanted by the seemingly benevolent Belgian king. Sir Rutherford Alcock, for one, reported to the Royal Geographical Society of Britain that "in no country and on no occasion has so grand and Royal a hospitality been exercised. Science and philanthropy could not have been united under higher or better auspices. Distinguished among the crowned heads of Europe for his devotion to objects of general utility and international scope for the betterment of mankind at large, his action in so great a scheme as the opening of Africa and the suppression of a slave trade which devastates the whole continent, and fills it with bloodshed and suffering, was singularly appropriate."

Armed with the world's deluded belief in his altruism, King Leopold successfully infiltrated the Congo, made it his private property, and, for the next three decades, in what author Paul Theroux called "one of the strangest and most violent episodes of empire the world has known," proceeded to enslave, murder, and maim millions in his unquenchable lust for profit through rubber and ivory.

SEPTEMBER 13, 1988

GI NO!!! The Campaign Photo That Tanked

In politics, image is just about everything. John F. Kennedy's was famously enhanced by the power of television when he debated Richard Nixon in 1960. The handsome young senator seemed confident and vigorous, while his opponent's wan appearance and sweaty upper lip made him look untrustworthy and something less than presidential. Television viewers concluded that Kennedy won the debate, while those listening to it on the radio had the opposite impression.

Nixon's telegenic disadvantage was but a pale comparison with some of the image-drubbing debacles many modern politicians have endured: President George W. Bush's strutting around the deck of the U.S.S. *Abraham Lincoln*—in a flight suit, under the banner "MISSION ACCOMPLISHED"—right in the middle of a ruinous war in Iraq. Dan Quayle schooled on the proper spelling of "potato." Sarah Palin's infamous interview with Katie Couric, during which the Alaska governor struggled to name any of the periodicals she read to keep abreast of events, and her declaration of the close eye she kept on neighboring Russia. Then there was almost everything poor Jimmy Carter ever did (see December 29).

Sometimes all it took was a single photograph to cause irreparable damage. Michael Dukakis learned this hard lesson during his 1988 presidential campaign after participating in an unfortunate photo-op staged on September 13, 1988.

The photo op that instantly transformed presidential hopeful Michael Dukakis into a dork

The Democratic candidate, long derided as soft on defense, was photographed riding in an M1 Abrams tank outside a General Dynamics plant in Michigan. Rather than conveying the image of a military tough guy, however, Dukakis came off looking like a twit. The high-tech helmet he wore was way too big and seemed to shrink his face—some observed he looked like Snoopy—while the goofy thumbs-up he offered the photographers only seemed to diminish him more.

"He said he wanted to hear what the other guys in the tank were saying [in donning the oversize helmet]," one aide later told the *Los Angeles Times*. "Fine. But he looked like an idiot." The campaign staff of Dukakis's rival, George H. W. Bush, agreed with that assessment and gleefully ran ads featuring the extremely awkward photo. Since then, such ill-conceived photo-ops have often been referred to by pundits as "Dukakis in the Tank" moments.

The candidate, who was trounced by Bush in the election, later reflected on the infamous incident in a 1998 interview with *U.S. News & World Report.* "Now, should I have been in the tank?" Dukakis said. "Probably not, in retrospect. But these days when people ask me, 'Did you get here in a tank? I always respond by saying, 'No, and I've never thrown up all over the Japanese prime minister.'" In making such reference to an embarrassing moment for his former rival, President Bush (see January 8), Dukakis came off looking *almost* as lame as he did in the tank.

SEPTEMBER 14, 1899, 1927,
and 1982

Over and Over,
a Wheely Bad Day

Something sinister seemed to happen on September 14—at least when it came to historic automobile fatalities. It was on this date in 1899 that a New Yorker by the name of Henry Bliss became the first person in the United States (and one of the first in the world) to be killed by a car; a taxicab, to be exact. Then there was the actress turned princess, Grace of Monaco, who died on the same day in 1982 after her Rover P6 plunged down a French mountainside. But perhaps eeriest of all was the sudden demise of the renowned dancer Isadora Duncan on that luckless September day in 1927.

She was wearing around her neck her favorite shawl—an elaborate, draping accessory designed by a friend*—when she hopped into the racing car of a companion and sped away. Alas, the tassels

---

* *"This shawl is magic, dear,"* Duncan wrote to her designer friend. *"I feel waves of electricity coming from it . . . What a red—the color of heart's blood."*

of the shawl whipped back in the wind and got caught in the spokes of the left rear wheel. The dancer was yanked out of the car, hurled to the street, and dragged some 60 feet before the driver finally stopped. Mercifully, her neck had been broken in an instant. "Affectations can be dangerous," Gertrude Stein remarked of the lethal shawl. But maybe it was just September 14 that proved perilous.

SEPTEMBER 15, 2008

Here's Looking at Hubris: The Lehman Debacle

When it came to the executives working beneath him, there was little that escaped the attention of Lehman Brothers CEO Dick Fuld—or "Gorilla," as he was called because of his intimidating demeanor. He expected them to be the best-dressed men and women on Wall Street, specified to which charities they would donate, spelled out where and with whom they would socialize, and even kept close tabs on the state of their marriages, which he insisted be happy ones.

But there was one thing the fastidious master seemed to miss while exercising nearly complete control over his people, and that was the looming financial crisis that would drive Lehman Brothers into ruin and help trigger the deepest recession in seven decades.

Fuld blithely ignored, or denied, the ominous signs that Lehman's subprime lending and leveraged loan practices, as well as its risky real estate ventures, had pushed the kingdom he ruled for 15 years to the brink of collapse. In the face of disaster, the cocksure CEO contemptuously dismissed a number of offers to buy Lehman assets that could have potentially saved the company.

In the end, though, no amount of foolish bravado, or cleverly disguised accounting, could stave off the inevitable. On

September 15, 2008, Lehman Brothers was forced into bankruptcy—the largest in American history, with $613 billion in debts outstanding. "I feel like I want to throw up," Fuld said at the time—a sentiment no doubt shared by the 26,000 Lehman employees who, after months of soothing reassurances by their leader, lost their jobs, their benefits, and the entire value of their company stock.

"There were people here who just a few weeks ago would go through hell for Dick Fuld," a former Lehman executive told CNBC. "That has changed. People want his head."

As it turned out, they would have to settle for a punch in the face, which one employee duly delivered to Fuld when the bankruptcy was announced.

SEPTEMBER 16, 2007

He's Finally Licked— They Did Convict

There was none of the drama of the slow-speed police chase that preceded O. J. Simpson's 1994 arrest on charges of double homicide. Nevertheless, his far more subdued second arrest on September 16, 2007, came with significantly graver consequences for the disgraced former football star. Charged with multiple robbery, assault, burglary, and conspiracy charges, stemming out of what one witness described as a "military-style invasion" of a sports memorabilia dealer's Las Vegas hotel room three days earlier, Simpson was convicted of all ten counts against him. The verdict, delivered exactly 13 years after his acquittal in the murders of Nicole Brown Simpson and Ron Goldman, abruptly ended the Juice's golf-playing days of leisure. And, barring any unforeseen reversals, it ensured that he would rot in jail until he's at least 70.

SEPTEMBER 17, 2002

Fools Gush Out:
The Best Bushism Ever?

"There's an old saying in Tennessee—I know it's in Texas, probably in Tennessee—that says, fool me once, shame on—shame on you. Fool me—you can't get fooled again."
—*President George W. Bush*

President Bush faced enormous challenges during his two terms in office, but one of the greatest for the self-proclaimed "Decider" was translating his thoughts into comprehensible English. The famously "misunderestimated" president mangled the language in many a speech, like the one he delivered in Nashville on September 17, 2002.

SEPTEMBER 18, A.D. 96

Emperor Domitian: Time Out!

Although he declared himself to be a god, the Roman emperor Domitian still had a mortal's fear of death—particularly since the precise date and time of his demise had been long prophesied: the fifth hour of September 18, A.D. 96. As the dreaded day approached, Domitian was understandably on edge. He executed his secretary Epaphroditus, who had reportedly helped Nero commit suicide nearly three decades earlier—just to remind those around him that it was *never* okay to countenance the killing an emperor, no matter what the circumstances. And, as the ancient chronicler Suetonius also reported, he installed highly polished stones around his gymnasium so he could see what was happening behind him.

On the eve of his predicted assassination, Domitian was presented with some apples. "Serve them tomorrow," he reportedly said, adding, "if tomorrow ever comes." The next morning, after a night of terror, the emperor condemned to death a soothsayer from Germany who had declared that a recent spate of lightning in the capital portended a change in government. Then, picking at a pimple on his forehead, which bled, he remarked, "I hope this is all the blood that is required."

After an extraordinarily tense morning, Domitian was thrilled to learn that the appointed hour of his death had come and gone. Gleefully, he went to take a bath—no doubt contemplating whom he was going to execute next. But what the emperor didn't know was that someone had lied to him about the time. And as he dried himself, one of his assassins entered the room under the pretext of informing him of dire news regarding a planned uprising. Then, as Domitian studied the report, the killer stabbed him in the groin.

A struggle between the two men ensued, during which the wounded emperor screamed for a servant boy to deliver the dagger he kept hidden under his pillow. But the weapon had been already removed. Hearing the desperate noise inside Domitian's chamber, the rest of the assassins entered and pounced, slaying the monarch at the exact time his murder had been foretold.

SEPTEMBER 19, 1952

Charlie Chaplin: Filmed in Black and White, and Painted Red

Charlie Chaplin was America's most cherished comic actor, at least for a time, but to U.S. authorities there was nothing remotely funny about him. With his sympathetic portrayals of the underdog, and hilarious skewering of the highfalutin, there was something subversive about the Little Tramp—Chaplin's most enduring and beloved character—that made the authorities see red. Early in Chaplin's film career, which was launched in 1914, FBI director J. Edgar Hoover dubbed him a "parlor Bolsheviki" and would hound him for decades to come—eventually right out of the country.

The Little Tramp's spell over his massive and adoring audiences, which the government was happy to use to its advantage to sell war bonds during World War I, also made him a most frightening figure—one who could use his insidious power over the people to foment class warfare. Indeed, FBI agents investigating Chaplin in Los Angeles dutifully reported to their boss in 1922 that he was part of a Communist conspiracy to make a "propaganda appeal for the cause of the labor movements and the revolution."

As Hollywood's silent era came to a close, Chaplin's films did begin to deliver more serious messages about peace, justice, and human dignity. Some called them dangerously political. In the 1940 film *The Great Dictator*, for example, Chaplin lampooned Hitler and Mussolini, with one character crying out, "Greed has poisoned men's souls—has barricaded the world with hate—has goose-stepped us into misery and bloodshed."

The increasingly somber tone of this and other Chaplin films of the period did not sit well with audiences comfortably cocooned in the isolation of pre–World War II America. Critic Bosley Crowther later summed up the sentiment: "What right has he, a comedian, to go solemn, they rancorously inquire. Climb back into that tramp costume, they thunder, and take those kicks in the pants of yore! Stop making us feel uncomfortable by provoking us to think!"

The government, however, was not content to let audiences determine the fate of Chaplin's films. Representative John Rankin, for one, called for his deportation. Chaplin "has refused to become an American citizen," the congressman thundered. "His very life in Hollywood is detrimental to the moral fabric of

America. [If he is deported] . . . his loathsome pictures can be kept from before the eyes of the American youth."

In 1947, Chaplin learned from newspaper reports that he was to be called before the House Un-American Activities Committee, and he wrote to the committee chairman, J. Parnell Thomas, in response: "In order that you be completely up-to-date on my thinking I suggest that you view carefully my latest production 'Monsieur Verdoux.' It is against war and the futile slaughter of our youth. I trust you will not find its humane message distasteful. While you are preparing your engraved subpoena I will give you a hint on where I stand. I am not a Communist. I am a peace-monger."

The committee delayed his testimony three times and Chaplin ultimately never appeared. But the government's final assault was still in store. On September 19, 1952, while Chaplin was sailing to England for the premiere of a new film, Attorney General Thomas McGranery revoked his permit to reenter the United States.

"If what has been said about him is true," McGranery remarked, "he is, in my opinion, an unsavory character [who] has been publicly charged with being a member of the Communist Party, with grave moral charges and with making statements that would indicate a leering, sneering attitude toward a country whose hospitality has enriched him."

Other than to receive an honorary Oscar for his life's work in 1972, Chaplin never did return to the United States. "I wouldn't go back there if Jesus Christ were president," he said at the time of his banishment, adding: "My prodigious sin was, and still is, being a non-conformist."

SEPTEMBER 20, 1737

Pulling a Fast One on the Indians

William Penn had been a relatively benevolent governor of the royal colony bearing his name, but his efforts to deal fairly with the Lenape, or Delaware, Indians who had long inhabited the region were not emulated by his sons. Eager to grab more territory from the natives, Thomas and John Penn produced what many historians consider an entirely bogus document, supposedly from their father's day, under the terms of which the Indians would cede as much land as a man could walk in a day and a half.

The Lenape leaders reluctantly agreed to the terms of the so-called treaty, but they hadn't counted on a scheme concocted by the crafty colonialists to gain maximum value for what became known as the Walking Purchase. Lured by the promise of rich rewards, three of the heartiest men in Pennsylvania were rounded up to make the trek, the path of which had been preciously marked and cleared of brush to ensure the greatest distance. Then, on the morning of September 19, 1737, the men sped off—literally *sped,* as mere walking would defeat the purpose of the land grab. The natives reacted with disgust. "You run. That's not fair. You was supposed to walk." But the protest was to no avail, and by the next afternoon, more than 60 miles had been covered—representing to the Delaware an enormous chunk of their homeland.

SEPTEMBER 21, 1327

Up and Died: Edward II's Ignoble End

Other than his good looks, almost everything else about the tumultuous reign of England's King Edward II was, quite simply, horrid: his fawning indulgence toward his arrogant male favorites; bitter feuds with England's barons; a humiliating military defeat at the hands of the Scots; dethronement by his own wife and her lover. And, if contemporary chronicles are to be believed, most ghastly of all was Edward's murder at Berkeley Castle on September 21, 1327. According to the *Historia Aurea* of 1346, among other period sources, the king "was killed . . . by the introduction of a hot iron through the middle of a horn inserted into his bottom."*

Incredibly, Edward wasn't the first English monarch reportedly done away with under such ignominious circumstances. After being forced to cede half his kingdom to the invading Danish prince Cnut (or Canute) the Great in 1016, King Edmund II briefly ruled the remnants of his former realm. But then he had to go to the bathroom. Henry of Huntingdon relayed what happened next:

"One night, this great and powerful king having occasion to retire to the house for receiving the calls of nature, the son of the ealdorman Eadric, by his father's contrivance, concealed himself in the pit, and stabbed the king twice from beneath with a sharp dagger, and, leaving the weapon fixed in his bowels, made his escape."**

The Housewife Who Couldn't Shoot Straight: Target President Ford

After one assassination attempt by Lynette "Squeaky" Fromme —a follower of the murderous cult leader Charles Manson— in Fresno, California, it was virtually inconceivable that another woman, in the same state, would try to kill President Gerald R. Ford the very same month. And yet it happened, just 17 days later, on September 22, 1975.

---

* *Some modern historians discount the popular notion that Edward was killed in this manner, and a few dispute that he was murdered at all.*
** *Another medieval source says the assassin hiding in the cesspool below used a spear; still another, more fanciful report insists that a crossbow had been rigged below and was triggered the moment Edmund sat down.*

President Ford after yet another September assassination attempt

Sara Jane Moore, a recently radicalized 45-year-old suburban housewife, with no coherent cause, shot at the president with a .38-caliber revolver she had purchased that morning as he exited a San Francisco hotel. The bullet, fired from 40 feet away, and in the midst of a large crowd, just narrowly missed Ford's head, perhaps due to Moore's unfamiliarity with her new weapon. Before she could fire a second shot, a bystander named Oliver Sipple knocked her arm away as the president was hustled to safety.

Incredibly, the would-be assassin had called the police on herself the day before she tried to kill the president, but all they did was confiscate her .45 revolver. The Secret Service then interviewed Moore, but deemed her "not of sufficient protective importance to warrant surveillance during the president's visit." The oversight nearly cost Ford his life, but not his sense of humor.

"I'm going to have to review my support for the Equal Rights Amendment," he later joked. "These women are trying to kill me."

SEPTEMBER 23, 2008

Bailed Out Straight Into
the Lap of Luxury

What to do with an $85 billion government bailout? Well, less than a week after avoiding total financial ruin, executives of the insurance giant AIG headed off to de-stress themselves for a week at a luxury resort in Monarch Beach, California. The bill: $443,343.71, which, in addition to their rooms, included $150,000 for banquets, $10,000 in bar bills, $3,000 on tips, $7,000 in greens fees, $23,000 at the hotel spa, and $1,400 at the salon. "They were getting their manicures, their pedicures, massages, their facials while the American people were paying their bills," thundered Representative Elijah E. Cummings during a Capitol Hill hearing in the aftermath, prompting the chastened executives to cancel another planned retreat, to the swanky Ritz Carlton spa resort at California's Half Moon Bay. But at least they still got their bonuses—and an additional $37.8 billion in bailout money.

SEPTEMBER 24, 1780

Benedict Arnold:
When the Rat Jumped Ship

It was a rat's response to the perceived slights and lack of appreciation he felt for the great sacrifices he had made for freedom: to deliver West Point, then under his command, to the British enemy. But when American general turned traitor

Benedict Arnold learned his treacherous plot had been discovered, he immediately scurried from his home on the morning of September 24, 1780. It was right before a planned breakfast with his onetime commander George Washington, the man Arnold considered most responsible for his chronic low standing among his countrymen.

Rowed out from the banks of the Hudson River, the self-aggrandizing Judas boarded the appropriately named British sloop of war H.M.S. *Vulture*—"It might be truly said that one vulture was receiving another," as Thomas Paine wrote—and sailed away into infamy. But Benedict Arnold, whose name became synonymous with betrayal, would be back—this time under the British flag, to lead a raid on his former neighbors in Connecticut, burning the town of New London to the ground. The irony was that the treacherous Arnold enjoyed no more regard in his adopted country than in the one he sold out. No one likes a snitch.

SEPTEMBER 25, 1980

Saturday Night Libel?
Chevy Chase Takes
Another Fall

The 2002 New York Friars Club Roast of Chevy Chase was an unusually ferocious affair; a nonstop, withering assault on the actor-comedian's faded star, chemical dependency, and, most frequently, his total lack of humor. "Chevy is living proof that you could actually snort the funniness right out of yourself," spat Greg Giraldo in one of many venomous barbs along similar lines—delivered not by Chase's peers, few of whom deigned to show up for the event (due comeuppance, perhaps, for Chase's own notorious mean-spiritedness), but by lesser known, particularly vicious comics.* Yet no matter how painfully unfunny the roasters insisted Chevy Chase was in 2002, silver-screen star Cary Grant had the same sentiment more than two decades before—and that was accompanied by a $10 million lawsuit.

Though Chase's spectacular career flameout has largely overshadowed it—"You've been in over 40 films and the biggest movie star up here [on the dais] is Al Franken," Giraldo hissed during the roast—there was actually a period when the *Saturday Night Live* alum seemed poised for greatness, with real leading man potential, some said, in the tradition of Cary Grant. In fact, *Tomorrow* host Tom Snyder asked the *Caddyshack* star about the comparison to the film legend in a fateful interview that aired on September 25, 1980.

"He really was a great physical comic," Chase said of Grant, "and I understand he was a homo . . . What a gal."

Grant was entirely unamused by the crack and promptly sued for slander. It was "the only time I ever heard Cary really angry," recounted film director Peter Bogdanovich in his book *Who the Hell's in It: Conversations With Hollywood's Actors.* "Cary told me he wasn't 'going to let him get away with that,' and slapped Chase with a lawsuit. 'I don't have anything *against* homosexuals,' Cary said to me, 'I just don't *happen* to be one.'"

Grant eventually settled for a reported $1 million, which was about ten times what Chevy Chase earned for being so mercilessly flambéed during the Friars Roast.

---

* *Brighter stars have weighed in on Chevy Chase as well. Johnny Carson, for one, reportedly said of the failed talk show host, "He couldn't ad-lib a fart after a baked-bean dinner."*

Perfection Blown to Bits:
The Bombing of the Parthenon

"Earth proudly wears the Parthenon as the best gem upon her zone," poet Ralph Waldo Emerson wrote of the proud ruin atop the Athens Acropolis. Yet the crumbling edifice of architectural perfection so lauded by Emerson and others was just a shell of what it had once been—due almost entirely to the events of a single catastrophic day in September 1687, when the forces of war all but destroyed this marble shrine to Western civilization.

Athens was occupied at the time by the Ottoman Turks; the Venetians formed part of a Holy League against them. In the midst of a clash between them on September 25, the ancient Parthenon fell instantly into ruins. The Turks were using it as an ammunition depository, as well as a shelter for women and children—perhaps, as historians have speculated, with the belief that their Christian enemies would never fire on the classic structure that had at one time been a consecrated church. Alas, the besiegers had no such scruples and bombarded the building.

One of the many hundreds of cannonballs fired at the Parthenon connected with the gunpowder stored inside, causing a massive explosion. Walls and perfectly proportioned columns came crashing down, as did the roof, while ancient statuary was blown to bits. An estimated 300 refugees were killed, and the fires that resulted raged for two days. "In this way," recorded one eyewitness, "the famous temple of Minerva [Athena], which so many centuries and so many wars had not been able to destroy, was ruined."*

---

* Further damage was made to the art of the Parthenon by the Venetian general Francesco Morosini when he subsequently looted the site of its larger

SEPTEMBER 27, 1942

Ship Happens, Part IV:
Willie Dee's Loose Cannon

If ships had brains, the U.S.S. *William D. Porter* would surely have been the nitwit of the U.S. Navy. Almost from the day the destroyer nicknamed "Willie Dee" was launched on September 27, 1942, one ridiculous mishap seemed to follow another.

In November 1943, the newly commissioned ship was assigned a vitally important secret mission—to escort the battleship U.S.S. *Iowa,* with Franklin D. Roosevelt on board, across the Atlantic to the president's summit with his fellow Allied leaders at the Tehran Conference. It seemed simple enough, but for the *Willie Dee,* simple was relative. Just before joining the convoy, the ship managed to smash into a fellow destroyer while backing out of its berth in Norfolk, Virginia. From there, it only got worse.

Having joined the convoy, in which stealth was paramount in a sea full of enemy U-boats, the *Willie Dee* caused quite a racket when one of its unsecured depth charges slipped off the destroyer and exploded. Then a freak wave washed a sailor overboard and the engine room lost power for a time, causing the *Willie Dee* to lose pace with the *Iowa.* With all that trouble aboard, the career-oriented captain, Wilfred Walter, was mortified, especially as he was under the watchful eyes of both his commander in chief and the head of the Navy. Perhaps some practice drills would improve the situation.

To that end, Walter organized a battle simulation as a torpedo exercise. With the *Iowa* chosen as the "target," crewmen removed

---

sculptures. His tackle was faulty and snapped, dropping a large statue of Poseidon and the horses of Athena's chariot from the west pediment to the rock of the Acropolis 40 feet below. Then, of course, there was Lord Elgin (see July 31).

the primers that were necessary to actually launch the torpedoes from the *Willie Dee*'s four tubes. Well, almost all of them. With the order to "fire," the first de-primed torpedo was given a simulated launch, and then the second. But with the third, something unexpected happened. Instead of the silence that was supposed to accompany a fake firing, a *whooooooosh* was heard. The *Willie Dee* had just launched a live torpedo at the president of the United States and the entire Joint Chiefs of Staff.

Panic naturally ensued. With only minutes before the torpedo was to strike, the *Iowa* had to be warned. But how? Strict radio silence had been ordered, so as not to attract enemy attention, which left only a signalman to alert the massive battleship to get out of the way. The young and inexperienced sailor flashed the wrong message, however: that the torpedo was heading *away* from the *Iowa*. Then, flustered, he signaled that the *Willie Dee* was going full speed, in reverse. Finally, there was no alternative but to get on the radio. The message was received with only moments to spare, and the *Iowa* turned sharply right, full speed ahead—its guns trained on the *Willie Dee*. The abrupt change in direction listed the battleship to such an extreme degree that President Roosevelt, who was watching the torpedo from the side of the ship, was nearly knocked out of his wheelchair. The crisis was averted with an explosion in the *Iowa*'s wake.

After the debacle, and with a strong suspicion that an assassin may have been on board, the *Willie Dee* was ordered out of the convoy and back to Bermuda. There the entire crew was arrested. The unfortunate crewman who had forgotten to remove the primer, and then lied about it, was sentenced to 14 years of hard labor, a sentence President Roosevelt sympathetically ordered set aside. And though the whole episode was eventually chalked up to a massive mistake by an inexperienced crew, the shame of the much derided *Willie Dee* lingered—with the often hailed greeting, "Don't shoot! We're Republicans!"*

* *The* William D. Porter *eventually met its demise in the Pacific, sunk by*

SEPTEMBER 28, 1597

Paying the Ultimate Price...
Through the Nose

They call it the *Mimizuka,* or Ear Mound, but it was mostly noses—thousands and thousands of them, lopped off soldiers and civilians alike during Japan's massive invasion of the Korean peninsula late in the 16th century. Normally, Japanese samurai would take entire heads as war trophies, for which they were paid, but that became impractical during this particular onslaught because there were simply too many heads to conveniently haul all the way back to Japan. So the samurai simplified things, as historian Samuel Hawley described in his book *The Imjin War:* "Noses hacked off the faces of the massacred were submitted by the thousands at the nose collection stations set up on the way, where they were carefully counted, recorded, salted, and packed." After shipment, multiple barrels of pickled noses were then buried at a shrine in Kyoto, dedicated on September 28, 1597. And there they remain, a testimony to Japan's wartime savagery—not that the government always saw it that way. A plaque at the rarely visited Mimizuka shrine,* since removed, once read: "One cannot say that cutting off noses was so atrocious by the standard of the time."

Japanese kamikazes. Yet despite its blundering history, the destroyer went down in 1945 without the loss of any of its crew members.

* *The Ear Mound was apparently once known by its proper name,* Hanazuka, *or Nose Mound, but was reportedly changed several decades after its dedication because it sounded too cruel.*

September

He's Ex-Ex-Ex-Excommunicated

B eing excommunicated by the Catholic Church was a big deal for a medieval monarch. It meant that his subjects no longer owed him fealty, and in essence it encouraged his removal from the throne—by any means necessary. So, Holy Roman Emperor Frederick II felt the heavy weight of papal wrath the *first* time he was excommunicated, on September 29, 1227.* And perhaps the second and third time, as well. But by the fourth, the imposition of the pope's most powerful weapon was no doubt beginning to feel just a tad redundant.

Wynn's Loss: How the Casino Mogul's Misdirected Elbow Cost Him $54 Million

I n the annals of great "Oh *NO!*" moments, few have been more forehead-slapping than Steve Wynn's accidental puncture of his own Picasso in 2006. The Vegas mogul had just made a deal to sell the 1932 masterpiece "Le Rêve," a portrait of the artist's young

---

* *The ostensible reason for Frederick's first excommunication was his failure to honor a pledge to go on crusade against the Muslim occupiers of the Holy Land. In reality, however, the emperor and the pope were locked in a fierce power struggle over territory, which informed the subsequent excommunications as well.*

mistress, Marie-Thérèse Walter, for a record $139 million when he brought some friends into his office for a private viewing before the sale. While offering the group an impromptu lecture on the painting's provenance and its erotic features, including the phallus jutting out from the subject's chin, Wynn gesticulated broadly with his arms. Then, suddenly, "there was a terrible noise," as one of the guests, writer Nora Ephron, recounted in *The Huffington Post.*

"Wynn stepped away from the painting," Ephron wrote, "and there, smack in the middle of Marie-Thérèse Walter's plump and allegedly erotic forearm, was a black hole the size of a silver dollar—or to be more exactly [*sic*], the size of the tip of Steve Wynn's elbow—with two three-inch-long rips coming off it in either direction. Steve Wynn has retinitis pigmentosa, an eye disease that dam-

ages peripheral vision, but he could see quite clearly what had happened. 'Oh shit,' he said. 'Look what I've done.'"

Needless to say, the sale was canceled. Wynn then had the painting repaired, after which its value plummeted by a whopping $54 million. Yet not all was lost. After settling with his insurer, the legally blind casino magnate decided to keep the damaged "Le Rêve" in his own collection.*

---

* *Wynn's penchant for grand gestures aside, the painting probably fared no worse than the Picasso damaged at the Metropolitan Museum of Art after a tourist stumbled into it early in 2010, or the one in Houston spray-painted by a vandal in 2012.*

October

"[Fall] hurries you along as you walk the roads,
crunching the leaves that have fallen in mad
and variegated drifts. The wind makes you ache
in some place that is deeper than your bones.
It may be that it touches something old
in the human soul, a chord of race memory that says
Migrate or die—migrate or die."

—STEPHEN KING,
Salem's Lot

OCTOBER 1, 1961

*-Crossed Slugger: The Record That Ruined Roger Maris

It was a blighted triumph for New York Yankee Roger Maris. On October 1, 1961, the right fielder broke Babe Ruth's 1927 record for the most home runs (61!) in a single season—a sensational accomplishment that few, it seemed, wanted to happen, let alone wanted to celebrate. And it gave fresh meaning to "bittersweet."

The reserved, sometimes sullen Maris was a relative newcomer to the Yankees and nothing like the legendary Bambino, whose record many considered sacrosanct. He was even less like his colorful, charismatic teammate Mickey Mantle, who vied with Maris that season to surpass the historic benchmark. Baseball legend Rogers Hornsby summed up a near-universal sentiment: "Maris had no right to break Ruth's record."

Baseball commissioner Ford Frick, an old pal of Ruth's (and his ghostwriter, as it turned out), stepped in to protect Ruth's legacy in July 1961, when the very real possibility that Maris might eclipse him became apparent. Because the number of games in a regular season had been increased since Ruth's time, from 154 to 162, Frick ruled that any new record would have to be established within 154 games. Otherwise, it would be classified separately— with what became known as "the asterisk" (although that actual symbol was never used). Frick "threw a protective screen" around Ruth's record, as *The New York Times* noted—and a pall on Maris's achievement, before he even made it.

Worse, though, than the attempts to qualify his success—or even the hate mail Maris received as he approached the magic number—were the sportswriters, the majority of whom seemed to abhor the very idea of a Roger Maris breakthrough and created a loathsome caricature of the man to conform to their distaste. "I find his whole big-headed attitude rather insufferable," sniffed Oscar Fraley, while Jimmy Cannon manufactured a rivalry with Mickey Mantle and wrote: "One fact is clear. Maris isn't a Ruth or a DiMaggio. He isn't a Mantle either. That's what seems to annoy Roger the Whiner most."*

* *Contrary to contrived reports of an ugly rivalry between Maris and Mantle, the two players were great friends. "There might have been better players, but no one was a better man," Mantle once said of his teammate. "When Roger hit his sixty-first home run, I was the second happiest person in the world."*

For a man as essentially shy as Maris, the predatory press became overwhelming. "It was as if I were in a trap and couldn't find an escape," he later wrote. "It was really beginning to get to me now. I was even afraid to go out for a haircut." Stress took care of that particular form of grooming, as his hair actually began to fall out. "It was only when Roger started losing his hair that we understood what kind of pressure he was under," recalled teammate Clete Boyer.

Turning to his good friend Mickey Mantle at one point, Maris exclaimed, "I'm going nuts, Mick. I can't stand much more of this."

"For those six weeks he went through an ordeal such as no athlete has experienced before," wrote Arthur Daley in *Columbia* magazine. "He was harassed, heckled, tormented, tortured, bewitched, bothered, and bewildered. Day after day he was mercilessly grilled by writers and radio-television inquisitors, probing for his secret thoughts. A few questions were sharp, penetrating. But most ranged from the inane to the insulting. He had to fence his way warily past the booby traps in the first category and suffer through the second."

The sportswriters who crucified the upstart Yankee, and contributed to his unsavory legacy, are also part of the reason only the ball and bat from his historic 61st home run of the 1961 season are on display in the Baseball Hall of Fame. Roger Maris himself remains excluded.

OCTOBER 2, 2013

Adventures in Hypocrisy, Part I: Did Someone Say "Shutdown"?

The Scene: Grandstanding congressman Randy Neugebauer (R-Texas), an oversize American flag poking out of his lapel, confronts a National Park Service employee at the World War II

Memorial on the Mall in Washington, D.C., which was closed to the public because of the recent government shutdown.

"How do you look at them and . . . deny them access?" Neugebauer demanded of the park ranger in the middle of a crowd of tourists that she had been charged with keeping out of the shuttered memorial. (An exception had been made for World War II veterans.)

"It's difficult," responded the employee.

"Well, it should be difficult," the congressman huffed.

"It is difficult," said the park ranger. "I'm sorry, sir."

"The Park Service should be ashamed of themselves," Neugebauer continued to press.

"I'm not ashamed," replied the ranger.

The Problem: Just days before, Neugebauer had voted on a funding measure that led to the government shutdown, which among other things, closed the memorial. Fortunately, the whole episode was captured on tape, fully documenting Neugebauer's idiotic hypocrisy.

OCTOBER 3, 1977

No Encore for Elvis

Elvis was fortunate enough to be dead when CBS aired several of his last concert performances on October 3, 1977. Otherwise, his waning career may have been dealt a killing blow. His voice was in fairly decent shape, but "the King" was clearly in decline—a bloated mass of sweat and confusion, slurring some verses and forgetting others entirely. CBS had reportedly considered shelving the project before Elvis's death that August, sparing the world the sad spectacle, but the opportunity for ratings beckoned in the aftermath. Mercifully, the late singer's estate has had better sense and has steadfastly refused to release the abysmal broadcast, only the soundtrack—leaving the King with a little more dignity. Now if they could just bury some of those bad movies.

OCTOBER 4, 1976

Barbara Walters's Weally Bad Day

Nineteen seventy-six was supposed to be a banner year for television personality Barbara Walters. But it sure didn't turn out that way. Hoping to beef up the dismal ratings for its evening news broadcast with Harry Reasoner, ABC lured Walters away from NBC's *Today* show, which she had co-hosted for 13 years, and gave her the opportunity to become the first woman to ever anchor a network news program. They offered a then staggering salary of $1 million a year. But no sooner was the announcement made in April of that year than the backlash began.

The press had a field day with the salary, neglecting to mention that half of it was to be paid by the network's entertainment division for a series of specials. "A Million-Dollar Baby Handling 5-and-10-Cent News," declared *The Washington Post,* while Richard Salant of CBS asked pointedly, "Is Barbara Walters a journalist, or is she Cher?" Then, just as the press was piling on, comedian Gilda Radner introduced "Baba Wawa," a new character on NBC's *Saturday Night Live* who, like Walters herself, had a bit of a speech impediment.

"Hewwo! This is Baba Wawa hewe to say faweweww," Radner held forth in a parody of Walters's departure from the *Today* show. "This is my wast moment on NBC. I want to wemind you to wook fow me awong with Hawwy Weasoneh weeknights at seven o'cwock . . . I want to take this oppohtunity to apowogize to NBC. I don't wike weaving. Pwease twust me—it's not sowuh gwapes, but, rathaw, that anotheh netwohk wecognizes in me a gweat tawent for dewivewing wewevant news stowies with cwystal cwahity to miwwions of Amewicans. It's the onwy weason I'm weaving."

All the derision Walters faced early in 1976 was merely a preview of actually working with Harry Reasoner, who made no secret of his displeasure at the prospect of sharing anchoring duties with a woman he considered to be a lightweight. The veteran newsman strenuously objected to being forced into what Walters described as something like an arranged marriage. As the date for their first broadcast together approached, Walters was a wreck: She recalled in her autobiography: "After all the hype and press about my move to ABC, millions of people all over the country would be watching to see if I succeeded or fell on my face."

On October 4, 1976, the ill-paired duo made their debut. In what turned out to be a temporary ratings boost for ABC News, hundreds of thousands of new viewers tuned in to see a broadcast brimming with tension. "I've kept time on your stories and mine tonight," Reasoner said to Walters, in front of their viewers. "You owe me four minutes."

"I hoped he was kidding," Walters later wrote. "He wasn't."

The on-air atmosphere only grew more strained, and as the on-screen relationship floundered, along with their ratings, pundits began sounding the death knell. After *New York* magazine declared the pairing "a flop," Walters recalled running into the magazine's editor, Clay Felker. "I had known Clay for a long time," she wrote. " 'What you wrote was very painful,' I said to him. 'Well,' he answered with a shrug, 'you *are* a flop.' "*

---

* *The ill-starred duo both left the ABC anchor desk in 1978: Reasoner returned to CBS's* 60 Minutes, *and Walters went on to achieve success in a*

OCTOBER 5, 1988

He Knew Jack

"Senator, I served with Jack Kennedy. I knew Jack Kennedy. Jack Kennedy was a friend of mine. Senator, you're no Jack Kennedy."

—Senator Lloyd Bentsen's withering retort
to his Republican opponent, Senator Dan Quayle,
after Quayle compared his length of service in
Congress to that of John F. Kennedy during the debate
of vice presidential candidates on October 5, 1988

"That was really uncalled for, Senator," was all the visibly flustered Quayle could reply amid the audience cheers and applause that greeted Bentsen's devastating rejoinder.

OCTOBER 6, A.D. 23

Emperor Wang Mang's
Deadly Shebang

History is rich with stories of valiant men and women who, with all hope lost, nevertheless stared down certain defeat and death with defiant final stands. Wang Mang, the first and only emperor of China's Xin (or Hsin) dynasty, was not one of them. Confronted with an overwhelming rebellion early in the first century, Wang Mang opted not to fight: Rather, he retired

---

number of television ventures, including the ABC news magazine program 20/20, and the female-paneled talk show The View.

to his harem and, according to some historians, got blissfully stoned.

In his drug-induced stupor, the once energetic and engaged reformist emperor lolled about with his wives and concubines, consorting with magicians and conjuring up trippy names for his army commanders—like "The Colonel Holding a Great Ax to Chop Down Withered Wood," or "The General for Whom Jupiter Rests in the Sign of Shen, With the Assistance of the Watery Element."

Perhaps it was better that Wang Mang's mind was too clouded to really contemplate his inevitable end, which turned out far more grim than he might ever have imagined. After the rebel army stormed his palace on October 6, A.D. 23, the emperor was cut into pieces, with his head on display in a public market. There it was pelted with rocks and garbage, after which someone tore out the tongue—and ate it.

OCTOBER 7, 1974

Washington Bombshell: The Congressman and the Stripper

Representative Wilbur Mills and stripper Fanne Foxe were quite happily carousing with friends during the early morning hours of October 7, 1974—until U.S. Park Police officers pulled their car over near the National Mall in Washington and a panicked Foxe jumped out and took a dive into the Tidal Basin. The sensational splash embarrassed the powerful chairman of the House Ways and Means Committee when it made the news the next day, but, curiously enough, didn't kill his career. Forgiving Arkansas voters reelected Mills the next month. But that December, the inebriated and apparently unrepentant congressman bounded up on a stage in Boston to join his old pal Fanne Foxe—who now billed herself as the "Tidal Basin Bombshell."

"I told him not to," the stripper said in an interview with *The Washington Post*. "But I am sure he wanted the audience to see him . . . He was saying, 'I have nothing to hide.'"

Now, it seemed, Mills had finally gone too far—even for his tolerant electorate. "If Mr. Mills cannot forgo his public indiscretions," the Arkansas *Gazette* editorialized, "and if he prefers the life of show business to the life on Capitol Hill, then let him select the former and resign his seat in Congress to devote full time to his new line of work. Whichever course Mills prefers it is past time that he made a choice."

The wayward congressman, who was hospitalized in the aftermath of his strange stage appearance and claimed to have no recollection of it, did manage to ride out the rest of his term—albeit stripped of his powerful position. He was still in office—and reportedly in treatment for alcohol abuse—when his notorious shenanigans were entirely eclipsed by his congressional colleague Wayne Hays (see May 23).

OCTOBER 8, 1871

The Cow That Ruined Chicago— and Mrs. O'Leary

Imagine going about life normally one day—just an ordinary soul, unknown to most except family and friends. Then suddenly becoming infamous the next day—scorned, ridiculed, and even hated for a lie told about you in the news. Such was the surreal situation Catherine O'Leary faced in 1871, when she was blamed for the devastating fire that took up to 300 lives and destroyed much of downtown Chicago. Her reputation was as surely ruined as the great city itself.

The fire originated in a barn where Mrs. O'Leary, a door-to-door milk seller, kept her cows, although no one knew then, or now,

precisely how it started. Mrs. O'Leary claimed to have been fast asleep when the conflagration began. That didn't matter to the Chicago press, however. They found the perfect scapegoat in the poor Irish immigrant woman, at a time when the ugliest stereotypes about such people abounded.

Some papers painted Mrs. O'Leary as a buffoon, who stood by, drunk and gaping, after one of her cows kicked over a lantern and started the blaze. The *Chicago Times* went as far as to accuse her of malice: "The old hag [she was 44] swore she would be revenged on a city that would deny her a bit of wood or a pound of bacon."

A subsequent investigation by the board of Police and Fire Commissioners was inconclusive as to the actual cause of the great fire. Nevertheless, Mrs. O'Leary remained the culprit in the mind of the public. And for the next 23 years of her life she was tormented by the charge, yet defiant in the face of the persistent efforts to make sport of her. Sometime before her death in 1895—of a broken heart, one of her descendants later said—her physician spoke to the press:

"It would be impossible for me to describe to you the grief and indignation with which Mrs. O'Leary views the place that has been assigned her in history. That she is regarded as the cause, even accidentally, of the Great Chicago Fire is the grief of her life. She is shocked at the levity with which the subject is treated and at the satirical use of her name in connection with it."

OCTOBER 9, 1919

Mighty Lefty Has Sold Out

If the fix was in—and people were whispering to that effect—there was scant evidence of it leading into Game 8 of the infamous 1919 World Series, which was supposedly being thrown by eight dirty players from the Chicago White Sox for a fee from underworld gambling interests. The Sox had just won Games 6 and 7 against the Cincinnati Reds, as well as Game 3, leading to speculation that any number of the so-called Black Sox either had their consciences pricked or weren't being paid as promised. With the Cincinnati Reds now ahead only 4-3, Arnold Rothstein, reputed kingpin of the whole illicit operation, wanted such nonsense stopped—immediately. To that end, a dark character whom *Eight Men Out* author Eliot Asinof called "Harry F." and described "as a man schooled in the finer arts of persuasion" was enlisted to convince Sox pitcher Claude "Lefty" Williams that the health of his wife and children depended on his performance the next day. Whether Williams took the mysterious man at his word remains a matter of conjecture almost a century later. But the fact is that on October 9, 1919, Chicago lost Game 8, and, with it, the Series—adding an indelible stain onto America's favorite pastime.

OCTOBER 10, 1793

The Reign of Terror: Madness in the Name of "Reason"

In the aftermath of the French Revolution, a violent retribution known as the Reign of Terror was launched against perceived enemies of the new state—including God. Thousands were sent to the guillotine, while the Almighty was officially banished. Reason was to be France's new deity, revolutionary leader Joseph Fouché decreed on October 10, 1793, and the only acceptable worship would be that of "universal morality." Fouché even ordered the Supreme Being out of graveyards, with the Christian promise of resurrection replaced at their entrances with the atheistic message "Death Is an Eternal Sleep." Then, after desecrating the Cathedral of Notre Dame and transforming it (along with other former places of worship) into a "Temple of Reason," Fouché headed to Lyon to instill his particular form of "universal morality."

The people of France's second largest city had been slow to accept the new order of things and actually had the audacity to rebel. Fouché arrived to guide them back to reason. He started by parading the local bishop on a donkey that was dressed in the cleric's vestments and miter, with a chalice around its neck and a missal tied to its tail. Then, he got down to the real business of reprisals, a task pursued with all the zeal of the truly enlightened. "Let us strike like lightning," Fouché proclaimed, "and let the very ashes of our enemies disappear with the approach of freedom."

Men and women of the rebellious southern capital were lined up by the hundreds and blasted with grapeshot—an impressive means of execution, but, as historian David Andress wrote, "grotesquely ineffective." The rebels fell, but they didn't all die, resulting in "heaps of mutilated, screaming, half-dead victims, who had to be finished off with sabres and musket fire by soldiers physically sickened by the task." Furthermore, all the spilled blood and gore was making a huge mess in the streets of Lyon, a problem Fouché addressed reasonably by moving the mass murders outside the city.

Yet despite these pesky inconveniences, the "Butcher of Lyon," as Fouché came to be called, was delighted by the progress being made in the noble cause of *Liberté, Égalité, Fraternité*.

"Terror, salutary terror, is here in truth the order of the day," he wrote triumphantly; "it represses all the efforts of the wicked; it divests crime of all covering and tinsel! . . . We are causing much impure blood to flow, but it is our duty to do so; it is for humanity's sake."

OCTOBER 11, 1991

Adventures in Hypocrisy, Part II: I Have Sinned... but So What!

H is was a message of hellfire and brimstone, especially for his fellow evangelical preachers who succumbed to demon lust, or "That Thing," as he called it in one of his published discourses. When, for example, televangelist Jim Bakker infamously fell for the charms of his secretary, Jimmy Swaggart immediately pounced, calling the disgraced preacher "a cancer on the body of Christ."

As for his own moral turpitude, the leader of one of the world's largest Pentecostal congregations deemed himself beyond reproach. "It is impossible for me to stray sexually," Swaggart insisted. "My wife Frances is with me all the time. If she can't go on Crusade with me, I have several people who go with me. I'm never alone."

A TV monitor captures Jimmy Swaggart blubbering in false repentance.

Armed with such apparent purity, Swaggart aimed his godly wrath at yet another adulterous preacher, Marvin Gorman, who was emerging as a rival with his own budding television ministry. In July 1986, Swaggart charged Gorman with a number of extramarital dalliances and led the crusade to have him defrocked. There would be no mercy for this loathsome sinner, Swaggart made certain, and Gorman was ultimately ruined by what he described as a brotherly lynch mob. But soon enough he would have his revenge.

The fallen minister began to receive anonymous tips that Swaggart was in the habit of visiting a prostitute. Accordingly, he set up his own surveillance at a seedy motel near Swaggart's Family Worship Center and was eventually rewarded with a damning set of photographs of Swaggart calling on prostitutes. Now came the reckoning. "I have sinned," a blubbering Swaggart declared before his congregation, his wife, and the world on February 21, 1988. "I have sinned against You, my Lord, and I would ask that Your Precious Blood would wash and cleanse every stain until it is in the seas of God's forgiveness, not to be remembered against me anymore."

It was an episode of staggering comeuppance for the self-righteous preacher, but apparently not one from which any enduring lessons were learned. Three years later, on October 11, 1991, Swaggart was caught *again*—which, arguably, made him twice as stupid. This time, however, there would be no tearful public repentance. As he announced to the congregation that regularly give him sizable chunks of their paychecks, "The Lord told me it's flat none of your business."

OCTOBER 12, 1492

Columbus Day of Reckoning

Christopher Columbus received the warmest of welcomes when he first arrived in the New World that he immediately claimed for Spain on October 12, 1492. The native people of that Bahamian island were so excited to see him that they swam out to his ship to offer greetings. The explorer, in turn, was much impressed by their gentle hospitality:

"They . . . brought us parrots and balls of cotton and spears and many other things, which they exchanged for the glass beads and hawks' bells. They willingly traded everything they owned . . . They were well-built, with good bodies and handsome features . . . They do not bear arms, and do not know them, for I showed them a sword, they took it by the edge and cut themselves out of ignorance. They have no iron. Their spears are made of cane."

Columbus also saw the vast potential in the natives he met that fateful day: "They would make fine servants . . . With fifty men we could subjugate them all and make them do whatever we want."

And so he did.

OCTOBER 13, 1992

Admiral Stockdale's Most Telling Questions

"Who am I? Why am I here?"
—*Opening statement of the seemingly befuddled*
Adm. James Stockdale, running mate of H. Ross Perot
on an independent ticket, at the vice presidential
debate of October 13, 1992. As a result of his fumbled
performance, the political unknown was instantly
transformed from a highly decorated naval officer
into a doddering, out-of-touch laughingstock.

OCTOBER 14, 2007

The Komplete Kollapse of Kulture

There was a time, in a brighter age, when fame was accompanied by at least a whisper of accomplishment. But then along came the Kardashians to prove once and for all that the quaint concept of earned renown was truly and unmistakably dead. " 'Keeping Up With the Kardashians, is, as the title suggests, a window into a family," wrote Ginia Bellafante in her *New York Times* review of the show that debuted on October 14, 2007—"a family that seems to understand itself only in terms of its collective opportunism." There's Kim, the starlet famous only for her "stolen" sex tape and abundant derriere; her vacuous sisters Kourtney and Khloe; her manager/mother, Kris, struggling in the first episode with the maternal instinct to protect her daughter from exploitation while simultaneously drooling over the potential windfall of Kim's compromising video. And haplessly watching all the Kardashian zaniness from the sidelines is Kris's husband, Bruce Jenner, the Olympic gold medalist who is, as Bellafante noted, "the only person in his household to have actually accomplished anything."

OCTOBER 15, 1863

Ship Happens, Part V:
That Re-Sinking Feeling

Among the many ironies of history are those occasions when, like the fictional Dr. Frankenstein, great innovators have fallen victim to their own creations. Call it death by lethal invention. Thomas Andrews, the chief naval architect of the *Titanic,* went down with his own ship in 1912. Marie Curie won two Nobel

Prizes for her pioneering studies of radiation, only to succumb to its deadly effects in 1934. Li Si, the first prime minister of a unified China, devised a monstrous means of law enforcement—the Five Punishments (which included the removal of the nose, lopping off a hand and a foot, then the genitals, and finally slicing the victim in two at the waist)—only to be executed by this very method after being charged with treason in 208 B.C.

Then there is the sad story of Horace Lawson Hunley, a Confederate patriot who helped finance and develop the first successful combat submarine. It was an awkward contraption, built from a cylinder boiler and operated by an eight-man crew—one who steered, while the other seven turned a crank that propelled it underwater. The "fish boat," as it was called, worked just fine when it was tested in the calm waters of Alabama's Mobile Bay—so well, in fact, that Confederate general P. G. T. Beauregard was convinced it might just be the perfect weapon to break the Union blockade of Charleston Harbor.

The submarine, now named the C.S.S. *H. L. Hunley* for its inventor, was transported to South Carolina by train, but that's when the trouble began. During a trial run, a crew member got tangled in part of the vessel's mechanisms, which caused it to dive with its two hatches open and sink. Only one man survived the debacle. And though the submarine was raised from the bottom of the harbor and cleaned, few were willing to risk their lives in what

was now seen as a submersible death trap. That's when Hunley stepped in. To inspire confidence in the craft he had devised, he agreed to helm it with another crew assembled from Mobile. On October 15, 1863, before a large crowd of spectators, the *Hunley* slipped below the surface. It never reappeared.

"I CAN HAVE NOTHING MORE TO DO WITH THAT SUBMARINE BOAT," General Beauregard telegraphed in the aftermath of the disaster. "TIS MORE DANGEROUS TO THOSE WHO USE IT THAN TO ENEMY."

Yet while the inventor and the rest of the crew perished—in the agony of slow asphyxiation, as their corpses revealed—not all was lost. Beauregard relented and salvaged the *Hunley* once again. Then, on February 17, 1864, it attacked and sank the powerful Union sloop of war U.S.S. *Housatonic* in shallow water, finally proving itself effective in warfare. Yet right after this pioneering demonstration of its lethality, the *Hunley* and its crew disappeared. Almost a century and a half later it was found on the bottom of the harbor and is now on display in Charleston.

OCTOBER 16, 1998

Oprah's "Beloved" Self

"I'm having my baby!" Oprah Winfrey brayed to her TV audience in one of several shows she devoted to the upcoming release of *Beloved*—the film she had nurtured to the screen after buying the rights to Toni Morrison's unsettling novel of slavery a decade before.

And just so there would be no mistaking the artistic merit of the $83 million project, her starring vehicle, the talk show legend made it abundantly clear to an interviewer: "This is my *Schindler's List.*" So worthy was the film to Oprah that its mere existence was satisfaction enough. "I don't care if two people come to see it or two million," she said. Had that sentiment been genuine, perhaps it might have sustained Oprah when *Beloved* opened on Friday, October 16, 1998, and proceeded to bomb—beaten handily that weekend by the horror romp *Bride of Chucky.* Oprah's baby, it turned out, had been a stillbirth that stayed in theaters for only four weeks.

At first blush, *Beloved* should have been a smash. First and foremost, it had the mighty Oprah behind it—an imprimatur that had made best sellers out of many an obscure book, and transformed everyday goods into objects of desire after being deemed "Oprah's Favorite Things." Plus, the Disney-driven media campaign surrounding the film was relentless—countless commercials, endless interviews, and Oprah on 11 magazine covers, including *Vogue* (with an entire show dedicated to the star's weight loss routine in preparation for that one cover).

Yet all this failed to sell tickets—and landed Oprah in a personal valley of darkness. The humbled auteur admitted that it was the lowest point in her career: "It sent me into a massive, depressive, macaroni-and-cheese-eating tailspin—literally!" she confessed on CNN's *Piers Morgan.*

Winfrey blamed audiences repelled by the subjects of race and slavery because of the culpability they felt. "The whole country was in denial," she told Britain's *Sunday Express*—perhaps overlooking the fact that 130 million guilt-ridden Americans had tuned in to the epic miniseries *Roots* two decades before.

Others had a much simpler answer for the total failure of *Beloved:* Oprah had made the film all about Oprah. "It is my history. It is my legacy. It is the capital WHO of who I am," she grandly pronounced. And to one congregation, with the civil rights icon Rosa Parks sitting right in the front row, she declared, "*Beloved* is my gift to you."

Frank Rich later concluded in *The New York Times,* "The real problem—and it was true from the day 'Beloved' opened, before 'word of mouth' could be the culprit—was that the audience feared more sermon than drama from the increasingly more preachy Oprah." Then, quoting Tom Shales of *The Washington Post,* Rich concluded, "'Winfrey playing national nanny is getting to be a drag.'"

OCTOBER 17, 1733

Titan Leeds Is Dead—
Long Live Titan Leeds

There was only one thing standing in Ben Franklin's way as he prepared to launch his *Poor Richard's Almanack:* a man named Titan Leeds, who, inconveniently, was publishing a successful almanac of his own. So Franklin killed him—not by any conventional murderous means—but by simply declaring Titan Leeds dead.

Writing in the voice of his fictional alter ego, the lowly, henpecked Richard Saunders, Franklin pretended to have high regard "for my good Friend and Fellow-Student, Mr. Titan Leeds," which is why he claimed to have held off publishing his own almanac for so long. But then he added, "this Obstacle (I am far from speaking it with Pleasure) is soon to be removed, since inexorable Death, who was never known to respect Merit, has already prepared the mortal Dart, the fatal Sister has already extended her destroying Shears, and that Ingenious Man must soon be taken from us." Franklin went on to predict the exact date and time of his rival's "inexorable Death": October 17, 1733, at precisely 3:29 p.m.

Of course when that day came and went, Leeds took great relish in excoriating Franklin in the 1734 edition of his almanac as a "conceited Scribbler" who had "manifested himself as a fool and a liar." Ah, but Poor Richard was ready for that predictable response. Surely the real Titan Leeds must be dead, he insisted later that year, and impostors taken his place, for his friend would *never* attack him so cruelly.

"Mr. Leeds was too well bred to use any man so indecently and scurrilously," he wrote, "and moreover his esteem and affection for me was extraordinary."

Franklin continued to bury Leeds literarily until 1738, when the poor man really did pass away. At that point Poor Richard commended the impostors for ending their charade, and printed a letter from the ghost of Titan Leeds, admitting "that I did actually die at that time [October 17, 1733], precisely at the hour you mentioned, with a variation of only 5 minutes, 53 seconds."

A Cult Above the Rest

The California State Senate capped off a rather heady year for the Reverend Jim Jones—one that began with his designation as "Humanitarian of the Year" by the now defunct *Los Angeles Herald Examiner*—by adopting a resolution on October 18, 1976, commending Jones and his Peoples Temple congregation "for their exemplary display of diligent and devoted service to and concern for their fellow man, not only in this state and nation, but throughout the world." Just over two years later, the great "humanitarian" would oversee the mass murder-suicide of more than 900 of his cult followers in Jonestown, Guyana.

The Lindy Flop: A Reputation Suddenly Loses Altitude

Looking at the life of Charles Lindbergh, it's difficult to pinpoint when exactly the great aviator went from what one columnist described as "Public Hero No. 1" to "Public Enemy No. 1." From his bizarre notions about racial purity to the fierce isolationism he advocated for America as Hitler rampaged through Europe, the man affectionately known as the Lone Eagle managed to alienate his once adoring public in an extended spiral of disgrace. There were so many ill-received statements and unsavory associations, but two events in particular stand out as perhaps the most unfortunate in the corrosive decline of not-so-Lucky Lindy.

A decade after he successfully piloted the *Spirit of St. Louis* solo over the Atlantic and became an instant hero in 1927, Lindbergh made several trips to Nazi Germany. There, as an honored guest at the Berlin Olympics, among other events, he extolled (and exaggerated) the strength of the German Luftwaffe and praised Hitler's leadership. "The organized vitality of Germany was what most impressed me," Lindbergh later wrote in his autobiography: "the unceasing activity of the people, and the convinced dictatorial direction to create the new factories, airfields, and research laboratories."*

Then, on October 19, 1938, the world-renowned aviator accepted, "by order of the Führer," Hermann Göring's presentation of the Service Cross of the German Eagle. Germany was not yet a formal enemy of the United States, but American critics bristled at how their hero was cozying up to the Nazis, whose assaults against humanity were already well under way.

Lindbergh rejected the notion of returning the medal. "It seems to me that the returning of decorations, which were given in times of peace and as a gesture of friendship, can have no constructive effect," he wrote. "If I were to return the German medal, it seems to me that it would be an unnecessary insult. Even if war develops between us, I can see no gain in indulging in a spitting contest before that war begins."

Secretary of the Interior Harold Ickes, among others, vehemently disagreed. "If Mr. Lindbergh feels like cringing when he is correctly referred to as a knight of the German eagle," Ickes wrote, "why doesn't he send back the disgraceful decoration and be done with it? Americans remember that he had no hesitation about

---

* *Lindbergh's affinity for Germany apparently extended to the women there. Long after his death in 1974, it was revealed that the all-American hero had fathered a number of children by three different women, two of them sisters.*

sending back to the President his commission in the United States Army Air Corps Reserve. In fact, Mr. Lindbergh returned his commission [in 1941] with suspicious alacrity and with a total lack of graciousness.* But he still hangs on to the Nazi medal!"

The nadir of Lindbergh's public career came during a speech delivered on September 11, 1941, in which he delivered a profoundly tone-deaf condemnation of the British, Jewish people, and the Roosevelt Administration. The reaction to the speech was immediate and devastating to Lindbergh's reputation. The onetime hero faced what his biographer Scott Berg described as "a Niagara of invective . . . Few men in American history had ever been so reviled." *Liberty* magazine called him "the most dangerous man in America," while residents of Lindbergh's hometown, Little Falls, Minnesota, even removed his name from their water tower. The Lone Eagle, unrepentant to the end, had finally crashed.

OCTOBER 20, 1986

Princely Sums From the Sultan's Prodigal Brother

On October 20, 1986, the Sultan of Brunei made his kid brother, Prince Jefri Bolkiah, finance minister of the tiny yet

---

* *Lindbergh resigned his commission in the United States Army Air Corps Reserve in response to President Roosevelt's public criticism of him as a "defeatist and appeaser" in the face of Hitler's aggression. Though he was by no means the lone voice in advocating for nonintervention in Europe—auto pioneer and fellow Service Cross of the German Eagle recipient Henry Ford was another prominent isolationist, as was Joseph P. Kennedy, patriarch of the political dynasty and ambassador to Great Britain—his was among the most incendiary.*

oil-rich kingdom on the coast of Borneo. And from that near-bottomless cookie jar, Prince Jefri managed to bilk the government of nearly $15 *billion*—perhaps the largest embezzlement in history. The epic theft was accompanied by an equally impressive spending spree, during which the prince at one point reportedly spent $50 million a month on such essentials as yachts, one of which he tastefully named *Tits* (and its two tenders *Nipple 1* and *Nipple 2*), polo ponies, pounds of jewelry (including $10 million worth of watches depicting couples having sex), private planes, and a fleet of more than 2,000 Bentleys, Ferraris, and Rolls-Royces. Alas, he had to give it all back when the irritated sultan—*finally*—took a good look at the books.

No Lobe Lost in the Getty Family

Oil baron J. Paul Getty, one of the richest men in the world, didn't seem to grasp the very real peril his grandson John Paul Getty III faced in the hands of his Italian kidnappers. Or, just as likely, he simply didn't care. After all, the old man's talent for accumulating vast wealth correlated perfectly with his chronic inability to develop or maintain tender family relationships—a trait he apparently passed down to his estranged son, J. Paul Getty II, who appeared as disinclined as his father to come up with the money the kidnappers demanded. That might mean sacrifice. "Do you realize that if I have to pay the ransom, I'd have to sell my entire library for that useless son?" he reportedly complained to his mistress.

Frustrated by the recalcitrant Gettys, the kidnappers delivered on their long-standing threat to cut up their 16-year-old captive, bit by bit, until their demands were met. On October 21, 1973, John Paul Getty III was given a few steaks as a treat, then blindfolded and muffled. The terrified young man knew what was coming next. "Is it going to hurt?" he asked his captors. "Of course it's going to hurt," one of them replied. With that, the boy's ear was sliced off with two strokes of a razor, preserved in formaldehyde, and sent to a newspaper in Rome with a warning that more body parts would be on the way.

The ghastly delivery finally got the Gettys' attention. The old man reluctantly agreed to cough up the ransom, but only that portion of it that would be covered as an insurance loss. The rest he would loan to his son, at 4 percent interest. Released at last, the hideously maimed young man telephoned his grandfather to thank him for his help. Asked if he wished to take the call, J. Paul Getty responded without even looking up from his newspaper: "No."

OCTOBER 22, 2012

How Lance Armstrong Lost Seven Races in One Day

There was one less hero in the world when on October 22, 2012, supercyclist Lance Armstrong was officially stripped of his seven Tour de France titles—the first of which he won in 1999, just three years after being diagnosed with testicular cancer that had spread to his lungs and brain. For years Armstrong was dogged by accusations that he used performance-enhancing drugs, a charge he repeatedly and vehemently denied as he parlayed his cycling success into lucrative endorsement deals, a successful cancer foundation, and nearly universal acclaim for his courage and tenacity. Eventually, though, the United States Anti-Doping

Agency issued a damning 202-page report detailing pervasive drug use by Armstrong and his teammates, the penalties for which the International Cycling Union opted not to appeal. "Lance Armstrong has no place in cycling" said Pat McQuaid, president of the union; "he deserves to be forgotten in cycling."

OCTOBER 23, 1812

Napoleon, Out in the Cold

After his sensational rise to power in postrevolutionary France, Napoleon Bonaparte cast his greedy eye on the rest of Europe, gobbling up huge chunks of the continent—barely pausing to burp. But the potbellied emperor bit off much more than even he could manage when his voracious appetite for conquest led him straight into the gaping maw of Russia.

On June 24, 1812, Bonaparte began his journey across the Nieman River into the forbidding land that would eventually consume his proud Grande Armée alive. There was no enemy to confront when he arrived in the burned and abandoned Lithuanian city of Vilna, which had been depleted by the retreating Russians of all resources. There was little food for the starving French soldiers and their horses. One observer reported, "They were dying like flies and their carcasses were thrown in the river." And so it would be for the rest of the French expedition—only so much worse. It was all part of Russian emperor Alexander I's strategy—to keep his forces in retreat, destroying everything along the way, letting Napoleon chase him deeper and deeper into the heart of Russia. The weather would take care of the rest. "Our climate, our winter will fight for us," Alexander declared.

Eventually the French made it to Moscow, the ancient seat of the Russian tsars, which had been all but abandoned by its inhabitants, leaving no people, no supplies, and no enemy to confront. "Napoleon is like a torrent that we cannot yet stop," announced the head of Russia's forces. "Moscow will be the sponge that absorbs it." The French soldiers barely had time to start looting before Moscow was in flames. The inferno raged for days, and the eerie red glow it produced could be seen for miles around; the sound was like a hurricane.

"So now the horde of barbarians is lodged in the ruins of that beautiful capital," Empress Elizabeth wrote. "Every step that [Napoleon] takes in Russia brings him nearer to the abyss. We shall see how he endures the winter!"

Bonaparte desperately wanted an end to the Russian campaign and to come to some kind of truce, but Emperor Alexander wouldn't give "the Corsican Ogre" such an easy exit. Thus Napoleon was stuck with only the most odious of options: retreat. And on October 23, 1812—just four months after crossing the Nieman River—he marched out of the remnants of Moscow to face his doom.

Winter, Emperor Alexander's greatest ally, was coming. And the wrath of an outraged populace would aid its lethal scourge. For the once Grande Armée, Russia became, in the words of one, "this

Napoleon's bitter retreat from Moscow depicted in Adolph Northen's etching

enormous tomb." In all, 400,000 French soldiers died; 100,000 more were taken prisoner. Some of those who managed to survive recounted the horror of that unforgiving retreat: tales of frozen bodies, half-eaten by wolves, of menacing peasants quick to torture, of starvation so severe that dung became nourishment.

"The route over which the Grande Armée was hurrying to Smolensk was strewn with frozen corpses," one French soldier wrote. "But the snow had soon covered them like an immense shroud, and little mounds, like the tombs of the ancients, showed us only faint traces of our buried comrades in arms."

When Nature Calls, It Pays to Listen: The Astronomer's Unheavenly End

Tycho Brahe was one of the most brilliant astronomers of the late 16th century—in addition to being something of a swashbuckler who once had his nose sliced off in a duel (over some dispute involving a mathematical equation, of all things). In the era before telescopes, the sniffer-less Brahe reimagined the heavens through scrupulous observation and paved the way for the laws of planetary motion set forth by his protégé, Johannes Kepler. Unfortunately, though, he didn't have enough sense to answer the call of nature— or, more precisely, he was too polite to pee—and it cost him dearly.

The esteemed scientist was dining in Prague as the guest of a great nobleman when the urge to urinate became overwhelming. Yet according to the mores of the era, a guest was never supposed to excuse himself from the table before the host had finished his own meal.

"Holding his urine longer than was his habit, Brahe remained seated," recounted Kepler. "Although he drank a little over generously and experienced pressure on his bladder, he felt less concern for the state of his health than for etiquette. By the time he returned home, he could not urinate anymore."

Brahe suffered terribly over the next 11 days as he was slowly poisoned by the unflushed toxins overwhelming his system. Finally, on October 24, 1601, he died after supposedly composing his own epitaph: "He lived like a sage and died like a fool."*

"Terror of the High C's": Screeching to Stardom

It was an artistic triumph . . . yet not. On October 25, 1944, 76-year-old opera "star" Florence Foster Jenkins made her one and

---

* There the strange story might have ended, with the moral "When you gotta go, you gotta go." But an exhumation of Brahe's corpse in 1901 suggested that something more sinister might have caused the great astronomer's demise. Traces of mercury were found in his beard, which led to speculation that he may have been poisoned. One possible suspect was Kepler, eager to get his hands on Brahe's meticulously kept notes and make a name for himself. Another was King Christian IV of Denmark, who, it was said, may have sent an assassin to kill Brahe in retaliation for bedding the king's mother (a story of illicit royal romance that supposedly inspired Shakespeare's Hamlet).

It was not until the corpse was again exhumed in 2010 that the murder theories were finally put to rest. In addition to learning that the prosthetic nose worn by Brahe wasn't made of silver, as long believed, but actually brass, scientists also determined that there wasn't nearly enough mercury present in the remains to kill him. Instead, they essentially confirmed the original diagnosis: death by burst bladder.

only appearance at New York's famed Carnegie Hall. The audience hadn't packed the house to hear the so-called soprano warble, however; they came to make fun of her—just as they had at all the other stage appearances she had made leading up to this grand debut. The fact was, Jenkins couldn't sing—not a note. But the wealthy socialite *believed* she could, and that was the beauty of it; it's what made audiences line up to watch her earnest performances, complete with elaborate costume changes and diva-like flourishes.

The "Terror of the High C's," as she was called behind her back, didn't disappoint that evening at the sold-out Carnegie Hall. There she was, the septuagenarian in her glittering angel costume, with full-length golden wings, to screech her signature number, "Angel of Inspiration." And back she popped as the Spanish coquette, jeweled comb and red rose in her hair, strewing petals out of a wicker basket. Hearing the roaring howls she always interpreted as rapturous approbation, Jenkins finally left the stage after several encores, knowing she had awed yet another audience. It was the pinnacle of a not-so-glorious career and she died happy, just a month later.

OCTOBER 26, 1928

Somehow, We Don't Weep for Goebbels

Call it schadenfreude, but there's just something delicious about a Nazi having a bad day—like this one, recorded by Hitler's propagandist Joseph Goebbels in a diary entry dated October 26, 1928:

"I have no friends and no wife. I seem to be going through a major spiritual crisis. I still have the same old problems with my foot, which gives me incessant pain and discomfort. And then there are the rumors, to the effect that I am homosexual. Agitators are trying to break up our movement, and I'm constantly tied up in minor squabbles. It's enough to make you weep!"

Boo-hoo!

From U.S.S.R. to … Just Bizarre: Turkmenistan's Lunatic Leader

October 27 is a special day on Turkmenistan's calendar, celebrating the Central Asian country's independence from the U.S.S.R. in 1991. But freedom is a relative concept, for although the new nation escaped the Soviet yoke, it was left saddled with a leader whom writer Paul Theroux described as "one of the wealthiest and most powerful lunatics on Earth"—a thieving dictator (or "president for life") whose cult of personality made Stalin's seem subtle by comparison.

The few Western journalists allowed in Turkmenistan under Saparmurat Niyazov's repressive regime were all left with vivid impressions of a nation gone insane. "Loonistan," Theroux called it in his book *Ghost Train to the Eastern Star: On the Tracks of the Great Railway Bazaar,* "less like a country than a gigantic madhouse run by the maddest patient, for whom 'megalomaniac' sounded too affectionate and inexact."

Reminders of Niyazov's omnipotence, and preening narcissism, were found virtually everywhere, starting with the giant portraits. The oversize mug of the man who dubbed himself Turkmenbashi, Leader of All the Turkmen, was found on banners hung from buildings, on billboards, on paper currency, in shops and schools—even on the bulkhead walls of all Turkmenistan Airlines planes. Of course there were statues as well, hundreds of them in various shapes and sizes, with perhaps the most gaudy of them all standing atop the

Arch of Neutrality in the capital city of Ashgabat—a 250-foot gold-plated monstrosity that constantly rotated to face the sun.

"I admit it," Niyazov once told a journalist, "there are too many portraits, pictures and monuments [of me]. I don't find any pleasure in it, but the people demand it because of their mentality." Presumably the people also required their leader to rename the month of January after himself, and April after his late mother.

The great leader acquiesced to these popular "requirements," but much was expected in return. Indeed, the Turkmenistan national oath included the phrase "[if] I betray . . . Turkmenbashi, may my breath stop." For many it did, in the dank prison cells in which uncooperative citizens often found themselves.

Turkmen were cowed into submission by Niyazov's idiosyncratic laws, most of which reflected his own unsettled state of mind. Beards and ballet were banned, along with car radios, the opera, and even gold teeth, which were ordered to be extracted.

Like the god he hoped to convince the people he was, Niyazov raised wondrous creations out of the desert that is Turkmenistan—or at least he tried—with a little help from the vast wealth he plundered from his impoverished country's natural gas profits. "Let us build a palace of ice," he declared in 2004, "big and grand enough for 1,000 people." Then there was the huge man-made lake planned in the Garagum Desert and the planting of a vast cypress forest that was intended to modify the arid climate but which quickly succumbed to it.

With a wave of his mighty hand, the great leader laid waste to acres of the capital—displacing thousands—and rebuilt in a unique style that one foreign diplomat described as "Soviet-Vegas." Among Niyazov's inspired projects, so helpful to his suffering people: a 130-foot pyramid, an Olympic Stadium that never saw the Olympics, a vast amusement park called the World of Turkmen Fairy Tales, and the Kipchak Mosque, a behemoth that most Muslims consider blasphemous. Indeed, chiseled into the walls, right beside excerpts from the Koran, are extensive passages of drivel from Niyazov's *Rukhnama,* or *Book of Spirit*—described by Theroux as a "hefty-sized farrago of personal history, odd Turkmen lore, genealogies, national culture, dietary suggestions, Soviet-bashing, insane boasting, wild promises, and his own poems, one beginning, 'Oh, my crazy soul . . .'"*

Fortunately for his people, he now lies buried beneath them.

OCTOBER 28, 1871

Ulysses S. Graft?

Ulysses S. Grant went from being one of the most acclaimed generals of his era—of *any* era, really—to one of the worst presidents the United States has ever known. And for that he had to blame his corrupt Cabinet members, as well as his own failure to check their outrageous chicanery. Although the president never personally benefited from any of the financial misdoings, "Grantism," nevertheless, was the word Senator Charles Sumner coined to describe the chronic malfeasance that ran through a number of federal departments—including War, Treasury, Interior, and State—fatally undermining the 18th president.

---

* *This tedious tome—Niyazov's own blathering bible, after which both Saturday and September were renamed—was required reading for all citizens.*

"Grant is now more unpopular than Andrew Johnson was in his darkest days,"* Vice President Henry Wilson, a bit of a shady character himself, told future president James Garfield early in 1875. His political appointments were "getting worse and worse," and, Wilson added: "He is the millstone around the neck of our party that would sink it out of sight."

So widespread was the criminal behavior that on any given day of Grant's eight-year administration someone close to him was almost guaranteed to be up to something crooked. Take October 28, 1871—at random. Secretary of War William W. Belknap had been supplementing his income quite nicely with kickbacks from one John Evans, a sutler, or supply merchant, he had appointed to operate the Fort Sill trading post on the Western frontier. But then Evans drew some unwelcome attention after bringing a large quantity of liquor into the Indian Territory to sell.

On October 28, the U.S. Treasury Department asked Belknap whether Evans even had a license to sell liquor. With his illicit income threatened, the secretary responded by issuing Evans a permit that same day—an act that illustrated, as his biographer Edward S. Cooper wrote, "the extent to which Belknap was willing to prostitute himself for his $1,500 quarterly payment."**

Less than two weeks later, Belknap wrote to the Treasury Department solicitor: "I have the honor to inform you that Mr. John S. Evans . . . through his friends, denies taking liquor into Indian country without authority . . . I therefore request that no proceedings be commenced against him."

---

* *See February 24.*

** *Cooper also noted the irony in the fact that Belknap need not have "prostituted" himself, for if he had checked, he would have found that Evans had already been issued a permit. The secretary of war was eventually impeached in Congress, but having abruptly resigned his position shortly before and now a civilian, he was acquitted.*

Well, It Was True for a While . . .

Many lost fortunes after the massive stock market crash, but a group of Washington bankers also lost face. Just ten months before—while the 1920s were still roaring—*The Washington Post* polled a group of financial leaders and asked them for their predictions for the year ahead. Their opinions were so glowingly positive that the newspaper featured them on the front page, under the banner headline "GOOD TIMES ARE PREDICTED FOR 1929."

Mis-Lead: The Chemist's Lethal Lie

Thomas Midgley "was an engineer by training," Bill Bryson wrote in *A Short History of Nearly Everything,* "and the world would no doubt have been a safer place if he had stayed so." Of course Midgley had no way of knowing the hideous effect his incarnation as a chemist would eventually have on Mother Earth—when he discovered that lead added to gasoline solved engine knocks. But considering the performance Midgley gave for the media on October 30, 1924, there's good indication that he simply wouldn't have cared.

More than a half century before the detrimental impact of poisonous lead spewed from automobile exhaust pipes became a major environmental and public health concern, the debilitating effects of the known neurotoxin on refinery workers were being widely reported in 1924. And that's when Midgley came up with a stunt to appease the braying media. Standing before a group of reporters at Standard Oil's headquarters in New York City, the scientist proceeded to pour a clear, thick liquid infused with lead over his arms. Then, after drying himself, he inhaled deeply from a jar of the same liquid for a minute—proof, he declared, that there was no danger associated with limited exposure to diluted lead, and that the dead and dying refinery workers had obviously not followed basic safety precautions.

What Midgley neglected to mention was that just a year earlier, he had become gravely ill himself from lead poisoning and had to take six weeks off work as a result. And a few months after the press conference, Midgley was sick again with lead poisoning. But the irrepressible scientist returned better than ever, with a brand-new chemical refrigerant he had discovered: chlorofluorocarbons, those pesky little ozone chewers better known as CFCs.*

OCTOBER 31, 1961

New Digs—Literally— for Stalin's Body

F ew would have dared tangle with Soviet dictator Joseph Stalin while he was still alive, loath as they were to join the millions of others the despot had murdered, starved, or sent away to die in frozen Siberian gulags. But it was an entirely different matter when the monster was felled by a cerebral hemorrhage in 1953. Only then did it become open season on the once invincible Stalin. His successor, Nikita Khrushchev, led the charge in what became known as his "Secret Speech," delivered before the 20th Congress

---

* *Midgley, who died in 1944, would never know what he had wrought. But that doesn't mean the scientist entirely escaped his own inventive legacy. Having contracted polio, Midgley devised a complex pulley-and-harness lifting mechanism that helped him get in and out of bed. On November 2, 1944, he became entangled in the mechanism and strangled himself to death.*

Former Soviet leader Joseph Stalin, temporarily at peace before "de-Stalinization"

of the Communist Party in 1956. In it, Khrushchev denounced the cult of personality his predecessor had so assiduously cultivated, and the terrible power he wielded so ruthlessly.

It was, he declared, "foreign to the spirit of Marxism-Leninism to elevate one person, to transform him into a superman possessing supernatural characteristics, akin to those of a god. Such a man supposedly knows everything, sees everything, thinks for everyone, can do anything, is infallible in his behavior." The Stalin cult, Khrushchev continued, was "the source of a whole series of exceedingly serious perversions of party principles, of party democracy, of revolutionary legality."

Having thus launched the process of what became known as "de-Stalinization," Khrushchev took a final step that left the dead dictator not so much spinning in his grave—but right out of it. His body had been carefully embalmed and placed under glass right next to Vladimir Lenin in his tomb, where the party faithful could stream past and view the preserved corpses of the two revolutionary leaders. But in a well-orchestrated scene, an old, devoted Bolshevik woman named Dora Abramovna Lazurkina stood up before the 22nd Congress in 1961 and, claiming to have a direct spiritual channel to Lenin, declared unequivocally that he hated being next to Stalin, "who did so much harm to the party."

Following that performance, Stalin's body was unceremoniously removed from Lenin's tomb on October 31 and quietly reburied near the Kremlin Wall. It was the final humiliation of a man whose presence had once permeated virtually every aspect of Soviet life—that is, until the city of Stalingrad was renamed Volgograd less than two weeks later.

November

NOVEMBER 1, 1861

General Incompetence:
George McClellan, Lincoln's Migraine

On November 1, 1861, President Abraham Lincoln gave himself a massive headache. On that day Lincoln handed Gen. George B. McClellan, already commander of the Army of the Potomac, additional responsibility as the supreme commander of the entire Union Army. "I can do it all," McClellan jauntily promised the commander in chief. Yet, when it came right down to it, the Young Napoleon, as McClellan was known, did nothing—and he did it with a bad attitude to boot.

Less than two weeks after McClellan's promotion, Lincoln was given a taste of his general's surliness and insubordination when he paid a visit to the Young Napoleon at home. Upon his arrival, the president was told that the general was at a wedding, but would be returning shortly. After about half an hour, McClellan did return and was informed by a servant that his commander in chief was waiting for him. McClellan ignored the summons and marched right past the president upstairs to his bedroom. He never came back down.

Lincoln overlooked the egregious insult with typical benevolence, but what he could not ignore was the troubling fact that four months after the Union defeat at Bull Run, McClellan seemed not the least bit inclined to confront the enemy still ensconced so close to the nation's capital.

After months of inertia, and with McClellan down with typhoid, the president at last had enough and called a meeting of the supreme commander's subordinate generals, Irvin McDowell and William B. Franklin. Lincoln told them he was "greatly disturbed by the state of affairs." He then famously suggested that if General McClellan did not want to use the army, he "would like to borrow it, provided he could see how it could be made to do something."

Suspicious about what might be going on behind his back, McClellan roused himself out of his sickbed and attended the next meeting at the Executive Mansion. But he wasn't about to share his war plans with "the gorilla"—one of his pet names for the president.

At the meeting, Quartermaster Montgomery Meigs implored McClellan to share his plans with his commander in chief, but McClellan refused, claiming they would be front-page news if he did so.

Instead, McClellan opted to blab his war plans the next day—to the *New York Herald*. And by the time he was relieved of his new position as supreme commander in March 1862, the Young Napoleon *still* hadn't made a move.

Army + Artillery vs. Emus:
And the Winner Is...

The enemy was formidable—20,000 strong, each standing six feet tall, proudly plumed, with fierce reddish brown eyes, and talons that could gut a man with a single swipe. But the farmers of the Campion district of Perth, Australia—most of them battle-hardened veterans of World War I—believed that their feathered foes, whose great numbers were wiping out their wheat crops, could easily be subdued with that most fearsome weapon of the day, the machine gun. Faced with ruin, the farmers appealed to the Australian defense minister, Sir George Pearce, who promptly assigned Maj. G. P. W. Meredith of the Seventh Heavy Battery of the Royal Australian Artillery to lead a pair of soldiers in the military assault against the massive birds. And, on November 2, 1932, what became known as the Great Emu War began.

From the beginning, the flightless avian army proved superior warriors—particularly with their evasive tactics and apparent indestructibility. At the sound of machine-gun spray, the horde of birds immediately scattered into smaller groups, which made them harder to hit, while their jaunty gait almost seemed a taunt to their pursuers. Those animals that were struck kept running, as if the bullets had no effect on them. Only a few were killed.

On the third day of the conflict, Meredith and his men set up an ambush near a fence. But as a large group of emus came within firing range, the machine gun jammed after a few rounds and most escaped. With mounting frustration, Meredith next ordered a machine gun placed on the roof of a truck. But the infernal creatures outran the vehicle. Plus, the truck jostled so much that the gunner was barely able to get off a shot anyway. They were losing the war to a bunch of birds, and after less than a week were forced to withdraw. Hostilities resumed briefly the next week, but with no better results. Hundreds of thousands of rounds had been fired in the conflict, with only a relative few emu casualties.

"If we had a military division with the bullet-carrying capacity of these birds, it would face any army in the world," Meredith later remarked. "They could face machine guns with the invulnerability of tanks."*

NOVEMBER 3, 1988

Lie Down With Dogs, Get Up With a Bloody Nose

Ersatz journalist Geraldo Rivera had an unerring nose for sensationalism, which, ironically, was smashed in a broadcast brawl. Following the laughably anticlimactic opening of Al Capone's vault (see April 21), Rivera was given his own television program, in which human freaks were showcased for ratings. "Men in Lace Panties and the Women Who Love Them" was one

---

* *Though the military professionals lost the Great Emu War, local farmers were more successful in the ensuing years, when they culled tens of thousands of the birds with government-provided ammunition.*

illustrative episode of the trashy spectacle, but at least lingerie couldn't hurt Rivera. Racist skinheads, on the other hand, could. And when Rivera invited these toxic guests on to confront civil rights leader Roy Innis on November 3, 1988, mayhem not surprisingly ensued. When Rivera leaped into the melee and scuffled with one of the white supremacists—or "roaches," as he called the ratings-boosting racists with faux indignation—another hit him in the shoulder with a chair and then punched him in the face, breaking his nose in two places.

Perhaps the host was just lucky he hadn't become possessed during the previous episode of *Geraldo:* "Devil Worship: Exposing Satan's Underground."

NOVEMBER 4, 1979

After the Kennedy Interview, Whose Name Was Mud?

It's been called the interview that killed Ted Kennedy's candidacy for president. In the fall of 1979, the Massachusetts senator sat down for several interviews with Roger Mudd of CBS News and proceeded to babble his way out of contention—even before he formally declared his intention to run.

"Senator, why do you want to be president?" Mudd asked during the television special, *Teddy,* which aired on November 4. Kennedy was apparently befuddled by the simple question "Well I'm . . . ah . . . were I to . . . to make the . . . ah . . . the announcement and to run . . ." the soon-to-be candidate stammered, before launching into a rambling, incoherent monologue that made it seem as if he'd never seriously considered the essential question before.

Kennedy appeared equally at sea, and visibly agitated, after Mudd asked him if he had anything more illuminating to say about the

infamous Chappaquiddick incident of a decade before. For the few
who don't know the story, he had driven his car off a narrow bridge,
into the water, and escaped safely back to his hotel room, leaving
his young passenger, Mary Jo Kopechne, trapped in the submerged
vehicle, to drown. It took nearly ten hours for him to call the police:

"Oh, there's . . . the problem is . . . from that night . . . I found the
conduct, the er, ah, er, the behavior almost beyond belief myself. I
mean that's why it has been . . . but I think that's . . . that's . . . that's
the way it was. That . . . that happens to be the way it was. Now
I find it as I have stated that I have . . . that the conduct that . . .
that evening in . . . in this as a result of the impact of the accident
of the . . . and the sense of loss, the sense of hope and the . . . and
the sense of tragedy and the whole set of . . . circumstances, that
the er, ah, behavior was inexplicable."

Two months after the television debacle, for which he was duly
excoriated in the press and elsewhere, Kennedy became the third
member of his famous family to officially seek the White House.
He lost the Democratic primary to the incumbent president,
Jimmy Carter, however, and three decades after the fact, his feelings against Roger Mudd were apparently still raw.

In his posthumously published memoir, *True Compass,* Kennedy
suggested that the interview had been an ambush; that he had
done it as a personal favor to Mudd, who was then in contention
to succeed Walter Cronkite as the anchor of CBS News, and that
he had expected his participation to be limited to a puff piece on
his mother, as well as the Kennedy family's long relationship with
sailing and the sea off Cape Cod. "I should have had my political
antennae up," he wrote. "In retrospect, it is almost inconceivable
to me that I did not."

Mudd, however, vehemently disputed Kennedy's account in a
letter to *The New York Times,* calling it "a complete fabrication."
The parameters of the interview were clear from the beginning,
Mudd insisted, and neither Rose Kennedy nor the sea was ever
considered to be the subject. "I remain mystified, perplexed,

angered, and saddened that the senator would have endorsed such a false account in what amounted to his last testament."

Slimed With Orange: No Dutch Treat for James II

James II might have taken a clue from the decapitation of his father, Charles I, that the English didn't take kindly to autocratic behavior by their monarchs. But, alas, that sharp lesson was lost on the king, and after more than three years of high-handed rule, his subjects had had quite enough. In fact, to rid themselves of their obstinate sovereign, they went so far as to actually invite an invasion from Holland.

It was bad enough for James that his own nephew, William of Orange, led the massive Dutch force that landed in England on November 5, 1688. But it was so much worse that William was also married to the king's daughter Mary.

"I easily believe you are embarrassed how to write me, now that the unjust design of the Prince of Orange is so public," James wrote to his daughter in Holland before the arrival of William's armada. "And though I know you are a good wife, and ought to be so, yet for the same reason I must believe you will be still as good a daughter to a father that has always loved you so tenderly, and that has never done the least thing to make you doubt it . . . I shall say no more, and believe you very uneasy all this time, for the concern you must have for a husband and a father. You shall find me kind to you, if you desire it."

Mary never bothered to respond.

Meanwhile, the king declined to confront his nephew on the battlefield, and instead fled back to London, where he was

Sir Peter Lely's rendering of James II with his double-crossing daughters, Mary and Anne

horrified to learn that his younger daughter, Anne, had defected to the enemy. "God help me!" he cried. "My own children have deserted me."

At least James was spared the knowledge that Anne had written William of Orange on the eve of his invasion, wishing her brother-in-law "good success in this so just an undertaking." Or that she had greeted his arrival in a dress festooned with orange ribbons.

The betrayed king was gone by then, escaping to exile in France while his nephew and daughter were jointly crowned in England as the co-monarchs William III and Mary II. As for Anne, who would also one day rule, her father's ignoble flight apparently had little effect. According to one of her maternal uncles, the Earl of Clarendon, "She was not one jot moved."

Dick Morris's Clouded Crystal Ball

"Yup. That's right. A landslide for Romney approaching the magnitude of Obama's against McCain. That's my prediction."

—*Dick Morris,* The Hill

"No single human made as many wrong, botched, bogus, and stupid predictions about the 2012 election as Dick Morris," Dave Weigel wrote in *Slate*—a statistically unverifiable assertion, but a delightfully pointed one nevertheless. The self-proclaimed political "insider" and unrelenting gasbag capped off his erroneous year with a foolhardy declaration in an Election Day column for *The Hill* published on November 6.

The pudgy pundit wrote with smug satisfaction: "On Sunday, we changed our clocks. On Tuesday, we'll change our president . . . More about what Mitt [Romney] did right in my post-election column on Thursday. But for now, let's celebrate the new president we are about to elect."

(For an apt metaphor of the post-election fallout for Morris, see November 12.)

Hail to the Chaff: A String of Loser Presidents

On November 7, 1848, Zachary Taylor was elected the nation's 12th chief executive—launching an unprecedented succession of *really* bad presidents, men whom historians consistently rank among the ten worst. Taylor, who died in office before he could do *too* much damage, was succeeded by the equally incompetent Millard Fillmore, champion of the calamitous Compromise of 1850. Then there was Franklin Pierce, a chronic drinker mocked by his political adversaries as "the hero of many a well-fought bottle." Rounding out this quartet of presidential duds was James Buchanan, who sat idly by as the nation careened toward civil war. Mercifully, Abraham Lincoln replaced him, thus ending the disastrous White House losers streak—albeit only briefly. Alas, Honest Abe was immediately followed by two more historic bottom dwellers: Andrew Johnson (see February 24) and Civil War hero turned presidential flop Ulysses S. Grant (see October 28 and December 17).

NOVEMBER 8, 1519

Beware of Spaniards Bearing Greed

The Spanish conquistador Hernán Cortés had already left a bloody trail of corpses behind him as he marauded through Mexico, and his smug sense of cultural superiority, demonstrated at every opportunity, was matched only by his insatiable greed for gold.* Yet despite all that, the Aztec ruler Moctezuma II allowed Cortés inside the capital of Tenochtitlan for some reason when the conquistador came calling on November 8, 1519.

One contemporary recorded the excitement of Cortés and his men when they were given gifts of gold: "[They] appeared to smile, to rejoice exceedingly. Like monkeys, they seized upon the gold. It was as if then they were satisfied, sated and gladdened. For in truth they thirsted mightily for gold, they stuffed themselves with it, and starved and lusted for it like pigs. They went about moving the golden streamer back and forth, and showed it to one another all the while babbling."

Tradition has it that Moctezuma believed his visitor was the human incarnation of the great god Quetzalcoatl, although many historians now dispute that. Whatever the reason the gates were opened, it was a colossal blunder. Cortés accepted the king's gracious hospitality, as well as his lavish gifts (except the women proffered; *that* would have been a sin). Then, as a thank-you, he made his host a prisoner in his own palace. Less than eight months later, Moctezuma II was dead,* with the Aztec Empire quickly to follow.

NOVEMBER 9, 2001

Well, **** a Duck!

S cientific journals are not usually known for their general interest reporting ("Reproductive Sequences of the Sumatran Sand Flea" . . . Anyone?) But *Deinsea,* the journal of the Rotterdam Natural History Museum, took esoteric to a whole new (and, some might say, disturbing) level on November 9, 2001, when it subjected readers to the published article "The first case of homosexual necrophilia in the mallard *Anas platyrhynchos* (Aves: Anatidae)."

C. W. Moeliker, a scientist at the museum, related in the piece how six years earlier he had witnessed a dead male mallard duck—referred to clinically throughout as "NMR 9997-00232"—being repeatedly raped by another male mallard, "with great force." The unfortunate NMR 9997-00232 had apparently crashed into one of the museum's reflective windows and dropped dead as a result. Within moments, his companion swooped on top of the corpse and did his business.

Accounts vary as to how Moctezuma died. The Spanish chroniclers say he was killed by his own people, enraged by his easy capitulation. Native reports said it was Cortés.

"Rather startled," Moeliker wrote, "I watched this scene from close quarters behind the window until 19.10 h during which time (75 minutes!) I made some photographs and the mallard almost continuously copulated his dead congener. He dismounted only twice, stayed near the dead duck and picked the neck and the side of the head before mounting again. The first break (at 18.29 h) lasted three minutes and the second break (at 18.45 h) lasted less than a minute."

NOVEMBER 10, 1879

Western Union STOP You Blew It STOP: A Bad Call on the Telephone

Western Union, as it became known, was *the* communications behemoth in the years following the Civil War—"the nervous system of commerce," as William Orton, president of the mighty telegraph company, once crowed. Supremely confident in its status as one of the world's richest and most powerful corporations, officials at Western Union dismissed the recently patented telephone as a "toy" when Alexander Graham Bell and his associates approached them in the fall of 1876 with an offer to sell it outright for $100,000.

"The idea is idiotic on the face of it," an internal Western Union memo reportedly read.* "Furthermore, why would any person want to use this ungainly and impractical device when he can send

---

* *Some historians question whether such a memo actually existed, but the essence of the message Western Union sent to Bell and his associates was unmistakable: no deal.*

a messenger to the telegraph office and have a clear written message sent to any large city in the United States?"

The rejection stung, but as Bell's assistant Thomas Watson later noted, it turned out to be "another piece of good fortune for us all. Two years later those same patents could not have been bought for twenty-five million dollars."

Watson was right, as Western Union quickly came to realize and regret. But it was too late. In a futile gesture of breathtakingly bad sportsmanship, the company tried to challenge Bell's patent in a most unscrupulous manner: by joining forces with Elisha Gray, the loser in an earlier telephone patent race with Bell, and even Thomas Edison, who had made some significant improvements on the telephone transmitter. Together, they claimed Bell had in essence stolen the idea for the telephone, and began marketing their own system. "The more fame a man gets for an invention, the more does he become a target for the world to shoot at," Bell lamented in a letter to his wife.

The inventor was so disgusted by the whole ugly business that he was ready to walk away. But the partners with whom he formed the Bell Telephone Company were by no means prepared to concede. Instead, they sued Western Union for patent violations, and eventually persuaded Bell to join the battle. His reluctant preliminary statement to the court was filed just in time, and after invigorating himself for the fight, he went on to serve as a remarkably effective witness. Western Union never stood a chance.

On November 10, 1879, the company agreed to withdraw from the telephone business altogether. Today it limps along as a wire transfer and money order business. The patent issued to Bell, on the other hand, emerged as one of the most valuable ever issued in U.S. history.

NOVEMBER 11, 1861

The "Mere Woman's" Elegant— but Deadly—Efficiency

Death came with a delicate touch when Empress Dowager Cixi completed her unlikely rise from a low-ranking imperial concubine to the virtual ruler of China as regent for her young son on November 11, 1861. Having staged a bloodless coup against the Board of Regents the late emperor had put in place to guide the realm, Cixi now had to dispose of them. For having essentially stood in her way, the men were charged with treason—the penalty for which was the fearsome Death by a Thousand Cuts, which, as the name suggests, was very slow and torturous. But the dowager empress was feeling benevolent and amended the sentences with a more feminine touch. Instead of being sliced and diced to death, the regents' ringleader was quickly decapitated. He howled at the scene of his demise, not out of pain, for he had been spared that, but only with regret that he had underestimated "this mere woman." Two of the other fallen regents were each sent a long, white silk scarf, with a sweet message to hang themselves in private, without all the muss and fuss of a public execution. And, with that, the minimally invasive, but no less lethal, work was done.

They Couldn't Leave
Whale Enough . . .

The lot of the spectator is not always an easy one. Consider those poor souls bopped on the head by errant baseballs, run over at racetracks, singed in firework spectacles, or, in the case of ancient Rome, occasionally dragged from their arena seats by mad emperors and fed to wild beasts. But on November 12, 1970, a group of gawkers in Oregon experienced something unique—and most unsavory—when they were hit head-on with bloody bits of blubber, bone, and guts from an exploded sperm whale.

The eight-ton, 45-foot-long cetacean had washed up on a Pacific Ocean beach just south of Florence, Oregon, and soon enough the putrid smell wafting from the whale carcass became overwhelming. It fell to the state Highway Division to do something about it. But what? Burying the remains on the beach was not deemed an option because the tides would gradually uncover them. So it was decided to simply blow the rotting behemoth to smithereens and let the seagulls feast on the remnants—a good idea, in theory.

Assistant district engineer George Thornton was put in charge of the operation. "Well, I'm confident that it'll work," he told Paul Linnman, a reporter for KATU-TV in Portland. "The only thing is we're not sure how much explosives it'll take to disintegrate this thing." Ah, and therein lay the problem. Thornton, a novice at explosives, figured a half ton of dynamite would do the trick.

Walter Umenhofer, a businessman traveling through the area, recognized Thornton's miscalculation immediately. Umenhofer had received explosives training during his service in World War II, and he knew Thornton should use either a lot less dynamite, so that the whale would just be pushed out to sea, or a whole lot more, so that it would be torn into tiny pieces. According to Umenhofer, Thornton brushed off his warning.

"The guy says, 'Anyway, I'm gonna have everyone on top of those dunes far away,'" Umenhofer told reporter Wayne Freedman of San Francisco TV station KGO in an interview 25 years later. "I says, 'Yeah, I'm gonna be the furtherest SOB down that way!'" Unfortunately, though, Umenhofer didn't move his brand-new Oldsmobile 88 Regency.*

Thornton then detonated the half ton of dynamite that had been shoved in and around the dead whale's remains. "Suddenly, it just happened," Florence local Jim "Skip" Curtis recalled to Dave Masko, a blogger for the Eugene *Examiner*. "The whale's body just imploded, and there was this 100-foot-high column of sand and smoke. Then I remember screaming as everyone ducked for cover as pounds and pounds of yucky guts and bones and chunks of the whale went just about everywhere. It was gross and so sad at the same time."

As onlookers peeled rancid whale remnants out of their hair and off their clothes, Umenhofer went back to his new car to find it had been hit by a huge chunk of blubber and ruined. "I don't want that car," he said days later. "It still stinks of the whale. I went down to the shop the other day to get something out of the glove box, and the car was covered with a tarp because it smelled so bad."

The Highway Division's insurance eventually covered Umenhofer's loss. But George Thornton's self-esteem was another matter. Years after the botched explosion he was still in deep denial about what had happened. Revisiting the event he had first covered decades earlier, Paul Linnman asked Thornton what had gone wrong. His response: "What do you mean, 'What went wrong?'"

---

* He had just purchased the car—and this is absolutely true—under a "Get a Whale of a Deal on a New Oldsmobile" promotion.

NOVEMBER 13, 2013

Oops, Our Bad. Here's Your Head.

The band of Syrian terrorists, bent on avenging themselves on the Shiite sect of President Bashar al-Assad, triumphantly held aloft the severed head of Mohammed Fares Maroush on November 13, 2013. "They [the Shia] will come and rape the men before the women, that's what these infidels will do," one of the jihadists, linked to al Qaeda, crowed before the gathered crowd. "God make us victorious over them!" There was just one problem with the ghoulish demonstration: They had accidentally decapitated one of their own.

Maroush had been injured fighting beside his fellow rebels against the Assad regime, but he inexplicably began muttering Shiite phrases while under anesthesia in the hospital. His Sunni killers then did what only came naturally to religious fanatics. They cut off his head. In the aftermath of the mix-up, the rebel spokesman Omar al-Qahtani made a plea for forgiveness on Twitter: "O respectful readers, I remind you that this mistake happens and repeats itself in the battlefields and in Jihad spots as people of Jihad do know."

NOVEMBER 14, 1908

The Kaiser's Tutu Sorry Day

It was the last thing Kaiser Wilhelm II needed after a gay sex scandal had already embroiled not only the highest echelons of imperial Germany but also the sovereign himself. On November 14, 1908, Dietrich Graf von Hülsen-Haeseler, chief of the German Imperial Military Cabinet, dropped dead at a private party for the kaiser while performing a balletic *pas seul,* or solo dance—in a tutu.

Homosexuality had long been an unmentionable subject in Germany, one that the press avoided assiduously—until 1906, that is, when a journalist by the name of Maximilian Harden launched a campaign to expose the sexual proclivities of the kaiser's inner circle. And much of his scoop was provided by none other than Otto von Bismarck, the "Iron Chancellor," who, like Harden, had vigorously opposed Wilhelm II's policies and was dismissed by the kaiser as a result. In a letter to his son, Bismarck wrote of the relationship the kaiser enjoyed with his devoted friend Philip Frederick Alexander, Prince of Eulenburg and Hertefeld—the details of which could "not be confided to paper."

Harden was wise enough to know that any compromising insinuations about the monarch's personal life with Eulenburg would be foolhardy, so he opted to discredit Wilhelm by disclosing instead the homosexual relationship between Eulenburg and the kaiser's adjunct, Count Kuno von Moltke—or "Sweetie," as Harden referred to him—the military commander of Berlin. In so doing, historian Alexandria Richie wrote, Harden "broke one of the most sacred taboos in imperial Germany."

Kaiser Wilhelm sought to insulate himself from the emerging scandal by distancing himself from his loyal friend Eulenburg and dismissing Moltke. But neither man was prepared to slink away with his reputation so thoroughly shredded. What resulted was a flurry of libel suits, filled with salacious details, that sent the press into an unprecedented feeding frenzy.

"German newspapers were full of the story," wrote historian James Steakley, "and it dominated their headlines for months; an anti-homosexual witch-hunt of unparalleled proportions was unleashed. Nearly every high government official and military officer was suspected or accused of homosexuality." A number committed suicide in the face of such shame; Wilhelm II suffered a nervous breakdown.

"It has been a very difficult year which has caused me an infinite amount of worry," the kaiser wrote in December 1907. "A trusted group of friends was suddenly broken up through . . . insolence, slander and lying. To see the names of one's friends dragged through the gutters of Europe without being able or entitled to help is terrible."

Then, just as the scandal seemed to be simmering down, Dietrich Graf von Hülsen-Haeseler performed his fatal pirouette. Worse, rigor mortis set in before he could easily be extricated from his tutu.

NOVEMBER 15, 1986

No Splainin' Lucy's Final Try

It was a sad coda to a brilliant career, when poor Lucy came to believe no one loved her anymore. On November 15, 1986, after only eight episodes, ABC ran its last episode of *Life With Lucy*, Lucille Ball's attempted return to sitcom glory. Five more episodes of forced zaniness had been filmed, but the show was such an abysmal failure, pounced on by critics and shunned by viewers, that the network mercifully pulled it before the 75-year-old comedy legend suffered any further humiliation. Ball reportedly took to her bed in despair, thoroughly convinced she had been abandoned by her legion of fans—and never quite reconciled to the fact that her better days, permanently enshrined on film, would endear her to the world forever.

NOVEMBER 16, 1849

Ready ... Aim ... Dostoyevsky's Cold Day in Hell

Tsar Nicholas I of Russia had a surprise in store for Fyodor Dostoyevsky, a diabolical twist with just one intent: to traumatize. On November 16, 1849, the writer and a group of fellow intellectuals were condemned to the firing squad for their participation in activities the repressive Russian state government considered subversive. For well over a month, the specter of death loomed implacably. Then, on the appointed day, the condemned were taken to the place of execution at St. Petersburg's frigid Semenovsky Square, where three stakes had been erected for the occasion.

"The horrible, immeasurably horrible minutes of awaiting death began," Dostoyevsky wrote. "It was cold, so terribly cold. They removed not only our coats, but our jackets. And it was minus twenty degrees."

As Dostoyevsky and the others stood shivering upon a black-draped scaffold awaiting their fate, the men of the first group were tied to the stakes and hoods placed over their heads. "We were taken in threes," the writer recalled. "I was in the second group. I had no more than a minute left to live." Yet just as the firing squad raised their rifles and took aim, a sudden reprieve came from the tsar. Rather than a lethal lesson in the perils of independent thought, it was a cruel charade with the same message, orchestrated by Tsar Nicholas himself.

Ralph Bruce's painting shows Dostoyevsky's 11th-hour reprieve.

"I received the news of the termination of the execution dully," Dostoyevsky remembered. "There was no joy at returning to the living. People around me were shouting and making noise. But I didn't care. I had already lived through the worst. Yes, the very worst. Wretched Grigoryev went mad . . . How did the others survive? I don't know. We didn't even catch cold."

It was only after being returned to his prison cell that Dostoyevsky came to fully embrace the joy of having his life restored— even though he now faced four years of hard labor in Siberia, followed by a forced induction into the army. He was alive. And Russian literature would be far richer for it—with *Crime and Punishment, The Brothers Karamazov,* and other classics yet to be written.

NOVEMBER 17, 1968

The Heidi Game: NBC's Fumble
of the Century

How in the world could anyone hate Heidi? Well, with one ill-timed flick of the switch, NBC television managed to turn millions against the plucky Swiss miss on November 17, 1968. Football fans were tuned in to one of the most exciting games of the season—an epic clash between the New York Jets and the Oakland Raiders, during which the two teams had traded the lead eight times. With little more than a minute left to play, the Jets kicked a 26-yard field goal that gave them a 32-29 lead. What happened next was one of the most astonishing climaxes in football history: Oakland managed to score twice in nine seconds to win the game 43-32. But no one saw it. Instead, at precisely 7 p.m. (EST) Heidi began her wholesome romp through the Alps in NBC's remake of Johanna Spyri's classic children's story.

Football fans were incandescent with rage, both at the orphaned little heroine on their television screens and the stupid network execs who put her there. "Men who wouldn't get out of their chairs in an earthquake rushed to the phone to scream obscenities at the man responsible for cutting off the game," wrote humor columnist Art Buchwald.

That man happened to be NBC programmer Dick Cline, who was acting on a previous order from his bosses at NBC that the heavily promoted *Heidi* must begin as scheduled. Cline, however, was unaware that the executives had changed their minds during the riveting fourth quarter of the game: Because of jammed phone lines, he couldn't be reached in time. "I waited and waited," he said later, "and I heard nothing. We came up to that magic hour and I thought, 'Well, I haven't been given any counter-order so I've got to do what we agreed to do.'"

Compounding the colossal blunder, NBC ran a crawl announcing the stunning Raiders turnaround during a dramatic moment in the film when Heidi's paralyzed cousin Klara tumbles out of her wheelchair and tries to walk. "The football fans were indignant when they saw what they had missed," observed sportswriter Jack Clary. "The *Heidi* audience was peeved at having an ambulatory football score intrude on one of the story's more touching moments. Short of pre-empting *Heidi* for a skin flick, NBC could not have managed to alienate more viewers that evening."

NOVEMBER 18, 1985

Even Worse Than *Heidi:*

Joe Theismann's Sick Sack Crack

For a game as rough as football, an injury has to be spectacular for responders to an ESPN poll to decree it the most shocking

November

moment in NFL history. (The so-called Heidi Bowl made the list as well.) And Joe Theismann's certainly was: a horrific moment on November 18, 1985, when millions of *Monday Night Football* viewers saw the career of the Washington Redskins quarterback end with a grotesque, bone-protruding leg fracture. In what *The Washington Post* dubbed "The Hit That No One Who Saw It Can Ever Forget," Theismann went down in a heap after being sacked by New York Giants linebacker Lawrence Taylor, his leg twisted sideways and pinned beneath him. Then, with a pile-on, came the cringe-inducing snap. "When I heard a crack, it went right through me," Taylor said after the game. "It felt like it happened to me. It made me sick."*

NOVEMBER 19, 1919

Woodrow Wilson, Out of His League

P resident Woodrow Wilson had enough trouble herding three recalcitrant, often self-interested allies (France, Britain, and Italy) to a peace agreement that reflected his own grand ideals in the wake of World War I. Yet no matter how torturous the peace process had been in Paris, it was but a frolic compared with the fierce resistance Wilson met when he returned home with his hard-won settlement—which would be shot down by the U.S. Senate on November 19, 1919.

The compound leg fracture was so nauseatingly memorable that, when writing about another gruesome football injury—the incident in 1978 when Chicago Bears cornerback Virgil Livers took a devastating knee to the gonads, literally exploding one of them—ESPN columnist David Fleming described Livers as "the Joe Theismann of testicle trauma."

The Treaty of Versailles, especially its provision for a League of Nations, was precious to Wilson—"one of the greatest documents of human history," he called it—reflecting as it did his grand (some said idealistic) vision for a new world order, where nations in harmonious union would prevent another senseless war like the one just concluded. And the president advocated for his treaty with uncompromising, near-messianic zeal, at one point prompting French prime minister Georges Clemenceau to refer to him contemptuously as "Jesus Christ."

The problem was that Woodrow Wilson fell short of the divine when it came to dealing with his political adversaries—particularly Henry Cabot Lodge, the Republican Senate majority leader he personally despised. And the feeling was mutual, as Lodge made clear to his friend and confidant Theodore Roosevelt: "I never expected to hate anyone in politics with the hatred I feel toward Wilson."

Foolishly, Wilson neglected to include Lodge or any of his other Republican opponents in formulating the treaty in Paris, thus dooming it at home. As Franklin D. Roosevelt, then assistant secretary of the Navy, reported at the time: "[Republican party chairman Will] Hayes, Lodge and others made up their mind before they knew anything about the Treaty or the League of Nations that they were going to wreck it whether their consciences demanded it or not."

On July 10, 1919, Wilson went to Capitol Hill to personally deliver the treaty—the first president ever to do so. In a speech to the Senate that day, he asserted that the treaty "constitutes nothing less than a world settlement," with its provision for a League of Nations an essential responsibility for men of good will. "Shall we or any free people hesitate to accept this great duty?" the president said in conclusion. "Dare we reject it and break the heart of the world?"

The answer from the Republicans was a resounding yes. Lodge was especially outspoken about his objections to the League, which he felt obligated the United States to intervene in international quarrels in which it had no interests, and, worse, entirely bypassed Congress. "I have always loved one flag and I cannot share that devotion and give affection to a mongrel banner created for a League," he declared.

With his cherished treaty imperiled, Wilson determined to go on a tour of the West and sell his vision directly to the American people. The president, however, was in no condition to make such an arduous trek. A series of small strokes and other ailments had significantly weakened him, and he was urged by his doctor to stay home.

But on September 3, the president set off on his mission, one he considered the most important of his life. The tour proved an impressive success, with Wilson greeted by enthusiastic crowds in every city and strong indications that the treaty's fortunes were tilting his way. But it took a heavy toll. With only a few stops left to go, the president's health finally betrayed him and he was forced to return to Washington. "This is the greatest disappointment of my life," he told his doctor. Soon after, he suffered a massive, debilitating stroke.

As Wilson was all but paralyzed, so were the affairs of the nation—and, most important, the fate of the treaty. Lodge sensed a new opportunity to either gut it with a number of his reservations, which he knew the one-track-minded president would never accept, or kill it altogether.

On November 19, for the first time in its history, the Senate voted against a peace treaty—both with the Lodge reservations included and without. The following March, another vote was held with the same result. As far as the United States was concerned, the League of Nations was dead. Four years later, so was its unflagging champion.

When the president's widow learned that Henry Cabot Lodge was planning to represent the Senate Foreign Relations Committee at his funeral, she sent him a curt note: "Realizing that your presence would be embarrassing to you and unwelcome to me, I write to request that you do not attend."

NOVEMBER 20, 1992

When She Reigns, It Pours: Adding Inferno to Injury at Windsor Castle

The symbolism was unmistakable as Windsor Castle erupted in flames on November 20, 1992. Since it was first constructed by William the Conqueror late in the 11th century (and continuously improved by subsequent sovereigns), the massive stone structure, high on a hilltop, stood as the physical embodiment of the British monarchy —a continuous residence of kings and queens for nearly a millennium, and the very place from which the current royal family drew its name and called home. Now the castle's imminent demise seemed to coincide with the declining fortunes of Queen Elizabeth II, whose 40-year reign had been rocked in the months preceding the inferno by endless scandals in her family—most notably the final breakdown of her eldest son and heir's marriage to Diana, Princess of Wales.

The fire apparently started in the Queen's Private Chapel, when a heat lamp came into contact with some curtains. It then spread with astonishing speed to other rooms, more than 100 in all, many of them historically significant. The grim-faced queen was captured on film as she tried to help rescue some of the castle's priceless works of art, as scores of firefighters valiantly fought the relentless blaze. When it was all over later that night, huge swaths of Windsor Castle lay in ruins.*

---

* *There were some bright spots in this otherwise dismal day. Fortuitously, some of the castle's most valuable art had been removed the day before in preparation for extensive electrical work. Only a few pieces were destroyed, including Sir William Beechey's equestrian portrait "King George III at Review," which was too large to remove from its frame. And though fire and water took their toll, the castle itself stood sturdy and was restored by expert craftsmen within five years.*

Four days later, Queen Elizabeth, her voice raspy from a cold, spoke at London's ancient Guildhall. "Nineteen ninety-two is not a year on which I shall look back with undiluted pleasure," she said with characteristic understatement. "In the words of one of my more sympathetic correspondents, it has turned out to be an *annus horribilis*."

NOVEMBER 21, 1916

Franz Josef: The Final Blow to a Cursed Reign

F ew monarchs in history reigned as long as Austria's Franz Josef, or endured quite as much heartache. During his nearly seven-decade rule, the emperor saw his wife, Elisabeth, stabbed to death by an anarchist; his son, Rudolf, commit suicide with his mistress in a lurid sex scandal; his brother Maximilian, the puppet emperor of Mexico, executed by firing squad (see June 19); his nephew Franz Ferdinand assassinated in Sarajevo (see June 28); and countless other relatives bring shame upon the glorious House of Habsburg—including another brother, Ludwig Viktor, a flamboyant cross-dresser known as Lutziwutzi, whose public shenanigans forced the emperor to finally banish him from Vienna, along with his nephew Otto, a syphilitic prone to public nudity.

Longevity alone would explain at least some of the emperor's seemingly endless stream of bad days, but a supposed curse by a Countess Karolyi, whose son was executed during the Hungarian uprising at the beginning at Franz Josef's reign, may have made things that much worse. "May heaven and hell blast your happiness," the countess reportedly shrieked at the young sovereign at a state ball in Vienna; "may your family be exterminated; may you be smitten in the persons of those you love best; may your children be brought to ruin and your life wrecked; and yet may you live on in lonely, unbroken, horrible grief, to tremble when you recall the name of Karolyi!"

So effective was the countess's curse—or maybe it was just cruel fate—that even in death poor Franz Josef couldn't catch a break. After succumbing to pneumonia on November 21, 1916, at age 86, the emperor was embalmed using a newfangled technique that distorted his features to such an extent that his coffin had to be kept closed—depriving his grieving subjects of one last look at the sovereign who had ruled over them for so many years, and perhaps providing Countess Karolyi with her final triumph.*

NOVEMBER 22, 1963

RFK to LBJ: You're No JFK

"Do it. President Kennedy isn't president anymore. I am!"

—*Lyndon B. Johnson, barking an order to Robert F. Kennedy*

Attorney General Robert F. Kennedy had to contend not only with the loss of his beloved brother but with a new boss he thoroughly despised, Lyndon B. Johnson. "This man," Kennedy said of the new president after the assassination of John F. Kennedy on November 22, 1963, "is mean, bitter, vicious—an animal in many ways." For his own part, Johnson thought no more highly

---

* Despite all his troubles, death did at least spare Franz Josef from having to witness the fall of the Austro-Hungarian monarchy two years later in the wake of World War I.

of Kennedy, whom he referred to as a "snot-nosed little son-of-a-bitch" (among his more generous epithets). The mutual animosity between the two men resulted in Kennedy's resignation as attorney general and his decision to oppose Johnson as the Democratic nominee for president.*

NOVEMBER 23, 1921

Adventures in Hypocrisy, Part III: Prohibition? I'll Drink to That!

With Prohibition now the law of the land, Congress closed a lingering loophole with the Willis-Campbell Act, which strictly limited the amount of liquor that physicians could prescribe for medical purposes. On November 23, 1921, President Warren G. Harding signed the bill—no doubt with a chuckle, as the man ultimately charged with enforcing Prohibition kept the White House cabinets filled with intoxicating "medicine," always at the ready for the enjoyment of the president and his corrupt, poker-playing pals.

Alice Roosevelt Longworth, the tart-tongued daughter of President Theodore Roosevelt, described one evening as a guest in the Harding White House: "The

---

* *Johnson ultimately declined to run, and Kennedy was assassinated before securing the nomination.*

study was filled with cronies . . . trays with bottles containing every imaginable brand of whiskey stood about, cards and poker chips ready at hand—a general atmosphere of waistcoats unbuttoned, feet on the desk, and spittoons alongside."

A year after signing the restrictive law, the liquor-swilling president stood before Congress and delivered this breathtakingly hypocritical message: "Let men who are rending the moral fiber of the republic through easy contempt for the prohibition law, because they think it restricts their personal liberty, remember that they set the example and breed a contempt for law which will ultimately destroy the republic."

NOVEMBER 24, 1832

Burning Up Old Hickory: Andrew Jackson's Dixie Nemesis

President Andrew Jackson was not having a good fall. The simmering tension between South Carolina and the U.S. government in late 1832 was mirrored in the deteriorating relationship between Jackson and his own vice president, John C. Calhoun, a native son of the Palmetto State. The issue that divided the two men had profound implications for the future of the young republic. It concerned whether an individual state had the right to disregard, or nullify, a federal law. Calhoun sincerely believed the state had every right to reject what it found odious, and, if it came down to it, even to secede. To Jackson, such a concept was tantamount to treason.

At the annual Jefferson Day dinner in 1830, the president raised a toast: "Our federal Union, it must be preserved." To this, Calhoun rejoined with a message of his own: "The Union, next to our liberty, the most dear." And that was just about as congenial as either man ever behaved during the emerging crisis—particularly the notoriously hot-headed president.

And so when a South Carolina convention had the audacity to pass an Ordinance of Nullification on November 24, 1832, Jackson went ballistic. He threatened to hang the nullification leaders as traitors—including Calhoun, who wisely resigned the vice presidency in the immediate aftermath to serve South Carolina in the Senate. Given the president's homicidal history, few doubted his sincerity.*

"The wickedness, madness, and folly of the leaders and the delusions of their followers in the attempt to destroy themselves and our Union has not its parallel in the history of the world," Jackson wrote. "The Union will be preserved." And to that effect, the president was fully prepared to use military force—to "crush the monster in its cradle."

Despite his fury, Jackson was politically astute enough to recognize the delicacy of the situation. If he should act too precipitously, it might ignite a civil war, with other southern states joining South Carolina's rebellion. Therefore, swallowing his indignation, he gently (at least for him) tried to coax the recalcitrant state back to its senses, reminding the people of the blessings of union and the shared perils the young nation had overcome by standing together. Still, he remained firm in his warning that dissent would be crushed—even if it meant spilling the blood of his countrymen.

---

* *In addition to Charles Dickinson (see May 30), the seventh president had taken other men's lives. In 1818, for example, when Jackson was fighting the Seminole in Florida, he ordered the court-martial and summary execution of two British citizens, Alexander Arbuthnot and Richard Ambrister—"unprincipled villains," as the general called them, charged with assisting the Indian enemy. Although a report by the House Committee on Military Affairs condemned the executions of Arbuthnot and Ambrister as unauthorized by any law of the United States and illegal under the laws of war, Jackson escaped censure and remained a hero in the minds of many.*

The crisis was eventually averted by compromise: A hated federal tariff that prompted South Carolina's defiance was modified and the state rescinded its Nullification Ordinance. There would be no civil war—for the time being—yet in spite of the resolution, the president still seethed. Asked on his deathbed his greatest regret, Jackson reportedly replied, "That I didn't hang John C. Calhoun."

NOVEMBER 25, 1970

Guts (Galore) but No Glory: The Misguided Samurai

It had been a while since the first Japanese samurai ritually disemboweled himself in the 12th century. And though the practice, known as seppuku, had largely fallen out of favor eight centuries later, the Nobel-nominated Japanese novelist Yukio Mishima* spectacularly revived it on November 25, 1970. There were just a few hitches, however: The reverence that once would have accompanied such an act of Bushido was decidedly missing this time—as were the skill and precision necessary for a clean dispatch.

The novelist, who had a sideline as a successful film star, had emerged as an ultranationalist determined to revive Japan's pre–World War II glory—with the emperor's divinity restored, the military strong again, and the flaccid constitution imposed upon his country abolished. It was an ambitious agenda, to be sure, but one Mishima pursued with the gusto of a true believer—by attempting a coup. He and a handful of fellow fanatics managed to take over the Defense Ministry—not by storming it, but as a celebrity and his entourage simply waltzing in, swords in hand.

---

* *Pen name of Kimitake Hiraoka*

After tying the stunned commandant to his chair, Mishima stepped outside his office and onto a balcony. There he tried to deliver a rousing speech to the soldiers massed below, but he was drowned out by jeers. Taken aback yet undeterred by the rude reception, Mishima declared, "I am going to shout 'banzai' for the emperor," then went back into the commandant's office to sacrifice himself—samurai-style—for the cause.

Cleanly gutting himself proved problematic, however. Traditionally the task was handled by another samurai, known as a *kaishakunin,* who was on hand to swiftly decapitate his disabled companion at the moment of his agony. That role was left to

Japanese author Yukio Mishima tries to inspire nationalism with a pre-seppuku speech.

Masakatsu Morita. But after several botched attempts to slice off Mishima's head, Morita proved to be a most ineffective kaishakunin. The task was finally completed by Hiroyasu Koga, who then proceeded to behead Morita after his own seppuku.

Alas, the whole spectacle was for naught. As Japanese prime minister Eisaku Sato said of Mishima, "I can only think he went out of his mind."

NOVEMBER 26, 1095 *and* 1648

Unchristian Christianity, Part III: Bloodthirsty Popes

On November 26, 1095, Pope Urban II issued his famous war cry, *"Deus volt,"* or "God wills it," thus launching the first of seven major crusades (and an endless series of historically bad days) against Muslims in the Holy Land. Five and a half centuries later, the Vatican was still beating the war drum—only this time, Christians were being urged to kill Christians in the Thirty Years' War, one of the most destructive conflicts in European history, fought in the midst of the so-called Enlightenment, when some of history's worst acts of human depravity were committed.

Like his predecessor from the Dark Ages, Pope Innocent X considered the war God's work, and he was thus immensely displeased when relative harmony was restored to the devastated continent with the Treaty of Westphalia. Indeed, the Vicar of Christ was so unhappy with the peace compromising his own interests that on November 26, 1648—exactly 553 years after Urban II's call to slaughter—he issued a blistering condemnation of the treaty. It was, he declared, "null, void, invalid, iniquitous, unjust, damnable, reprobate, inane, empty of meaning and effect for all time"—just as Jesus would have wanted.

Whitewash Those Redcoats...
Or Else!

The Birth of a Nation, D. W. Griffith's 1915 film, was a well-crafted, epically racist celebration of the emergence of the Ku Klux Klan after the Civil War. It was such a commercial success—the world's first "blockbuster"—that it inspired Robert Goldstein, who had worked with Griffith on the film, to produce his own historical extravaganza, focused on the Revolutionary War. *The Spirit of '76* contained none of the themes that made *The Birth of a Nation* controversial enough to spark riots in some cities. Goldstein's film was an earnest (some said schmaltzy) re-creation of such all-American episodes as Paul Revere's midnight ride, Valley Forge, and the signing of the Declaration of Independence. There were also depictions of the villainous British, bayoneting babies and dragging away good American girls by the hair to be ravished. And that's where Goldstein and his film ran afoul of the U.S. government, leading to what historian David Hackett Fischer called "one of the strangest acts of federal tyranny in American history."

The United States was just entering World War I when, in May 1917, *The Spirit of '76* was first screened in Chicago. The debut of the film, with its patriotic, apple-pie themes, seemed perfectly timed. The authorities thought otherwise, however. Goldstein was ordered to cut the scenes of British atrocities lest they inflame the public at a time when the country was fighting in Europe by Britain's side. The producer complied, but when the film premiered in Los Angeles on November 27, the excised scenes had been restored. Goldstein was arrested and charged under the recently passed, broad-sweeping Espionage Act. His stilted representations of British atrocities—ones committed almost a century and a half earlier—essentially made him an enemy of the state. For that Goldstein was sentenced to ten years in prison (a sentence later upheld on appeal), was fined heavily, and had his film confiscated without compensation.

Although Goldstein was released from prison after three years, he was entirely ruined. "I am merely a lone man suffering a great wrong for no reason whatever, can you refuse to help me obtain justice?" he wrote to the Academy of Motion Picture Arts and Sciences in 1927. "I have never done the slightest thing to warrant this persecution and prejudice against me, which denies the very right to exist. What, in the name of common sense, can be the reason for such wanton injustice?"

NOVEMBER 28, 2000

Big Tobacco: We're Basically National Heroes, See

Philip Morris executives got a big boost from the November 28, 2000, report the giant cigarette manufacturer had commissioned from Arthur D. Little International, Inc. It turned out that smoking in the Czech Republic, where the study was focused, actually had "positive effects" on that nation's economy. There was the revenue from excise and other taxes on cigarettes before smokers met their demise, and, as the consulting firm reported, "health-care cost savings due to early mortality." When those savings were weighed against the costs of treating smoking-related illnesses, and the lost taxes no longer paid by dead smokers, the Czech Republic actually came out ahead, the report concluded—to the tune of about $147 million.

Certainly Philip Morris, manufacturer of about 80 percent of the cigarettes smoked in the Czech Republic, couldn't keep such great news to itself and widely disseminated the Little report in the subject country. "This is an economic-impact study, no more, no less," Robert Kaplan, a spokesman for Philip Morris's international tobacco unit, told *The Wall Street Journal.* "We're not trying to suggest that there would be a benefit to society from the diseases related to smoking."

No, of course not.

NOVEMBER 29, 1968

Ono You Didn't!

In November 1968, the Beatles released their classic, eponymously titled double album—the one noted for its entirely white cover. Would that John Lennon and his then paramour Yoko Ono had opted for a similarly stark design for their own effort, *Unfinished Music No. 1: Two Virgins,* which was unleashed on an unsuspecting public the very same month. That way, the only horror would have been the relentless sounds of Yoko screeching over John's experimental instrumentation. But the couple went for an album cover they considered as avant-garde as their "music": a shudder-inducing, full frontal nude photograph of themselves, with another shot on the flip side featuring their saggy rear ends.

John Lennon said the album was recorded in one night, just before the adulterous couple first went to bed together (although given Yoko's yelping vocal spasms, it sounds like it could have just as easily been recorded during). "She was doing her funny voices and I was pushing all different buttons on my tape recorder and getting sound effects," he recalled. "And then as the sun rose we made love and that was *Two Virgins.*"

EMI, the Beatles' record label, refused to have anything to do with the finished product, which was released independently. ("Why don't you use Paul [McCartney] instead?" EMI chairman Joseph Lockwood reportedly commented on the nudie cover. "He's much better looking.") Meanwhile, police in numerous jurisdictions did the public a huge favor by seizing album shipments, deeming the cover pornographic. For those who did get their hands on *Two Virgins,* whatever message John and Yoko were trying to convey was lost in the noise. "Dilettante garbage, simply," Lester Bangs wrote in *Rolling Stone.* Still, the couple was successful in one aspect:

"What we did purposely is not have a pretty photograph," Lennon said later, "not have it lighted so as we looked sexy or good . . . We used the straightest, most unflattering picture just to show we were human."

NOVEMBER 30, 1977

Father of the Year (to Some)

Something about starting new families after remarriage has given many a famous father selective amnesia about the children they sired first. Henry VIII of England cruelly cast aside his daughter Mary—once his "chieftest pearl"—when he married his second wife, Anne Boleyn. Their daughter, Elizabeth, suffered the same fate when Henry had Anne beheaded. It was only when the king's third wife, Jane Seymour, gave him the son he had long desired that Henry showed himself a proud and consistent papa. Similarly, Russia's Peter the Great doted on the children he had by his second spouse, but entirely ignored the son he had by his despised first wife—until he found a good reason to have the young man tortured to death in 1719.

More recently, celebrity dads have replaced royal ones in paternal favoritism. John Lennon (yes, *him* again) adored his second son, Sean, by Yoko Ono, yet all but abandoned his firstborn son, Julian. Legendary *Washington Post* editor Ben Bradlee, of Watergate fame, dedicated his autobiography to his youngest boy, Quinn, while overlooking his other two sons and daughter from previous marriages. Bradlee even co-wrote a book with Quinn—alone among his offspring—ironically titled *A Life's Work: Fathers and Sons*. Then there was the most unlikely of forgetful fathers, beloved crooner Bing Crosby—once named Movie Father of the Year—whose four sons by his first marriage were all but erased when the star started a new brood with second wife, Kathryn. It was this fresh batch of Crosbys who appeared with Bing in all his Christmas specials and ubiquitous orange juice commercials.

During one rare television appearance with his oldest son, Gary, in 1969, Crosby responded to a compliment from the young man with unintentional poignancy: "Well, that's high praise, coming from a complete stranger." Father and son then proceeded to sing a song together: "Hey Jude" by the Beatles—a song written by Paul McCartney for John Lennon's sadly neglected son Julian.

On November 30, 1977, the last Bing Crosby Christmas special aired, once again featuring only his three youngest children. The star had died just weeks before the broadcast, and with him any hope of ever celebrating a White Christmas with all *seven* of his kids.

December

DECEMBER 1, 2006

Mexico's Inaugural Brawl

The inauguration of Felipe Calderón as president of Mexico had all the dignity of a barroom brawl—perhaps that's because it closely resembled one. While rioters ran amok on the streets outside, lawmakers opposed to Calderón's assumption of the presidency exchanged punches and hurled chairs at their political rivals during a joint session of the Mexican Congress—a chaotic scene described by movie star turned California governor Arnold Schwarzenegger, an invited guest, as "good action." Then, when Calderón briefly took the dais to be sworn in, he was greeted with piercing whistles and screams to "get out!" After four minutes, the new president was hustled away to safety, making his inaugural ceremony perhaps the briefest on record—and almost certainly the rowdiest.

DECEMBER 2, 1974

In the Literary Boxing Ring— Down Goes Mailer!

Years before trashy television talk shows like *Jerry Springer,* a battle erupted on the normally staid *Dick Cavett Show* in 1974. And it wasn't between pregnant mistresses or cuckolded husbands. Rather, two literary giants, Gore Vidal and Norman Mailer, engaged in what might be best described as the egghead equivalent of a trailer park smackdown.

The mood was set before either man even stepped foot in front of the cameras. Mailer was a bit miffed over Vidal's scathing review of his polemic on feminism, *The Prisoner of Sex,* which, Vidal wrote in the *New York Review of Books,* "read like three days of menstrual flow." Before the taping began, Mailer—already buzzing from a few pre-program cocktails—head-butted Vidal offstage in the Cavett show's greenroom.

If Mailer hoped his sudden head blow would daze Vidal and throw him off his game onstage, as he later claimed, it was a wasted effort. Vidal showed no evidence of having just been assaulted backstage, ably deflecting Mailer's attempts to unnerve him. When Mailer maintained that Vidal's writing was "no more interesting than the contents of the stomach of an intellectual cow," the audience booed heartily. But Mailer was undeterred, suggesting that if Vidal could teach him something about writing, then he would look up to him. When Vidal then riposted that he wasn't the Famous Writers School, the audience laughed, while Mailer seethed.

"Why don't you try to talk just once, Gore, without yuks?" he snarled. "Why not just talk to me instead of talking to the audience?"

"Well," Vidal responded, "by a curious thing we have not found ourselves in a friendly neighborhood bar, but both, by election, are sitting here with an audience, so therefore it would be dishonest of us to pretend otherwise."

Having lost that round, Mailer redirected the conversation to Vidal's *Prisoner of Sex* review. Mailer had taken offense at a great many things in the review, but asked for an apology for Vidal's comparing him to murderer Charles Manson. (Mailer, years earlier, stabbed his wife Adele, the second of his six spouses.)

Vidal answered, "I would apologize if—if it hurts your feelings, of course I would."

"No," Mailer retorted, "it hurts my sense of intellectual pollution."

"Well," Vidal answered to audience laughter, "I must say as an expert, you should know about such things."

"Yes, well," Mailer weakly riposted, "I've had to smell your works from time to time, and that has helped me to become an expert on intellectual pollution, yes."

And things only got worse as Mailer proceeded to insult—or tried to insult—not only Vidal but also host Dick Cavett. "Why don't you look at your question sheet and ask a question?" Mailer growled at Cavett, who promptly responded, "Why don't you fold it five ways and put it where the moon don't shine."

As the audience members howled in appreciation, Mailer turned to them and asked, "Are you all really, truly idiots or is it me?"

"You!" they shouted, after which Cavett piped up:

"Oh, that was the easy answer."*

---

* *Years later, Mailer was apparently still miffed at Vidal and punched him in the face at a New York party. Vidal countered with an intellectual blow to the gut: "Once again, words have failed Norman Mailer."*

No LOL Matter

O n December 3, 1992, Neil Papworth sent the world's first text message, making it a very bad day for the English language indeed. Since that day, teenagers have stopped actually speaking to one another, proper spelling has become obsolete, and driving while texting has now far surpassed driving while drinking as the most lethal activity on the road. 4COL.

Of Cannibals and Kings

O n December 4, 1977, an accused cannibal crowned himself emperor of the Central African Republic. Given the abject poverty of the nation over which he was now sovereign, Jean-Bédel Bokassa's coronation might have been a modest affair. But His Imperial Majesty wouldn't stand for that. With an ego as outsize as his hero Napoleon's, he insisted on a ceremony as lavish as that French emperor's had been more than a century and a half before. Bokassa's "clowning glory," as Kenya's *Sunday Nation* contemptuously called it, would cost nearly $25 million, or a quarter of his nation's annual income, and make the self-proclaimed monarch an international laughingstock.

To prepare for his narcissistic extravaganza, Bokassa turned to France, the country that had backed his coup in 1966 and supported his brutal regime ever since. Sculptor Olivier Brice was retained to construct an enormous, two-ton gilded throne in the shape of an eagle sitting upright with outstretched wings, as well as the ornate, empire-style carriage that would carry the sovereign and his favorite wife to the ceremony. Scores of soldiers from the newly renamed

Central African Empire, who would serve as Napoleonic "hussars," were sent to Normandy to learn how to actually ride horses.

On the scorchingly hot coronation day, Bokassa exercised his right as emperor to be late for the ceremony, leaving his guests wilting in the sun. When he did finally arrive, His Imperial Majesty was bedecked in regal attire designed by the 200-year-old French firm that had once dressed Napoleon. There he stood, proud as a peacock, in a floor-length toga decorated with tens of thousands of tiny pearls, over which was draped a 30-foot-long mantle of crimson velvet, embroidered with gold imperial eagles and trimmed with a wide ermine border. Adding just a touch of Caesar, the emperor's head was adorned with a wreath of golden laurels, which would soon be exchanged for the actual crown—a grandiose accent created by the French jeweler Arthus-Bertrand.

Bokassa had hoped Pope Paul VI would come for the ceremony and witness him crowning himself, just as Pius VII had been there for Napoleon. Not surprisingly, His Holiness declined the invitation, as did most of the world's other leaders—including those

Self-proclaimed emperor Jean-Bédel Bokassa preens in front of his gaudy throne.

from other African nations. "They were jealous of me because I had an empire and they didn't," Bokassa later reflected.

When the faux-Napoleonic ritual concluded, guests were escorted away to celebrate in the fleet of 60 new Mercedes-Benz automobiles imported for the occasion. And while there was little enthusiasm from the local people as the emperor's retinue passed— no doubt a result of hunger—the invited were about to feast on heaping piles of caviar and sturgeon, among other delicacies, all washed down with thousands of bottles of vintage wine and champagne . . . French, of course.

Apparently, there was one other item on the menu, as well. After the guests had consumed their fill at the coronation banquet, the emperor whispered into the ear of French cooperation minister Robert Galley, "You never noticed, but you ate human flesh!"

DECEMBER 5, 1484

Unchristian Christianity, Part IV: Witches Brewhaha

Heinrich Kramer was having a devil of a time. Central Europe was teeming with witches who were wreaking havoc in a number of regions. Worse, local ecclesiastical authorities actively resisted his efforts to confront such evil. So, as a dutiful inquisitor, Kramer appealed to the pope for help. On December 5, 1484, His Holiness Innocent VIII obliged his loyal witch hunter by issuing the papal bull *Summis desiderantes affectibus.*

The pope's message not only acknowledged the existence of these malevolent creatures, who at the "instigation of the Enemy of Mankind . . . do not shrink from committing and perpetrating the foulest abominations and filthiest excesses," but also warned local bishops not to interfere with Kramer's holy mission under pain of "excommunication, suspension, interdict and still other more terrible sentences, censures, and penalties."

The fanatical inquisitor—described as "a furious misogynist" by historian Edward Peters—was thrilled with the pope's sanction and immediately set about compiling a handy guide to identifying, torturing, and killing the (mostly female) servants of Satan.

Malleus maleficarum, or *Hammer of the Witches* (published in 1487 and nominally co-written with Jacob Sprenger), was filled with such insightful declarations as "all witchcraft comes from carnal lust, which is in women insatiable," and, of particular interest to men, that witches "are able to vitiate the natural use of any member."

With the advent of the printing press, *Malleus maleficarum* became a massive best seller and the authoritative source upon which many a judge relied over several centuries of successive witch crazes to kill thousands of innocent people. And faithfully reproduced in each copy of this blood-soaked book was Pope Innocent's so-called Witch Bull and its endorsement of "our beloved son" Kramer.

DECEMBER 6, 1741

Ivan the Terribly Treated:
A Baby Tsar in Misery

Poor little Ivan VI had no idea he was having a bad day when he was suddenly swept off the Russian throne on December 6, 1741. After all, he wasn't even 16 months old. But the baby's misfortune would become painfully apparent in the years that followed.

The infant emperor was sound asleep when his distant cousin Elizabeth, escorted by armed Imperial Guards, swooped into the Winter Palace to claim his crown. It was a bloodless coup, but in an instant young Ivan VI went from emperor to prisoner. Taking the baby up to her breast, Elizabeth said to him, "You are not guilty of anything, little one!" She then handed him off to his horrible fate.

The new empress, Peter the Great's daughter, was relatively benevolent at first, allowing the deposed tsar to live with his parents and siblings in remote captivity. But at age four, the child was torn from his family and forced into isolation—never to see them again. The cruel irony was that for one extended period Ivan was kept in the same prison home as his loved ones, having no idea that on the other side of the thick wall that separated them he had two new baby brothers or that his mother was dying of fever in 1746.

Two years later, when the little boy was himself deathly ill with both measles and smallpox, Empress Elizabeth refused to allow treatment. Miraculously, the ex-emperor survived, but only to exist alone in a gloomy cell, deprived of every childhood joy.

Such extreme isolation gradually made itself manifest in the boy, who began to show signs of mental damage—particularly after he was moved at age 15 to the notorious island prison of Shlis-selburg. As one guard reported: "His articulation was confused

to such a degree that even those who constantly saw and heard him could understand him with difficulty . . . His mental abilities were disrupted, he had not the slightest memory, no ideas of any kind, neither of joy nor of sorrow, and no special inclinations." The guard also noted that in June 1759 "his fits became more violent: the patient shouted at the guards, quarreled with them, attempted to fight, twisted his mouth, and threatened to hit the officers." Of course this behavior may have had something to do with the fact that the guards liked to torment the helpless young prisoner mercilessly.

Through three reigns Ivan lived in this dank prison. Peter III even came to visit him shortly before he was deposed (see August 21). But it was under Catherine the Great that he finally perished. The empress had ordered that if any attempt were ever made to free the royal prisoner—referred to as "the nameless one"—he should be killed immediately. And when one misguided officer tried to do just that in 1764, Ivan VI met his end.

DECEMBER 7, 1941

"A date which will live in infamy"
—*President Franklin D. Roosevelt, in his response
to the Japanese attack on Pearl Harbor*

DECEMBER 8, 1941

MacArthur Parked: In Manila, a Pearl Harbor II

When it comes to history, the end of the story has already been written. Thus it's an entrenched fact that the Allies triumphed over evil in World War II and Gen. Douglas MacArthur emerged as a hero who did as he promised and returned to liberate the Philippines. But on the first day of the war, such an outcome was hardly assured. Indeed, it was a complete fiasco, with *another* devastating aerial attack by Japan that caught MacArthur—warned hours earlier of a likely onslaught on the Philippines in the wake of Pearl Harbor—entirely unprepared.

The Japanese bombers were surprised to find such a vulnerable target when they flew over Clark Field, outside Manila—nearly half the entire U.S. Air Force in the Far East, just sitting there parked in peacetime formation, wing to wing, in neat rows. They destroyed the base in a few hours, and with it any viable defense of the Philippines. As one Japanese officer later recalled: "We were very worried because we were sure after learning of Pearl Harbor you would disperse your planes or make an attack on our base at Formosa [present-day Taiwan]." For some reason, which still bewilders historians, MacArthur had done neither.

The general's biographer William Manchester called MacArthur's inaction "one of the strangest episodes in American military history. He was a gifted leader, and his failure in this emergency is bewildering. His critics have cited the catastrophe as evidence that he was flawed. They are right; he was."

DECEMBER 9, 2002

A Lott of Explaining to Do

Yes, it was bad when Senate Majority Leader Trent Lott appeared at the 100th-birthday party of his colleague Strom Thurmond and seemed to pine for the good old days down South that the centenarian once represented. "When Strom Thurmond ran for president [in 1948], we voted for him," Lott said of the onetime "Dixiecrat" whose platform at the time was the strict segregation of the races. "We're proud of it. And if the rest of the country had followed our lead, we wouldn't have had all these problems over all these years, either." But what was *really* embarrassing was Lott's increasingly ineffective apologies in the midst of the hullabaloo caused by his apparently racist remarks.

The first attempt at contrition was made on December 9, 2002—four days after the birthday celebration, and just hours after he seemed to brush away the controversy, insisting that his remarks were made in the spirit of "a lighthearted celebration," an apology that didn't quite cut it. And neither did the errant senator's next two stabs at atonement on December 11—made on both Fox News and CNN.

By the time Lott tried for a fourth time, during a speech in his home state of Mississippi, even conservative columnist George Will seemed to have it out for the majority leader, whom he dubbed "the serial apologizer." In his speech, Lott had said he had been "winging it" during the Thurmond celebration, which explained why his words came out all wrong. Will pounced: "It is dangerous for Republicans to have a leader who not only cannot be trusted without a script but who is utterly unembarrassed about citing scriptlessness as an exculpation for any embarrassment he causes." The columnist proceeded to attack Lott for the artlessness of his three previous apology attempts as well.

Finally, on December 16, Lott made one more stop on the atonement tour, this time to Black Entertainment Television, where he informed the host that he now supported a holiday honoring Martin Luther King, Jr.—only a few years *after* the commemorative day was officially established in all 50 states. Alas, all the groveling did little to save the majority leader, who resigned from his position four days after his BET appearance. Nevertheless, as authors Arleen Sorkin and Paul Slansky wrote, it did give the fallen politician the distinction of being "the twenty-first century's reigning king of contrition, the ayatollah of atonement, the rajah of regret."

DECEMBER 10, 1918, 1949, 1994, *and* 1997

Less Than Nobel:
Some Prize Bloopers

And the Oscar went to Elizabeth Taylor for her work in *Butterfield 8,* a film so dreadful even the actress herself dismissed it as "a piece of obscenity." A Grammy was given to Baha Men for "Who Let the Dogs Out," a song that asked the probing question "Who? Who? Who? Who? Who?" Madonna, whose portrayal of Eva Perón came off stiffer than the corpse of Argentina's once celebrated first lady, nevertheless won a Golden Globe for her "acting" in *Evita.* Yet no matter how colossally ill chosen the award winners were, nobody (except perhaps the worthier competition) was too adversely affected by these aberrations. "That's entertainment," as the saying goes.

The Nobel Prize, however, is a different matter entirely. The award, given every year on December 10, is supposed to recognize the very best in human accomplishment in various fields of endeavor. Giants like Einstein, Mandela, Churchill, and Curie have all been named Nobel laureates. But so have some vastly less deserving folk who, by virtue of winning the Nobel, gave the prestigious prize a bit of a black eye. Among them:

- Fritz Haber, 1918, chemistry, for the synthesis of ammonia from nitrogen in the air. Thanks to Haber's discovery, which allowed for the development of industrial fertilizers, the world became far better fed. Yet this immensely beneficial contribution to mankind was made well before World War I, by which time the chemist was redirecting his creative energy toward something his own wife condemned as "perversion of the ideals of science" and "a sign of barbarity, corrupting the very discipline which ought to bring new insights into life"—the annihilation of

Germany's enemies on the battlefield with poisonous gas.*

- António Egas Moniz, 1949, medicine, for pioneering the lobotomy. Besides the fact that this radical brain procedure turned many patients—including President John F. Kennedy's sister Rosemary**—into near zombies, there was nothing particularly inventive about drilling holes into the skull and shoving in an instrument to disable the frontal lobes. In fact, it was kind of medieval—not like, say, creating the artificial heart (a feat for which Robert Jarvik was

---

* On April 22, 1915, during the Second Battle of Ypres, the Germans first utilized Haber's lethal innovation and released more than 168 tons of chlorine gas from nearly 6,000 canisters. A ghastly cloud, described by one witness as "like a yellow low wall," began to drift toward some 10,000 troops in the French trenches. When it settled over them, more than half the soldiers reportedly died by asphyxiation within minutes. One survivor of the chemical attack, Lance Sgt. Elmer Cotton, described the ordeal as "an equivalent death to drowning only on dry land. The effects are these—a splitting headache and terrific thirst (to drink water is instant death), a knife edge of pain in the lungs and the coughing up of a greenish froth off the stomach and the lungs, ending finally in insensibility and death. The colour of the skin turns a greenish black and yellow . . . and the eyes assume a glassy stare. It is a fiendish death to die."

** Rosemary Kennedy may have become difficult as she grew older, with mood swings her father found intolerable, but she was most definitely not mentally retarded, as the family has long maintained. Her detailed diary entries prove that. Nevertheless, Ambassador Joseph P. Kennedy found his 23-year-old daughter deficient enough to subject her to a lobotomy in the fall of 1941. The results were disastrous, reducing the once vibrant Rosemary to a near-vegetative state. Banished from the family bosom, she spent the rest of her life in a Wisconsin convent.

egregiously overlooked by the Nobel committee). And when a place as oppressive and cruel as the Soviet Union bans lobotomies as "contrary to the principles of humanity," as it did in 1950, that might be taken as an indication that this monstrous procedure was bad medicine indeed.

• Yasser Arafat, 1994, Peace Prize (shared with Shimon Peres and Yitzhak Rabin of Israel). Yes, it's true that one man's terrorist is another man's freedom fighter. And certainly the Palestinian people have had plenty of legitimate beefs with Israel. Yet when the massacre of innocents—coupled with hijackings, kidnappings, political assassinations, and other mayhem—becomes the paramount means to an end, as it did for the Palestinian leader, it tends to make a mockery of the Nobel *Peace* Prize— especially considering the fact that Mahatma Gandhi was never awarded one.

• Myron Scholes and Robert Merton, 1997, economics. Less than a year after receiving their prize, "for a new method to determine the value of derivatives," as the Nobel announcement read, the laureates' esteemed hedge fund, Long-Term Capital Management, lost $4 billion in six weeks.

DECEMBER 11, 1951

A Twist in the Helix: Crick and Watson Get Off Track

On December 11, 1951, after a disastrous demonstration of what they *thought* was the model for the structure of DNA, Francis Crick and James D. Watson were ordered to cease their research in that arena by Sir Lawrence Bragg, director of Cambridge University's Cavendish Laboratory, where both men worked.

"No attempt was made to appeal the verdict," Watson later wrote with characteristic edge. "An open outcry would reveal that our professor was completely in the dark about what the initials DNA stood for. There was no reason to believe that he gave it one hundredth the importance of the structure of metals, for which he took great delight in making soap-bubble models. Nothing gave Sir Lawrence more pleasure than showing his ingenious motion-picture film of how bubbles bump into each other."

Watson did acknowledge that the partners' passive acceptance of the verdict was based on self-interest, not on protecting Sir Lawrence. "Lying low made sense because we were up the creek with models based on sugar-phosphate cores. No matter how we looked at them, they smelled bad."

Within a few years, however, Watson and Crick resumed their work in DNA and soon arrived at a solution—the mystery of life, in essence—which has often been called the most important biological discovery of the last century.

DECEMBER 12, 1937

Suddenly Shocked! Shocked! at Mae West

On December 12, 1937, sex symbol Mae West was invited to perform her usual shtick of purring enticements and double entendres on radio's *Chase & Sanborn Hour,* a weekly variety show broadcast on Sunday nights. Playing a seductive Eve in one sketch, and flirting with ventriloquist Edgar Bergen's wooden sidekick, Charlie McCarthy, in another, the sultry actress delivered as bawdily as might be expected. At one point, for example, she reminded the puppet that he had already kissed her in her apartment. "I got marks to prove it," she said. "An' splinters, too."

Mae West infuriates NBC suits with her radio seduction of a dummy.

NBC had approved the script, but when a coordinated protest by the Legion of Decency and other morality groups erupted, the network immediately disowned the star and declared her an "unfit radio personality." In a spineless attempt to shift the blame, network executives claimed West took the script they had found acceptable to unexpected levels of indecency by the way she delivered her lines. Subsequently, even the mention of her name was banned on NBC radio. Fortunately, there were more reasonable observers, like the *Chicago Daily News,* which excoriated the network's cowardice in an editorial:

"NBC and the commercial sponsors of the program knew Mae West. They knew her technique. They'd heard her and seen her. They coached her in rehearsals. But when the public protests swamped them they pretended they had Mae all mixed up with Mary Pickford or Shirley Temple."

DECEMBER 13, 1974

Clattering Pan: The *Times* Disses a Future Film Classic

The quality of art may be in the eye of the beholder, but it must also be said that many a critic has suffered from severe astigmatism and other sensory impairments. And more than a few of them have written for *The New York Times*. (The author of this book was called "deliberately naive" in a *Times* review of the History Channel's *The French Revolution,* but he digresses . . .) Consider the paper's critical take on the Beatles' masterpieces *Abbey Road,* an "unmitigated disaster," and *Sgt. Pepper's Lonely Hearts Club Band:* "There is nothing beautiful on 'Sergeant Pepper.' Nothing is real and there is nothing to get hung about." Or the review for Nabokov's classic, *Lolita:* "Dull, dull, dull in a pretentious, florid and archly fatuous fashion." Or of Salinger's *Catcher in the Rye:* "Gets kind of monotonous. And he should've cut out a lot about these jerks and all that crumby school. They depress me."

One of the greatest critical blunders, published in the *Times* on December 13, 1974, was Vincent Canby's scathing review of *The Godfather, Part II,* which has since received nearly universal acclaim as one of the greatest films ever made.

"The only remarkable thing about Francis Ford Coppola's *The Godfather, Part II* is the insistent manner in which it recalls how much better his original film was," Canby began. "It's a Frankenstein's monster stitched together from leftover parts. It talks. It moves in fits and starts but it has no mind of its own . . . Everything of any interest was thoroughly covered in the original film, but like many people who have nothing to say, Part II won't shut up . . . Even if Part II were a lot more cohesive, revealing and exciting than it is, it probably would have run the risk of appearing to be the self-parody it now seems. Looking very expensive but spiritually desperate, Part II has the air of a very long, very elaborate revue sketch. Nothing is sacred."

Indeed not, he said naively—at least at *The New York Times*.

DECEMBER 14, 1861

Mourning Noon and Night— for Decades

The death of Queen Victoria's beloved consort Prince Albert on December 14, 1861, plunged the British monarch into decades of obsessive, crepe-draped mourning. But his passing wasn't easy on the children, either—of that, Mum made certain. First, she blamed her eldest son and heir for essentially killing his father. The Prince of Wales had recently been caught up in a youthful indiscretion with an actress, mortifying the prudish Albert, who succumbed to typhoid soon afterward. Victoria, however, insisted that it was the trauma of their son's immorality, not disease, that killed her husband, and loudly proclaimed that she could never again look at the young man "without a shudder." And shudder she did—for the next 40 years.

Then, just to make sure everyone knew how sad she was, Victoria ruined the wedding of her daughter Alice with her weeping and wailing. The queen described the small, private ceremony—held seven months after Albert's death—as "more like a funeral than a wedding." She had that right; it was, after all, the atmosphere *she* had created, forlornly sitting apart from the rest of her family, protectively flanked by her four eldest sons.

"Fortunately for the bride and groom, who were much less the focus of attention than the huddled figure in black, the Archbishop of York kept the service short," wrote biographer Stanley Weintraub. When it was all over and Alice was off on her honeymoon, the queen recorded in her diary: "I hardly miss her at all, or felt her going, so *utterly* absorbed am I by that one dreadful loss."

DECEMBER 15, 2013

Dying to Upstage Her Sister: Joan Fontaine's Finale

Olivia de Havilland and Joan Fontaine were Hollywood's feuding sisters—leading ladies locked in a bitter rivalry that reportedly went all the way back to childhood. "I married first," Fontaine once commented on the enduring sibling spat, "won the Oscar before Olivia did, and if I die first, she'll undoubtedly be livid because I beat her to it!" On December 15, 2013, at age 96, Fontaine did indeed beat de Havilland to the grave.

DECEMBER 16, 1997

Pokémon Attacks 600 Children!

That classic parental admonition "Television will rot your brain" was given sudden urgency in 1997 when more than 600

Japanese schoolchildren became dizzy and nauseated while watching an episode of the popular Japanese cartoon series *Pokémon*. Some even had seizures. Hospitals across the country were inundated with retching, convulsing kids, and a few parents, in scenes reminiscent of a really bad Japanese sci-fi flick.

"I was shocked to see my daughter lose consciousness," said Yukiko Iwasaki, whose eight-year-old suffered a seizure. "She started to breathe only when I hit her on the back."

The spasmodic mass reaction was triggered about 20 minutes into *Pokémon* episode 38, "Computer Warrior Porigon," which, like other episodes of the top-rated show, was produced in an intense version of animation known as anime. A vivid explosion, with pulsating strobe-light effects, apparently walloped those kids with their eyes glued to their television sets on the evening of December 16. "I must say that as an adult that part made me blink, so for a child the effect must have been considerable," said TV Tokyo programming division manager Hironari Mori.

Amid the ensuing uproar, the show was suspended and Japanese authorities launched an investigation, which proved inconclusive. Nevertheless, the offending episode was never aired again.

DECEMBER 17, 1862

General Grant's Medieval Measure

While civil war raged between the states, cotton still remained king. The commodity was the South's economic engine, and northern manufacturers absolutely depended upon it for survival. And though the U.S. government allowed some restricted trade, controlled by the Treasury Department and enforced by the Army, a lucrative black market nevertheless thrived—fueled, or so Gen. Ulysses S. Grant believed, by that most reliable of scapegoats, the unscrupulous Jew.

"Give orders to all the conductors on the [rail]road that no Jews are to be permitted to travel on the railroad southward from any point," Grant ordered in November 1862. "They may go north and be encouraged in it; but they are such an intolerable nuisance that the department must be purged of them."

The following month, on December 17, Grant strengthened his restrictions against "the Israelites" with an old-fashioned expulsion order of the kind European monarchs had issued in their kingdoms for centuries.* General Order No. 11 read, in part: "The Jews, as a class violating every regulation of trade established by the Treasury Department and also department orders, are hereby expelled from the Department [of the Tennessee, then under Grant's command] within twenty-four hours from the receipt of this order."

Fortunately, Grant had a commander in chief with a far more evolved sense of fairness, and by the following month General Order No. 11 had been officially revoked.

DECEMBER 18, 1912

Skullduggery: The Piltdown Man Hoax

The buzz of anticipation filled the packed meeting of the Geological Society of London on December 18, 1912, as amateur paleontologist Charles Dawson took the podium to announce his remarkable discovery: the long-elusive "missing link" between man and ape. It was a scientific bonanza—"the most startling and

---

In 1290, for example, King Edward I ordered all Jews expelled from England. Ferdinand and Isabella of Spain did the same thing with their Alhambra Decree of 1492.

significant fossil bone that has ever been brought to light," wrote scientist Ray Lankester in his 1919 book *Divisions of a Naturalist*—made all the more gratifying by the fact that the ancient remains had been found right in England. *Eoanthropus dawsoni* ("Dawson's dawn-man")—or Piltdown Man, as the humanoid was popularly named*—could now be proudly claimed as a proper Englishman.

In the midst of all the excitement—with scientists writing scholarly papers on Piltdown Man and people actually making pilgrimages to the discovery site—a few skeptics emerged. One of them, Gerrit S. Miller of the Smithsonian Institution in Washington, D.C., noted the incongruity between the skull and apelike jawbone. Such a combination, he concluded, would produce a freakish specimen that would never be found in nature. For his efforts, Miller was immediately and ferociously attacked.

It was Charles Dawson himself who managed to silence any further criticism when he produced more bone fragments, matching Piltdown Man's, that he claimed to have uncovered two miles away from the original site. A second "missing link" specimen seemed to confirm the existence of the first. And with that firmly established, there would be no more questions for decades to come—until Joseph Weiner, a professor of physical anthropology at Oxford University, came along.

Several aspects of Dawson's discoveries troubled Weiner, who began a careful examination of the evidence. It eventually led to

---

* For the village in southern England, near where the fossils were found

the complete unraveling of what he called "a most elaborate and carefully prepared hoax," the perpetration of which was "so entirely unscrupulous and inexplicable, as to find no parallel in . . . paleontological history."

In short order, Weiner deduced that Piltdown Man's teeth had been chiseled down to resemble a humanlike chewing pattern and had been stained with what appeared to be ordinary house paint to give them a patina of age. Other fossils recovered from the discovery site, such as ancient elephant and hippopotamus teeth, were determined to have been planted, as were some Paleolithic tools. The cranium, stained like the teeth, was judged to be about 500 years old, and the jaw apparently belonged to an orangutan. Thus, wrote John Evangelist Walsh, "Piltdown Man, the most famous creature ever to grace the prehistoric scene, had been ingeniously manufactured from a medieval Englishman and a Far Eastern ape."

This was no merry prank, however. One scientist called it "the most troubled chapter" in the study of man's origins. It set back for years the search for understanding, compromised reputations, and, in the process, really gave creationists something to crow about. The deception "was nothing short of despicable," opined Walsh, "an ugly trick played by a warped and unscrupulous mind on unsuspecting scholars."*

DECEMBER 19, 211

The Brother's Grim Fate

Motherhood certainly was a burden to Julia Domna, the wife of Roman emperor Septimius Severus. Her two sons, Antoninus (better known by his nickname Caracalla) and Geta, were brats. They

---

* *The perpetrator of the fraud has never been discovered, but many assume it was Dawson, eager to make a name for himself among the scientific elite.*

abused boys, outraged women, embezzled money, often kept unsavory company, and generally loathed one other. The Roman consul and historian Cassius Dio reported that they were "full of strife in their rivalries; for if the one attached himself to a certain faction, the other would be sure to choose the opposite side." The two sons also shared a claim to their father's throne and both stood to rule after his death. Before Septimius Severus died, he pleaded with his sons to "be good to each other." But momma probably knew better.

Less than a year into their joint, tension-filled reign, Caracalla moved to do away with his brother once and for all—and he used Julia Domna to perpetrate the wicked deed. Caracalla ordered his mother to summon Geta to her chambers, for the ostensible purpose of arbitrating the differences between her sons and orchestrating peace between them. Thus, on December 19, in the year 211, Geta responded to his mother's call, unarmed. A pack of centurions, under Caracalla's command, awaited him in ambush. Seeing his murderers upon entering the room, Geta rushed to his mother's arms for safety. But the killers were undeterred by Julia's protective embrace. Cassius Dio related the rest of the story:

> And so she, tricked in this way, saw her son perishing in the most impious fashion in her arms, and received him at his death into the very womb, as it were, whence he had been born; for she was all covered with his blood, so that she took no note of the wound she had received on her hand. But she was not permitted to mourn or weep for her son, though he had met so miserable an end before his time (he was only twenty-two years and nine months old), but, on the contrary, she was compelled to rejoice and laugh as though at some great good fortune; so closely were all her words, gestures, and changes of color observed. Thus she alone, the Augusta, wife of the emperor and mother of the emperors, was not permitted to shed tears even in private over so great a sorrow.

Ho Ho Oh No! The Poison Christmas Present

There was one tiny problem with one of the holiday season's most popular toys—a minuscule yet highly carcinogenic problem: asbestos, found in the fine dusting powder of the "CSI: Crime Scene Investigation Fingerprint Examination Kit." And though the Asbestos Disease Awareness Organization had earlier discovered the microscopically lethal substance in the kit, which allowed kids to emulate the investigative heroes of the hit CBS television show, it would take almost a month before the network succumbed to pressure and quietly—*very* quietly—ordered a recall on December 20, 2007. By then, however, the toxic toy—hazmat suits *not* included—was under countless Christmas trees, just waiting to be unwrapped by unsuspecting junior crime solvers. Merry Mesothelioma!

Every Christmas, Ladling Out Holiday Sneer

Self-parodying daytime talk show co-host/chanteuse Kathie Lee Gifford took her first stab at yuletide cheer with a primetime Christmas special in 1994. *Washington Post* television critic Tom Shales promptly shredded it. In the review, published on December 21 and headlined "Kathie Lee's Blight Before Christmas," Shales described the special as "ghastly, hideous and downright nightmarish in its desperate cheerfulness," and wrote of the plucky star: "Naturally she sings, sings, sings—or rather, not so naturally, just in that excruciatingly bland and vapid way of hers."

Poor Kathie Lee might have taken some comfort in believing that Shales was just being a Grinch that year. Little could she have known that the Pulitzer Prize–winning critic had just launched a new Christmas tradition of making his reviews of her subsequent holiday specials a blood sport. A few excerpts:

- **1995 Kathie Lee: The Grin That Stole Christmas**

  Give her enough tinsel and she'll hang herself. And she does.

  Kathie Lee Gifford's second annual CBS Christmas special is perhaps even worse than her first—a sickeningly saccharine vanity production that should really have been titled "O Come, Let Us Adore Me."

- **1996 Kathie Lee's Christmas: Mistletoe by a Mile**

  In a brief monologue, Gifford said Christmas was, among other things, the one time of year when we think about "how much we have to be grateful for." What about Thanksgiving? Ah, of course: At Thanksgiving we get to be grateful that Kathie Lee doesn't do a Thanksgiving special.

  It was often said that Christmas wouldn't be Christmas without Bing Crosby. But oh brother, would Christmas ever be Christmas without Kathie Lee Gifford.

- **1997 Another Chestnut Ready to Roast: Kathie Lee Gifford's "Little Christmas"**

  Kathie Lee Gifford sings songs like she's mad at them. What did they ever do to her? Maybe she was frightened by a song as a child. And by Christmas, too, because each year on television she wreaks a bit more revenge.

- **1998 Kathie Lee? Bah Humbug!**

  What's the difference between the 24-hour flu and a Kathie Lee Gifford Christmas special? Twenty-three hours.

  The special had more aura de horror than holiday glow and proved punishingly similar to previous efforts. In other words, it might have been called "I Saw What You Did Last Christmas." And the one before that.

Please, one might have prayed, in the name of all that's holy: Let it stop, let it stop, let it stop.

DECEMBER 22, 1995

A Huge, Spectacular, Unprecedented... Flop!

Director Renny Harlin was very specific about his philosophy for the film *Cutthroat Island.* In a memo to studio executives, he insisted: "No matter what the budget limitations or the physical handicaps are, we've got to offer the audience an unprecedented milestone in action and movie spectacle. Our imagination and sense of invention can not be limited by mundane reality."

He went on:

"I don't want big, I want huge. I don't want surprising, I want stunning. I don't want fast, I want explosive. I don't want accidents, I want disasters. I don't want dirt, I want filth. I don't want a storm, I want a hurricane. I don't want hills, I want mountains. I don't want groups, I want crowds. I don't want fear, I want panic. I don't want suspense, I want terror. I don't want fights, I want battles. I don't want beautiful, I want awesome. I don't want humor, I want hysteria. I don't want horses, I want stallions. I don't want boats, I want ships. I don't want events, I want action. I don't want good, I want great. I don't want interesting, I want mind boggling. And, I don't want love, I want passion."

What Harlin got when *Cutthroat Island* opened on December 22, 1995, wasn't just a failure, but the biggest, most expensive bomb in Hollywood history. The career of leading lady Geena Davis wasn't just damaged by the flop, but bludgeoned beyond repair. And the studio wasn't just pushed to the financial brink, but hurled into a bottomless pit of bankruptcy.

DECEMBER 23, 1883

John Wilkes Booth's Other Victim

The psychic scars that the assassination of Abraham Lincoln left on the nation were deep and enduring, but for the president's companions that fateful evening at Ford's Theatre—Maj. Henry Rathbone and his fiancée, Clara Harris—the trauma proved particularly tragic.

Rathbone didn't hear John Wilkes Booth sneak into the president's box during the performance of *Our American Cousin,* and, right after shooting Lincoln, the assassin immediately disabled him with a deep knife slash to the arm. As Rathbone stood there bleeding and helpless, Booth made his famous escape by leaping onto the stage and slipping out of the theater. It was a moment of horror from which the Civil War veteran would never recover.

As President Lincoln lay dying at a home across the street from the theater, Rathbone, who had helped bring him there, drifted in and out of consciousness from blood loss—his head resting on his fiancée's lap. As it turned out, Booth's knife attack had severed an artery. Nevertheless he eventually recovered—at least physically—and married Clara Harris.

In 1882, the couple, along with their three children, moved to the German state of Hanover, where Rathbone had been appointed U.S. consul. But there was little relief from the mental agony of the assassination and his inability to stop it. "I understand his distress," Clara wrote to a friend. "In every hotel we're in, as soon as people get wind of our presence, we feel ourselves become objects of morbid scrutiny . . . Whenever we were in the dining room, we began to feel like zoo animals. Henry . . . imagines that the whispering is more pointed and malicious than it can possibly be."

On the evening of December 23, 1883, Rathbone, his mental state always fragile, finally snapped. Clara sensed something was wrong when her husband tried to force himself into their children's bedroom. When she tried to stop him, he shot her, and then repeatedly stabbed her before turning the knife on himself. Clara died, but Rathbone survived to spend the remaining 27 years of his life in a German asylum for the criminally insane.

DECEMBER 24, 1865

Christmas Evil

"'Twas the night before Christmas,
at a town in the South,
A band of ex-Confederates gathered,
down in the mouth;
That the black man was now free,
they felt was unfair,
An abomination they'd address
with terror to spare;
Crosses they'd burn with white hoods
on their head,
Spreading their message of hate
with horror and dread."

Yes, ringing in the season with Yuletide cheer, the Ku Klux Klan was officially organized in Pulaski, Tennessee, on December 24, 1865.

DECEMBER 25, 2002

The Windfall That Blew Everything Away

Take trouble and multiply it by $315 million and that's the Christmas present Jack Whittaker received in 2002. While horror stories of sudden lottery wealth gone bad are legion—broken relationships, stupid spending, and rapid bankruptcy—the spiral of death and destruction that accompanied Whittaker's staggering windfall made it seem as though the devil himself had delivered the winning ticket.

It all started well. "I want to be a good example," Whittaker said when he became the single largest lottery winner in history. "I want to make people proud of what happens with this winning. I want to promote goodwill and help people."

By all indications, the 55-year-old West Virginia native might have made good on his lofty intentions. He was a self-made man, already wealthy from his construction business. Everything seemed just fine as Whittaker made the rounds of the network morning shows, accompanied by his wife, Jewell, daughter Ginger, and his beloved 15-year-old granddaughter, Brandi. Sharing the bounty in a Christian way, it seemed, would be the Whittaker legacy.

"We pay tithes to three churches," he told Matt Lauer of NBC's *Today* show, "and we're going to take care of those pastors with 10 percent of the money." Another chunk would go to his own charitable foundation.

But then things took a turn for the worse. Jack Whittaker started hitting a local strip joint called the Pink Pony—throwing around wads of cash and making a terrific nuisance of himself pawing at the entertainment. It was as if his unimaginable wealth gave him license to do as he pleased.

"It was like the money was eating away at whatever was good in him," one employee of the Pink Pony told *The Washington Post.* "It reminds me, like, 'Lord of the Rings,' how that little guy—what's his name? Gollum?—was with his Precious. It just consumes you. You become the money. You are no longer a person."

Drunk-driving arrests and car crashes followed, but Whittaker was unapologetic. Nevertheless, the money was beginning to take a ghastly toll: countless strangers seeking financial salvation, a cascade of lawsuits, several robberies—including $500,000 in cash stolen from his car parked in front of the Pink Pony—and even the breakup of his 40-year marriage to Jewell. "I don't know if life will ever be normal again," Whittaker told a reporter for Channel 13 in Charleston.

Worst of all, though, was the toxic effect Whittaker's extravagant wealth had on those with whom he shared it—like evil seeping down from its source. This was particularly true of his granddaughter, Brandi, who lived with her "Paw-Paw" off and on while her mother suffered from lymphoma. "She was the shining star of my life, and she was what it was all about for me," he later said. "From the day she was born, it was all about providing and protecting and taking care of her." And later showering her with cash and cars.

The once bright-eyed, blond young girl who had happily declared that her only wishes were to get a new Mitsubishi Eclipse and meet the rap star Nelly almost instantly became a jaded, paranoid drug addict with unlimited resources. False friends flocked to her. "They want her for her money and not for her good personality," Whittaker complained to an Associated Press reporter a year after his win. "She's the most bitter 16-year-old I know."

Just over two years after Whittaker hit the jackpot, Brandi was dead of a drug overdose. The death of his granddaughter drained the last bit of joy from Jack Whittaker's life. Looking back, he said sadly, "I wish I'd torn that ticket up."

DECEMBER 26, 1919

Curses! The Red Sox Owner's Ruthlessly Dumb Deal

Perhaps it really was the "curse of the Bambino," as some have called it, or maybe just a terrible coincidence. But the fortunes of the Boston Red Sox plummeted so precipitously after owner Harry Frazee sold superhitter Babe Ruth to the New York Yankees on December 26, 1919, that the events seemed inescapably entwined. For nearly nine decades after the sale, the "Dead Sox" would remain one of the most snakebit teams in Major League Baseball while the previously moribund Yankees rose to glory with Ruth.

Frazee's motives for selling his most valuable player, in an all-cash deal, were mixed. Certainly the extraordinary price he commanded (more than twice the amount ever paid for a player) would fund the club owner's true passion for producing Broadway musicals—even as he presented the sale to Sox fans as a means of eventually financing an improved roster of players. But there was something else: Frazee's animosity toward his star player, whom he publicly disparaged as "a one-man team" after the deal with the Yankees was sealed.

"While Ruth is undoubtedly the greatest hitter the game has ever seen," Frazee declared, "he is likewise one of the most selfish and inconsiderate men ever to put on a baseball uniform. Had he possessed the right disposition, had he been willing to take orders

Babe Ruth poses in 1919, his last season in a Boston Red Sox uniform.

and work for the good of the club like the other men on the team, I never would have dared let him go."

The Sultan of Swat, as Ruth came to be called, immediately called foul on his old boss. "If not for Frazee, I would be content to play with the Red Sox to the end of my baseball days," he told the press. "Frazee sold me because he was unwilling to meet my [salary] demands, and to alibi himself with the fans, he is trying to throw the blame on me."

Frazee's feeble attempt to vindicate himself flopped. Outraged New Englanders derided the move as "a second Boston massacre," while *The Boston Post* called it "a tremendous blow to the army of loyal fans."

The thoroughly excoriated Red Sox owner had said at the time of the sale that the Yankees were taking a big gamble in paying such a steep price for Ruth. But the risk paid off splendidly with seven pennants and four World Series titles during Babe Ruth's 14-year tenure with the team. Meanwhile, the Sox finished dead last in 9 of the next 11 seasons.

DECEMBER 27, 1979

Sure We Will! And Here's Some Nice Soup for You...

"The Soviets will help us."
—*President Hafizullah Amin of Afghanistan, still clueless about the Soviets on the same day they tried to assassinate him by poisoning his soup, then, hours later, fatally shot him in a palace coup that accompanied their disastrous nine-year incursion into the strife-torn nation*

DECEMBER 28, 1984

"You Think It's Fake?" Stossel's Smackdown

Probing reporter John Stossel was having a marvelous time ripping the mask off pro wrestling for the ABC news magazine program *20/20*. But then he got a little too penetrating with Dave "Dr. D." Schultz, and was left with a sharp ringing in his ear as a memento of his encounter with the six-foot-six-inch 268-pounder.

"I'll ask you the standard question," Stossel ventured. "You know: 'I think this is fake.'"

"You think it's fake?" Schultz replied, while boxing the reporter on the right ear and knocking him to the ground. "What's that? Is that fake? Huh? What the hell's wrong with you? That's an open-hand slap. You think it's fake? I'll fake you." As Stossel regained his footing, Schultz hit him on the left ear, flooring him once again. As the thoroughly chastised reporter tried to flee the scene, Schultz followed after him. "Huh?" he taunted. "What do you mean, fake?"

DECEMBER 29, 1977

Lust in Translation: President Carter's Polish "Desire"

A long with a few of his 19th-century predecessors, such as James Buchanan, Jimmy Carter's administration was one of the most bedeviled in American history. Soaring inflation, a debil-itating gas crisis, and the hostage crisis in Iran all converged on the hapless president, who also had to contend with his embar-rassing brother, Billy—a beer-swilling, hillbilly cartoon of a char-acter noted not only for his buffoonery but also for accepting a $200,000 "loan" from the outlaw nation of Libya.

But as much as outside events seemed to conspire against Presi-dent Carter, there was just something about the man himself—well-meaning though he was—that inspired ridicule. There was that toothy grin, flashed at the most incongruous moments, combined with a seemingly endless stream of humiliating gaffes. Start with the "killer" rabbit the president claimed tried to attack him while he was fishing in a pond near his hometown of Plains, Georgia. Then there was his earnest declaration to a debate audience: "I had a discussion with my daughter, Amy, the other day, before I came here, to ask her what the most important issue was. She said she thought nuclear weap-onry and the control of nuclear arms." Amy was all of 13 at the time. And this much mocked gem from a 1976 *Playboy* magazine inter-view: "I've looked on many women with lust. I've committed adultery in my heart many times. God knows I will do this and forgives me."

Carter's lusty heart inadvertently popped up again on December 29, 1977, during a visit to Poland. Of course the president had to speak through an interpreter, but the man chosen wasn't quite up to the job. What resulted may count as the most mortifying foreign address by a U.S. president—ever. "I left the United States this morning," Carter said. The interpreter translated it as, "When I abandoned the United States." It only got worse. When the president declared, "I have come to learn your opinions and understand your desires for the future," it was translated—amid much audience tittering—into "I desire the Poles carnally."

DECEMBER 30, 2013

Along Came a Snyder

On December 30, 2013, the Washington Redskins ended their worst season in over half a century by firing Mike Shanahan—the team's *seventh* head coach in the 14.5 years since a diminutive young billionaire by the name of Daniel Snyder purchased the franchise in 1999. With his dictatorial style, shameless gouging of fans on everything from stadium parking to stale peanuts, and, most vitally, the pathetic showing of the Redskins during his reign, "Mister" Snyder, as he insisted he be called, made himself one of the most hated owners in the NFL—pilloried even in the comic strip *Tank McNamara,* where he was dubbed "Sports Jerk of the Year." As *Washington Post* sports columnist Thomas Boswell wrote after the firing of Shanahan, "What Washington has endured for 14-plus years of the Daniel Snyder era is a morbid laboratory experiment in mass alienation of football affection."*

---

* *Perhaps the most scathing indictment of Daniel Snyder came from his*

Name Your Poison:
The Feds' Deadly "Morality"

Prohibition had been in effect for seven years, but people were still slurping down illicit booze like never before. Frustrated, Uncle Sam was determined to spoil the party—even if it meant poisoning the punch bowl from which millions of Americans imbibed.

The Volstead Act of 1919 had provided for the continued production of alcohol for industrial purposes, as long as it was rendered "unfit for use as an intoxicating beverage." Nasty substances like kerosene and brucine (a plant alkaloid closely related to strychnine), gasoline, benzene, cadmium, iodine, zinc, mercury salts, nicotine, ether, formaldehyde, chloroform, camphor, carbolic acid, quinine, and acetone were added to make it so. The problem was, though, much of this legally tainted alcohol found its way to bootleggers, who in turn hired chemists to remove the array of toxins mandated by the government. A kind of escalating chemical warfare ensued as the authorities concocted ever more noxious additives while the criminals managed to diminish their effectiveness. Still, the government had one particularly lethal weapon in its arsenal—a vicious agent known as methyl, or wood alcohol, which even in small amounts caused blindness, hallucinations, paralysis, and, not uncommonly, death.

On New Year's Eve, 1926, enforcement agents announced that they were going to double the already dangerous amount of methyl in

---

childhood hero, former Redskins running back John Riggins. "This is a bad guy that owns this team," Riggins said on Showtime's Inside the NFL *in 2009. "I'll just tell you that upfront. Bad guy." Asked to elaborate, Riggins continued, "Let me put it to you this way . . . this person's heart is dark."*

industrial alcohol—and, if necessary, quadruple it. This is what had become of Prohibition, the moral crusade once described by future president Herbert Hoover as an "experiment noble in purpose."

The government's announcement came as holiday revelers were already staggering into city hospitals, quite literally blind drunk from the effects of methyl, or half dead. Bootleggers, after all, never felt compelled to withhold tainted liquor they couldn't fully purify. New York's chief medical examiner Charles Norris, for one, was appalled by the carnage wrought by the state-sanctioned contamination—especially on the unsuspecting poor.

"The government knows it is not stopping drinking by putting poison into alcohol," he said in a press conference the day after Christmas. "It knows what the bootleggers are doing with it and yet it continues its poisoning process, heedless of the fact that people determined to drink are daily absorbing that poison." Later, he added, "There is practically no pure whiskey available. My opinion . . . is that there is actually no Prohibition. All the people who drank before Prohibition are drinking now—provided they are still alive."

A report issued by Norris on the staggering toll the poisoning policy had already taken—and the projected devastation that would accompany the government's recently

announced plans to add even more methyl—was met with outrage from many quarters. "The Eighteenth is the only amendment which carries the death penalty," wrote columnist Heywood Broun of the New York *World*.

"Murder!" declared Nicholas Murray Butler, president of Columbia University. "Just plain, unadulterated murder by our glorious Government, is what I think of the deaths attributed to the consumption of liquor manufactured from poison alcohol!"

Members of Congress had similar reactions. As Senator James Reed of Missouri told the *St. Louis Post-Dispatch,* "Only one possessing the instincts of a wild beast would desire to kill or make blind the man who takes a drink of liquor, even if he purchased it from one violating the Prohibition statutes."

Yet there were still those who insisted that the legions of sick and dying Americans got exactly what they deserved. "Must Uncle Sam guarantee safety first for souses?" asked *The Omaha Bee*. Wayne Wheeler, the powerful leader of the Anti-Saloon League, which had lobbied extensively for Prohibition, responded to the uproar with this statement to the press: "The government is under no obligation to furnish people with alcohol that is drinkable when the Constitution forbids it. The person who drinks this industrial alcohol is a deliberate suicide."

Though Wheeler and his movement lost a great deal of credibility in the wake of his callous remarks, it would take another seven years and the repeal of Prohibition before Americans could once again safely celebrate the New Year and assuredly toast one another's health.

Selected Bibliography

January

Ambrose, Stephen E. *Eisenhower: Soldier and President.* New York: Simon & Schuster, 1990.
Carter, Bill. *Desperate Networks.* New York: Doubleday, 2006.
Durant, Will. *The Story of Civilization: The Reformation.* New York: Simon & Schuster, 1957.
Hastings, Max. *Armageddon: The Battle for Germany, 1944–1945.* New York: Knopf, 2004.
McCullough, David. *The Great Bridge: The Epic Story of the Building of the Brooklyn Bridge.* New York: Simon & Schuster, 1972.
Pry, Peter Vincent. *War Scare: Russia and America on the Nuclear Brink.* Westport, Conn.: Praeger, 1999.
Stumbo, Bella. "Barry: He Keeps D.C. Guessing." Editorial. *Los Angeles Times,* January 7, 1990.
Tuchman, Barbara. *A Distant Mirror: The Calamitous 14th Century.* New York: Knopf, 1978.

February

Cohen, Jon. *Almost Chimpanzees: Redrawing the Lines That Separate Us From Them.* New York: Henry Holt and Company, 2010.
Goodrich, Lloyd. *Thomas Eakins.* Cambridge, Mass.: Harvard University Press, 1982.
Harrison, George. *I, Me, Mine.* New York: Simon & Schuster, 1981.
Macaulay, Thomas Babington. *The History of England From the Accession of James II.* Philadelphia: Porter & Coates, 2000.
Pepys, Samuel. *The Diary of Samuel Pepys: A New and Complete Transcription.* Berkeley: University of California, 1970.
Wise, David. *Spy: The Inside Story of How the FBI's Robert Hanssen Betrayed America.* New York: Random House, 2002.

March

Dundes, Alan, ed. *The Blood Libel Legend: A Casebook in Anti-Semitic Folklore.* Madison: University of Wisconsin, 1991.
Offit, Paul A. *The Cutter Incident: How America's First Polio Vaccine Led to the Growing Vaccine Crisis.* New Haven, Conn: Yale University Press, 2005.
Onoda, Hiroo. *No Surrender: My Thirty-Year War.* Annapolis, Md.: Naval Institute, 1999.
Park, Robert L. *Voodoo Science: The Road From Foolishness to Fraud.* New York: Oxford University Press, 2000.
Roberts, Sam. *The Brother: The Untold Story of Atomic Spy David Greenglass and How He Sent His Sister, Ethel Rosenberg, to the Electric Chair.* New York: Random House, 2001.
Updike, John. *Endpoint and Other Poems.* New York: Knopf, 2009.

April

Matovina, Dan. *Without You: The Tragic Story of Badfinger.* San Mateo, Calif.: Frances Glover, 1997.
Munn, Michael. *John Wayne: The Man Behind the Myth.* New York: Penguin, 2003.

Selected Bibliography

Prawy, Marcel. *The Vienna Opera*. New York: Praeger, 1970.

Rivera, Geraldo, and Daniel Paisner. *Exposing Myself*. New York: Bantam, 1991.

Wilde, Oscar. *De Profundis*. New York: Vintage, 1964.

May

Churchill, Winston. *Their Finest Hour: The Second World War*. Boston: Houghton Mifflin, 1949.

Elegant, Robert S. *Mao's Great Revolution*. New York: World Publishing Company, 1971.

Harris, Robert. *Selling Hitler: The Story of the Hitler Diaries*. London: Arrow, 1986.

Moran, Mark, and Mark Sceurman. *Weird N.J., Vol. 2: Your Travel Guide to New Jersey's Local Legends and Best Kept Secrets*. New York: Sterling, 2006.

Rivera, Diego. *My Art, My Life: An Autobiography*. New York: Dover, 1991.

June

Dash, Mike. *Batavia's Graveyard: The True Story of the Mad Heretic Who Led History's Bloodiest Mutiny*. New York: Crown, 2002.

Davies, Peter J. *Mozart in Person: His Character and Health*. Westport, Conn.: Greenwood Press, 1989.

Dickey, Colin. *Cranioklepty: Grave Robbing and the Search for Genius*. Denver: Unbridled Books, 2009.

Dinwiddie, James. *Biographical Memoir of J. Dinwiddie*. Liverpool, England: Edward Howell, 1868.

Evelyn, John. *Diary and Correspondence of John Evelyn*. London: H. Colburn, 1854.

Gibbon, Edward. *The Decline and Fall of the Roman Empire, Volume 3*. New York: Knopf, 1993.

July

Connors, Jimmy. *The Outsider: A Memoir*. New York: Harper, 2013.

McCullough, David. *John Adams*. New York: Simon & Schuster, 2001.

Powers, Richard Gid. *Broken: The Troubled Past and Uncertain Future of the FBI*. New York: Free Press, 2004.

Purvis, Alston, and Alex Tresniowski. *The Vendetta: Special Agent Melvin Purvis, John Dillinger, and Hoover's FBI in the Age of Gangsters*. Philadelphia: Perseus, 2005.

Wyman, Bill, and Ray Coleman. *Stone Alone: The Story of a Rock 'n' Roll Band*. New York: Viking, 1990.

August

Baden-Powell, Robert. *Scouting for Boys: A Handbook for Instruction in Good Citizenship*. Oxford: Oxford University Press, 2004.

Blake, John. *Children of the Movement*. Chicago Review Press, 2004.

Blumenson, Martin. *The Patton Papers: 1940–1945*. Boston: Houghton Mifflin, 1974.

Coleman, Ray. *The Man Who Made the Beatles: An Intimate Biography of Brian Epstein*. New York: McGraw-Hill, 1989.

Froissart, Jean. *Froissart's Chronicles*. Ed. John Jolliffe. New York: Penguin, 2001.

Warhol, Andy. *The Andy Warhol Diaries*. Ed. Pat Hackett. New York: Warner, 1989.

Wolf, Leonard. *Bluebeard: The Life and Crimes of Gilles de Rais*. New York: Crown, 1980.

September

Bogdanovich, Peter. *Who the Hell's in It: Conversations With Hollywood's Legendary Actors*. New York: Knopf, 2004.

Bonner, Kit. "The Ill-Fated USS *William D. Porter*." *Retired Officer Magazine*, March 1994.

Hawley, Samuel. *The Imjin War: Japan's Sixteenth-Century Invasion of Korea and Attempt to Conquer China*. Seoul: Royal Asiatic Society, Korea Branch, 2005.

Hochschild, Adam. *King Leopold's Ghost: A Story of Greed, Terror, and Heroism in Colonial Africa*. New York: Houghton Mifflin Harcourt, 1999.

October

Andress, David. *The Terror: The Merciless War for Freedom in Revolutionary France*. New York: Farrar, Straus, and Giroux, 2006.

Bad Days *in* History

Asinof, Eliot. *Eight Men Out: The Black Sox and the 1919 World Series.* New York: Ace, 1963.
Berg, A. Scott. *Lindbergh.* New York: Putnam, 1998.
Bryson, Bill. *A Short History of Nearly Everything.* New York: Broadway, 2003.
Cooper, Edward S. *William Worth Belknap: An American Disgrace.* Madison, N.J.: Fairleigh Dickinson University Press, 2003.
Lindbergh, Charles A. *Autobiography of Values.* New York: Harcourt Brace Jovanovich, 1992.
Maris, Roger and Jim Ogle. *Roger Maris at Bat.* New York: Duell, Sloan, and Pearce, 1962.
Theroux, Paul. *Ghost Train to the Eastern Star: On the Tracks of the Great Railway Bazaar.* Boston: Houghton Mifflin, 2008.
Walters, Barbara. *Audition: A Memoir.* New York: Knopf, 2008.

November

Clary, Jack. *30 Years of Pro Football's Greatest Moments.* New York: Rutledge, 1976.
Fischer, David Hackett. *Liberty and Freedom: A Visual History of America's Founding Ideas.* New York: Oxford University Press, 2005.
Kennedy, Edward M. *True Compass: A Memoir.* New York: Twelve, 2009.
Richie, Alexandra. *Faust's Metropolis: A History of Berlin.* New York: Carroll & Graf, 1998.
Steakley, James D. *The Homosexual Emancipation Movement in Germany.* New York: Arno, 1993.

December

Cassius, Dio. *Roman History, Volume IX, Books 71–80.* Trans. Earnest Cary. Cambridge, Mass.: Harvard University Press, 1927.
Manchester, William. *American Caesar: Douglas MacArthur, 1880–1964.* Boston: Little, Brown, 1978.
Peters, Edward. *Inquisition.* New York: Free Press, 1988.
Slansky, Paul, and Arleen Sorkin. *My Bad: The Apology Anthology.* New York: Bloomsbury, 2006.
Walsh, John Evangelist. *Unraveling Piltdown: The Science Fraud of the Century and Its Solution.* New York: Random House, 1996.
Watson, James D. *The Double Helix: A Personal Account of the Discovery of the Structure of DNA.* New York: Atheneum, 1968.
Weintraub, Stanley. *Victoria: An Intimate Biography.* New York: Dutton, 1987.

Photo Credits

Index

Index

Index

Index

Paris, France 219
Parker, Richard 185–186
Parthenon, Greece 275–276, **276,** 347
Passenger pigeons 317–318
Patton, George S. 23, 282–284
Pearl Harbor, Hawaii 439
Penises, disappearing 98
Penn family 340–341
Périsset, Jocelyne 162
Peter, Walter G. "Gip" 213
Peter III, Emperor (Russia) 305–306, 439
Peter the Great, Tsar (Russia) **214,** 214–215, 428
Philip II, King (Spain) 290–293
Philip IV, King (France) 326–327
Philip Morris 426–427
Philippines 99–100, 202, 439–440
Pickering, Timothy 14–15
Pierce, Franklin 147, 400
Piltdown Man hoax 451–453
Plagiarism 37–38, 64–65
Pluto (dwarf planet) 307–308
Poe, Edgar Allan 30, 186
Poisonous alcohol 467–469
Poisonous toys 455
Pokémon (cartoon series) 449–450
Pole, Margaret 195–196
Polio vaccines 121–122
Polk, James K. 178
Pons, B. Stanley 116–117
Powell, Lewis 145–146
Prague Spring 304
Prescott, Richard 247–248
Presidents, bad 399–400
Presley, Elvis 207–208, 356–357
Prohibition 123, 419–420, 467–469
Pueblo, U.S.S. 44–45, **45**
Pulitzer Prize 142–144
Purvis, Melvin 263–265

Q

Qín Shǐ Huáng, Emperor (China) 272, 329
Quayle, Dan 332, 359

R

Radner, Gilda 357–358

Raleigh, Sir Walter 117–120, **119**
Rappe, Virginia 323–325
Rathbone, Henry 458–459
Razzies (Golden Raspberry Awards) 127
Reagan, Nancy 137–138
Reagan, Ronald 83, 257
Reasoner, Harry 357–358
Reign of Terror 363–364
Revere, Paul 296–298, **297**
Richard I, King (England) 135–136
Richard III, King (England) 138–139, **139**
Richardson, J. P. "the Big Bopper" 57
Rivera, Diego 168–169
Rivera, Geraldo 154, 394–395
Robison, Frank DeHaas 105–106
Rockefeller, Nelson 168–169
Rockets 30–31, 47
Roebling, Washington 28
Rolling Stones 241–243
Roman Empire 13, **13,** 46, **46,** 101–102, 124, 296, 453–454
Roosevelt, Eleanor 141–142
Roosevelt, Franklin D. 75, 82, 111, 121, 141–142, 175, 348–349, 375, 414
Rosenbaum, Joseph Carl 203–206
Rosenberg, Ethel & Julius 102–104, **103**
Rumsfeld, Donald 140
Russia 47, 378–380, **379**
Ruth, Babe 353–355, 462–464, **463**
Rwandan genocide 215–216

S

Salem, Mass. 115, 303–304
Salk, Jonas **121,** 121–122
Samurai 422–424
San Diego Free Speech Fight 181–182
Saudi Arabia 25
Sauk Indians 206–207
Scholes, Myron 444
Schott, Marge 217
Schultz, Dave "Dr. D." 464–465

Schwarzenegger, Arnold 93, 431
Scott, Robert Falcon 35–36, **36**
Seagulls 284–286, **285**
Sedition Act (1798) 253–254
Seizures, from *Pokémon* 449–450
Semmelweis, Ignaz Phillipp 273–275
Severus, Septimius, Emperor (Rome) 124, 453–454
Seward, William H. 145–146
Sex scandals 84–86, 191, 360–361, 407–409
Shah Jahan, Emperor (India) 325–326, **326**
Shales, Tom 371, 455–457
Shark attacks 239–240, **240**
Sharpeville, South Africa 113–114
Shetty, Shilpa **158,** 159
Shields and Yarnell **218,** 218–219
Shuster, Joe 89–90
Sickles, Daniel 84–86, **85**
Siegel, Jerry 89–90
Simpson, O. J. 336
Skyscrapers 62–64, **63**
Slavery 247
Smoking 160–161, 426–427
Snyder, Daniel 466
Soccer 112, **112,** 165–167, 241
South Pole 35–36, **36**
Soviet Union 304, 306–307, 464
Space flights and research 30–31
Spanish Armada 290–293, **292**
Spanish Inquisition 185
Spies 71–72, 102–104, 213
Stalin, Joseph 76, 306–307, 388–390, **389**
Stallone, Sylvester 59, 127, 160–161
Stein, Gertrude 152–153, 335
Stock market crash (1929) 387
Stockdale, James 367
Stoker, Bram 222, 223
Stossel, John 464–465
Stravinsky, Igor 198–200

Index

Acknowledgments

It was my lucky day when Lisa Thomas came to me with her idea for this project, which she subsequently shepherded through with such grace and good humor. I am also grateful for the valuable contributions of two other brilliantly funny women: Marguerite Conley and Pat Myers.

A number of people kindly offered great suggestions for bad days. My deepest appreciation to Tom Dodd, Lee Doyle, Mary Farquhar, Billy Foote, Johnny Foote, Ann Marie Lynch, Paul Maloney, Nelson Rupp, Kevin Tierney, and Evan Wilson.

Huge thanks to the *Bad Days* team at National Geographic: Amy Briggs, Anne Smyth, Melissa Farris, Katie Olsen, Susan Blair, Zachary Galasi, Erin Greenhalgh, and Susan Nguyen, and to Giulia Ghigini for her wonderful illustrations.

Finally, I am blessed to have a friend like Sarah Hennessey, who rallied herself from her own rotten days of illness to lend me such enthusiastic support for this book. Thank you, Bones!

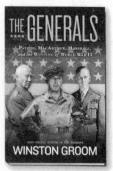
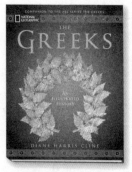
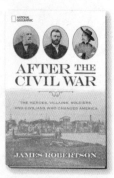